REFRAMING THE
PRACTICE OF PHILOSOPHY

SUNY series, Philosophy and Race

Robert Bernasconi and T. Denean Sharpley-Whiting, editors

REFRAMING THE PRACTICE OF PHILOSOPHY

Bodies of Color, Bodies of Knowledge

EDITED BY

GEORGE YANCY

STATE UNIVERSITY OF NEW YORK PRESS

Published by
STATE UNIVERSITY OF NEW YORK PRESS, ALBANY

© 2012 State University of New York

For information, contact
State University of New York Press, Albany, NY
www.sunypress.edu

Production, Laurie Searl
Marketing, Anne M. Valentine

Library of Congress Cataloging-in-Publication Data

Reframing the practice of philosophy : bodies of color, bodies of knowledge / edited by
George Yancy.
    p. cm. — (SUNY series, Philosophy and race)
Includes bibliographical references and index.
ISBN 978-1-4384-4002-6 (pbk. : alk. paper)
ISBN 978-1-4384-4003-3 (hardcover : alk. paper)
1. Philosophy and social sciences.   2. Minorities—United States.   I. Yancy, George.

B63.R42 2012
108—dc22   2011010849

10 9 8 7 6 5 4 3 2 1

To philosophers of color not yet born

CONTENTS

ACKNOWLEDGMENTS

The contributors within this volume are thanked for their collective effort to produce a text that fills an important philosophical gap. I recall sharing this project with the noted literary figure and philosopher Charles Johnson. Aware of my other edited volumes, Johnson said, "You're filling in whole quadrants of philosophical exploration that have for too long been neglected!" His expression and insight brought home to me my own sense of purpose. I thank Chuck for that. I also thank Philosophy and Race Series editors T. Denean Sharpley-Whiting and Robert Bernasconi for their initial assesment of the importance of this project. I would like to thank Jane Bunker, former Associate Director and Editor-in-Chief of SUNY Press, for her leadership in terms of promoting excellence in publishing, her encouragement, and especially her patience. I also thank Andrew Kenyon, Assistant Acquisitions Editor, for his support and Laurie Searl, Senior Production Editor, for her energy and creative ideas. I thank a number of colleagues for their continued insights and support: James G. Spady, Fred Evans, Jim Swindal, Kathy Glass, Steve Martinot, Manomano M.W. Mukungurutse, Maria Del Gaudalupe Davidson, Janine Jones, J. Everet Green, Mariana Ortega, Clevis Headley, Robert E. Birt, Lucius T. Outlaw Jr., Cornel West, and Anita Allen. I would like to especially thank Joyce M. Cook. She is a dear friend and an enviable philosopher; indeed, one of a kind. Ruth, my mother, is thanked for the breath (the life) that she gave me. The Yancy boys are products of that same loving breath. And to Susan, my wife, thanks for your endurance and work ethic, but especially for your patience with a man who continues to learn how to *unlearn*.

INTRODUCTION

INAPPROPRIATE PHILOSOPHICAL SUBJECTS?

George Yancy

I found that it was extremely important to legitimate the production
of philosophical knowledge in sites that are not normally considered
the philosophical sites.

—Angela Davis

It is difficult to hate people whose culture is understood, but easy to
hate people who are imagined to embody a label that means "inferior"
or "dangerous."

—Naomi Zack

The vision for *Reframing the Practice of Philosophy: Bodies of Color, Bodies of Knowledge* emerged from a conversation with Jorge J. E. Gracia. We discussed the paucity of African Americans and Latinos/as in the field of philosophy in the United States despite the fact that the twenty-first century had arrived. Our goal was to create a critical space where both groups would come together to discuss critically a collectively important defining theme, a common problem—our marginalization within the profession of philosophy, which is one of those "inappropriate" philosophical subjects. We conceived that this critical cadre would come together in the form of a session at one of the American Philosophical Association (APA) meetings. The idea was exciting and the fruitful possibilities endless.

As we continued to think about this, I thought that I would also edit a text that brought together African American and Latino/a philosophical voices. Initially, I thought that the text principally would reflect the concern that Jorge and I had contemplated with respect to the APA session—the concern regarding such appallingly low numbers of African Americans and

1

Latinos/as in the field of philosophy. The book would function as a textual site that raised critical questions about the status of African Americans and Latinos/as in the predominately *white* and *male* field of philosophy. The idea was to locate and interrogate ways in which the profession of philosophy actually militates against the presence of these two groups. After thinking through the project with greater conceptual precision, however, it grew into its current form.

The text indeed does succeed in bringing together African American and Latino/a philosophers within a single text. Yet, the critical and conceptually complex and diverse yield was unexpected. In this sense, the project itself is truly dynamic. The attempt to explore and explicate the lack of African Americans and Latinos/as in the field of philosophy actually resulted in a much broader and comprehensive text that uncovered complex and multifaceted issues such as alienation, institutional prejudices, insidious racism, canonical exclusion, linguistic exclusion, nonrecognition, disrespect, white hegemony and power, discursive silencing, philosophical territorial arrogance, and indignation. In short, what emerged was a powerful and multilayered exposure—by these two collective critical philosophical voices—of the implicit and explicit ideologically and philosophically myopic exclusionary practices that shape and inform contemporary philosophy as practiced in North America.

I began to see just how important the text had become beyond the scope of low numbers, particularly in terms of the text's forward-looking dimensions. The text constitutes an important site—a textual balm of sorts—for blacks and Latinos/as currently pursuing degrees in philosophy and who, as a result, may feel isolated, "out of place," and marginalized. Moreover, the text speaks to future philosophers of color who might need confirmation of their sanity, a collective voice that says, "We also know your pain, your blues." Yet, it is a text that encourages—valorizes—the importance of "talking back." As bell hooks writes, "It is that act of speech, of 'talking back,' that is no mere gesture of empty words, that is the expression of our movement from object to subject—the liberated voice."[1]

As the text continued to take shape, what also began to emerge was a parallel between many of the issues that black and Latino/a bodies experience within the everyday world of social perception as linked to pervasive de facto racism, and the refined and intellectually highfalutin world of professional philosophy. This confirmed what I had always thought to be the case. Philosophical academic spaces are, in so many ways, continuous with everyday, politically invested, racially grounded, prejudicial, social spaces. Such normative (white) academic spaces are shot through with much of the same racist toxicity that configures black and brown bodies as outside the normative (white) Demos. Blacks and Latinos/as are seen/depicted as possessing an "essential" (noncontingent) tendency toward "laziness, drug abuse and dealing, poor linguistic skills, unreliability, and so on."[2]

White-dominated intellectual spaces permeate with such stereotypical perceptions. In the halls of academia, black and Latinos/as continue to be made to feel like outsiders, as unwanted, as unfit, unprotected. They are deemed lazy and unreliable as agents of knowledge production. So, black and Latinos/as traverse both academic and nonacademic social spaces where the white gaze continues to operate, to deform, and to depict them/us in degrading ways, perhaps as "niggers" and "spics"/"wetbacks," as exotic bodies fit for "different" work, but *not* philosophical work. As Linda Alcoff relates, "As a new assistant professor, I was loudly called a 'bush' in front of graduate students by a senior colleague, and my complaints to the chair seemed to have no effect on his subsequent regular editorial comments."[3] Anita Allen relates how her white dissertation advisor, philosopher Richard Brandt, positioned her as a maid, a stereotyped mammy figure. According to Allen, after tilting her face up to his, he said, "Anita, you look just like a maid my family once had."[4] In 1981, Allen, while in Washington, DC, also relates how she was stopped by white police officers as she walked alongside of a white male philosopher named Harold Hodes. She says that "they suspected we were prostitute and John! They forced me to show identification and asked me where I worked."[5]

Within this context, the image of black and Latina women as sexual objects and sexual workers abound. In the white imaginary, African Americans and Latinos/as are stereotyped as dangerous dysfunctional criminals on a par with our so-called dysfunctional and criminal hoods and barrios—places that many of us affectionately call home, places where many of our loved ones continue to live. As Ofelia Schutte notes, "Many of us [both blacks and Latinos/as] are part of nonacademic communities where the 'we' includes people who are oppressed and/or discriminated against on a daily basis."[6] Hence, blacks and Latinos/as often experience nonacademic and academic spaces as a distinction without a difference. Writing of his identity as a Latino faculty member in philosophy, Eduardo Mendieta discloses, "I have suffered racism, both overt and covert, tolerably subtle and snarlingly blatant."[7]

It is important to note that it is not my aim to reinscribe a black–white binary, where anti-Latino/a forms of racism are subsumed under anti-black racism, where racism shown toward Latinos/as is the same as racism shown toward blacks. Such a view would only further the logic of the black–white binary, grouping Latinos/as on the black side, as it were, and would fail to give critical attention to the *different* (while certainly overlapping) ways in which black and Latino/a bodies experience white racism, cultural exclusion, philosophical exclusion, and so on. Within the context of this introductory framing, I only wish to create a space for intersubjective recognition of overlapping configurations of alienation, marginalization, and caricature experienced by Black and Latino/a philosophers vis-à-vis racist normative assumptions and circuits of desire that are operative within white hegemonic philosophical spaces.[8]

The voices within *Reframing the Practice of Philosophy: Bodies of Color, Bodies of Knowledge* are multiple; they provide clarity and unearth deep layers of disciplinary hegemony, sites of crisis, and inspiration. For example, one layer of disciplinary hegemony is revealed through interrogating certain assumptions regarding canon formation and biases against certain languages. Spanish, for example, often is scorned. Joe R. Feagin notes, "Mocking Spanish involves whites, frequently in the middle and upper classes, creating derisive terms like 'no problemo,' 'el cheapo,' 'watcho your backo,' and 'hasty banana,' as well as phrases like 'numero uno' and 'no way, José.' Such mock Spanish by white English speakers generates, overtly or subtly, a negative view of Spanish, those who speak it, and their culture."[9] Such biases that stipulate certain languages as *the only* legitimate media for philosophical expression are revealed as sites governed by raced (white) conceptions of linguistic intelligibility. Elizabeth Millán argues that such forms of exclusion result in the deformation of the spirits of those *who* exclude. Part of what constitutes such exclusions, according to her, include "historical myopia, an exclusionary gaze, and rigidly prohibitive borders for a field that should be ever striving to expand and grow."[10]

Many of the voices critically deploy autobiography as a way of articulating the *lived* interiority of what it means to be black and Latino/a within the field of philosophy. Alcoff argues that "Latinas in philosophy often live without the sort of cultural and social recognition that would provide an uptake or confirmation of our interior lives."[11] As a black woman, Donna-Dale Marcano reveals how she walks into introductory philosophy courses and how young white boys in those spaces take up the role of philosopher with ease vis-à-vis the complicated way in which she takes up that role. Drawing from black women's standpoint epistemology, she argues that philosophy has failed black women, and, I argue, other women of color as well, because they are situated vis-à-vis gender and race and various ostracized communities.[12] Oscar R. Martí notes that "Everyone who works in an 'ethnic' philosophy—Black, Chicano, Latin American, and so forth—is familiar with the blank stares or dismissive smiles from colleagues when we talk about our fields."[13] Martí captures what it no doubt feels like to be a Latina/o philosopher and to do Latin American philosophy in the following expression—illegal alien worker. Nelson Maldonado-Torres found it necessary to do philosophy *elsewhere* as he faced forms of epistemic exclusion from "the sacred space of Euro-versal reason."[14] Charles Mills suggests what he calls *conceptual* tokenization in the profession of philosophy. It is a process "where a black [and I would add a Latino/a] perspective is included, but in a ghettoized way that makes no difference to the overall discursive logic of the discipline, or subsection of the discipline, in question: the framing assumptions, dominant narratives, prototypical scenarios."[15] So, even as we gesticulate, voice, write, publish important articles and monographs, and physically move into historically white academic spaces, we remain on the margins. We might be physically present, but still epistemological outsiders. Gregory Fernando Pappas is succinct, "Hispanic philosophers suffer from marginalization. I have experienced this in my own career and in the lives of the few Hispanic graduate students that I have directed."[16]

What became clear is that for both groups the color line continues to thrive within philosophical spaces. And even as Black and Latino/a bodies attempt to make their presence felt and to usher in different philosophical voices, traditions, epistemic assumptions, it is important to remain cognizant of John McClendon's warning that the mere inclusion of blacks or Latinos/as into philosophical spaces, say, philosophy departments, sessions at the APA, editorial boards, and organizational positions, does not necessarily create a shift in *power*. Hence, if inclusion "does not change the balance of power relationship central to white supremacist oppression then the Color Line remains intact despite the occasional appearance that the line had been broken by the entrance of individuals into white academic [spaces] organizations."[17]

Reframing the Practice of Philosophy: Bodies of Color, Bodies of Knowledge is an eye opener. The idea of "reframing" suggests the sense in which one steps back and takes another look, realizing that the current frame excludes all that does not fit within the demarcated limits of that frame. In fact, that which is outside the frame is constituted as that which is unintelligible and ersatz. This form of framing actually deforms, delimits, and truncates the very power of philosophical imaginings. To reframe the current practices of philosophy, then, functions to reveal the limits of its current practices, its current assumptions, its current conceptual allegiances, and its current self-images. The aim is to expand the hermeneutic horizons of what is possible, philosophically. The text challenges fundamental normative assumptions about philosophy, *doing* philosophy, *coming* to philosophy, and *staying* in philosophy. The voices within the text speak to various gate-keeping assumptions and practices that actually thwart the love of wisdom, diminish the capacity to "world travel" and to be critically self-reflexive.

I suspect that many white readers (philosophers or not) are not familiar with the ways in which philosophers of color face their "professional dilemmas."[18] I have attempted, with varying degrees of success, to get my white philosophy graduate students to grapple with the ways in which philosophers of color face various professional and personal challenges and dilemmas by encouraging the former to think about exactly why they do philosophy, why they desire to do philosophy, and how they see themselves within the overall context of philosophy as a site of various critical discourses, professional practices, values, assumptions, and worldviews. I often begin by asking them to discuss openly their philosophical interests. Some are very clear and specific about what they want to do, how they desire to flesh out some particular philosophical issue. Others are somewhat inchoate and often have a rather broad range of philosophical interests. Nevertheless, they usually respond without much hesitation. I then request that they relate their philosophical interests to their identities. I ask, "So, how do your philosophical interests relate to how *you* understand who you are, how you see yourself, the person that you take yourself to be?" From the appearance of scrunched eyebrows I assume that the question is not often asked of them or considered by them. I find myself looking for any response, no matter how vague, that will provide me with a sense of how they understand their identities vis-à-vis their philosophical concerns. Perhaps they think that I mean for them to reveal some personal idiosyncrasy, some quirk. And although I do not rule this out, I am more interested in how such specific identity markers as race, gender, and sex inform, mediate, shape, and encourage their philosophical concerns.

As a way of getting them started, I begin by openly exploring significant links between how *I* am raced (as black) and what *I* do in philosophy, the philosophical issues that *I* think are important, the philosophical issues about which *I* write, and the philosophical issues about which *I* have a passion. Of course, this does not mean that absolutely *everything* that I find of value philosophically is related to how I have been raced and how I understand myself as raced. And although I have argued elsewhere[19] for the important dynamics between philosophical reflection, on the one hand, and doing philosophy from a specific *positional here*, on the other hand, and how philosophy is not something done from nowhere, there is no attempt to maintain that *all* that is of philosophical importance must be linked to one's raced/ethnicized and gendered identities. After all, our identities are more complex than our specific raced/ethnicized and gendered identities. Yet, I am critical of those who argue that our raced/ethicized and gendered identities have entirely no connection to our philosophical intuitions, sensibilities, and worldviews. Indeed, I argue that many of our philosophical sensibilities are precisely and fundamentally linked to such sites of identity.

I suspect that many of my white students are seduced by the idea that they can rise above such identity designations because such markers are believed to have no purchase on their "real" selves.[20] The invocation of an autonomous liberal self—a "nontribal" self, one that is cosmopolitan—within the dynamic context of race suggests forms of obfuscation and bad faith. As *white* graduate students studying philosophy, the social world of philosophy will typically open up differently to them than for persons of color studying philosophy. As white, as socially located, my students' (white) *visual* bodies signify a multiplicity of meanings that are always already stacked against the *visual* bodies (and the *audible* voices—think about Spanish accents and the so-called Negro dialect) of persons of color. If white students move and have their being within predominantly white philosophical spaces where there are social interactions through their (white) visible identities that work "to organize the social world's responses to and interpretations of [their] behavior, this is surely what it means to be [them], this is [their own-ness]."[21]

After I have explored how I understand the connection between my black embodied existence *and* my own philosophical passions and concerns, my students begin to appreciate, even if at times vaguely, what is at stake meta-philosophically. Questions about their own whiteness begin to emerge. I ask, "So, how do you think that *your* whiteness relates to *your* philosophical passions?" Then again, it is the *problem*, the *conceptual conundrum*, which really matters—so, one might claim. It is about attempting to gain intellective clarity about some philosophical issue, to make a contribution to philosophical perennial problems that we "all" face, problems that are uppermost for "all" epistemic subjects. There often is the hidden presumption that the concerns that they deem philosophically worthy are universal concerns, the intelligibility and meaningfulness of which are supposed to be given as such. In other words, my sense is that many of my white students understand the importance of certain philosophical problems and the practice of philosophy itself as disconnected from *their* raced, gendered, and sexed embodied selves. Hence, there is no real appreciation for interrogating various complex markers of identity vis-à-vis how certain philosophical problems become valorized *by them* and of significance *to them*.

I often have shared with my white students what it is like to move in and out of spaces at APA conferences.[22] I share with them how alienating this experience can be for someone of color—in my case, black—within such monochromatic (white) spaces, how it feels, existentially, to be an "inappropriate" subject situated within a sea of white faces. Some look puzzled. Others look with new insight. None of them, however, have experienced this feeling of alienation, a reality, I might say, that makes *my* experiences stand out, even more hyperbolically, as simply anomalous and marginal, something of no real importance. Often, there doesn't appear to be any shared points of meaning. Alcoff also has expressed this sense of alienation. She notes, "Neither my general lived experience, nor my reference points in argumentation, nor my routine affective responses to events, nor my philosophical intuitions are shared with most people in my immediate milieu."[23]

African American philosopher Jacqueline Scott also expresses a sense of fragmentation, how philosophy militates against her identity. For Scott, "The discipline [of philosophy] in which I house myself does not want all of me to settle in and fully join the community."[24] Scott finds, as with Alcoff, that the complexity of her identity, with all of its rich epistemic importance, is placed under erasure within academic spaces governed by white normative frames of reference. As black, as Latina, from the perspectives of many white gatekeepers, these women did not fail (through their own acts of agency) to be "appropriate" subjects fit for philosophy; rather, they were never fit to be "appropriate" subjects for philosophy in the first place. The indictment of their philosophical competence was not *a posteriori*, but *a priori*.

I encourage my white students to think about the fact that so many philosophers of color feel this incredible sense of alienation. I also encourage them to interrogate how the *absence* of this feeling of alienation speaks to their lives, their philosophical identities, how they see themselves, and how they are positioned by various assumptions that shape the professional field of philosophy itself. There is often silence. Typically, someone will say, perhaps fueled with some nervous hesitancy and self-doubt: "Because we're white?" I reply, "But of course!"

The absence of this feeling of alienation is further teased out. My white students come to recognize that they are the "philosophical (*white*) we." The history of philosophy—from Plato to Derrida—is a family relationship; one that welcomes them *a priori*. My white students' feelings of ownership of "genuine" philosophy and "real" philosophical texts is a given. After all, they are *white*. They are thinkers, potential philosophical geniuses. The philosophers who they have seen look like them; the philosophical traditions are populated by *raced* (white) bodies that resemble their own bodies: Plato, Friedrich Nietzsche, Simone de Beauvoir, Michel Foucault, Willard Quine, and Luce Irigaray. Whether analytic or continental, the monochromatic philosophical players remain the same, even as their philosophical orientations differ fundamentally. There is still the fact that white philosophy graduate students' perceptual expectations (what "real" philosophers look like, what "real" philosophers sound like, and what "real" philosophers smell like) are shaped through the value-laden mobilization of texts, texts that were written by bodies that reflect their own (my students') raced (white) body images. In this way, my students come to cognize themselves as the genuine audience to whom these texts speak and for whom they were written. The presence of epidermal sameness becomes normative and thus invisible; the specific whiteness of the philosophers' flesh becomes transfigured as *the* universal body. Hence, white bodies become universal bodies, whereas various raced epistemic orders and institutional practices that sustain and reinforce the epidermal sameness of these bodies go un-interrogated.

Through critical lines of questioning, through encouraging them to reframe their expectations regarding the "philosophical we," there are times when the "curtain," as it were, is removed, although all too infrequently. And although there is no deceptive wizard discovered, there are forces, historical, epistemic, axiological, and racial. The relationship of a few of my white students' with the canon, with philosophical texts and philosophical figures, begins to shift, radically so. They begin to uncover and nominate complex layers of privilege, power, and hegemony. They begin to uncover how I am implicated within these texts. As black, I was never even imagined as a philosophical interlocutor, a discussant, part of the audience, part of the conversation. Often through the *particularization* of my absence, the *particularization* of their presence is revealed. Hence, their white privilege vis-à-vis philosophical texts and the historical stream of white bodies engaged/engaging in philosophical thought and philosophical scholarship becomes all too uncomfortably visible. As Peggy McIntosh would no doubt concur, my white students can be sure that they will be given *philosophical* "curricular materials that testify to the existence of their race."[25] They also can remain oblivious to the philosophical ideas embedded in "the language and customs of persons of color who constitute the world's majority without feeling in [their] culture penalty for such oblivion."[26]

It is unsettling to read a text, to engage it, to feel its texture, its spine, and yet to realize that such a text—say, Kant's *Critique of Pure Reason*—wasn't written for your eyes, but written on the assumption that you were not one of its "appropriate" subjects, *could not* have been one of its "appropriate" subjects/readers. As I have emphasized, my white students have always already been "appropriate" subjects. Even my white female students are not "black from head to toe"[27]—clear proof that what they say and think have some level of epistemic credibility. Alexis Shotwell argues that it is important not to slide from "'women in philosophy to women and minorities in philosophy.'"[28] It creates a form of elision that fails to take into consideration the differential negative implications of specific processes of racialization on people of color vis-à-vis philosophy. According to Shotwell, "Failing to attend to the real differences between white women, racialized women, racialized men, and other people who fall into the category of the philosophical minority, replicates implicitly the effects of more explicit decisions to focus attention on winning a place at the table for white women in philosophy."[29]

Despite what my white students might think, what metaphors might govern their self-understanding, they are not abstract minds who simply carve out their philosophical identities *ex nihilo*. The simple act, one that is mundane, but not trivial, of a white hand reaching for a philosophical text is a relationship mediated by history, sanctioned by a philosophical anthropology steeped in whiteness as normative. Relaxingly reading Aristotle in some monochromatic (white) philosophy graduate lounge is a complex site of effective history—years of repetition, years of calcified habits mediated by raced norms. In fact, to see a white body reading a philosophical text is *uneventful*. This, after all, is what white bodies do. And even if the white body is *poor*, it is still white and is thus granted a certain presumptive capacity to transcend its economic circumstances. Bodies of color are not believed circumstantially incapacitated, but ontologically so. Historically, white bodies read books with no fear of punishment, unless, of course, they read to blacks. As well-known as this point is, it is important to recall that it was once illegal for black people to read, prohibited by (white) law. Hence, a black hand reaching for *any* book, let alone a philosophical text, is an act referentially linked to America's racist history, to the myth of black inferiority and the reality of white power. Furthermore, from the perspective of this history, and from the presumptions about who can and can't do philosophy (or who should and should not do philosophy), sitting in a philosophy lounge reading Aristotle—as a black or Latina—is a sight to behold, something of a spectacle, something of an oxymoron, an aberration, perhaps even a miracle. Indeed, an *event*.

The majority of my white students resist the implications of their normative whiteness vis-à-vis their engagement with philosophy or they fail (or refuse) to bring their new insights to bear upon other philosophy courses. In this way, they elide their whiteness, lie to themselves, and continue to do philosophy as presumed race-less *thinkers*, pure and simple. Even this move, however, is itself a function of whiteness. Bodies of color, however, cannot elide their appearance within contexts that always already mark them as alien, as outsiders. Bodies of color are marked against a background of unmarked normative white bodies. White bodies move through the pristine halls of academia in the mode of ownership. Philosophy departments, philosophy meetings, and philosophy social gatherings are sites of white bonding, forms of bonding that function as confirmation that one has come to the "right place." The casualness of these mundane situations actually militates against the recognition of various absences—that is, the absence of bodies of color, the absence of philosophical and conceptual points of view informed by the social location of philosophers of color. After all, there is nothing out of place; all that matters has already been framed. As suggested, my white students would rather see these spaces as racially unmarked. It is easy for them to do this because their white bodies have been historically constructed as *just* human bodies. They soon forget about (refuse *to know* any longer) the ways in which they are constituted by power relations and discursive frames of reference. The *self-knowledge* that they come to construct about themselves as philosophers, how they come to *feel* about the profession of philosophy, the *ease* with which they enter into the profession, is linked to an overall meta-narrative that forms the backdrop of whites' pursuit of philosophy as *their* exclusive (white) destiny.

Charles Mills notes that when it comes down to it "a lot of philosophy is just white guys jerking off."[30] Imagine the scene: white guys engaging in forms of self-stimulating discourse, articulations that speak to their experiences, theorizations of philosophical frameworks that speak to their existential predicaments and their normative status as epistemic subjects. The scene is one of group self-pleasuring, philosophical narcissism, and philosophical debauchery. All of this is done publicly and rarely with a hint of shame. This is why it is so important to nominate and to mark sites of white hegemony and white myopia publicly once we come to recognize them. Reframing white bodies engaged in philosophy as public displays of moral indecency—something akin to Mills' imagery—might trigger the recognition that it has always been about "us white folk," our white intellectual titillation, our white mental ejecta. Perhaps they might come to recognize themselves, as James Baldwin wrote, "as the slightly mad victims of their own brainwashing."[31] As philosophers of color, we mustn't forget that we are not deemed liberal subjects residing above the markers of racial particularity. To engage in public displays of philosophical self-pleasuring, we may find ourselves in the hands of a white lynch mob, the victims of *castration*—cut off from those (whites) who see themselves as giving birth to a nation that sees us (you) as racially antithetical, abhorrent, and nugatory.

Critically engaging my white students, the aim is *not* to stifle their philosophical growth. On the contrary, my objective is to encourage them to think meta-philosophically, to begin thinking critically about how history, a specifically racist history, impacts their lives, how it impacts what they think is philosophically valuable and also what they fail to think is philosophically valuable, how they have come to think and judge what are "appropriate" philosophical subjects and how they have come to think and judge what are "inappropriate" philosophical subjects. As I have intimated throughout, the notion of "inappropriate"/ "appropriate" philosophical subjects is not simply about subjects qua items to be studied; rather, "inappropriate"/ "appropriate" philosophical subjects raises the very question of personhood. Blacks and Latinos/as continue to fight mightily to protect their sense of personhood, to debunk racist images (illegal, uneducated, loud, lazy, fit for menial labor, inarticulate, exotic, etc.) that demean and dehumanize, and to resist a legal system that disproportionately criminalizes and punishes them. *Reframing the Practice of Philosophy: Bodies of Color, Bodies of Knowledge* is a text that consciously acknowledges the political as profoundly ingrained in the philosophical. Questions of personhood, power, canon formation, identity, marginalization and alienation, the privileging of certain languages as philosophical over others, whiteness and philosophical normativity, and more, are themes that are raised within this text. The text is an effort to reframe, to rethink certain philosophical assumptions and to show how certain bodies and philosophical traditions have been narrowly and problematically conceived. This book refuses the *imperial* philosophical route, refuses its colonial imaginary, its hegemony, and its misanthropy. The text accomplishes exactly what Jorge J. E. Gracia and I initially discussed and does so much more.

SUMMARY OF CHAPTERS

Reframing the Practice of Philosophy: Bodies of Color, Bodies of Knowledge is divided into five sections. However, they are not pure or strict demarcations, but fundamentally overlap in terms of capturing the mutually reinforcing multidimensionality of philosophical themes, concerns, and insights of African American and Latino/a philosophers.

I. Colonization/Decolonization: Philosophy and Canon Formation

Linda Martín Alcoff opens this section with an insightful exploration of the dynamics of alienation and marginalization and the impact of these on Latino/a philosophers vis-à-vis their hermeneutic horizons. Alcoff contextualizes the problem of alienation against the backdrop of a more global disrespect for Latin America and the alarming conditions that Latinos/as face in the United States. She rightfully calls into question the idea that de-alienation is to be purchased through assimilation. She also recognizes that hegemonic frameworks, those that often demand assimilation, also suffer from foreclosing other philosophical voices. Through the work of Ofelia Schutte, Alcoff shows that "otherness" is not the only problem facing Latinos/as, but that cultural subordination compounds the problem. Alcoff suggests that integration ought to be a valorized goal, but not at the expense of Latino/a self-erasure.

Charles W. Mills opens his chapter on a somewhat pessimistic note regarding the influence of Africana philosophy within the profession of philosophy, its assumptions and aims. Deploying his own personal journey through philosophy as an important lens, Mills provides keen observations regarding important moments in the progression of Africana philosophy. However, his pessimism is fundamentally linked to the structural hegemony of whiteness within the academy and philosophy's self-conception. Through a critical and astute analysis of problematic issues around placement, black philosophers employed at top-ranked institutions, questions involving conference presence and publications, and so on, Mills makes the case that

Africana philosophy faces serious long-term marginalization. Drawing on his experiences as the author of the academic bestseller, *The Racial Contract*, Mills argues that the text has had close to zero influence on the way mainstream political philosophy continues to be done. This, among other things, leaves one with a confirmed sense of Mills' pessimism.

Ofelia Schutte's chapter importantly poses the question of Latinos/as in philosophy against the backdrop of the problem of the canon, the issue of "prestige," and the problem of the "we" of philosophy. Speaking in her own critical and wise Latina philosophical voice, Schutte argues against the (white) North American and western European philosophical approaches that refuse to engage in a process of epistemic reciprocity. She critiques the racist and procrustean assumptions that define prestige, assumptions that actually exclude Latino/a philosophical voices. She also insightfully discusses what it is like *not* to feel like the philosophical "we." Schutte ends by critically reflecting on the possibilities of the future of philosophy where the face of the field and its methodologies are more variegated, and where what she calls the "knowledge-regime of Anglocentric androcentricity" effectively loses its power and illusions of a disembodied form of reason.

Jorge J.E. Gracia correctly points out that philosophers are not often drawn to critical questions regarding philosophical canon formation. With the growing number of women and other minorities within the field, however, this question has become a salient one. Gracia raises important questions about canon formation and specifically explores reasons why Latin American philosophy has been generally excluded. He raises many significant concerns regarding the fact that Latin American philosophy is not even part of the philosophy college curriculum in the United States, that there is a paucity of dissertations that explore issues within Latin American philosophy, and the fact that *Jobs for Philosophers*, in the last few years, have had only six job advertisements for philosopher's specializing in Latin American philosophy. When one thinks about the few faculty who are actually trained to teach or direct dissertations in Latin American philosophy, the picture gets gloomier. Gracia goes on to explore and critique reasons why Latin American philosophy has been excluded from the canon. He takes up an important discussion around the issue of tradition and its role vis-à-vis philosophical canons, revealing important implications for Latin American philosophy's exclusion, particularly the fact that the philosophical canon is constituted within "familial" groups linked by practices, that is, traditions. Gracia's chapter both complicates philosophical canon formation vis-à-vis Latin American philosophy and demonstrates various complex factors regarding its inclusion.

Jesús H. Aguilar's chapter explores the possibility of a *distinctive* Latin American philosophy. Aguilar's analytically complex piece shows that such a possibility is by no means simple. He explores an "externalist" approach

to the issue of a distinctive Latin American philosophy and finds it wanting. He then examines an "internalist" approach to the issue, methodically
detailing its problems. He concludes the bulk of his chapter by exploring
the possibility of using the notion of style as a meta-philosophical category
to provide a justification concerning the existence of a Latin American
philosophical tradition. He draws the source of this conceptual approach
from the way in which the notion of style is employed in the arts and sciences to distinguish different traditions. Aguilar's chapter places the reader
within the fray of some very complex meta-philosophical issues around the
existence of a distinctive Latin American philosophy.

II. Racism, the Academy, and the Practice of Philosophy

John H. McClendon III opens this section with a powerful critique of the
profession of philosophy vis-à-vis African Americans in the field. He argues
that the present deplorable status of African American philosophers in the
profession is a function of how institutionalized racism is intractably tied
to power within the academy and the profession. He also explores how the
professionalization of philosophy is a class phenomenon rooted in a bourgeois social division of labor. McClendon delineates the specific impact of
institutionalized racism through an insightful historical overview of African
American philosophers before the 1970s and links this historical overview
to the context of Historically Black Colleges and Universities, showing that
it is not by happenstance that this link exists, especially within the context
of the existence of the racist Color Line.

     Eduardo Mendieta powerfully links autobiographical reflections with
meta-philosophical reflections. He explores his experiences as a Latin Amer-
ican/Latino philosopher, who is *Mestizo*. He explores the complexity of the
fact that he can pass for a swarthy Mediterranean European, or a South East
Asian. Yet, he observes that he is not a U.S.-born Latino, pointing out that
this duality has been both exploited and used against him. Mendieta also
discusses his experiences in the profession in the role of a philosophy professor, who, like the ubiquitous Mexican, doubles as a race, Latin Americanist,
continentalist, and the like, expert. Given his identity as a Latin American,
and Latino, he argues that he fulfills many rolls: diversity hire, affirmative
action hire, and ethnic hire. His chapter provides the much needed *internal*
exploration of the complexity of being a Latino in the profession of philosophy as practiced in the United States.

     Gregory Fernando Pappas explores the very common explanation that
Latin American philosophers do not often get "invited or welcomed to the
table" because they are Latinos/Latinas and because the "mainstream" in philosophy is white. Pappas recognizes that philosophy in America continues to

be a de facto predominantly white male profession, and recognizes that there are power structures that work against Latin American voices. Although he recognizes the truth in these claims, he worries about the tendency of philosophers to be reductionist regarding the social problems related to the profession of philosophy and Latin American/Hispanic-American philosophers. Hence, Pappas explores how multiple prejudices operate in philosophy, such as *professional* prejudices, *Eurocentric* prejudices, and prejudices in the form of philosophical *methods* and *styles*. Pappas ends his chapter with some important ameliorative suggestions.

Bill Lawson insightfully deploys a linguistic expression, used within African American communities, to speak to the profession of white philosophers/philosophy: "Don't hate the playa, hate the game." Lawson argues that white philosophers who are colleagues, who dislike the accomplishments of minority philosophers and minorities in the academy, more generally, are guilty of "playa hatin'." Instead of questioning the existence of racism in the academy, which Lawson sees as a significant systemic problem within philosophy, white philosophers would rather disparage the abilities of their colleagues of color. Through an analytical discussion of issues around the concept of respect, Lawson unpacks the experience of disparagement as a large part of the academic life of scholars/philosophers of color.

III. Gender, Ethnicity, and Race

Like other philosophers within this text, Jacqueline Scott opens this section by weaving her personal reflections into larger philosophical and meta-philosophical themes within the profession of philosophy. Scott explores her identity formation as a black, female philosopher in terms of its perils and promises, recognizing that because black, female philosopher is not a ready-made category that one is forced to create and maintain such an identity in the face of both hostility and indifference. She sees this lack of fixity as also holding the promise of creating one's own identity as one sees fit. Drawing from the work of Linda Alcoff among others, Scott contributes to the discourse around making sense of the intersecting identities of black, woman, and philosopher. She concludes by arguing that the creation and embodiment of such a hybrid identity potentially allows for a healthy type of subject formation which in turn could allow for the possibility of creating more vibrant, elastic communities that openly and lovingly reflect the complex identities of their members. She sees this investigation as potentially changing not only the way many in philosophy think about issues such as race, subjectivity, and identity, but changing the philosophers who carry out such investigations.

Donna-Dale Marcano theorizes black women within the context of philosophy through the lens of Back women's lives as raced and sexed, and as both political and personal. Hence, for Marcano, this leaves black women beyond the universality of whiteness or maleness or "objectivity" within the discipline. Through an insightful analysis of Plato's *Symposium*, she draws an important parallel between Alcibiades and black women in philosophy. She says that like Alcibiades, black women are "outsiders" to philosophy, especially as they refuse to pursue only the transcendent without the particular, without the physical, and without appearance. Marcano opens up the discussion for an "erotic mode" of engaging philosophy, one that allows for black women to grasp the greatness of philosophy as well as its failures.

Oscar R. Martí also is cognizant of the fact that racialized women philosophers and "ethnic" philosophers are often perceived as abandoning the "noble" philosophical tradition established through the practices and assumptions of white male philosophers. Martí critically explores some of the reasons why "gender and ethnicity philosophers" (his phrase) are deemed ersatz and claimed to be doing "illegitimate" philosophy. For example, he critically and insightfully engages such presumptive claims as "gender and ethnicity philosophers" are opportunistic and ideologically driven, that their arguments are poorly made, that their methods deviate from traditional ("better") forms of philosophizing, and that their way of doing philosophy violates "good" philosophy.

IV. Philosophy and the Geopolitics of Knowledge Production

Nelson Maldonado-Torres opens this section by tracing his identity as a Puerto Rican/U.S. Latino of mixed African descent. He thinks through this identity and explores the discovery that he had to find alternative spaces to satisfy his interests in the field of philosophy. He argues that what he began to find of value in philosophy could only be continued in Religious Studies and Ethnic Studies—two of the fields that many philosophers, as he argues, would consider to be related to a less "genuine" philosophical enterprise. He became interested in modern religious thought and non-Western philosophies and religions, and important questions about the legacy of Western imperial projects and their impact on political life, the academy, and thinking in general. He found that the questions that he valorized as philosophically significant connect with fundamental questions raised by subjects from the Third World and marginalized communities in the First. Philosophy, as he found it, and as it continues to exist in its current constitution could not accommodate questions of liberation, race, and empire. Maldonado-Torres concludes that such shortcomings provide an opportunity to reach out to new associations that help to open up new possibilities for doing work in the discipline, what he sees as characteristic of the Caribbean Philosophical Association (CPA) where African, Afro-Caribbean, Latin American, Euro-Caribbean, and U.S. scholars meet to discuss, among other things, the decolonization of philosophical reflection by "shifting" of the "geography of reason."

Lewis Ricardo Gordon takes up the theme of his own identity within the context of shifting geographical and linguistic spaces. He offers insights concerning the arguments that he advanced for the motto (i.e., "Shifting the Geography of Reason") of the CPA, and also draws attention to the ways in which his own identity underwent/undergoes various shifts. Both Gordon and Maldonado-Torres' chapters function within the context of larger, transversal connections, philosophical, political, and geographical, especially as both traveled through subaltern regions as a way of meeting other philosophers/thinkers and engaging in South–South dialogues without, as Gordon argues, forming a reactionary relationship with *el Norte*. What Gordon sees as the three dynamics of "subaltern" thought, namely, questions regarding philosophical anthropology, philosophies of freedom, and the meta-critiques of reason, I take to be important discursive and existential sites shared by black, Latino/a philosophers in the United States. Hence, Gordon's reflections function as an inclusive site, combining insights grounded in terms of his experiences through communities that were not only Afro-Latin American but also Afro-Indigenous Latin American.

V. Philosophy, Language, and Hegemony

In this last section, George Yancy raises the issue of African American vernacular speech as a neglected topic within the field of African American philosophy in particular and philosophy of language more generally. Yancy argues that black philosophers have not as of yet seriously grappled with the potential meta-philosophical implications embedded within the assumption that African American vernacular speech has the capacity to articulate modes of cognition that are not necessarily captured by so-called Standard American English. This raises significant issues regarding how black English is linked to particular ways of existentially or social ontologically engaging the world. Yancy pulls from the important work of African American linguist Geneva Smitherman to help in framing his argument.

Drawing on the fact that it is no secret that philosophy in the United States is far from inclusive, Elizabeth Millán's chapter critiques the pernicious exclusionary practice of assuming that only French, German, and English are *the* linguistic sites of philosophical expression, which she argues is the status that they receive in graduate programs where the study of such languages is part of the serious training students undergo to become masters or doctors of philosophy. Millán sees this as a fundamental limitation, one that assumes that philosophy was born with the Greeks, and reached its culmination in Europe, and then in the United States. Although there are many exclusions made on the way to creating the canon of philosophy in the United States, Millán specifically examines the exclusion of Spanish as a philosophical language. She views the exclusion of Spanish as a philosophical language as resulting in a high cost: the silencing of important philosophical voices from which all of us still have much to learn.

Last but not least, José Medina ends this section and the book. Medina is cognizant of the ways in which Hispanic philosophers lose linguistic capital on the basis of speaking with an accent or if they allow Spanish to impact their discourse within academic settings, specifically within the context of philosophy. Along with this, from his own experiences, he is aware of those who ask questions like: Is there a philosophical tradition in Spanish? The privileging of linguistic sites (say, English, German, and French) is linked to the privileging of philosophical traditions and cultural hegemony. On the way toward locating and examining significant forms of linguistic resistance and subversive negotiations, Medina critiques what he sees as inadequate semantic views, the Monopoly Model and the Free Trade Model. He proposes a Negotiating Model that he argues provides for linguistic interaction without assuming the exclusivity or the universality of linguistic resources. He argues against the constraining and disciplining of diversity and valorizes the importance of linguistic differences and the worldviews that the latter may embody. For Medina, this process of valorization constitutes a site of the proliferation of diversification, and, to use his language, one that is required by justice—one that attempts to heal various omissions and silences.

NOTES

1. bell hooks, *Talking Back: Thinking Feminist, Thinking Black* (Boston: South End Press, 1989), 9.

2. Jorge J.E. Gracia, "Race or Ethnicity? An Introduction," in Jorge J.E. Gracia (ed.) *Race Or Ethnicity?: On Black and Latino Identity* (Ithaca, NY: Cornell University Press, 2007), 11.

3. Linda Martín Alcoff, "Of Philosophy and Guerilla Wars" in George Yancy (ed.) *The Philosophical I: Personal Reflections on Life in Philosophy* (Lanham, MD: Rowman & Littlefield, 2002), 185.

4. George Yancy, "Situated Black Women's Voices in/on the Profession of philosophy, in *Hypatia: A Journal of Feminist Philosophy*, 23, no. 2, (2008): 171.

5. Yancy, "Situated Black Women's Voices in/on the Profession of philosophy," 171.

6. See Schutte's chapter, this volume.

7. See Mendieta's chapter, this volume.

8. For more on the importance of avoiding conflating forms of racism and avoiding the black–white binary, see Linda Alcoff, "Latinos Beyond the Binary," under articles: http://www.alcoff.com/.

9. Joe R. Feagin, *The White Racial Frame: Centuries of Racial Framing and Counter-Framing* (New York: Routledge, 2010), 118–19.

10. See Millán's chapter, this volume.

11. See Alcoff's chapter, this volume.

12. See Marcano's chapter, this volume.

13. See Martí's chapter, this volume.

14. See Maldonado-Torres's chapter, this volume.

15. See Mills' chapter, this volume.

16. See Pappas' chapter, this volume.

17. See McClendon's chapter, this volume.

18. See Ofelia Schutte's chapter, this volume.

19. See George Yancy, "Introduction: Philosophy and the Situated Narrative Self," in George Yancy (ed.) *The Philosophical I: Personal Reflections on Life in Philosophy* (Lanham, MD: Rowman & Littlefield, 2002). Also, see George Yancy, "Introduction: No Philosophical Oracle Voices," in George Yancy (ed.) *Philosophy in Multiple Voices* (Lanham, MD: Rowman & Littlefield, 2007).

20. Part of this formulation is taken from Linda Alcoff's work where, within a larger critical discussion about visible identities, agency, resistance, and what it means to be a self, she offers three very insightful responses to her critics. See her "Three Responses," in *Philosophy Today*, 53, (2009): 63.

21. Alcoff, "Three Responses," 63.

22. I have written about this in my authored book, *Black Bodies, White Gazes, The Continuing Significance of Race* (Lanham, MD: Rowman & Littlefield, 2008), especially in chapter 2.

23. See Alcoff's chapter, this volume.

24. See Scott's chapter, this volume.

25. Peggy McIntosh, "White privilege and Male Privilege: A Personal Account of Coming to See Correspondences through Work in Women's Studies," in Rechard Delgado and Jean Stefancic (eds.) *Critical White Studies: Looking Behind the Mirror* (Philadelphia: Temple University Press, 1997), 293.

26. McIntosh, "White privilege and Male Privilege," 294.

27. Immanuel Kant, *Observations on the Feeling of the Beautiful and the Sublime*, trans. John T. Goldthwait, 1764; (Berkeley: University of California Press, 1960), 113.

28. Alexis Shotwell, "Appropriate Subjects: Whiteness and the Discipline of Philosophy," in George Yancy (ed.) *The Center Must Not Hold: White Women Philosophers on the Whiteness of Philosophy* (Lanham, MD: Rowman & Littlefield, 2010), 124.

29. Shotwell, "Appropriate Subjects," 124–25.

30. Charles W. Mills, *Blackness Visible: Essays on Philosophy and Race* (Ithaca, NY: Cornell University Press, 1998), 4.

31. James Baldwin, *The Fire Next Time* (New York: Random House, 1963/1995), 101.

PART I

COLONIZATION/DECOLONIZATION:
PHILOSOPHY AND CANON FORMATION

CHAPTER ONE

ALIEN AND ALIENATED

Linda Martín Alcoff

I

Some years ago, while discussing with my continental philosophy class the famous claim by Walter Benjamin that the "hatred . . . nourished by the image of [one's] enslaved ancestors"[1] provides the most powerful motivation possible for revolutionary action, I allowed myself to imagine (out loud) tying a rope around the well-known local statue of Christopher Columbus, pulling the statue over, and dragging it to the ground. The students sitting in the classroom, only one of whom was a Latina, stared at me with blank perplexity, their foreheads creased with the effort to understand. Some of them literally had their mouths open. How could I possibly make an analogy between the "discoverer" Christopher Columbus and the statues of tyrants that have been torn down in recent memory, from Saddam Hussein to Stalin? Have I lost my marbles?

As a Latina in the academic world of North American philosophy, I regularly feel that, indeed, I have lost, or am in the process of losing, my marbles. Neither my general lived experience, nor my reference points in argumentation, nor my routine affective responses to events, nor my philosophical intuitions are shared with most people in my immediate milieu. Miranda Fricker calls this situation "hermeneutic marginalization" to name the effects of inequality on the domain of socially available meanings.[2] Like Roquentin, Sartre's anti-hero in his early novel *Nausea*, Latinas in philosophy often live without the sort of cultural and social recognition that would provide an uptake or confirmation of our interior lives, a fact that might indeed cause one to hallucinate, as he did, grotesque images when looking into the mirror.

23

In this chapter, I explore the problem of alienation for Latinos/as in academic philosophy in north America (a problem that is obviously analogous to the alienation of many other groups). Given our alienation, one might reasonably come to believe that assimilation is the natural and even just solution, since assimilation would decrease the experience of dislocation and enhance effective communication. But it remains open to question whether assimilation is either possible *or* desirable, or whether assimilation is even an alternative to alienation rather than in reality a form of alienation itself. If assimilation requires self-alienation from one's own hermeneutic horizon, for whom is it a solution? I suggest there are philosophical reasons, as well as political ones, to resist assimilation, given that coercive one-way assimilation forecloses what we might choose to read, teach, cite, and argue.

Yet on the other side, one might argue that if we militantly reject assimilation we will undoubtedly exacerbate our alienation from the Anglo majority in the profession. And anyway, what if assimilation simply involves an acclimation to majority conventions: Is that so unjust? Without assimilating, we cannot formulate arguments that will be meaningful or intelligible within the dominant domain of discourse, and thus we will not be able to expand or alter that domain. And one might argue further that the quest to resist assimilation embroils us in assumptions about neat Latino/Anglo divisions and "authentic" Latina/o dispositions. Can't a Latino just study Davidson if he or she wants to without having to engage in political self-examination?

II

These are the sorts of internal debates I suspect many of us have in our heads, especially as we enter the profession in graduate school and have to make decisions about dissertation topics, language-proficiency exams, and the cultivation of areas of competence and specialization. And our philosophical and political evaluations of these choices are always circumscribed by the pressing goal of academic success, which in our profession usually is measured simply by a tenure-track job at any institution anywhere for whatever pay is offered (as a former chair once told me, entering philosophy is like entering the priesthood; it requires a vow of poverty).

In order to even begin answering such questions about the harmfulness, legitimacy, or advisability of assimilation, we need to begin with an exploration of alienation. The particular level of alienation that I experienced may well be due to the sort of private, expensive, largely white-Anglo institution at which I was teaching at the time of the unfortunate Columbus statue-defacement example; I do not experience such alienation today teaching at the City University of New York (CUNY; now I just have the usual sorts of generational alienation from students who know more about reggaeton than about reggae). But outside of CUNY and a few other places, Latino students are scarce in U.S. higher education, no doubt affected by the fact that Latinos also are the group most likely to drop out of high school (I didn't know I was simply manifesting a statistical likelihood when I dropped out). Only 12% of Latinos in the United States graduate from college, as compared with 30% of whites and 17% of blacks (and all of these numbers—whites included—are of course much lower than they should be).[3] Although we currently represent about 15% of the U.S. population (and rising), we make up less than 3% of the philosophy profession. Is there a relationship between Latino difficulties in educational institutions and our social and cultural alienation? Duh?

Africa and Latin America are alone among the continents of the globe that engender an alarming level of disrespect, ignorance, and contempt in north America.[4] Military dictatorships, corruption, poverty, disease, and regularly occurring revolutions are the stuff of comedy when white North Americans land unhappily in one of these backward parts of the world, from Woody Allen cavorting with the revolutionary guerillas in *Bananas*, to Richard Dreyfuss haplessly forced to imitate a crazed dictator in *Moon Over Parador*—astoundingly in brown face. It is all good for a laugh. When Chinua Achebe's manuscript of his masterful novel, *Things Fall Apart*, was first reviewed by a publisher in 1958, Alan Hill, one of the editors, recalled the initial response: "Would anyone possibly buy a novel by an African?" Western reviewers later praised the book for its portrait of rural Igbo life, as if it was a piece of anthropological documentation. Its literary qualities were ignored.[5]

Can there be any coincidence about the fact that Latin America and Africa are viewed either contemptuously or paternalistically in the United States, and the fact that Latin American and African philosophy is invisible in Anglo-American philosophy curricula? Malcolm X motivated his pan-Africanism by the claim that the ways in which your nations of origin are viewed will determine the status of minority communities in the diaspora. African and Latin American intellectual cultures have not yet been accorded what Arturo Arias calls "the privilege of recognition" in the United States.[6] This is to say that our philosophical traditions are *not even represented badly* in the mainstream U.S. philosophy curriculum: *They are not represented at all*. No wonder we hardly feel at home in institutions of learning, or that we are so often tempted to downplay our backgrounds, if not join in the derision of them.

For many Latinos/as I know who teach in colleges and universities, daily social alienation is so normal that they begin to see it as normative. One thing many of us have in common is that we have come a long distance to be where we are today—a social and cultural distance as well as a geographical one. The distance we have come is in fact rarely a mere matter of geography but more often a combination of geography, race and ethnicity, culture, nationality, first language, and class, some or all of which mark us as different from the majority. Given this distance, the alienation we experience might be interpreted—by others as well as by ourselves—as simply the expected price of travel.

Yet our very experiences of alienation can be quite useful at times in developing, and motivating, philosophical analysis, as well as in our pedagogy. When I teach the Marxist theory of alienation, I always use the example of the shirt factory where I worked as a piece-rate seamstress (after I dropped out of college, another statistical regularity!). I was assigned to sew the top stitch on collars for a rate per piece that required me to produce one perfect collar every seven seconds of my eight-hour shift in order to make minimum wage. I use this experience to provide a vibrant picture of the four forms of alienation Marx describes in *Economic and Philosophic Manuscripts of 1844*: the alienation from the product I produced, from the process of producing it, from other workers, and from my own "species-being." And yet I know that the use of this example, while vivifying the analysis and giving students something that helps them to both understand and remember Marx's ideas, risks alienating me from my students even further (and in ways Marx himself did not theoretically elaborate). The alienating aspects of working conditions that I describe for my students sometimes resonate with their own experiences of manual or otherwise proletarianized jobs. But there are other experiences of alienation that could prove similarly useful and illuminating although they may be less commonly shared, such as linguistic, religious, sexual, and cultural alienation. For example, the peculiar challenges of bicultural and cross-racial negotiations within one's own immediate family provide much interesting fodder for considerations of the effects of hermeneutic and phenomenological differences in baseline knowledge.

As philosophically useful as it may be, however, the experience of alienation has many negative ramifications both for one's personal well-being as well as for one's ability to perform one's job in the academy. If students do not understand what I am talking about, or perceive me as biased, "too" political, or an unlikely prospect to be a qualified professor of philosophy, my teaching evaluations might show signs of strain. My ability to work with colleagues may show similar strain if my point of view on matters of departmental concern cannot be made intelligible because of my hermeneutic marginalization. Fricker defines the "hermeneutically marginalized" as those who "participate unequally in the practices through which social meanings are generated" with the result that the experiences of the members of such groups "are left inadequately conceptualized and so ill-understood, perhaps even by the subjects themselves."[7] Hermeneutic marginalization disables participation in the construction of new meanings and new languages, which results in an interpretive incapacity to render one's experiences intelligible to others. To be marginalized from the construction of meanings and terms can produce what Fricker calls a "hermeneutic gap" of intelligibility, and she notes that this can affect content—the absence of available terms—as well as style, the manner in which we communicate. The adverse effects here tend to amalgamate and feed on each other, such as in the case she discusses of a woman who is sexually harassed before the second wave of the feminist movement invented this concept. Because the woman is unable to name her problem or its source in a way that will be understood correctly and taken seriously, she is then further cut off from social participation: She quits her job, cannot obtain unemployment benefits because she quit rather than was fired and cannot name the cause, and continues to fall in a spiraling effect. The end result of such amalgamating effects is a deflation of the very hermeneutic community that might be engaged in the work of developing new meanings and terms as well as more effective manners of redress.

III

These are the kinds of problems that create a motivation to assimilate. One is assimilated if one is absorbed or incorporated and thus comes to resemble the larger body, as when a food is assimilated when eaten. In this sense, assimilation is often distinguished from integration, which is a way of making room for a new entity, or of unifying a set of parts into a coherent whole. The term assimilao can connote a process of hybridization and bilateral influence, as Paula Moya argued using the famous lines of Tato Laviera's poem: "assimilated? Que assimilated, brother, soy asimilao."[8] But the dominant North American understanding of assimilation signifies a one-way accommodation, a process in which a minority adopts the majority mode of thinking, acting, even being. Given the receding percentages of the white Anglo majority, however, that "majority point of view" is losing its stability and meaningfulness; increasingly, the culture of U.S. urban life constitutes a pluritopic, rather than monotopic, hermeneutic horizon, inclusive of multiple and conflicting points of view, narratives of history, and opinions about the salience of race and the value of such things as markets, religious practice, and multiculturalism. These substantive differences sometimes result in differences in philosophical intuitions on topics as esoteric as intrinsic properties or the nature of ideal justice or the flexibility of linguistic contexts. I recently attended a talk on philosophy of language where Gricean concepts of implicature were being debated with the example of police interrogation techniques, and the philosophical differences in the room were interestingly correlated to those who referred to the subjects of police interrogation as "criminals" and those who referred to them as "the accused."

What is clear is that the question of assimilation and alienation are not simply of concern to the minorities who must adapt, but also to the majority whose cultural and political dominance may be at risk. If we continue to assume that assimilation is the natural and rightful solution to alienation, and the justifiable price for traveling the distance from Latin America to the United States or from factory to college classroom, then we will foreclose the possibility of having a discussion about hermeneutic inequality and its effects on the norms of current practices in all areas of social life, including academic philosophy. I am suggesting, in short, that we shift away from debating the psychic cost of assimilation, and whether its benefit for individuals outweighs its costs to the collective. Rather, we need to be asking whether philosophy itself suffers when we accept assimilation as, to quote Baldwin, the "price of the ticket."

Thus, the issues of alienation and assimilation are not only relevant to the daily grievances of our working conditions, such as those that concern social interaction, chilly climates, and one's ability for effective pedagogical communication. There also are philosophical issues at stake. I suggest that this claim is less antithetical to the traditions of Latin American philosophy. Such thinkers as Sarmiento, Bolivar, Martí, Mariátegui, Vasconcelos, Ramos, and others threw doubt on the assumption that the sphere of ideas operates above and beyond the fray of cultural imbrication. For Bolivar, for example, one cannot answer the question "What is the best or most just form of government?" in the abstract, without carefully assessing the local, historical conditions. Well before the American pragmatists, he argues that an idealized approach to political theory would be empty and useless. Similarly for Ramos, the nature of the self and mind cannot be approached as generic universals, but should rather be understood as constitutively related to the social conditions in which they emerge. Martí claimed that philosophy itself can be alienated.[9] What this tradition suggests is that the cultural identity of philosophers will not be irrelevant to the philosophies they develop, a belief that is implicitly accepted in Anglo-American circles, as we teach about the "Scottish Enlightenment," "British Empiricism," and "German Idealism." And yet rarely are the implications of this connection between philosophy and culture overtly explored.

In what follows, I explore both the philosophical and the everyday experiential issues involved in alienation and assimilation, as well as the interactions between these levels. In the conclusion, I suggest some remedies.

IV

When we consider the condition of Latinos in north American philosophy departments, we need to disaggregate between those from Latin America and those who were born and raised in the United States. We also might disaggregate further along region, race/ethnicity, and nationality, but this first distinction is highly significant.[10] Latinos are among the most under-represented groups in philosophy, and if one eliminates from this group those who were raised and educated in Latin America, the numbers *vastly* drop. This has something to do with the likely class background this distinction tracks, but also may well be because Latin Americans, as opposed to U.S. Latinos, are likely to experience less *culturally based* alienation, of the sort that can deprive one of the conceptual repertoire necessary for a minimal understanding of one's own experience. That is, Latin Americans who grew up in Latin America will likely learn something of their own political, intellectual, and cultural history, will likely come into contact with some articulations of what it means to be Bolivian or Nicaraguan, or to be Quechua or mestizo. Despite the gender and racial hierarchies and exclusions, national narratives of *latinidad* assume that Latin American countries are sites of cultural and intellectual production.[11]

If Hegel is to be believed, all knowledge requires some level of self-knowledge given the ineliminable historical and cultural positioning of the knower. Knowing is a relational category, and one needs to train our critical analysis on both sides of the relation. It is just common sense that some self-examination is necessary in order to ensure that one's argumentative responses to philosophical ideas are not based on irrational prejudice, ideology, artificially induced limits on one's imaginative capacity, monocultural blindspots, emotional projections, or limited experience. No one believes the process of self-knowing can achieve perfect transparency or completion, and yet a rational approach to the pursuit of knowledge should clearly include the pursuit of self-knowledge as a necessary, and necessarily ongoing, component. This has implications for both the alienated and the nonalienated among us: Latinos need to have a sufficiently sizable hermeneutical territory in order to be able to flex their relevant muscles and develop concepts that can explain and analyze our specific experiences. Anglos or non-Latinos also need to lose their blindspots and overcome their ignorance about Latino realities in order to increase their own self-knowledge as well as their ability to have effective dialogical encounters in an increasingly diverse academic environment. By learning about Latinos, or others, non-Latinos may come to realize, for example, that some concepts and assumptions they operate with are not universally shared or presumed to be obviously true by all.

Ofelia Schutte's work on cultural alterity is a useful place to begin an exploration of Latino alienation and its effects on self-knowledge. Schutte's analyses help to amplify and expand on Fricker's conceptual definition of hermeneutical inequality, especially given that her account of cultural alterity emerges out of her work on cross-cultural communication and the possibilities for negotiating political unity across difference. Schutte's work has been concerned about the political, ethical, and epistemic implications of otherness, particularly for those who are put into the role of "the other."

For Latinos, of course, otherness is not the only problem. When cultural alterity is paired with cultural subordination, Schutte shows how it can lead to hermeneutic opacity, attributions of essentialized pejorative differences, and one's invisibility as a "producer of culture."[12] "[G]aps in communication may cause one speaker's discourse to appear incoherent or insufficiently organized."[13] If a dominant speaker finds a subordinate speaker unintelligible, he may be quick to judge the speech inadequate rather than motivated toward further exploration or an acknowledgment of his own possible limitations in understanding. Women in particular are generally viewed as "transmitters" of culture whose role is to conserve rather than challenge, interpret or create culture. This will make Anglo-dominant intellectual environments especially difficult for Latinas, who will tend to become invisible as thinkers.

Schutte shows how her own alienation in the Anglo-dominant world of philosophy operates to truncate her visible, public self. She explains that because:

> the local metanarrative exists in tension with what the Latina knows and experiences, . . . the former shuts out the latter. This is why sometimes, when some interlocutor responds to me (say, at the office) in reference to the self I perform there as a speaking subject, I get the sense that this colleague is not speaking to me at all; that my interlocutor is missing something, because the "me" that is culturally different is ignored, shut off, or bypassed.[14]

The silencing that occurs here is different from the sort of examples Fricker discusses, where a lifetime of hermeneutic marginalization and testimonial injustice wears down speakers, demolishes their confidence and linguistic capabilities, and disables conceptual formation. Schutte describes cases where the person is not silenced, but that what she says is only partially heard or understood. When cultural alterity exists in a context where one culture has hegemony, "there is always a residue of meaning that will not be reached in cross-cultural endeavors."[15] Partial understanding exacerbates the problem, because the dominant speaker may believe that he has understood everything that was said, although he actually understood only a part. The problem is both inequality and cultural marginalization. Although it is naïve to hope for a complete transparency of meanings across difference, Schutte's point is that it is possible to *improve* one's capacity for cross-cultural communication, and thus, perhaps, to overcome alienation without assimilation. Philosophers could, among others, attend to the processes by which concepts and meanings are made available, or not, for our theoretical uses, and could consider the impact that arbitrarily restrictive processes have on the epistemic status (i.e., degree of justification) that we can rightfully claim for our most cherished conclusions. How can we know whether we have consulted all of the relevant considerations that may disprove a thesis, a common point in justification theories these days, if we are operating in an arbitrarily restricted discursive environment? How can we claim to be enacting epistemic virtues when we neglect to pursue the self-knowledge that would make our othering practices more apparent? In a plurivocal culture, or university, justification requires gaining multicultural literacy.

Schutte suggests that the incommensurability that alienation can sometimes engender can actually provide a fruitful impetus for deeper critique, in the same way that anomalous experimental outcomes can instigate a shift in theoretical models. What if instead of a quick dismissal of incomprehensible or inadequate sounding claims, I allow the unfamiliar to "resonate in me as a kind of strangeness, as a kind of displacement of the usual expectation," she asks. What if we refuse to "bypass these experiences or subsume them under an already familiar category"?[16] This might inspire new thinking, as well as an enriched capacity for dialogue.

Such open and productive engagements with the strange are, as we know, all too rare. More often, subordinate interlocutors will have to do much of the work of cross-cultural communication by themselves if any dialogue is to be achieved. But Schutte's phenomenological description shows the costs of this unfair distribution of dialogical labor: Those individuals who operate in more than one culture will necessarily have to leave part of their selves behind each time they cross over, thus exacerbating the injustice. Her thick description of how this feels reminded me of Simone De Beauvoir's account of the inherent conflict between what is signified human and what is signified feminine. To be recognized in North American contexts, Schutte explains, "I must show that . . . I can perform, in my North American voice, a public erasure of my Latina voice. . . . My white Anglo-American counterpart is not called on to perform such a feat with respect to her own cultural background."[17] She goes on to acknowledge that, although her white counterpart may have to erase her working-class or lesbian background, still "she does not need to combine her cultural background with, say, that of Middle Eastern, Asian, African, or Latin American people before being accepted as an important contributor to society and culture."[18] In some cases, Latinas, in fact, may be valued only or primarily for their cross-over labor, for their ability to represent (and "explain") Latino culture to an Anglo-American world, which requires exceeding "the category of the national" and incorporating "two or more cultures into our way of being." But she points out that this is always accompanied by the demand to "demonstrate that the way we bring such cultures together can benefit the Anglo-American public."[19]

Schutte thus describes the alienating effects that result when Latinas achieve recognition, but in terms that are weighted toward the dominant culture. In order to gain recognition, she explains, "I need to be knowledgeable in the language and epistemic maneuvers of the dominant culture, the same culture that in its everyday practice marks me as culturally 'other' than itself." It is thus only when we transcend our culturally "other" self—when we assume the speaking voice of the dominant—that we gain recognition. The price for this is predictably high.

This description of alienation casts a different light on the claim that assimilation is innocuous or the simple price of inclusion or of success. In the experiences Schutte describes, one's Latina self is shown to be precisely *not* included and *not* successful. There is another self present in the Anglo-dominant room, recognized for her abilities and sound arguments, perhaps, but it is not the self with which one initially entered.

V

Crossover Dreams

Most viewers of the Academy Award-winning movie A *Beautiful Mind*, which told the story of John Nash, the brilliant and troubled mathematician, were probably oblivious to the neat trick of assimilation the movie performed. Nash was in real life married to Alicia Lardé, a *Salvadorena* whom he had met while she was studying physics at MIT in the 1950s. In the film, Lardé is referred to simply as "Alicia Nash," her identity and national origin from El Salvador is ignored, and she is played by a white Anglo actress, Jennifer Connelly. As Lisa Navarrete argued in her critique of the movie in the *Los Angeles Times*, North American audiences lost an opportunity to see an atypical Latina role model, and Latina actresses lost an opportunity for a potentially career-making part.[20] Lardé's *latinindad* was rendered invisible, or, in the parlance of Latin America, it was disappeared.

I find this a fitting metaphor for the condition of too many Latinos in philosophy, where the price of admission requires such an extreme assimilation that we may feel ourselves to have "disappeared." Sometimes this happens willingly, when we try to merge ourselves into the wallpaper, and other times unwillingly, as Schutte describes. But visibility and full presence is not easy to accomplish. Part of why it is difficult to be wholly yourself as a Latina or any person of color in the academy is because so much of our daily work life involves white racism and cultural chauvinism. Airing honest opinions about these experiences can put one in jeopardy. If you don't have job security you have to censor yourself constantly when asked ordinary questions like, for example, "how was the conference?" or "what did you think of that paper?" or "how is your class going?" Moreover, Spanish has not typically been accepted for the language requirement in philosophy programs, nor is Latin American philosophy acceptable as a concentration area for comprehensive exams. Those who write their dissertations in this area are still, to this day, taking a career risk. If we (or others) do have an interest in these philosophical traditions, it must be pursued on our own time, in effect, as an extra to the work of the "real" philosophy about which we are required to establish proficiency. Thus, we may be able to appear in the movie, or in the profession, but not as ourselves.

The question of assimilation is an every day affair. Every time I reject the use of the term *America* to refer only to the United States, or insist on the inclusion of my first surname and its accent mark, or purposefully allow myself to use classroom examples that reference Latino experiences, I am resisting assimilation. I am self-conscious about using Spanglish in class—students seem to enjoy my expressions of frustration (*Dios mio*), but then I wonder if they are enjoying it as an exotic or comic moment. I become so self-consciously self-conscious until every Spanish word feels like a studied performance. How do we distinguish voluntary assimilation from simple self-protection? How can we unravel our own motivations, or those of others, as if these are clear-cut?

Graduate study is an intense period of intellectual activity, and one often finds one's initial intentions giving way to new roads of inquiry opening up. I intended to write on Marx and ended up in epistemology (of all things). For some inexplicable reason, Wittgenstein inspired hours of delight and fascination. The vagaries of individual intellectual trajectories are too idiosyncratic to permit sociological studies that might look for intelligible patterns. Yet my friend Ofelia Schutte works on cultural alterity, Eduardo Mendieta works on the ethics of communication, Jorge Gracia works on national, ethnic, and cultural identity, Jorge Garcia on racism, Angelo Corlett on reparations, and so on, such that one begins to wonder. In some cases, the connections of their philosophical interests to their own experience is obvious, in other cases more oblique, such as Mariana Ortega who, as an exile, has worked for years on Heidegger's notion of home.

Searches for such patterns are dangerous, however. Would these suggest that Gomez, who works on fourth-dimensionality, is more alienated than the others? This raises the question that I raised earlier but have been skirting: What *is* assimilation? How can we tell the difference between assimilated behavior and autonomous choices? Does the very concept of assimilation embroil us in assumptions about neat Latino/Anglo divisions and "authentic" Latina/o dispositions (i.e., simplistic essentialisms about difference)? If we cannot make the distinction between assimilated and unassimilated behavior, then the evaluative question about whether assimilation is wrong may be a nonstarter.

I suggest a distinction between assimilation and integration that follows standard definitions but provides a useful demarcation. Assimilation is absorption, where a new item is transformed so as to become part of a whole. The larger whole is augmented, but not qualitatively changed if assimilation has occurred properly. It is only when assimilation fails—as when a new organ is rejected by the body, for example—that threatens qualitative change and the development of disease. Integration, by contrast, is a combinatory process that desegregates in order to produce a newly unified system. It is not an absorption of a smaller part by a larger whole, but a system modification that yields a new integrated unit.

Now let us take these machine and organic metaphors and transfer the ideas to political realities involving power and subordination. Forcible absorption of a subordinated minority involves coercion, hermeneutic inequality, a disappearing of fundamental characteristics, and injustice. Assimilation in this sense will necessarily involve a certain amount of invisibility and concealment of the aspects of the minority that cannot be absorbed without causing qualitative change. Where integration makes a space in the system for the new part, requiring some dialogue and negotiation from both parties based on equality, assimilation requires only compliance.

Thus, one way we might then demarcate assimilation is by whether our choices of dissertation topic, advisor, areas of specialization and competence, course topics, book projects, and so on have been made on the basis of some coercive aspects of our department, institution, or profession generally. Was Spanish allowed to fulfill the language requirement? Would Latin American philosophy be covered in the history of philosophy exam? Would the department support a course in Latin American philosophy, encourage students to take it, even include it in a distribution requirement for majors? Would a publication in Spanish in a leading journal in Latin America count toward tenure? Or is the answer to all of these questions, as is usual, no?

There are a number of philosophers publishing in English today who are defying the standard, coercive conventions and choosing to write about Latin American philosophy and about philosophical issues particularly of interest to Latinos. These include Schutte, Ortega, Mendieta, Gracia, Saenz, Vallega, Millán, Nuccetelli and Seay, Valadez, Corlett, Lugones, Vargas, myself, and others. But those who are untenured or still in graduate school may reasonably be uncertain about whether to follow this model, given the persistently narrow parameters of philosophy that gatekeeping journals operate within. Some come to us to ask about the advisability of doing this; others simply stay carefully away (perhaps from fear of the taint, perhaps from the happenstance that their own philosophical interests do not tend in this direction).

When I was a graduate student there were no such models to follow. My dissertation advisor, a highly respected Cubano, did not engage much with Latin American philosophers except those doing contemporary analytic epistemology, although he regularly traveled and gave papers in Spanish. Thus, the option of doing Latin American philosophy or philosophical issues related specifically to Latinos was not a visible option for me, or a viable one. I had children to support; I needed a job. I well remember my internal debates about whether to pursue my interest in feminist philosophy, another derided subfield viewed as politically motivated rather than philosophically respectable. I made the decision not to write a dissertation in this area, although my dissertation topic was motivated by issues that arose for me in my work on feminist philosophy. In that way, I ensured my enthusiasm about the project but in a way that would not harm me on the job market. Twenty-odd years later, it is still a gamble to write a dissertation on feminist topics. I argued with a colleague in a search recently that a candidate we were considering should be viewed as a good metaphysician; he had classified her as simply a feminist philosopher, because she worked on the metaphysics of gender. She never made it to our interview list. Nor did a top graduate I liked who was from one of the top two departments in the country, because her work in philosophy of language was centered on sexual justice.

The American Philosophical Association (APA) has supported a Committee on Latinos/ Hispanics since the early 1990s to provide some concerted work around issues affecting Latinos in the profession. I was chair of this committee from 1998 to 2001 and together with previous chairs worked to expand the opportunities to do philosophical work on Latin American philosophy and issues related to Latinos, to have Spanish count for language requirements, to have important work translated into English, and to overcome the prejudicial treatment Latinos sometimes receive in the profession. (Spanish now can count in some places for a language proficiency just as the general language requirement is being eliminated!) The national office of the APA during those years was very supportive of our efforts and those of the other "diversity committees," as we came to call ourselves. The APA Board of Officers was not always supportive although sometimes we could garner a majority of votes on the Board. I remember a luncheon of the Board I attended, at which I was seated next to someone who, in the course of a general discussion about Appiah's work, opined that Africa as a continent simply has no history. I argued with him; he argued back. He was a leading member of our profession.

In the course of my work as chair of the Committee on Latinos/Hispanics, I discovered that philosophy is woefully behind its colleague disciplines in taking proactive steps toward racial and ethnic inclusiveness. Political scientists, historians, and the English profession—the three groups I looked most closely at for comparison—have extensive programs of scholarship, statistical gathering, internships, institutes, awards and honors, disciplinary assessments, even assessments of introductory textbooks, all with the aim of enhancing diversity in their profession and all with major amounts of resources attached. These were programs organized out of the national offices of their professional associations. And to judge from the steadily climbing numbers in their disciplines, there was substantive empirical evidence that the strategies were paying off. They were light years ahead of philosophy, which at the time had only one such institute created in a grassroots way by Howard McGary and Jorge Garcia at Rutgers, developed and run on their own time and on a shoestring budget.

What is wrong with philosophy? What is distinct about philosophy in comparison to these other fields is its self-understanding as a universal abstract conversation founded by the Greeks and not too terribly changed since then (we are still trying to figure out what the ideal forms of knowledge and justice are, and love to quote Whitehead that all subsequent philosophy is a footnote to Plato). The inclusion of independent minority voices who may raise new questions threatens the dominant narrative of philosophy and its ability to cloak itself as universal and uncompromised by its cultural location or its racial and ethnic uniformity.

The work of institutional reform nonetheless is continuing in philosophy at a steady pace. We have a paper prize in order to promote and legitimate work in Latin American philosophy, we maintain a newsletter, there have been several excellent conferences, and there is an increasing amount of serious work being published. The APA national office is helping once again by providing access to course syllabi on their website, and funding a variety of initiatives to enlarge the stream of Latino applicants to graduate school.

Meanwhile, we need to consider our goals: more Latinos in the profession no matter what they work on? Or more options of philosophical traditions available to all?

VI

An Unassimilated Theorist

If integration is preferable to assimilation, we must learn to speak in our own voice(s). We might take the example of Gloria Anzaldua here. Although she was not a trained philosopher, Anzaldua was a theorist who was fully herself in her writing, unwilling to play the part of the assimilated Latina. Both her work and its reception make an instructive example.[21]

As a philosopher, I read Anzaldua for her insights about and analyses of multiple oppression, mixed identities, and alternative epistemologies. But as another Latina trying to write theory, I read her as one dying for thirst chokes on the first gulp of water. Her fearless accounts of violence *within* the Chicano/a community, her unapologetic disclosures of her spiritual faith, and her belief in the theoretical value of the personal voice, emboldened me to reveal parts of myself in my own writing that had felt incongruous in the professional discourses of the academy, even in the supposedly anticonventional circles of feminist theory. Anzaldua's work went beyond the usual conventions of academic writing in order to make visible the relations between self and world, feeling and thinking, personal experience and theory.

Anzaldua did not self-censor, and provided clear, strong, honest reflections on the real nature of what she experienced in the academy, in the movement, and in daily life. She also refused to self-censor her Spanglish, a derided language that remains the mother tongue of many of us. Since she repudiated the need for institutional acceptance, hers is not a model all of us can follow (e.g., if we needed health insurance for our children). But she nonetheless presented an idea of how to write, how to publish, and how to theorize that is both instructive and energizing.

Like Kafka, however, Anzaldua's iconic status within feminism resulted in the contradiction of an iconoclast becoming the new standard. The status she attained in the 1990s as the "authentic voice of the multiply oppressed" often was paradoxically used to provide an epistemological foundation for antifoundationalist, postmodern theories. In other words, her work was used to bolster some of the exclusionary and elitist theoretical fashions of the very institution that made her marginal. I worried not only for the effects of this on her personally, but also about the effects on the reputation of her work. I thought of her situation as similar to the Che Guevara or Frida Kahlo problem of overexposure and commodification—serious engagement with their intellect has seemed to decrease in proportion with their worldwide fame. In the latest Hollywood movie on Frida's life, viewers get zero information on what her political views were, or what intellectual reasons she had for the themes of self-representation she chose in her work. If Anzaldua was always read in Women's Studies 101, but rarely in higher-level theory courses, a similar flattening out of her theoretical legacy is to be expected. Often cited, she remains undertheorized.

In reality, Anzaldua's body of work is well known only in a few circles. The story of her reception is quite complex. Within women's studies,

where she is required reading, she is too often exoticized as the voice of
the authentic. In feminist theory, she is either used as expert authority on
multiplicity or ignored, but rarely critiqued as a serious thinker should be.
Within Latino studies, she remains a maverick figure, unorthodox in both
style and content, and the themes of lesbian experience and feminism that
she wrote about remain marginalized.[22] In postcolonial theory, astoundingly,
she is nearly unread, with a few important exceptions (e.g., Walter Mignolo).

Two aspects of her writings can illustrate both her unassimilated,
unorthodox approach and the tendency of her work to be misread and
misused: The conceptualization of mestizahe, and the use of the personal
voice for doing theory. Anzaldua's positive articulation of mestizahe has been
used to support the celebration of hybridity, even though her own treatment of it is far from celebratory. Her use of the personal voice has been
taken up as an example of situated knowing, which is itself a deservedly
popular (although underarticulated) epistemological position. Yet I would
also argue that the extent to which Anzaldua validated personal experience
contradicts the main currents in feminist and social theory, in which the
move to authorize one's claims through invoking personal experience and
one's social identity has been widely undermined.[23]

For Anzaldua, the principal meaning of mestizahe is inclusivity. Mestizo peoples are better, Vasconcelos argued, because they are inclusive of
more than one culture and way of being in the world. The multiple character of the hybrid makes for a stronger, more adaptable, and more resilient
form than the vulnerable, single-strand genealogy of the pure bred. *Borderlands* often is read for its similarly hopeful portrayal of the mestiza's social
positionality, as having an enhanced capacity for cultural translation and
flexibility. In this way, the book supports a current trend in continental
philosophy that celebrates hybridity as the political and theoretical antidote
to essentialism.

But in contrast to Vasconcelos, the Mexican philosopher she draws
from to develop this concept, Anzaldua wrote as a Chicana living north of
the border who experienced hybridity as a difficult and precarious political situation and psychic experience. The hybrid individual in the north
is marginalized everywhere, often vilified, and usually full of self-doubt.
This is the main theme of *Borderlands/La Frontera*: the immense difficulties
that Chicanas and Chicanos must endure because of their bridge position
between cultures and races. Contrast her account of mestiza consciousness
with Deleuze and Guattari's romanticized portrait of the nomad as a role
model for deterritorialized subjectivity, a subjectivity freed from the being of
identity to emerge into the becoming of possibility. Far from celebrating the
lack of identity, Anzaldua wrote, "The ambivalence from the clash of voices
results in mental and emotional states of perplexity. Internal strife results in

insecurity and indecisiveness. The mestiza's dual or multiple personality is plagued by psychic restlessness."[24] Thus, Anzaldua's description and analysis of mestiza consciousness is not at all in line with the postmodernist celebration of hybridity; the fact that she is used as support for this indicates that her work is not read carefully or critically enough.

Thus, Borderlands/La Frontera gives a detailed first-person phenomenology of just how painful and difficult hybridity can be. Furthermore, it proposes hypothetical explanations that link the insecurity of hybridity to various forms of violence. In particular, Anzaldua worried that the shame and rootlessness of the mestizo can lead to excessive compensation, especially in the form of machismo:

> In the Gringo world, the Chicano suffers from excessive humility and self-effacement, shame of self and self-deprecation. Around Latinos he suffers from a sense of language inadequacy and its accompanying discomfort; with Native Americans he suffers from a racial amnesia which ignores our common blood, and from guilt because the Spanish part of him took their land and oppressed them. He has an excessive compensatory hubris when around Mexicans from the other side. It overlays a deep sense of racial shame . . . which leads him to put down women and even to brutalize them.[25]

For Anzaldua, the positive articulation of mestiza identity is a project to be undertaken, rather than something that is already in existence. Given the painfulness of hybridity, she argued that it is essential to provide some degree of coherence in order to avoid the incessant cultural collisions or violent compensations that result from the shame and frustration of alienated self-negation. This project to achieve coherence also works against poststructuralist celebrations of incoherence. On Anzaldua's view, incoherence is neither inevitable nor acceptable, but coherence will only be achieved through conscious effort and political struggle, through resisting assimilation and instead demanding integration. By writing in Spanglish as an out lesbian Chicana critic of both Chicano nationalism and assimilation, she was helping to bring about the possibility of integration.

Anzaldua suggests that we can create a positive identity through seeing how the mestiza is engaged in the valuable though often exhausting role of border crosser, negotiator, and mediator between races, and sometimes also between cultures, nations, and linguistic communities. The mixed person is a traveler often within her own home or neighborhood, translating and negotiating the diversity of meanings, practices, and forms of life. This vision provides a positive alternative to the mixed race person's usual representation as lack or as the tragically alienated figure. Being mixed means having resources for communication and understanding that are vital for political movements.

Today, the idea of being mixed and having a hybrid identity may no longer seem to be the liability it was in the days of the "tragic mulatto." Being mixed has some political and cultural cache, and the mixed person sometimes even enjoys an enhanced credibility in the white-dominant world. Yet the experiential difficulties of being mixed can persist in this new status, and in fact be increased as we try to negotiate an unmerited credibility among whites. Whether Anzaldua's analysis of the particularities of Chicana hybridity is applicable to hybrid identities generally, or to hybrid identities specifically now, in the current climate of globalization, needs reflective analysis.

A second aspect of Anzaldua's work that is relevant here is the political importance and theoretical legitimacy she accorded to the personal voice. Within philosophy, the personal voice is rarely heard, and only recently have journal papers been discontinuing use of the royal, and impersonal, "we." Anzaldua wrote in not only a personal voice but a richly personalized voice, weaving together descriptive sociology, history, and political critique with recipes, personal narrative, poetry, dream images, and other unexpurgated elements of a lively intellect.

In Anzaldua's view, similar to Nietzsche's in this regard, theory necessarily begins with the body and the subjective experiences that only come in first person form. The personal is unavoidable, ineliminable, carried everywhere the mind travels, even though, as Anzaldua believed, the mind's imaginative capacities can travel quite far. Nietzsche wrote in *The Genealogy of Morals* that "There is *only* a perspective seeing, *only* a perspective 'knowing'; and the *more* affects we allow to speak about one thing, the *more* eyes, different eyes, we can use to observe one thing, the more complete will our 'concept' of this thing, our 'objectivity,' be."[26] For both Anzaldua and Nietzsche, the presence of a particular and situated body is not always or simply a drag on theory.[27] The assumption that the body *is* a drag on theory—that the embodied experience of the personal realm will provide a drag of the particular against the attempts of the mind to develop universalizable theory—remains powerfully influential in philosophy. Anzaldua's view, again similar to Nietzsche's, is that the body and its feelings are both resource and motivation for theory:

> I do not believe that "distance" and "objectivity" alone help us come to terms with our issues. Distancing cannot be a major strategy—only a temporary breather. Total feeling and emotional immersion, the shocking drench of guilt or anger or frustration, wakes us up to some

of our realities. . . . The intellect needs the guts and adrenaline
that horrific suffering and anger . . . catapult us into.[28]

Anzaldua allows that staying inside one's own subjective positionality may
limit what one can know, and she recommended at times the attempt to
empathically imagine oneself as another, and to stretch beyond the self's
boundaries.[29] But she also believed that a deliberately nondetached strategy
from one's own experiences has major theoretical and political benefits.
Feeling our feelings can clarify the nature of our reality, which is always a
shared, interdependent and social reality. It also can galvanize us into doing
the hard work that theory demands, to achieve understanding through a
rigorous and unedited reflection on experience. Coming to see the truth, the
truth of our own oppression and humiliation, for example, or of another's
fundamental discomfiture in our world, often is experienced as a kind of
shock. Shock is not something looked for, expected, or desired, but comes on
us without warning. Anzaldua is thus describing the similarity between and
interconnectedness of emotional and cognitive states, the multiple ways in
which theory "change[s] people."[30] This is strikingly in line with Nietzsche's
embrace of the power of painful emotions to become creative resources, and
strikingly at odds with his indifference to social oppression.

The personal is relevant for theory, on Anzaldua's account, because
of our tendency to live in what she called "'selective reality,' that narrow
spectrum of reality that human beings select or choose to perceive and/
or what their culture 'selects' for them to 'see.'"[31] Perception is already
interpreted and organized, and its manner of organization involves censoring. The possibility of becoming aware of and reflective about one's own
processes of censoring and interpretation requires bringing the personal in
at full throttle. Anzaldua believed in the possibility of change, but she also
believed that changing one's perceptual selectivity requires a change at the
level of our soul or spirit. It is this that will then bring our mind and body
along. I find such claims absolutely consistent with every experience I have
ever had in activism, in pedagogy, and in my own personal life.

Anzaldua was a pluralist about theory, theory making, and theoretical
language, just as one might expect from a theorist of borderlands and hybridity. She allowed that abstraction could be useful, even that distanciation
has its place, and she defended the legitimacy of a "specialized language"
for theorists in the academy who need it in the same way as other professionals, whether they are doctors or seamstresses. Her complaint was that
the academy itself did not support such pluralism.

Anzaldua claimed forthrightly that the goal of our theory is to "change
people and the way they perceive the world."[32] Reading this, I was struck by

its contrast to Wittgenstein's dictum that philosophy should leave things just as they were.[33] On his view, philosophical reflection should help to clarify the everyday lifeworld, and at the end of the day everything should stay just as it is. For Anzaldua, in contrast, the goal of theory is revolution, and reflection is useful to the extent it leads to a disruption of the everyday. Her pluralism might counsel us to let Wittgenstein have his method, to acknowledge that he is operating in a different realm. But her own theoretical efforts demanded a different outcome.

I suspect that although Wittgenstein himself shared Anzaldua's belief that the real work of the understanding occurs in the soul, his strict separation of theoretical knowledge and moral understanding prohibited his ability to comprehend the seat of his own brilliance. And thus, it was circumscribed. Anzaldua's abilities, thankfully, were not limited by an alienated self-understanding, or a censored self-expression, but only by the material limits put on her and her work by a hostile and uncomprehending Anglo culture.

NOTES

1. Walter Benjamin, "Theses on the Philosophy of History," *Illuminations*, ed. by Hannah Arendt, trans. by Harry Zohn (New York: Schocken Books, 1955), p. 260.

2. Miranda Fricker, *Epistemic Injustice: Power and the Ethics of Knowing* (Oxford: Oxford University Press, 2007).

3. These statistics come from the Pew Hispanic Center at www.pewhispanic.org.

4. When I express an interest in Latin American philosophy, I invariably get the response from Anglos and even some Latin Americans as well that this must be rooted in my biography. We never make such assumptions of those studying German idealism, French post-structuralism, the Scottish Enlightenment philosophers, even Chinese philosophy, since these areas are considered to have obvious intrinsic philosophical interest.

5. Ruth Franklin, "After Empire: Chinua Achebe and the great African novel," *The New Yorker* May 26, 2008, pp. 72–77.

6. Arturo Arias, "Central American Americans: Invisibility, Power, and Representation" in *The Other Latinos: Central and South Americans in the United States* (Cambridge: Harvard University Press, 2007, p. 104.

7. Fricker, p. 6.

8. Paula Moya, "Cultural Particularity vs. Universal Humanity: The Value of Being *Asimilao*," *Hispanics/Latinos in the U.S.: Ethnicity, Race, and Rights*, eds. Jorge Gracia and Pablo DeGreiff, New York: Routledge, 2000. 77–97.

9. There are now excellent sources and compilations in English of these philosophers and others; see e.g., *Latin American Philosophy for the 21st Century: The Human Condition, Values, and the Search for Identity* eds. Jorge J.E. Gracia and Elizabeth Millán-Zaibert (Amherst NY: Prometheus Books, 2004); and *Latin American Philosophy: An Introduction with Readings* eds. Susana Nuccetelli and Gary Seay

(Upper Saddle River, NJ: Pearson/Prentice Hall, 2004. See also Ofelia Schutte's masterful study, *Cultural Identity and Social Liberation in Latin American Thought* Albany: SUNY Press, 1993.

10. In reality, these two categories are poles of a continuum, and many of us fall somewhere in between.

11. There are of course differences, and inferiority complexes. Recently I spent some time in Panama and then Colombia, and was struck by how often (middle-class) Panamanians speak disparagingly of Panama, and how rarely Colombians do.

12. Ofelia Schutte, "Cultural Alterity: Cross-Cultural Communication and Feminist Theory in North-South Contexts," in *Decentering the Center: Philosophy for a Multicultural, Postcolonial, and Feminist World* eds. Uma Narayan and Sandra Harding (Bloomington: Indiana University Press, 2000), p. 53.

13. Schutte, p. 56.

14. Schutte. p. 60.

15. Schutte, p. 56.

16. Schutte, p. 50.

17. Schutte, p. 53.

18. Schutte, p. 59.

19. Schutte, p. 59.

20. See "Why the Whitewashing of Alicia Nash?" by Lisa Navarrete, *Los Angeles Times*, April 1, 2002, p. F3. Quoted in Arias, loc.cit., footnote 2.

21. Some of the following is taken from my "Anzaldua: The Unassimilated Theorist" in *Proceedings of the Modern Language Association*, January 2006, Vol. 121, No. 1, pp. 255–59.

22. See for example Edén Torres, *Chicana Without Apology: The New Chicana Cultural Studies* (New York: Routledge, 2003).

23. I develop this claim more fully in "The Politics of Postmodern Feminism, Revisited" *Cultural Critique* No. 36, Spring 1997, pp. 5–27; and in "Merleau-Ponty and Feminist Theory on Experience" in *Chiasms: Merleau-Ponty's Notion of Flesh*, edited by Fred Evans and Leonard Lawlor (Albany: SUNY Press, 2000), pp. 251–72.

24. Anzaldua, *Borderlands/La Frontera* (Spinsters/Aunt Lute: San Francisco, 1987), p. 78.

25. Anzaldua 1987, p. 93.

26. Friedrich Nietzsche, *On the Genealogy of Morals and Ecce Homo*, translated by Walter Kaufmann (New York: Random House, 1967), Bk. 3, Sec. 12.

27. See for example, her *Interviews/Entrevistas* edited by AnaLouise Keating (Routledge: New York, 2000), p. 178.

28. Anzaldua, "Preface," *Making Face, making Soul; Haciendo Caras: Creative and Critical Perspectives by Women of Color* (Aunt Lute Foundation Books: San Francisco, 1990). p. xviii.

29. See for example, 1987, p. 1.

30. Anzaldua, 1990, p. xxv.

31. Anzaldua, 1990, p. xxi.

32. Anzaldua, 1990, p. xxv.

33. See for example, Ludwig Wittgenstein, *Philosophical Investigations*, translated by G. E. M. Anscombe (New York: Macmillan, 1958, sec. 124.

CHAPTER TWO

PHILOSOPHY RACED, PHILOSOPHY ERASED

Charles W. Mills

I graduated from the University of Toronto in 1985, which (to my alarm) puts me in the category of really senior African American philosophers in the profession, junior only to such pioneering figures in the field as Bernard Boxill, Leonard Harris, Howard McGary, Al Mosley, and Lucius Outlaw, all 1970s graduates, and a few early 1980s graduates like Robert Gooding-Williams, Bill Lawson, Tommy Lott, and Cornel West. As I have recounted in greater detail elsewhere—indeed, in an earlier one of the indefatigable George Yancy's collections—I originally went to graduate school in philosophy in the hopes of exploring the issues of race and imperialism then being hotly debated in my native Jamaica.[1] Not finding any appropriate philosophical frameworks in a white field in an all-white department in a white Canadian university without even a black studies program to assist me, I decided to do a dissertation on Marxism instead. So in a sense, my 1990s turn to race in my work was a return, a coming back to what I had originally wanted to do. Because by many conventional measures—publications, recognition, visibility—I have succeeded, it might be illuminating to reflect on what this "success" is worth, and the changes I have seen, as well as the changes I have not seen, in academic philosophy over this period, and what they say about the profession. My conclusions are, unfortunately, somewhat pessimistic. I now believe that what has been self-satirizingly described as the "long march" through the academy for campus radicals wanting to transform their disciplines will be much longer and harder for blacks seeking to establish Africana philosophy than for theorists elsewhere. Whiteness has become—in effect, if not de jure—more structurally central to the very self-conception of the field than in other subjects, so that by pursuing this agenda one is, in a sense, challenging philosophy itself in a way that black scholars in other areas like, say, literature, history, sociology, are not challenging theirs.

PHILOSOPHY THEN AND NOW

Let me begin with the positives, looking at such representative indices as publications, conference visibility, and the placement of people in the academy. In 1985, there was only one really good anthology in African American philosophy, Leonard Harris' path-breaking *Philosophy Born of Struggle*, which came out in 1983.[2] (A second edition, so radically revised it might as well have been a different book, appeared in 2000.[3]) *The Philosophical Forum* had dedicated a special double issue to philosophy and the black experience in 1977–1978, guest edited by Jesse McDade, but it was never brought out in book form, although Rutledge later published a special triple issue of the journal on a similar theme in 1992–1993, edited by John Pittman.[4] Harris has recounted his experience of shopping the manuscript around to all the publishers at the American Philosophical Association (APA) book exhibit and being turned down by all of them, the consensus being that only black philosophy students and black philosophers would be interested in such a book, and clearly there weren't enough of either, or both put together, to make it a viable proposition. It was eventually published by Kendall/Hunt, a well-known firm in other areas but with no reputation in philosophy, and *not* one to be found at the book exhibit. Around the same time period, two other path-breaking texts would appear: Cornel West's first book, *Prophesy Deliverance!* (1982), which would launch the career of the person who would go on to become the best-known black philosopher in the country, and Bernard Boxill's *Blacks and Social Justice* (1984), which remained for many years the only text in analytic black normative political philosophy.[5]

But the point is that these were isolated works, each one by its very existence being a noteworthy event. Samuel Johnson is a man of many quotable lines, but one of my favorites, sexist and speciesist although it may be, is his comment about a woman preacher and a dog walking on its hind legs: "It is not done well; but you are surprised to find it done at all." To many white eyes of the time, black philosophy had that same kind of quasi-oxymoronic character: Its very existence (never mind its definition—an endless debate of the period) was remarkable. A bookshelf of contemporaneous monographs and anthologies on African American philosophy (as against classic writings by Douglass, Du Bois, et al.) would not have needed to be more than a few inches wide. Today, when books on race and Africana philosophy are being published by the most prestigious presses in the business—see such recent entries as Lewis Gordon's *An Introduction to Africana Philosophy*, Derrick Darby's *Rights, Race, and Recognition*, and Thomas McCarthy's *Race, Empire, and the Idea of Human Development* with Cambridge, Tommie Shelby's *We Who Are Dark* and Robert Gooding-Williams' *In the Shadow of Du Bois* with Harvard, Leonard Harris and Charles Molesworth's *Alain J.*

Locke: The Biography of a Philosopher with Chicago[6]—when the total over the past twenty years for single-author monographs and article collections, and edited general and thematic anthologies, is now (depending on how and what you count) approaching one hundred—when articles on race can appear in places like the *Journal of Philosophy*—when Africana philosophy is formally recognized as a category and a legitimate area of specialization by the APA—it would be difficult for contemporary graduate students to realize how radically different things were a mere quarter-century ago.

For it was not merely the absence of books in the area that marked this earlier period. The marginalization of race and Africana philosophy in the profession was, of course, also manifest in the content of APA meetings. As a graduate student in Canada, I was not in the United States in the 1970s and most of the 1980s. But people like Lucius Outlaw have given accounts of what it was like during the time.[7] To find the panel on race or African American philosophy one consulted the marginalized "group program," descended to the hotel basement for the special midnight session, followed the cockroaches to a cobwebbed door, whispered "Lucius sent me," and was then admitted to a broom closet—but nothing more than a closet would have been needed for an audience that was, if one was lucky, the same size as the panel, or, more frequently, *was* the panel. (OK, I exaggerate slightly, but not much.) Now, when panels on race are not only routinely on the main program but sometimes competing with one another, with scores of people (mostly white) in attendance, so that it is not possible to go to them all, the existence of this epoch may seem unbelievable.

What changed things was the determined activism of a handful of black philosophers, whether as caucuses within the APA, such as the Committee on the Status of Blacks in Philosophy (now the Committee on Blacks in Philosophy), or outside, such as the New York Society for Black (now Africana) Philosophy, usually assisted by committed black scholars without formal philosophical training, working sometimes with the aid of white sympathizers in organizations like the Radical Philosophy Association (RPA), continually lobbying for more room and representation in APA programs, while simultaneously organizing meetings and conferences in other venues, for example at historically black institutions such as Tuskegee and Morgan State, and at white institutions with friendly faculty.[8] Although it was long before my time there, the first-ever black philosophy conference at a "white" university was held in 1970 at the institution that I would later join in 1990, the University of Illinois at Chicago (then "Chicago Circle," now UIC), with the late Irving Thalberg being a key facilitator. In 2001, while I was still at UIC, I organized the second black philosophy conference there, including some participants like Bernard Boxill, Howard McGary, Al Mosley, Leonard Harris, and Lucius Outlaw, who were present at the first one, and were able to give some historical perspective on the event. Today, there is an annual Philosophy Born of Struggle conference, going steadily since 1994, inspired by Leonard Harris' anthology, under the guidance of Harris and J. Everet Green; the more recently inaugurated California Roundtable on Philosophy and Race, which holds annual workshops; and the "South"-oriented Caribbean Philosophical Association, seeking to "shift the geography of reason" and meeting annually in Caribbean and Caribbean diasporic locations (so far: Barbados, Puerto Rico, Montreal, Jamaica, Guadeloupe, Florida, Colombia); not to mention numerous ad hoc or special occasion events at different campuses on African American philosophy in general, or "whiteness," or on particular classic texts, or in honor of key past or contemporary figures in black philosophy, or other themes.

Moreover, progress has also been manifest in the greater visibility and prominence of black philosophers both within and outside the profession. In 1995, the irrepressible Leonard Harris published an infamous letter in the APA *Proceedings and Addresses* (for which, he reports in the second edition of *Philosophy Born of Struggle*, he received death threats[9]) in which he suggested that American Philosophy was so white that it was clearly a product of the Klan:

> The Ku Klux Klan secretly created a profession: American Philosophy. . . . The most noted Black philosophers are relegated to the status of kitchen help on the plantation: Cornel West, at Harvard, holds a joint appointment in African American Studies and the Harvard Divinity School. Anthony Appiah, also at Harvard, holds a full time faculty line in African American Studies. Neither costs philosophy any money.[10]

Harris pointed out that blacks only constituted 1 percent of American philosophers (only nine of whom were black women) and that apart from the question of numbers, black philosophers and black philosophy were generally not shown any respect.

Consider, by contrast, the situation today. As I was writing this chapter in winter 2010, the Eastern Division had recently had its first black president, in the person of that same (former "kitchen helper") Anthony Appiah, who is now at Princeton with an endowed chair as the Laurance S. Rockefeller University Professor of Philosophy and the University Center for Human Values. Appiah also is nationally—indeed internationally—visible and multiply honored, with numerous books and public appearances, honorary degrees, elected memberships to the American Academy of Arts and Sciences, the American Philosophical Society, and the American Academy of Arts and Letters, and holding the positions of current chair of the Executive

Board of the APA, chair of the Board of the American Council of Learned Societies, and president of the PEN American Center.[11] Who among us twenty-five years ago would have dreamed that a black philosopher could attain such status and honors, or that a book on black nationalism written by a black philosopher in Harvard's African and African American Studies Department would be published by Harvard University Press and reviewed by *The New York Times*, as Tommie Shelby's *We Who Are Dark*[12] was, gaining him tenure at Harvard and membership in the Philosophy Department, or that the Stanford University Philosophy Department, nationally ranked in the top ten, would for many years have a black chair, Kenneth Taylor, or that the most visible black intellectual in the country, veteran of thousands of conferences and campus appearances, a fixture on the talk-show circuit, would be a philosopher, Cornel West? Harris had complained that there were no blacks in philosophy at any of the eight Ivy League universities (Brown, Columbia, Cornell, Dartmouth, Harvard, Penn, Princeton, Yale). Today, by my count, there are eight (four of whom are at Columbia!). Harris had said that only two blacks had endowed chairs/distinguished professorships in philosophy departments. Today, by my count (including Kwasi Wiredu, emeritus), there are at least nine. Harris had listed only fourteen blacks empowered to sit on philosophy doctoral committees. Today, by my count, there are two to three times that number.

So given all this obvious progress, what could the grounds of my pessimism be?

YES, BUT . . .

Well, let's take them in reverse order: people and placement, APA presence, publications. To begin with, it has to be pointed out that the overall numbers have not changed, proportionally. Fifteen years ago, as Harris said, only 1 percent of U.S. philosophers were black; today, only 1 percent of U.S. philosophers are black. (And "black" here is being used so as to include not just African Americans but Afro-Caribbean and African immigrants to the United States. Restricting the count just to native black Americans would make it *less* than 1 percent.) Enough graduates are being produced that this percentage is being maintained; it is certainly in no danger of doubling, or tripling, or anything like that. And less than thirty of these black philosophers are women, doubly disadvantaged in the profession by the intersection of race and gender.

Moreover, it is instructive to look at the number of blacks in top-ranked institutions who are actually working *on* race and Africana philosophy. By no means do I want to prescribe that all black philosophers choose this specialization. Creating and expanding a black presence in the profession means encouraging people to go into a number of areas, especially because the reality is that blacks who succeed in "white" fields ("real" philosophy) will be taken more seriously than those working in Africana and race, and there might be an eventual halo effect by which their success validates the latter's research focus simply by demonstrating that, *mirabile dictu*, blacks are indeed capable of philosophizing. (Although it might instead work the other way: Those who continue to focus on race instead of following their wiser peers' example prove thereby that they are the subset of blacks *not* so capable.) But from the perspective of trying to diagnose the future of Africana philosophy, this is obviously the crucial question. So the issue of the representation of more black philosophers needs to be conceptually separated from the issue of the wider representation of black philosophy, even if there is considerable overlap. (In other words, I am rejecting the definition that says that anything black philosophers do is black philosophy. Not to mention the fact that some *white* philosophers, like Anna Stubble-field—past chair of the APA Committee on Blacks in Philosophy—have worked in the field.) Barriers to the former have come down considerably, but the question is what this means for barriers to the latter. Even if Africana *philosophers* (African American, Afro-Caribbean, African) are increasingly and more prominently represented in professional philosophy, to what extent will Africana *philosophy* be flourishing comparably?

Consider, in this light, the numbers of black philosophers in top institutions, and what their areas of specialization are. Here is my listing, using Brian Leiter's 2009 "Philosophical Gourmet Report." This ranking is, of course, very controversial, which has been criticized for its analytic bias (and indeed for its very existence). However, as is often pointed out, there is no real alternative—one cannot consult instead the current official APA or *Chronicle of Higher Education* or National Research Council listing, because there is none.

Leiter's 2009 ranking of the twenty-five top schools is as follows: no. 1: New York University; no. 2: Rutgers; no. 3: Princeton; no. 4: Pittsburgh; no. 5: Michigan; no. 6: Harvard and MIT; no. 8: Yale; no. 9: Stanford, Berkeley, UCLA, and University of North Carolina at Chapel Hill; no. 13: Columbia and Arizona; no. 15: CUNY Graduate Center and Notre Dame; no. 17: Brown, Cornell, and the University of Southern California; no. 20: University of Texas at Austin; no. 21: UC San Diego and the University of Chicago; no. 23: Indiana University at Bloomington, UC Irvine, and University of Wisconsin at Madison. My count of black philosophers in these twenty-five institutions is as follows: Rutgers: Howard McGary; Princeton: Kwame Anthony Appiah and Delia Graff Fara; Harvard: Tommie Shelby; Stanford: Kenneth Taylor; University of North Carolina at Chapel Hill: Bernard Boxill and Ryan Preston-Roedder; Columbia: Macalester Bell, Souleymane Bachir Diagne, Michele Moody-Adams, and Elliot Paul; Arizona: Joseph Tolliver; CUNY Graduate Center: Frank Kirkland (at Hunter College)[13]; UC San Diego: Michael Hardimon; University of Chicago: Anton Ford. (Cornel West is, of course, also at Princeton, but in African American Studies and religion, not philosophy; Robert Gooding-Williams is now at Chicago, but in political science, not philosophy.)

So to begin with, we're only talking about fifteen people total. Of these fifteen, Fara, Taylor, and Tolliver, senior scholars, work completely outside of African American philosophy and race (philosophy of language, philosophy of mind, epistemology), leaving just twelve. Bell, Ford, and Preston-Roedder, recent graduates, are just starting out, and their areas of specialization are ethics and moral psychology (Bell), action theory and ethics (Ford), moral and political philosophy, and philosophy of religion (Preston-Roedder). So given their interests, it is possible that their work might in the future develop so as to include Africana themes, but at this stage, obviously, we are not in a position to tell. Paul, another recent graduate, works in early modern philosophy and epistemology. Moody-Adams has done one or two pieces on race, but her sole book so far is on mainstream ethics, not on race, and it is noteworthy that on her Web site race is not even mentioned. Hardimon, likewise, has done a few articles on race, and he does mention race on his Web site, but his sole book so far is not on race either, and his list of sample publications does not include those on race. Appiah is, of course, well-known for his work on race, but (I say more about this later) from the beginning his project has been the discrediting of race as a category, and his work in recent years has shifted to issues of cosmopolitanism and liberal theory.

Of these fifteen black philosophers in the top twenty-five departments, then, only *five* people—McGary, Shelby, Boxill (all in ethics, political philosophy, and African American philosophy), Diagne (broad expertise, including African philosophy), and Kirkland (Hegel, Husserl, African American philosophy)—are really working centrally and currently on race and Africana philosophy, and two of them, McGary and Boxill, as 1970s graduates, will presumably be retiring in another few years. Even if we add Gooding-Williams as a possible future joint appointee with philosophy, Appiah *malgré lui*, and some of the others as competent supervisors even if they have not published recently in the field, this is only a handful. That is not to say, of course, that there are not many very good black philosophers making contributions at other institutions. But insofar as in any discipline the top departments tend to establish the norms for what is considered important and cutting-edge philosophy, one can easily see that Africana philosophy is going to be marginalized for a long time to come simply by virtue of these numbers.[14] As another sign of marginalization, it

is noteworthy that in the section of his report on specialization (top programs in particular areas), Leiter does not even list race or Africana philosophy, whereas he does list feminism. Lucius Outlaw, one of the pioneers
in establishing the field in the first place, is now at Vanderbilt, but taught
for most of his career at an undergraduate institution, Haverford College.
Lewis Gordon, one of the most active and prolific Africana philosophers—by
some estimates, the central figure in the field today—as well as a tireless
institution- and network-builder, was for many years at Brown (he is now
at Temple), but in Africana Studies, with no relationship (or a poisoned
relationship) with the Brown Philosophy Department. And in addition, of
course, both men are Continental philosophers, and are thus—quite apart
from Africana research focus—disadvantaged for that reason alone by the
prevailing North American analytic hegemony. Because the top schools tend
to hire from one another, PhDs in Africana philosophy produced by such
lower-ranked departments are unlikely to be hired "upstream."

So the figures are not encouraging. Partly the problem is just statistical,
an artifact of the interrelation of large and small numbers. If one starts with
a marginal subject area, that only attracts a small fraction of the applicant
pool to begin with, and then multiplies that fraction by the similarly small
fraction of applicants likely to be able to *get into* the best schools, and that
fraction by the fraction of top schools with qualified supervisors in the area,
then what one ends up with is a number quite tiny. Low numbers tend to
perpetuate themselves as low. (Howard McGary once told me that in all
his decades at Rutgers, he had only graduated two people working on race
and African American philosophy, Paul Taylor and Anna Stubblefield, and
Stubblefield did not originally go to Rutgers intending to work on race, but
only developed her interest once there. Both are success stories, certainly.
But think of it—just two people in all those years. And Stubblefield has
now shifted her research focus to other areas.)

Let me now say something about Appiah, an outlier whose case is
special enough that he deserves his own discussion. To be sure, as the first
black president of the Eastern Division, or of any APA division, and as a
very successful and well-published figure in the field, with a huge presence
outside the academy as a "public intellectual" as well, he helps to normalize
the very concept of a black philosopher. Here is a very smart guy who can
do philosophy—and, crucially, analytic philosophy (for some, coextensive)—
who happens to be black. So, one imagines white philosophers thinking,
perhaps Kant was, after all, wrong when he said, "This fellow was quite
black from head to foot, a clear proof that what he said was stupid." But
though Appiah's presence and prominence may legitimate blackness, albeit
a blue-blooded, Oxbridge, and non-American kind, they do not legitimate
race and African American philosophy. (They may legitimate African phi-

losophy.) For of course from the very beginning, the whole burden of his work—from In My Father's House to his contributions to the book with Amy Gutmann, Color Conscious[15]—has been the deflation of race. In his famous judgment: "The truth is that there are no races."[16] Basically, his position is an eliminativist one, and his current post-race work on cosmopolitanism and liberalism only elaborates on the themes already foreshadowed in his original critiques of Pan-Africanism and black nationalism. Race is a delusion and one we really need to get over.[17]

Although far more sophisticatedly, then, his view is unhappily convergent with the "color-blindness" that has increasingly become the default position of the white majority.[18] There is little sensitivity in his work to issues of social subordination, little recognition of the enduring structures that make race sociopolitically real. So far as I know, he has never engaged in print with the by now extensive anti-eliminativist literature of the 1990s and 2000s that makes the case for the socially constructed reality of race, for example in the work of people like Sally Haslanger, Ronald Sundstrom, Ron Mallon, George Yancy, Robert Gooding-Williams, Paul Taylor, and myself. His own achievements have, of course, been exemplary by any standards. Yet one cannot help but wonder whether he would have been so successful in the profession if, in his writings on race, his considerable intelligence, erudition, and eloquence had been turned instead to proving the continuing importance and reality of race in the United States and to indicting ongoing white racial domination. At any rate, independent of such speculations, the fact is that the black philosopher most respected by his white peers for his work on race is precisely the one for whose work what has been central is the denial of the reality of race and the disparagement of the black nationalist political tradition classically and distinctively linked to the Africana experience. (Cornel West, also at Princeton, and famous for his insistence that "race matters," is the most prominent black philosopher in the country, but he is not in the philosophy department—indeed he has never been employed by a philosophy department—and does not enjoy Appiah's standing in the profession.) And this is surely significant in terms of the long-term prognosis for the future of the field.

THE SUCCESS AND FAILURE OF THE RACIAL CONTRACT

That brings us to the issues of conference presence and publications. The concept of tokenization may be useful here. Personal tokenization is of course a familiar problem since the affirmative action debates of the 1970s onward: the black figure, sometimes prominent, whose hiring is supposed to prove the institutional commitment to nondiscrimination, but whose presence does nothing to change the reproductive dynamic of the underlying exclusionary structures. So we are all now sophisticated enough to be able to see through this kind of stratagem. I want to suggest (if no one else has already done so) the idea of *conceptual* tokenization, where a black perspective is included, but in a ghettoized way that makes no difference to the overall discursive logic of the discipline, or subsection of the discipline, in question: the framing assumptions, dominant narratives, prototypical scenarios. My fear is that the dramatically increased presence of black bodies and black panels in APA programs, and even black texts in philosophy, may in the end amount to no more than conceptual tokenization.

It is natural to use one's own work as illustrative, because one knows it and its fate best. So let me now do so. I have written five books (the fourth, *Contract and Domination*, being co-authored with Carole Pateman[19]). But what is and probably will always be my best-known book is my first one, *The Racial Contract*, which came out in 1997.[20]

The book was written out of my frustrations with mainstream political philosophy. I still recall my first encounter with Rawls, in a graduate seminar in the late 1970s at the University of Toronto taught by none other than David Gauthier, before his move to Pittsburgh. Looking back thirty years later, what I find most revealing is the utter disconnection I felt between Rawls' work and my interests, a disconnection so great that it did not even manifest itself in a feeling of disappointment. I had gone to graduate school hoping to explore philosophically issues of race and imperialism; I was working in social and political philosophy; I planned to do a dissertation that would address problems of social injustice. But at no stage in reading Rawls did it *remotely* occur to me that this was a book that could in any way be relevant to my project, even though its title was A *Theory of Justice*.[21] Admittedly, at the time I was not sufficiently sophisticated philosophically to appreciate how absolutely crucial to the architecture of the text was the distinction between the ideal theory on which Rawls focuses and the nonideal theory he virtually ignores, and would continue to ignore for the rest of his career. This was a revelation that would only come many years later.[22] But what did seem overwhelmingly obvious was that—whatever this book was about—it was not about anything that was going to be of any help to me. So to repeat, it is not that I was looking for guidance and was disappointed, but that I simply did not see Rawls' work as having anything to do with what I was concerned about. It seemed to exist in a different conceptual world altogether. And there is a sense in which—although my book with Pateman does self-consciously try to engage with Rawls—that simple episode sums up everything, thirty years later. With only apparent paradox, I will put it this way. Since its revival by Rawls, mainstream Anglo-American political philosophy's primary focus has been normative theory and social justice. However, *racial justice is not a species of justice but belongs in a different genus altogether.* And, as a corollary: *You can do political philosophy or race, but not both.*

Now I am sure that to an outsider, these claims will seem quite bizarre, just as, in a different but related way, nonphilosophers I have met at political science or sociology or interdisciplinary conferences have found it unbelievable that I did not have to deal with a storm of job offers from higher-ranked philosophy departments after *The Racial Contract* came out (in fact, I did not even receive one), or that in the ten-year period after it appeared, I did not have a single student doing his dissertation on race. (Now, at Northwestern, I recently supervised and graduated one, Chike Jeffers, for the first time, who in 2010 started as an assistant professor at Dalhousie in Canada.) But for black philosophers within the field, more knowing about our peculiar profession, I doubt that they are particularly controversial or surprising. That's the way the discipline works, and one needs to understand that.

Back to *The Racial Contract*, however. Far from expecting the book to have the success it has had, I had been unsure whether I would even be able to get it accepted by any reputable press in the first place. But my Cornell University Press editor Alison Shonkwiler's faith in the manuscript's potential turned out to be completely justified. It was reviewed very widely at the time, not just in philosophy journals, but in sociology, political science, and gender studies, and not just in the academy but in the popular press also, gaining positive evaluations from journals/newspapers as far apart politically as *In These Times* and *The Nation*, on the one hand, and the *Jerusalem Post*, on the other. As of December 31, 2010, the last date for which I received sales figures, it had sold more than 27,000 copies, making it an academic bestseller, with widespread and continuing course adoption across numerous disciplines and in scores of universities, at both the undergraduate and the graduate levels. Excerpts from the book have been reprinted in several anthologies, most recently in an Oxford Canada text, *Social and Political Philosophy*, a collection of classic and contemporary readings in political philosophy.[23] The online *Stanford Encyclopedia of Philosophy's* entry "Contractarianism" has a paragraph on Carole Pateman (author of *The Sexual Contract*[24]) and myself, under the subheading "Subversive Contractarianism." The online *Internet Encyclopedia of Philosophy's* entry "Social Contract Theory" has several paragraphs on the book, under the subheading "Contemporary Critiques of Social Contract Theory." Students can buy essays on the book at the appropriate Web sites, a sure sign, if a morally dubious one, of routine course adoption. Before it came out, I was averaging a pathetic three to four presentations a year (conferences, campus invitations). After it came out, my figures jumped for a while to nearly twenty a year—not remotely in the league of a Cornel West, of course (this would be a slow month for Cornel), but certainly very busy by my standards. As of December 2010, I had given nearly 250 presentations. And all this for a book dealing with race, imperialism, white supremacy, and genocide—the very kind of topics that mainstream white philosophy is reluctant to talk about.

What on earth could I be complaining about then, given this degree of success?

The problem is this. It seems to me that the simple and crucial test to be imposed is: what impact has the book actually had—a book that has now, to repeat, been out for more than a dozen years—on mainstream political philosophy in general and social contract theory in particular? This is the kind of criterion one would routinely use in other disciplines about work widely perceived to be successful and innovative. And I think the objective answer that has to be faced is: close to zero. I don't think I can truly say that the course of mainstream ("white") political philosophy has in any way been affected by the book's publication. So if a philosophy text on race that has sold at the time of writing more than 27,000 copies—almost certainly more than any other such academic philosophy book on the topic over the period (I am excluding, obviously, popular works like Cornel West's *Race Matters*[25])—a philosophy text that has been and is widely adopted in courses across the country—a philosophy text that tries to engage (albeit somewhat polemically) with the liberal tradition and a framework central to that tradition rather than simply arguing for the dismissal of liberalism as such—if such a text cannot affect the direction of white political philosophy, what can?

But what (you ask) about the online encyclopedia entries I cited? Well, it is noteworthy that both of them are by anti-racist white feminists (Ann Cudd, Celeste Friend), allies in the struggle for a more inclusive vision of philosophy (not to mention personal acquaintances), but hardly representative of the white male-dominated field as a whole. The Oxford (Canada) anthology also was edited by a progressive white woman, Andrea Veltman. Well, what about all the invitations I received at the time? Yes, but where did they come from? In general they were from second-tier institutions and liberal arts colleges or, when from first-tier institutions, from departments other than philosophy: for example, African American Studies at Princeton, or the Reproduction of Race and Racial Ideologies Workshop at the University of Chicago. What about all the book sales? Well, the book is sufficiently short and accessible that it can be used in introductory courses, which may have 100 to 150 students in them, so that a few such adoptions lead to huge sales. Moreover, as emphasized—again, because of its accessibility—where these course adoptions are at top universities, it is usually (apart from one's few sympathetic black philosophy colleagues in top programs) in disciplines *outside* of philosophy, for example in political science, sociology, African American Studies, Ethnic Studies, education, anthropology, literature, American Studies.

In other words, for many (nonphilosophy) people of color and white progressives in the academy, *The Racial Contract* has now become a standard text to assign as a self-contained crash course on imperialism, critical race theory, and white supremacy that exposes the hypocrisies of liberalism and the Western humanist tradition, and puts U.S. racism in a global and historical context. But the contract framework itself is quite dispensable for them except insofar as it provides another useful target to be trashed. It is not the case that most of these academics—certainly not those outside philosophy—are interested in the exercise of seeing how Rawlsian contract theory can be *revised* and *reconstructed* to deal with these issues. Indeed, I suspect that for many of them such an attempted reconstruction would be a disappointing *reneging on* (what they see as) the exuberant and uncompromising trashing mission of the book. This became evident to me at a panel on race at the 2005 meetings of the Association for Political Theory, when the negative reaction of most of the audience to my paper proposing a modification of a Rawlsian approach (see chapters 3 and 4 of *Contract and Domination*) made me realize that for many attendees, any such enterprise was a cop-out, a surrender to the Rawls establishment. Here I had given this wonderful demonstration of how to *épater la Rawlsoisie* and now I was turning tail and begging for readmission into the club.

But as emphasized, the clearest indicator of failure is the lack of engagement in the mainstream (i.e., white) political philosophy literature. Consider what I say in the introductory opening pages of *The Racial Contract*. I indict the whiteness of the "conceptual array and . . . standard repertoire of concerns" of mainstream political philosophy, and call on African American philosophers to follow the (white) feminist example and "aggressively engage the broader debate":

> What is needed is a global theoretical framework for situating discussions of race and white racism, and thereby challenging the assumptions of white political philosophy, which would correspond to feminist theorists' articulation of the centrality of gender, patriarchy, and sexism to traditional moral and political theory. What is needed, in other words, is a recognition that racism (or, as I will argue, global white supremacy) is *itself* a political system. . . . The "Racial Contract" . . . is intended as a conceptual bridge between two areas now largely segregated from each other: on the one hand, the world of mainstream (i.e., white) ethics and political philosophy, preoccupied with discussion of justice and rights in the abstract, on the other hand, the world of Native American, African American, and Third and Fourth World political thought, historically focused on issues of conquest, imperialism, colonialism, white settlement, land rights, race and racism, slavery, jim crow,

reparations, apartheid, cultural authenticity, national identity, *indi-genismo*, Afrocentrism, etc.[26]

So what I was trying to accomplish, through using while radically revising the device of a contract, was a desegregation, an integration, of these two conceptual and theoretical worlds, because in reality, of course, they are just *one* world in which one pole deludes itself about its relation to the other pole. I hoped that my book would be part of a dialogue on rethinking the canon and making it harder, if not impossible, to go on as before, with traffic going both ways, to and fro, on this "conceptual bridge."

But such discussions as have taken place have basically been organized and carried out by those on just one side of the bridge. On Lewis Gordon's initiative, the APA Committee on Blacks in Philosophy and the RPA arranged a very successful panel (in terms of turnout and participation) on my work at the 1998 Eastern APA meetings.[27] A related symposium on *The Racial Contract* was put together by the RPA and eventually published (the original arrangement for the RPA newsletter having fallen through) some years later in a collection of pieces based on a 1999 Michigan State interdisciplinary conference on race.[28] Another symposium appeared in *Small Axe*, the Caribbean postcolonial theory journal edited by David Scott.[29] Thus, neither symposium was organized by a mainstream philosophy organization or journal, or even appeared in a philosophy venue. The most detailed (published) critique is by Jorge Garcia, a black/Latino philosopher, again hardly a representative figure, and published in the main black philosophical journal still functioning, *Philosophia Africana*.[30] At least one dissertation has been done on it, but as a "Marxist-Leninist" critique by another black philosopher, Stephen Ferguson (so both red and black), it is doubly minoritarian.[31]

If we look instead at the response of the white political philosophy establishment, what do we find? Basically, nothing. Samuel Freeman's edited *Cambridge Companion to Rawls* has, unsurprisingly, no chapter on race (that would require there to be a secondary literature on Rawls and race).[32] But *The Racial Contract* is not even listed in the extensive thirty-page bibliography that Freeman provides. Brooke Ackerley—again, a white feminist—does at least mention it in a footnote to her introduction to a fifty-plus–page symposium on Rawls' legacy in *Perspectives on Politics*, but none of the other contributors cite it, or indeed talk about race and racial justice at all.[33] So the book is there as a standing challenge to mainstream contractarianism and liberalism—a challenge I have sought to develop further in my chapters in the follow-up book with Carole Pateman, *Contract and Domination*—but so far it is not a challenge that shows any sign of being taken up, or even noticed. (Of course, an ironist might point out that, given my claims in the book, such an ignoring is precisely what I should have *expected*, and that any other outcome, however academically satisfying, should actually be dreaded by me as a disconfirmation of my thesis! In other words, the failure of *The Racial Contract* to change anything is precisely a sign of the success of the Racial Contract.)

THE WHITENESS OF POLITICAL PHILOSOPHY

So what is the source of the problem? Let me conclude with an attempt to tease out the peculiar whiteness of philosophy in general,[34] and political philosophy in particular, and illustrate it with a recent standard reference work.

The exclusion of racial minorities from the academy is, of course, a complex phenomenon that is a function of numerous factors, including, historically, straightforwardly racist views of people's worth and competence, discriminatory practices, and limitations on opportunities both material and juridical. But in philosophy, as various people have pointed out, there is an additional factor that is more structurally related to the very nature of the subject. Contrast philosophy with, say, literature, sociology, history. If you think people of color are incapable of writing poetry or fiction or plays worth reading by anyone, then such work, having no aesthetic value, will naturally be excluded from the canon. But it is not part of the definition of literature that it be restricted, either formally or de facto, to whites. Insofar as literature is canonized as white, this rests on additional contingent claims. Moreover, there is nothing at all self-contradictory about the idea of different national literatures, or different ethnic literatures within one nation, that may provide us with different insights into the multifaceted human experience. In this sense, the flourishing of African American literature does not threaten *literature*. Or consider sociology. Sociology is, in Comte's famous formulation, the scientific study of society. Now one may, of course, have a sanitized picture of the centrality of racial subordination to modern society's origins and workings that black work on race may contest, as in the 1970s debates stimulated by Joyce Ladner's *The Death of White Sociology*[35] (reports of this demise were greatly exaggerated, as it turned out). So there will be both vested intellectual and material interests at stake in such disciplinary battles. But again, there is obviously nothing in the definition of the field itself which precludes taking objective account of the role of race, especially because one would expect that different societies in different time periods will have different social groups and social dynamics. Or take history. History is supposed to be the account of what happened. If you think people of color are incapable of making history, whether as "great men (and women)" or en masse, then they will play no part in your historical narratives. But once more, this is because of racist beliefs about nonwhite capabilities, not part of the definition of history itself. So in each case, a set of false empirical claims unrelated to the conception of the discipline is doing most of the exclusionary work.

What makes philosophy distinctive is that not merely have there been racist views in the tradition of the intellectual capacities of people of color, but that the conception of the discipline itself is inimical to the recognition of race. Philosophy is supposed to be abstracting away from the contingent, the corporeal, the temporal, the material, to get at necessary, spiritual, eternal, ideal truths. Because race as a topic is manifestly not one of those eternal truths, even by the claims of those insistent on its contemporary importance, it is necessarily handicapped from the start. (The simple fact that philosophy's past is so present is, in my opinion, another major factor. In philosophy, we are still reading texts from thousands of years ago, which make no reference to race, since, of course, it didn't exist then. So the sheer weight of tradition itself militates against the inclusion of race as a legitimate philosophical subject.) Philosophy aspires to the universal, whereas race is necessarily local, so that the unraced (whites) become the norm.

But political philosophy, it may be objected, is, even for its mainstream practitioners, necessarily more time-bound and local than, say, metaphysics and epistemology, because it formally recognizes a periodization (ancient, medieval, modern) that mandates sensitivity to different kinds of political systems. Yet insofar as contemporary political philosophy is largely focused on normative issues, justice for equal persons, these temporal and geographical contingencies tend to drop away. The ideal character of the enterprise lifts it above mere sociology and political science, even if such disciplines provide an empirical input, whereas location in the modern period is supposed to legitimate a framework predicated not merely on human moral equality but *socially recognized* human moral equality. We are no longer in ancient Greece and Rome, or feudal Europe, but in the world of the American and French revolutions. The quest for the good society, the just polis, can thus be framed in a way that emphasizes the transhistorical continuities and commonalities in the Western socionormative project, ignoring the reality that—*in this very same modern period*—race emerges as a new social category that radically and ineluctably differentiates the moral status and corresponding experience of whites and people of color.

Take one of the primary political debates of the last few decades, communitarianism versus contractarianism. Communitarians and contractarians may be in dispute over whether it is more illuminating to consider individuals as socially embedded Aristotelian *zoa politika* or the presocial and prepolitical atoms of Thomas Hobbes. However, they are both in agreement on the moral equality of these individuals, their requisite equal status before the law, and the protection of their interests by the state, not merely as a desirable ideal but (with a few anomalies) as an accomplished reality. But of course the existence of people of color necessarily transgresses and disrupts the key assumptions of *both* of these political framings. Expropriated Native

Americans and African slaves are clearly not part of the European and, later, Euro-implanted/Euro-imposed "community" in question. But neither can they be conceptualized as presocial and prepolitical atoms considering that their very existence *as* people of color arises from a particular sociopolitical history. In other words, this category would not even exist absent the history of European expansionism, colonialism, imperialism that transforms people from different Native American and African nations into "Indians" and "Negroes," reds and blacks.

So the seeming colorlessness of these competing political visions is revealed as white. They share common taken-for-granted assumptions even in their contestation with each other. Assimilating the experience of non-whites to either of these political frameworks necessarily distorts it because the political starting point is so different. Your moral equality and personhood are certainly *not* recognized; you are *not* equal before the law; and the state is *not* seeking to protect but to encroach upon your interests in the interests of the white population. This is not at all the anomaly, but rather the norm. So your whole political orientation as a person of color in modernity is oppositional in a way that the white political orientation is not, and this has obvious implications for your normative priorities. Making sense of your distinctive politics, understanding your particular perspective on justice requires—even for seemingly abstract philosophy—contextualizing it within this history, taking account of the input of other pertinent disciplines, and developing, accordingly, a set of categories sensitized to these differences. Any bracketing of this history and this input will in effect mean—even if it is not advertised as such (and these days, of course, it will *not* be advertised as such)—that it is the white experience of modernity, the experience of Europeans and Euro-Americans, that is tacitly shaping the narrative. Whether conceived of as a community or as a "contracting" population, both visions of the polity are framed as white. Thus Rawls, a citizen of the United States, tells us in the opening pages of *A Theory of Justice* that "a society is a cooperative venture for mutual advantage" governed by rules "designed to advance the good of those taking part in it."[36] Try telling that to expropriated Native Americans and enslaved Africans.

Consider, from this perspective, the second (2007) edition of the Blackwell *Companion to Contemporary Political Philosophy*,[37] an important reference work in Blackwell's invaluable "Companions" series that is particularly apropos here, in part because I commented on the first (1993) edition in an essay, "The Racial Polity," which appeared in 1998.[38] So because that was twelve years ago, and the second edition is appearing nearly fifteen years after the first, this will provide a useful benchmark of the progress (or not) in the subfield.

I wrote at the time, comparing gender with race:

There has been such a burgeoning of feminist scholarship in philosophy—articles, books, special journal issues, anthologies, series—that
it now merits its own category, whereas race (as against routine condemnations of racism) has yet to arrive. Thus, to cite one reference
work, Robert Goodin and Philip Pettit's nearly 700-page Blackwell
Companion to Contemporary Political Philosophy (1993) has feminism
as one of the six entries in the "major ideologies" section (along
with anarchism, conservatism, liberalism, Marxism, socialism), but no
entry on, say, black nationalism or Pan-Africanism. Nor does either
appear, or the related subjects of race, racism, and white supremacy,
in the subsequent list of twenty-eight "special topics," though this
list extends all the way to such nontraditional political topics as
environmentalism and sociobiology. Frantz Fanon and W.E.B. Du
Bois do not even make the index. . . . [A] political philosophy
necessarily involves factual (descriptive and theoretical) assumptions
as well as normative claims about the polity. . . . The Blackwell
editors' inclusion of entries on economics, history, law, political
science, and sociology shows that they recognize this descriptive
dimension of their subject. But as one would expect, these entries
are no more neutral and politically disengaged than the listing of
major ideologies. The economics and history of imperialism, colonialism, slavery—the law, politics, and sociology of imperial rule,
white settler states, Jim Crow, apartheid, racial polities—make no
appearance here either. The "whiteness" of the text, of this vision of
what political philosophy is and is not, inheres . . . in the political
whiteness and Eurocentrism of the outlook, one that takes for granted
the truth of a certain account of world history and the centrality
and representativeness to that history of the European experience.
The pattern of exclusion is thereby epistemically complete, the
theoretical circle closed.[39]

So that was then and this is now. What has changed in the nearly fifteen
years between editions? Thomas Pogge, well-known left-Rawlsian, has been
added to the lineup of editors, and the book has now been expanded to
two volumes, so that the total pagination is now nearly nine hundred pages.
The listing of "major ideologies" has been increased from six to eight, with
the addition of cosmopolitanism and fundamentalisms. The listing of "special topics" has been expanded from twenty-eight to thirty-eight, with the
addition of such topics as criminal justice, historical justice, international
distributive justice, personhood, and such recherché issues as intellectual
property, and trust and social capital. But there is still no recognition of
the black nationalist or Pan-Africanist traditions as ideologies worthy of

examination, or, more generally, any change in what I originally characterized as the "political whiteness and Eurocentrism of the outlook."

Consider, for example, as an appropriate stage-setter, Philip Pettit's
opening essay (in the "disciplinary contributions" section) on analytical philosophy. From the late nineteenth century to the 1950s, he tells us, "political
philosophy ceased to be an area of active exploration . . . there was little or
nothing of significance published in political philosophy."[40] The anticolonial
and antiracist tradition of people of color is, of course, simply erased by this
judgment.[41] But apparently there was no need for such a tradition, because
we later learn that over this same time period, "the majority of analytical
philosophers lived in a world where such values as liberty and equality and
democracy held unchallenged sway."[42] But didn't these philosophers live in a
world ruled by European colonialism, where hundreds of millions of people
were denied liberty, seen as unequal, and excluded from the democratic
process? Didn't these philosophers live in a world where, even in independent nations like the United States and Australia and the Latin American
countries, people of color were systematically racially subordinated, treated
as second-class or noncitizens? Obviously, the "world" that Pettit is talking
about only extends as far as the boundaries of white skin, the population
of the racially privileged. This is further confirmed when he later goes on
to cite Ronald Dworkin's suggestion that "all plausible, modern political
theories have in mind the same ultimate value, equality. . . . [E]very theory
claims to treat all individuals as equals."[43] But this is a completely anachronistic and sanitized reading of modern political theories, which, until very
recently, generally took the racial inferiority of people of color for granted.
It is an account of modernity from the white (really, white male) point of
view. If the right of each individual to be treated as an equal to others,
independent of race, was such an uncontroversial normative principle of
the modern period, embraced by all plausible political theories, then why,
at the 1919 post-World War I Versailles Conference, did the "Anglo-Saxon
nations" (where these same analytical philosophers mostly lived) veto the
Japanese proposal to include a "racial equality" clause in the League of
Nations' Covenant?[44] And why is this not-insignificant historical fact mentioned nowhere in the nine hundred pages of these two volumes?

So there is a mystification of the political, which is then further
complemented and compounded by the evasions in the "disciplinary contributions" of history, sociology, economics, international political economy,
political science, international relations, legal studies, and the silences (or
complete absences) in the "special topics" listing. Over the past two decades,
a large body of work has emerged across numerous disciplines that looks at
issues of race and racism; colonialism, anticolonialism, and neocolonialism;
and the role of Western ideology and Western legal systems in facilitating

white domination, both globally and nationally. And the point is that virtually *none* of this work is taken into account by the editors and the authors they have chosen.[45] The chapter on the history of political thought makes no reference to such works as Anthony Pagden's *Lords of all the World*, or James Tully's *Strange Multiplicity*, or Barbara Arneil's *John Locke and America*, or Uday Singh Mehta's *Liberalism and Empire*, or Jennifer Pitts' *A Turn to Empire*, or any of the philosophy anthologies on race, such as Emmanuel Eze's *Race and the Enlightenment* and Andrew Valls' *Race and Racism in Modern Philosophy*, or any of the other numerous recent books and essays exposing the interconnections between the development of modern European political theory, empire, and white racism. The chapter on sociology does not draw on such historical/sociological accounts as George Fredrickson's *White Supremacy*, or Frank Füredi's *The Silent War*, or Matthew Frye Jacobson's *Whiteness of a Different Color*, or Howard Winant's *The World Is a Ghetto*, or any of the huge literature on contemporary racism, like Douglas Massey and Nancy Denton's *American Apartheid*, or Stephen Steinberg's *Turning Back*, or Joe Feagin's *Racist America*, or Eduardo Bonilla-Silva's *White Supremacy and Racism in the Post-Civil Rights Era*, or Michael Brown et al.'s *Whitewashing Race: The Myth of a Color-Blind Society*, or any of the other numerous recent books and essays examining the centrality of white racial domination to recent global history and U.S. social structure. The chapter on economics takes no account of work like Melvin Oliver and Thomas Shapiro's *Black Wealth/White Wealth*, or Dalton Conley's *Being Black, Living in the Red*, or Thomas Shapiro's *The Hidden Cost of Being African American*, or Ira Katznelson's *When Affirmative Action Was White*, or Deborah Ward's *The White Welfare State*, or any of the other numerous recent books and essays showing how white political privilege makes possible the systemic white economic exploitation of blacks. The chapter on political science shows no awareness of Desmond King's *Separate and Unequal*, or Donald Kinder and Lynn Sanders' *Divided by Color*, or Michael Goldfield's *The Color of Politics*, or Rogers Smith's *Civic Ideals*, or Anthony Marx's *Making Race and Nation*, or Michael Dawson's *Black Visions*, or Anthony Bogues' *Black Heretics, Black Prophets*, or Linda Faye Williams' *The Constraint of Race*, or any of the other numerous recent books and essays demonstrating the racial nature of the U.S. state, its historic roots in the birth of the nation as a white settler state, and the concomitant systemic advantaging of whites in the polity, necessitating a black politics of resistance. The chapter on legal studies does have a paragraph on critical race theory (a few sentences out of an entire article), but it is ghettoized, with no exploration of the centrality of law in expediting European conquest, as documented in Paul Keal's *European Conquest and the Rights of Indigenous Peoples* and Lindsay Robertson's *Conquest by Law: How the Discovery of America Dispossessed Indigenous Peoples of Their Lands*, or any examination of the role of the legal system in establishing whiteness as a privileged juridical category, as shown in Ian F. Haney López's *White by Law*, and subordinating blacks, as exhaustively detailed in A. Leon Higginbotham's two-volume *Race and the American Legal Process*, leaving a legacy in which seemingly color-blind legislation functions to reproduce white privilege, as illustrated in the essays in Kimberlé Crenshaw et al.'s classic *Critical Race Theory* anthology. The chapters on international political economy and international relations make no reference to the Atlantic Slave Trade (indeed I don't think it is mentioned anywhere in these nine hundred pages), an institution lasting hundreds of years that was central to the shaping of the modern world, its currently racialized distributions of wealth and poverty, and its planetary stigmatization of blackness, nor any reference to imperialism and genocide, as in King Leopold II's Belgian Congo.

In other words, the political history of the West has been so reconstructed that race and racial domination, and the emancipatory struggles against them, have been eliminated from the record in an intellectual purge, a feat of intellectual falsification, as thorough and impressive as anything Stalin's history-rewriters could have engineered. In 1967, historian Geoffrey Barraclough wrote: "[W]hen the history of the first half of the twentieth century . . . comes to be written in a longer perspective, there is little doubt that no single theme will prove to be of greater importance than the revolt against the West."[46] But not, evidently, for white political philosophers. The anti-imperialist and anticolonial political struggle, that involved millions of people, finds no place in this text, any more than the racial legacy of the world created by the West. Instead, these configurations of power and subordination are presented as neutral, raceless, with no genealogical connection to their past history, approached through philosophical abstractions that carefully abstract away from the racial dimensions of virtually every major topic mentioned. And no, Fanon and Du Bois can still not be found in the index.

The pretensions of philosophy are to illuminate the world, factually and normatively, to show us what it is like and how it should be improved. But the abstraction that is structurally central to the discipline has, as a result of its overwhelming demographic whiteness, mutated into a lethal cognitive pattern of collective white self-deception and group evasion that inhibit the necessary rethinking long under way in other subjects. Far from being the queen of the sciences, far from being the vanguard of Truth and Justice, philosophy lags pathetically in the rear of the forces of intellectual inquiry in comparison to the progress being made elsewhere. Without a willingness to face how seemingly colorless abstraction is really generalization from the white experience, the discipline's exclusions, both demographic and theoretical, can only perpetuate themselves.

It's going to be a long haul.

NOTES

1. Charles W. Mills, "Red Shift: Politically Embodied/Embodied Politics," in George Yancy, ed., *The Philosophical I: Personal Reflections on Life in Philosophy* (Lanham, MD: Rowman & Littlefield, 2002), pp. 155–75.

2. Leonard Harris, ed., *Philosophy Born of Struggle: Anthology of Afro-American Philosophy from 1917* (Dubuque, IA: Kendall/Hunt 1983). However, there were at least two other earlier collections, Charles A. Frye, ed., *Level Three: A Black Philosophy Reader* (Lanham, MD: University Press of America, 1980) and Percy Edward Johnston, ed., *Afro American Philosophies: Selected Readings, from Jupiter Hammon to Eugene C. Holmes* (Upper Montclair, NJ: Montclair State College Press, 1970).

3. Leonard Harris, ed., *Philosophy Born of Struggle: Anthology of Afro-American Philosophy from 1917*, 2nd edn. (Dubuque, IA: Kendall/Hunt, 2000).

4. *The Philosophical Forum*, vol. 9, nos. 2–3 (1977–78), special double issue, ed. Jesse McDade, "Philosophy and the Black Experience"; *The Philosophical Forum*, vol. 24, nos. 1–3 (1992–93), special triple issue, ed. John Pittman, "African-American Perspectives and Philosophical Traditions"; John Pittman, ed., *African-American Perspectives and Philosophical Traditions* (New York: Routledge, 1996). As Lucius Outlaw has pointed out, the late Marx Wartofsky, editor of the journal, deserves considerable credit for this generous opening of his pages to African American philosophers, something very few if any other white editors of the time would have been prepared to do.

5. Cornel West, *Prophesy Deliverance! An Afro-American Revolutionary Christianity* (Philadelphia: The Westminster Press, 1982); Bernard R. Boxill, *Blacks and Social Justice*, rev. edn. (Lanham, MD: Rowman & Littlefield, 1992); orig. edn. 1984.

6. Lewis R. Gordon, *An Introduction to Africana Philosophy* (New York: Cambridge University Press, 2008); Derrick Darby, *Rights, Race, and Recognition* (New York: Cambridge University Press, 2009); Thomas McCarthy, *Race, Empire, and the Idea of Human Development* (New York: Cambridge University Press, 2009); Tommie Shelby, *We Who Are Dark: The Philosophical Foundations of Black Solidarity* (Cambridge, MA: Harvard University Press, 2005); Robert Gooding-Williams, *In the Shadow of Du Bois: Afro-Modern Political Thought in America* (Cambridge, MA: Harvard University Press, 2009); Leonard Harris and Charles Molesworth, *Alain L. Locke: The Biography of a Philosopher* (Chicago: The University of Chicago Press, 2008).

7. See, for example, Lucius T. Outlaw, Jr., "What Is Africana Philosophy?" in George Yancy, ed., *Philosophy in Multiple Voices* (Lanham, MD: Rowman & Littlefield, 2007), pp. 109–43.

8. Outlaw, "What Is Africana Philosophy?"

9. Harris, *Philosophy Born of Struggle*, 2nd edn., p. 345. The letter, under the heading " 'Believe It or Not' or the Ku Klux Klan and American Philosophy Exposed," originally appeared in the APA *Proceedings and Addresses*, vol. 68, no. 5 (May 1995): 133–37. It is reprinted in Harris, *Philosophy Born of Struggle*, 2nd edn., pp. 346–51.

10. Harris, " 'Believe It or Not,' " p. 346.

11. Kwame Anthony Appiah, Princeton University Web site.

12. Tommie Shelby, *We Who Are Dark: Philosophical Foundations of Black Solidarity* (Cambridge, MA: Harvard University Press, 2005).

13. However, Linda Martín Alcoff has recently joined Kirkland at Hunter College and the CUNY Graduate Center, so depending on what criteria we (and she) want to apply, she could be counted as Afra-Latina, and thus as one more black philosopher. Certainly she counts as a major theorist of race.

14. Admittedly, another route would be to get a PhD in a related area of philosophy and then simply educate oneself in the field through one's own reading—as indeed older figures in the field (such as myself) perforce had to do, since there *were* no appropriate courses and mentors at the time. And of course there are also a few white philosophers in these departments who are sympathetic to such scholarship, and have published in the area themselves, such as Sally Haslanger at MIT, and Elizabeth Anderson at Michigan, whose important work on racial justice, *The Imperative of Integration* (Princeton: Princeton University Press, 2010), has just appeared.

15. Kwame Anthony Appiah, *In My Father's House: Africa in the Philosophy of Culture* (New York: Oxford University Press, 1992); K. Anthony Appiah and Amy Gutmann, *Color Conscious: The Political Morality of Race* (Princeton, NJ: Princeton University Press, 1998).

16. Appiah, *In My Father's House*, p. 45.

17. In November 2009, Appiah was listed by *Forbes Magazine* as one of the world's "seven most powerful thinkers," a list selected by Princeton's president. The accompanying blurb states: "In his writings, he has powerfully rejected race as a meaningful way to construct one's identity."

18. See, for example, Eduardo Bonilla-Silva, *Racism without Racists: Color-Blind Racism and the Persistence of Racial Inequality in the United States*, 2nd edn. (Lanham, MD: Rowman & Littlefield, 2006), orig. edn. 2003, and Michael K. Brown, Martin Carnoy, Elliott Currie, Troy Duster, David B. Oppenheimer, Marjorie M. Schultz, and David Wellman, *Whitewashing Race: The Myth of a Color-Blind Society* (Berkeley and Los Angeles: University of California Press, 2003).

19. Carole Pateman and Charles W. Mills, *Contract and Domination* (Malden, MA: Polity Press, 2007).

20. Charles W. Mills, *The Racial Contract* (Ithaca, NY: Cornell University Press, 1997).

21. John Rawls, *A Theory of Justice* (Cambridge, MA: Harvard University Press, 1971).

22. See Charles W. Mills, "'Ideal Theory' as Ideology," *Hypatia: A Journal of Feminist Philosophy*, vol. 20, no. 3 (Summer 2005): 165–84, and chapters 3 and 4 of *Contract and Domination*.

23. Andrea Veltman, ed., *Social and Political Philosophy: Classic and Contemporary Readings* (Don Mills, ON: Oxford University Press Canada, 2008), pp. 350–68.

24. Carole Pateman, *The Sexual Contract* (Stanford: Stanford University Press, 1988).

25. Cornel West, *Race Matters*, with a new preface by the author (Boston: Beacon Press, 2001); orig. edn. 1993.

26. Mills, *The Racial Contract*, pp. 2–4.

27. Gordon gives an account in his book *Disciplinary Decadence: Living Thought in Trying Times* (Boulder: Paradigm Publishers, 2006), pp. 111–12, the point of which is to illustrate "Mr. X"'s (my) failure to recognize that it is through such organization and the building-up of social networks that antiracist progress is made, rather than trying to "use the liberal discursive practice of writing texts that would stimulate white guilt or simply rely[ing] on the reasonableness of white philosophers." Maybe my confession of failure here is a vindication of his point.

28. "Symposium on Charles Mills's *The Racial Contract*," in Curtis Stokes and Theresa Meléndez, eds., *Racial Liberalism and the Politics of Urban America* (East Lansing, MI: Michigan State University Press, 2003), pp. 11–50.

29. "The Racial Contract: A Discussion," Small Axe: A Journal of Criticism, no. 4 (1998): 165–201.

30. Jorge Garcia, "The Racial Contract Hypothesis," *Philosophia Africana: Analysis of Philosophy and Issues in Africa and the Black Diaspora*, vol. 4, no. 1 (March 2001): 27–42.

31. Stephen C. Ferguson, II, "Racial Contract Theory: A Critical Introduction," Ph.D. diss., University of Kansas, 2004.

32. Samuel Freeman, ed., *The Cambridge Companion to Rawls* (New York: Cambridge University Press, 2003).

33. Brooke Ackerley et al., "Symposium: John Rawls and the Study of Justice: Legacies of Inquiry," *Perspectives on Politics*, vol. 4 (2006), no. 1: 75–133.

34. For an earlier more detailed attempt, see Charles W. Mills, "Non-Cartesian *Sums*: Philosophy and the African-American Experience," in Mills, *Blackness Visible: Essays on Philosophy and Race* (Ithaca, NY: Cornell University Press, 1998), pp. 1–19, 201–05 (endnotes).

35. Joyce A. Ladner, *The Death of White Sociology: Essays on Race and Culture*, with an afterword by Becky Thompson (Baltimore: Black Classic Press, 1998); orig. edn. 1973.

36. Rawls, A Theory of Justice, p. 4.

37. Robert E. Goodin, Philip Pettit, and Thomas Pogge, eds., *A Companion to Contemporary Political Philosophy*, 2 vols., 2nd edn. (Malden, MA: Blackwell, 2007); orig. edn. (1 vol.) 1993.

38. Charles W. Mills, "The Racial Polity," in Mills, *Blackness Visible: Essays on Philosophy and Race* (Ithaca, NY: Cornell University Press, 1998), pp. 119–37, 220–24 (endnotes). It also appeared in Susan Babbitt and Sue Campbell, eds., *Philosophy and Racism* (Ithaca, NY: Cornell University Press, 1999).

39. Mills, "The Racial Polity," pp. 120, 125.

40. Philip Pettit, "Analytical Philosophy," in Goodin, Pettit, and Pogge, *Companion*, p. 6.

41. See, for example, Prasenjit Duara, ed., *Decolonization: Perspectives from Now and Then* (New York: Routledge, 2004).

42. Pettit, "Analytical Philosophy," p. 8.

43. Pettit, "Analytical Philosophy," pp. 22–23.

44. For the fascinating story of this revealing, and now deeply embarrassing to the West, historical episode, see Marilyn Lake and Henry Reynolds, *Drawing the*

Global Colour Line: White Men's Countries and the International Challenge of Racial Equality (New York: Cambridge University Press, 2008), ch. 12. The authors' (two Australian historians) title is, of course, a tribute to W.E.B. Du Bois.

45. See the following: Anthony Pagden, *Lords of All the World: Ideologies of Empire in Spain, Britain, and France, c. 1500–c. 1800* (New Haven, CT: Yale University Press, 1995); James Tully, *Strange Multiplicity: Constitutionalism in an Age of Diversity* (New York: Cambridge University Press, 1995); Barbara Arneil, *John Locke and America: The Defense of English Colonialism* (New York: Oxford University Press, 1996); Uday Singh Mehta, *Liberalism and Empire: A Study in Nineteenth-Century British Liberal Thought* (Chicago: University of Chicago Press, 1999); Jennifer Pitts, *A Turn to Empire: The Rise of Imperial Liberalism in Britain and France* (Princeton, NJ: Princeton University Press, 2005); Emmanuel Chukwudi Eze, ed., *Race and the Enlightenment: A Reader* (Malden, MA: Blackwell, 1997); Andrew Valls, ed., *Race and Racism in Modern Philosophy* (Ithaca, NY: Cornell University Press, 2005); George Fredrickson, *White Supremacy: A Comparative Study in American and South African History* (New York: Oxford University Press, 1981); Frank Füredi, *The Silent War: Imperialism and the Changing Perception of Race* (New Brunswick, NJ: Rutgers University Press, 1998); Matthew Frye Jacobson, *Whiteness of a Different Color: European Immigrants and the Alchemy of Race* (Cambridge, MA: Harvard University Press, 1998); Howard Winant, *The World is a Ghetto: Race and Democracy since World War II* (New York: Basic Books, 2001); Douglas S. Massey and Nancy A. Denton, *American Apartheid: Segregation and the Making of the Underclass* (Cambridge, MA: Harvard University Press, 1993); Stephen Steinberg, *Turning Back: The Retreat from Racial Justice in American Thought and Policy* (Boston: Beacon Press, 1995); Joe Feagin, *Racist America: Roots, Current Realities and Future Reparations* (New York: Routledge, 2001); Eduardo Bonilla-Silva, *White Supremacy and Racism in the Post-Civil Rights Era* (Boulder, CO: Lynne Rienner, 2001); Michael Brown, Martin Carnoy, Elliott Currie, Troy Duster, David B. Oppenheim, Marjorie M. Schultz, David Wellman, *Whitewashing Race: The Myth of a Color-Blind Society* (Berkeley and Los Angeles: University of California Press, 2005); Melvin L. Oliver and Thomas M. Shapiro, *Black Wealth/White Wealth: A New Perspective on Racial Inequality*, 10th anniversary edn. (New York: Routledge, 2006) (orig. edn. 1995); Dalton Conley, *Being Black, Living in the Red: Race, Wealth, and Social Policy in America* (Berkeley and Los Angeles: University of California Press, 1999); Thomas M. Shapiro, *The Hidden Cost of Being African American* (New York: Oxford University Press, 2004); Ira Katznelson, *When Affirmative Action Was White: An Untold History of Racial Inequality in Twentieth-Century America* (New York: W. W. Norton, 2005); Deborah E. Ward, *The White Welfare State: The Racialization of U.S. Welfare Policy* (Ann Arbor, MI: University of Michigan Press, 2005); Desmond King, *Separate and Unequal: African Americans and the U.S. Federal Government*, rev. edn. (New York: Oxford University Press, 2007) (orig. edn. 1995); Donald R. Kinder and Lynn M. Sanders, *Divided by Color: Racial Politics and Democratic Ideals* (Chicago: University of Chicago Press, 1996); Michael Goldfield, *The Color of Politics: Race and the Mainsprings of American Politics* (New York: The New Press, 1997); Rogers M. Smith, *Civic Ideals: Conflicting Visions of Citizenship in U.S. History* (New Haven, CT: Yale University Press, 1997); Anthony W. Marx, *Making Race and Nation: A Comparison of the United States, South Africa,*

and Brazil (New York: Cambridge University Press, 1998); Michael C. Dawson, Black Visions: The Roots of Contemporary African-American Political Ideologies (Chicago: University of Chicago Press, 2001); Anthony Bogues, Black Heretics, Black Prophets: Radical Political Intellectuals (New York: Routledge, 2003); Linda Faye Williams, The Constraint of Race: Legacies of White Skin Privilege in America (University Park, PA: Pennsylvania State University Press, 2003); Paul Keal, European Conquest and the Rights of Indigenous Peoples: The Moral Backwardness of International Society (New York: Cambridge University Press, 2003); Lindsay G. Robertson, Conquest by Law: How the Discovery of America Dispossessed Indigenous Peoples of Their Rights (New York: Oxford University Press, 2005); Ian F. Haney López, White by Law: The Legal Construction of Race (New York: New York University Press, 1996); A. Leon Higginbotham, Jr., In the Matter of Color: Race and the American Legal Process, I: The Colonial Period (New York: Oxford University Press, 1980) and Shades of Freedom: Racial Politics and Presumptions of the American Legal Process, II (New York: Oxford University Press, 1998); Kimberlé Crenshaw, Neil Gotanda, Gary Peller, and Kendall Thomas, eds., Critical Race Theory: The Key Writings that Formed the Movement (New York: The New Press, 1995); Adam Hochschild, King Leopold's Ghost: A Story of Greed, Terror, and Heroism in Colonial Africa (Boston: Houghton Mifflin, 1998).

46. Geoffrey Barraclough, "The Revolt against the West" (orig. 1967), in Duara, Decolonization, p. 118.

CHAPTER THREE

ATTRACTING LATINOS/AS TO PHILOSOPHY

Today's Challenges

Ofelia Schutte

This chapter focuses on three important problems that contribute to marginalizing the participation of Latinos/as in the profession of philosophy in the United States. These problems are as follow:

1. The problem of the canon, in particular the mainstream understanding of modern philosophy setting the ground for an Anglo/Eurocentric vision of philosophy as an epistemic field;

2. The problem of what counts as "prestige," which becomes a built-in expectation of performance for new practitioners entering the field as well as for attaining tenure, promotion, and honorary awards within the profession; and

3. The problem of the plural philosophical subject, the "we" of philosophy, which creates a symbolic field of expert interlocutors where—unless a concerted effort is made to change this—the weight of past practices and tradition privileges the white Anglo-centric male.

In each of these cases, I mention certain extra-philosophical factors and contexts that bear on the problems just identified, among them: with respect to the problem of the canon, European and British colonialism; with respect to "prestige," the desire of elite members of the profession to guard ever more intensely what generates "prestige" for the status of philosophy in the face of neoliberal market economies that are eroding the weight of tradition;

71

and with respect to the problem of the "we," the socioeconomic weight of ethnocentrism, racism, sexism, along with the racial and sexual division of labor. Regarding the question of prestige, my intention is not to object to philosophers' defense of the profession in the wake of the economic restructuring of higher education, but only to point out that philosophy needs to be defended in the spirit of inclusivity, not by dwelling on exclusionary identities. In conservative times, the public often fails to realize that, especially today, the ideals of justice and equality at the root of American society require the cultural recognition of underrepresented social groups. Upholding a qualitative (not merely a quantitative) ideal of social inclusion means that Latinos/as and African Americans, among others, need to be given the opportunity to acquire a legitimate place in knowledge and culture—and, closer to home, in the field of philosophy.

In what follows, I speak in my own voice and reflect on issues based on my lived experience. I do not speak in any official or unofficial capacity as a representative of my place of employment or any professional association or group. At the time these reflections are written, I am—at long last—happily employed in a philosophy department where my areas of specialization in continental philosophy, Latin American philosophy, and feminism are all in good standing. It is very gratifying to work in a department where several Latina/o graduate students are enrolled in the PhD program and to see enthusiastic student support (whether or not they are Latino/a) for the fall 2007 graduate seminar in Latin American philosophy, which attracted maximum enrollment.[1] Even in this positive climate, it is possible for Latino/a students to feel insecure about their future in a profession where our ethnic group is so visibly underrepresented. My reflections, therefore, touch on the analysis of key problems that require attention if we are to become a truly inclusive profession. In my comments, I try to be both critical and constructive. It is my hope that readers who are relatively unfamiliar with the professional dilemmas we face—here told not from a sociological perspective but in our own voices—will be motivated strongly to act on these pressing problems.

THE PROBLEM OF THE CANON

The canon, or set of texts and works thought to be central to the study of philosophy, constitutes the point of departure defining the contours of professional philosophy. The canon functions as the point of entry into the profession. Mastery of the canon, or representative works within it, is generally a basic requirement for obtaining the doctorate, or even an undergraduate college degree. The canon influences hiring, tenure, and promotion, insofar as it determines a set of priorities or order of rank among sets of works to be taught, studied, and critically reflected on. The canon strongly affects the reproduction of the discipline from one generation to the next, insofar as it constitutes the central body of texts and knowledge to be transmitted to future generations. Finally, the canon can even function as the limit of professional philosophy's reach, whenever the profession is susceptible to forces, whether material (scarcity of resources) or intellectual (dogmas, political purges), that try to keep the institution of philosophy within a tight or narrow grip. Granted, the canon does not necessarily imply an absolutely rigid limit, insofar as it is subject to a process of growth and transformation. In a discipline like philosophy, whose Western tradition is well over two thousand years old, however, change often is very slow. There is a noticeable lack of connection between the extra-fast pace of the postmodern world and the extra-slow pace in which change occurs and is recognized in the field of philosophy. It may be that philosophy tends to attract people who like the slow, sedimented accumulation of knowledge that our discipline represents, people who are attracted to our collective suspicion that the latest fads and values lack the proven sustainability to be included into the halls of knowledge. If so, it is all the more urgent that philosophers' insistence on not being driven by intellectual fads does not become complicit with a blindness toward meeting the challenges of constructing a truly diversified profession, in terms of ethnicity, race, gender, and North/South global awareness.

It is not my intention to claim that the canon is worthless, despite the shortcomings noted. The canon fulfills the function of giving philosophers certain common areas of knowledge that can ground and give stability to a philosophical community, including a diversified community. In this light, one way of promoting diversity in philosophy is to include works by women and ethnic/racial minorities within the canon. For example, if a course on ethics includes segments on feminist ethics and the philosophy of race, then we are at least taking an initial step toward acknowledging the existence of theoretical positions and perspectives that bear witness to voices that might otherwise be ignored or marginalized. The same, to a greater or lesser extent, can be said for other branches of philosophy.

Currently, I teach a course in contemporary political philosophy where the textbook I adopted contains a fairly adequate representation of feminist perspectives on major topics of discussion. A shortcoming of this text is that, for example, Latino perspectives on contemporary Anglo-American and European political philosophy are missing. As a Latina professor teaching the course, I often mention examples of issues involving Latinos/as or Latin Americans when I am explaining an interesting point discussed in North American political theory. Personally, I find many of the readings by North American philosophers intellectually fascinating. But I ask myself:

Why is it that every framework of discussion is so Anglocentric? Don't we live in a world where the United States is a cohabitant of the planet along with other nations and where, within the United States, there is such a diversity of cultures?

This question leads me to the extra-philosophical constraints that can be found to play a part in the determination of the canon. If the dominant culture itself, wherein we live and work, is Anglocentric, should we be surprised that the dominant knowledge taught at its universities replicates this fact? Does knowledge not end up representing dominant power structures, at least in terms of the assumptions and framing of the problems it addresses and seeks to solve? How could I even begin to speak of a Latin American perspective (any Latin American perspective because there are plenty of them) in a classroom where all the texts center on and presuppose either a (white) North American or a Western European approach to what counts as knowledge? And yet, consider how often it is the case that educated people in other parts of the world know *both* about their own cultural perspectives *and* those of various other countries. Why can't knowledge in the United States adopt a principle of reciprocity, where it recognizes the value of knowledge found in Asia, Africa, Latin America, and other nondominant parts of the world? Why does philosophy, a discipline that often takes itself to engage in universal claims to knowledge, in actuality confine itself to such partial interests in the United States, representing such a small portion of the world? Is it the case that the West's colonial legacy—which coexisted with the development of modern philosophy—continues to play a role in what is thought to be central to the canon, and what is not?

In the past, I have heard it said that there isn't enough time or space available to crowd into our courses the contributions to knowledge from the so-called underrepresented groups—women, Latinos/as, African Americans, or what-have-you. In this view, diversity takes up too much curricular space and therefore it is not cost-effective for the philosophy major. Are we to assume, then, that ethnocentric Anglocentric knowledge must be considered the paradigm of cost-effectiveness? Flip the coin, and see what happens when we eliminate knowledge that recognizes the contributions of women, African Americans, Latinos/as, Asians, Native Americans, and other "others." How cost-effective is it that we remain ignorant regarding the philosophical contributions of persons and cultures that do not fit into the dominant or mainstream molds? This line of reasoning regarding the lack of space for diversifying the canon, in my view, leads nowhere. In this Internet age, students in the United States, themselves diverse in background, are curious. It is not good pedagogy to narrow their interests to correspond with those of only a small (even if influential) part of the population.

THE PROBLEM OF PRESTIGE

There is another line of reasoning (or attack) that is used to hold back the presence of many Latinos/as, African Americans, and women in philosophy. This is the line that says, in one way or another, that our presence in philosophy detracts from philosophy's prestige. Of course, you will rarely hear it stated in such an explicit form. It is nothing personal, they will say. It is not a question of persons but of fields. What is meant is that fields composed primarily of members of underrepresented groups (Latin American philosophy, Latino/a philosophy, Africana philosophy, feminism, women, and gender studies), unlike such fields as philosophy of logic, epistemology, or philosophy of mind, fail to bring prestige to philosophy. This way of thinking puts a great deal of pressure on social minorities and women to disengage from the fields just mentioned, especially if they want to be taken seriously by peers who hold such prejudicial views. Yet even if one held that the fields in question need more development (especially considering how recently they have been established, compared with others in philosophy), the appropriate response is to give them more support, not refuse to grant them eligibility for tenured or tenure-track appointments, professional awards, and other recognition granted to philosophers.

Along with this line of thought regarding prestige some hold that some of the fields I just mentioned do not count as "philosophy" either because their content is too interdisciplinary (at worst, in their eyes, watered down) or because its peer review process is not sufficiently rigorous (meaning, the content of these fields is second- or third-rate). I have always been baffled by this line of thinking. The element of prejudice can be singled out by seeing the reaction of the critic when confronted with a truly excellent achievement in any of these underrepresented fields. No matter how good a specimen of philosophy it may be, objectors insist that it is not philosophy or that it fails to meet the "high standards" of the local philosophy unit. If pressed to identify what they consider a good model of philosophy, they often produce a sample as far removed as possible from the underrepresented field in question and/or its legitimation. For instance, when dismissing the value of a specimen of feminist philosophy, the objector takes as the model of philosophy a specimen as disconnected as possible from gender issues. Or when dismissing the significance of a specimen of Latin American philosophy, the critic selects as the model a specimen that rejects any philosophically significant connection between philosophy and culture. From such a standpoint, the appeal to "prestige" locks out whatever becomes "associated" with a questionable field, or source. In moral terms, it is at best an ascetic posture, at worst a discriminatory practice. In intellectual terms, it functions as a disguised (because rationalized) form of dogmatism.

Again, quite a number of extra-philosophical factors affect the problem of prestige. Value judgments and prejudices operating in the society at
large get transposed into the ranking of philosophical fields, with prestige
associated with certain social values rather than others. For example, the
appreciation of science, legitimate as it is, often results in the attitude that
fields such as the philosophy of mind, logic, science, and mathematics are
deemed far superior in importance to ethics, political philosophy, or the
philosophy of culture. "Hybrid" fields, or interdisciplinary crossings among
fields, are assessed comparatively, so that a cross between the philosophy of
mind and cognitive science is thought to enhance the prestige of philosophy, whereas a cross between epistemology and women's studies is thought
to devalue it unless its purpose is to expose the epistemic shortfalls of the
latter. Where this leaves the evaluation of what counts as prestige in the
humanities also is indicative of the prejudices found in society at large that
enter into academic discussions and curriculum programming.

One past incident of disagreements about the curriculum stands out in
my memory. It had to do with a Faculty Senate meeting where an important
vote was coming up to permit the category of "international and diversity"
courses—that is, courses whose content focused, for example, on gender,
race, ethnicity, or international affairs—to fulfill "double-duty" requirements
for graduation by fulfilling general education distribution requirements in
both the category of diversity and one other required category, such as the
humanities or the social sciences. This meant that at least six of twenty-
seven semester hours distributed among the humanities, the social sciences,
and the physical and biological sciences were to be doubly assigned to international and diversity courses. This proposal was seen as a way for diversity
to be accepted across the disciplines and to form part of a general core
identity for university instruction. Interestingly, three of my former philosophy colleagues (white males with administrative experience or ambitions)
attended the meeting presumably to object to the proposal, although only
two spoke against it and the third remained silent. One of these colleagues
objected that to allow a course to meet both a humanities and a diversity
requirement would, in effect, *water down* the humanities.

Fortunately for the supporters of diversity, the body of senators voted
in favor of the "double-duty" proposal. My former colleague's public stance
on this question, however, made it clear to me that according to his conception of diluted knowledge, courses I taught regularly, such as feminism and
Latin American social thought, could presumably be thought of, en masse,
not just marginal to philosophy but only nominally part of the humanities.[2] What is odd about the negative stereotyping of fields such as those I
was teaching is that my courses are often packed with humanities content,
considering the connections I am recurringly addressing among philosophy,

history, and culture. Curiously, one thing some critics of diversity appear not to have questioned at the time was their own attempts—at least in department policy—to associate philosophy ever more closely with science and mathematics (formal logic) as if *their* conception of philosophy was not in fact distancing philosophy from the humanities at the same time that they claimed to be its rightful guardians. Thus the breakdown in collegial respect for the diversity-associated fields on the ground that these would water down some valuable intellectual legacy that must be protected at all costs from contact with the diluting source makes little sense to me, in academic terms. I would rather think that this aversion to dilution has more to do with psychological and social factors. This takes me to the next topic, the question of the "we" of philosophy.

THE PROBLEM OF THE "WE" OF PHILOSOPHY

There is a sense in which every philosopher—more likely if she or he is professionally employed in the field—forms part of, or at the least, has every opportunity to form part of, a philosophical community. After all, even if a person is the sole philosophy professor in a small college where no philosophy department exists, that person has the option of joining professional philosophy associations, attending conferences with other philosophers, or, in this day and age, engaging in internet connections with other philosophers, whether in this country or abroad. Yet, it is possible to be a successful tenured philosopher, enjoy these extra-departmental links, and still, on a daily basis, feel deeply marginalized within one's "home" department. When this happens, a frequent reason is that the "we" of philosophy has been foreclosed at the department level, such that the person is habitually made to feel like an outsider. The type of alienating experience that I have lived through in earlier parts of my career could be summarized as effects of a dominant group ethos, whose unwritten message (to me) was: Your knowledge is irrelevant to us and we lose nothing valuable if you leave. Whatever the explanation for the practices undertaken in the effort to attain the much-coveted departmental identity, my fields of Latin American philosophy, continental philosophy (in the continental style), and feminism became its casualties.[3]

Today I am fortunate to work in a philosophy department for which—unlike in the previous case—the history of philosophy is a central focus, and where we have agreed to value both the continental and analytic traditions. It is understandable that everyone care strongly for the fields and methods that she or he practices. As everyone realizes, this can lead at times to differences of opinion. But we also understand that all of us form a philosophical community and that we have common goals allowing us to work together to

create the best learning environment we can for our students. In my department, I recognize a differentiated community of interests that finds ways of
working together for goals we value. We are diversified by ethnicity, gender,
and race. In this academic climate, a number of our graduate students are
producing impressive original work. As a member of the department, I feel
included and appreciated by my colleagues and I respond in turn. This makes
a great deal of difference in the quality of my life and in appreciating the
quality of our working relations, since as the reader probably has observed,
it is always a struggle to function in a general system that commodifies and
quantifies our endeavors.

Our department has attracted several Latina/o graduate students. Some
have shared with me a number of challenges they experience in the profession. Inevitably, one of the challenges (and this affects women as well, at all
stages of our careers) is looking for others like ourselves in our profession.
For example, we would like to see larger numbers from our diverse part of
the world to reassure ourselves that, yes, it is just a normal thing to be a
Latina/o philosopher in the United States. Of course, this goal continues to
elude us. It is not easy to be a member of an underrepresented group that
faces social or economic oppression in the nonacademic part of the world,
for the prejudices that befall these groups are like a social (and at times
emotional) deficit that affects us regardless of individual merit, whether or
not we are professors or highly talented students on scholarships. Many of
us are part of nonacademic communities where the "we" includes people
who are oppressed and/or discriminated against on a daily basis. Sometimes
it is our own parents, our relatives, friends, or even ourselves. For example,
the recent backlash in U.S. politics against "illegal aliens" (undocumented
workers) places Latinos/as in the category of Abject in the social imaginary
of a very vocal segment of native-born white Americans.

When we Latinas/os reach out to the philosophical "we," we have the
sound expectation that the discrimination, marginalization, and the dismissiveness of concerns that we have encountered in the larger society will not
be duplicated in our workplace, in the relations we have with others—teachers, students, peers, senior faculty. And yet this legitimate expectation on
our part is thwarted—sometimes more, sometimes less—depending on the
kinds and degrees of social and intellectual respect and acceptance each
person experiences. I am speaking about the human factor in the profession, which is very important, and yet is often neglected when we speak of
attracting and retaining members of underrepresented groups to philosophy.

On the positive note, Latinos/as and women, the two groups I know
the best, have come together in recent decades to implement at least an
informal, if not a formal, network of mentoring. These networks can be like
a lifeline keeping younger members of these groups, often vulnerable from

practices of social oppression, involved in philosophy. How does a young person whose parents may not have had a college degree, or at least a college degree from this country (if they are immigrants), learn how academic professions work and all the social and intellectual assets that help to embed some in, and disenfranchise others from, a profession? Is it that they learn by trial and error? Just think how difficult this will be, added on to all the normal challenges of earning a graduate education, or getting your work published, or speaking before an audience of experts? Is it that somehow we learn this through osmosis, by imitating various professors we have known or older graduate students further along in their studies? How precisely does this happen for the underrepresented student who is thriving to learn but does not quite have her foot in the door when it comes to understanding fully what is expected of her? Who will help her if the issue of attending to her cultural, social, gender, or racial difference—if that is a stated need—is not thought to be a matter of the highest priority in the profession? Who will know, if she does not say so, that just being treated as a person in the abstract, or a student in the abstract (precisely if the prevailing source for this abstraction is the white middle-class Anglo-American male) makes her feel rejected in terms of her diction, accent, color of skin and the specific person that she is, complete with a biography of having grown up in the barrio, or what-have-you? With whom will she be able to communicate on the faculty that, she will feel, will understand her?

It is very difficult for members of a mainstream or dominant group to understand what it is like to work in a profession where one is a single, socially marginal minority. Although it is true that some people or perhaps small groups are boastful (more likely behind closed doors) of their racist or sexist beliefs, it seems that, especially in universities and professional associations, the majority professes to stand against discrimination. The idea that they could be biased against Latinas/os, African Americans, gays and lesbians, or others, simply would not cross their minds. In fact they might even pride themselves in being egalitarian in ethnic, racial, and sexual matters. This notion of presumed fairness toward the socially marginal, no less than the explicit manifestations of sexism and racism (which, if documentable, may be subject to legal action), can work against Latinas/os and others, precisely because of well-intended persons' blindspots against their complicity in a hierarchized Anglocentric and androcentric profession.

Latina women are double minorities in the field of philosophy, at a minimum. Any other deviation from the local socially accepted norm—sexual orientation, age, and so on—risks further marginalization. Just what our role is, in the "we" of philosophy, is put in question—unlike the role, say, of white heterosexual males—when something we propose in good faith to our peers gets ignored or forgotten, or happens to get a negative answer.

For example, it occurs to me (although I cannot speak from that position) that when those in the mainstream are treated by collegial peers in some disappointing way, it does not need to cross their minds whether the treatment reflects a racial or gender prejudice. For example, just to keep the case simple, if a socially mainstream white male analytic philosopher is the recipient of a dismissive, negative, or professionally disappointing remark coming from peers of similar background, among the things he does not need to process or register psychologically is: Is my underrepresented (or "deviant"), racial, ethnic, or sexual status a trigger for this negative gesture? A number of personality factors or emotions might cross the person's mind, for example: Is the dismissiveness perhaps motivated by jealousy or envy? Did I step in at the wrong moment, when their attention was focused on something else? Did they misunderstand a point? The social privilege enjoyed by these individuals is evident (although perhaps not to them in their average daily awareness). The privilege rests on the fact that negation or disappointment, at their level, does not need to get confused with or imbricated in power relations where superior/inferior, accepted/dismissed, included/excluded fall on a psychic register marked by racial, gender, and ethnic difference. For the mainstream or dominantly socially positioned person, the negation experienced is explainable in terms of the idiosyncracies of interpersonal relations between two or more plain (i.e., equally privileged) persons, or at most in terms of a power struggle among groups where neither side is particularly marked by minority social status.

The case where the above interaction happens across racial, gender, and/or ethnic lines, however, is quite different. The person of minority, marginal, or unprivileged social status affected by the negative response faces a much more challenging psychological and emotional issue, as well as a much more complex problem when it comes to a strategic (often immediately demanded) response. As a Latina, I must ask myself whether my interlocutors' negative attitudes toward my good-faith proposal are devoid of sexist or ethnic prejudice, or not. Within a split second, sometimes, I may need to come up with a response. What if I sense a bias (assuming there is one) ahead of other members of the group who in the course of time might become sympathetic to my plight? Identifying a problem before others recognize it can get the first person to notice it in trouble, but someone has to speak up first. Much worse, I think, is to remain silent. The default position that all is well in our corner of the world is difficult to displace when one is the first to question an oppressive pattern and if, on top of this, one is speaking from the margins. Still, numbers and a collective effort are needed in order to change oppressive patterns. Embracing the project of maintaining a diverse and open-minded environment cannot be accomplished single-handedly. Just as with the lack of responsibility toward preserving a green environment, where small daily actions of individuals, taken collectively, have ominous consequences for the life of the planet, so do the day-to-day actions of professional philosophers, when their impact is felt collectively, serve either to enforce white Anglocentric masculine dominance or to place it behind us.

I do not mean to suggest, given my example here, that Latinas and other members of marginalized groups must never experience a professional disagreement, or disappointment, when engaging with mainstream or dominant members of the profession. None of us is, as the pope is alleged to be, infallible. Of course, neither are our more privileged interlocutors. The problem is that, all too often, those in power do not question their biases, particularly when academic and social prestige accrue to them directly as a result of exercising them (e.g., by promoting certain methods or fields vs. others; by delimiting the appropriate questions and borders of philosophy; by keeping those borders tightly under control). This observation takes me back to the three areas we have been analyzing: the problem of the canon, the problem of prestige, and the problem of the "we" of philosophy. Clearly, we can see how they all reinforce each other. In the next and final section, I offer a mix of commonsensical and unorthodox comments to address some of these issues.

TOWARD INCUSIVE PRIORITIES

The high regard and dedication we feel toward our designated areas of specialization should motivate us to expand the horizons of philosophy, not to narrow them. In my experience, it is just as important to involve women and members of social minorities in the profession as it is to develop fields such as feminist philosophy and Latin American philosophy in the United States. Of course, the first appears to be a precondition of the second, in that these fields would not have been developed without a strong and/or emerging "significant mass" of women and Latinos/as in philosophy. (I say "emerging" because our numbers as Latinos/as—and even as women—are still small.) We must bear in mind that not all women philosophers do feminism nor do all Latinos/as do Latin American philosophy. (It is also important not to "ghettoize" social minorities within underrepresented fields.) The struggle, then, is not just over the participation of these underrepresented groups in philosophy—which is an important goal in itself—but over the development of new methodologies or fields that in their very nature may focus on issues that are of socio-cultural or political importance to the groups in question. These subaltern groups have had little or no opportunity throughout previous history of contributing to the discussion and formulation of what philosophy means as a professional field, and whose interests it must serve.

Insofar as they have, they must face the question of the extent to which androcentric Eurocentrism—and more recently Anglocentrism—should be associated exclusively with the social prestige and academic substance of philosophy. Moreover, these are not the only problems stemming from weighted perspectives in society and in philosophy. We also have, among others, the problems of heterosexism as a dominant ideology of gender difference and of anthropocentrism as an obstacle to understanding the value and importance of non-human life and nature.

The weight of the past exercises its influential grip over philosophy's canon until we come to challenge the ahistoricity of reason (the so-called view from nowhere) and the androcentricity of professionally expert discourse. Decentering the latter by breaking or challenging the masculine/feminine binary, that is, by creating a more flexible and fluid subject position that can accept sexual/gender differences constitutes a first important step to overcoming androcentrism. Once this happens and the subject of philosophy recognizes that embodiment as such is not necessarily the feared distraction from or impediment to reasoning, a smaller step is all it takes to acknowledge the historicity and positionality of discursive reasoning.

Alas, it may seem as if the dream of objectivity would be foreclosed by this double ejection of the subject of philosophy from its transcendentally or methodologically privileged position, hovering as much as possible above embodiment and history. If we trust ourselves, however, we will find that the old dream of objectivity is an illusion (and, if Nietzsche was right, an exercise in ascetic self-deceit as well). Much better, even if less reassuring, is to think of claims to knowledge in terms of what Nietzsche called perspectivism, or what Foucault called a set of enunciatory acts within a discursive formation.[4] To fully understand our knowledge claims, it is important to be as cognizant as possible regarding the perspectival conditions from which we make them. And to understand the latter, we need to take a look beyond philosophy (as narrowly conceived) to the material, political, sociocultural, discursive, and other conditions that at any given time or moment of history enable, motivate, sustain or, on the contrary, limit or incapacitate, philosophers' claims to knowledge. It is when we are most attentive to the perspective from which we speak (as well as to its limits), and to the multiplicity of other perspectives from which a specific philosophical problem can be approached, that we come closer to the not-quite attainable, but still pursuable, ideal of objectivity—now understood and reconsidered in the sense of balance and fair-mindedness.

The practice of Nietzschean perspectivism requires an epistemic maturity that our culture as a whole, however, lacks. Just as many count on fast (or microwaved) meals and fast access to the internet, they become impatient with having to listen to perspectives that question or challenge the power or centrality of their own.[5] As for their own, they would rather not consider it a perspective, but rather the proven-and-reliable-track to knowledge or truth, the straight path from A to B. For this mindset, "democracy" allows for a little conflict of views: You have your straight path and I have mine, so we play it out and see who wins. Winners come out on top and nobody cares about the losers. In this kind of reductionist scenario, there is little room to notice, much less understand, those differences that can't be accommodated to this model. To correct this model we need to shift to a different paradigm. Unlike the generally idealistic paradigm about knowledge where truth and power are kept in separate quarters, in this alternative paradigm we must assume that there is no democracy in the realm of ideas, and that the weight of what is considered knowledge at any given time in our institutions of higher learning is the ongoing result of a set of material, ideological, and other complex factors among which the will to truth, as Nietzsche called it, although significant, is only one of several players.

As for what counts as knowledge, such questions are intimately bound up with power. This is not to say that all power is the same or that power is undifferentiated in its effects; nor is it to say that power is always corrupting or evil. Some forms and configurations of power and empowerment are arguably much better (and healthier) than others. It's in this debate (and the actions taken as its consequence) regarding the enablement of healthy forms of power in university lives and communities where these issues of ending the marginalization, devaluation, and/or exclusion of certain perspectives in philosophy directly associated with the cultures, lifestyles, and voices of those falling on the margins of the racial, sexual, and ethnic division of labor will ultimately be resolved. To achieve our goals, it is essential to have professional organizations, journal and editorial boards, fellowship foundations, faculty associations, university administrators, students, and other important constituencies supporting the inclusionary projects. The quality resulting from such projects will depend on the sensibilities and visions of leaders and participants who take the time and energy to contribute toward these efforts and to create links so that the talents of future generations poised to diversify and expand our profession will not be lost.

There currently sre two nationally competitive programs designed to interest talented undergraduates from underrepresented social backgrounds to pursue a graduate career in philosophy. The older one is the Summer Institute for Diversity in Philosophy offered at Rutgers University.[6] It seeks to acquaint students with various methodologies and fields of specialization in philosophy and to provide interaction with philosophers who practice them, along with offering relevant information about graduate programs and the application process. More recently (since 2006) the Philosophy in an Inclusive Key Summer Institute (PIKSI) has been developed at Penn State

University.[7] PIKSI also reaches out to students from underrepresented sectors and provides information on graduate programs, with the emphasis being on acquainting students, through local and guest speakers, with approaches to doing philosophy (as the title suggests) in an inclusive way. In 2007 I had the honor and opportunity of being a guest speaker at PIKSI.[8] I was very impressed by the motivational and intellectual energy of the participating students with whom I interacted. PIKSI was conceived as a project by the Association for Feminist Ethics and Social Theory and is made possible currently by support from Penn State's Rock Ethics Institute and College of Liberal Arts, the American Philosophical Association, and other donors. There needs to be more funding for programs like these along with efforts at all levels of professional incorporation to encourage a welcoming attitude toward diverse perspectives. I am fairly optimistic that with further critical discussion on the links between exclusionary practices and ignorance, and with the persistent dedication of those who believe in inclusion to bring such matters to light, the knowledge-regime governed by Anglocentric androcentricity will give way to a plurality of perspectives and distinct methodological orientations that will lend philosophy a more variegated, earthly, and colorful tone—something that will serve it well, considering the meager diet it has been fed, on the misguided belief that its proper and ultimate refuge was a disembodied reason.

NOTES

1. The syllabus for this graduate seminar as well as one for a recently taught undergraduate course in Latin American Social Thought appeared in the *APA Newsletter on Hispanic/Latino Issues in Philosophy* 7:1 (Fall 2007), now published electronically.

2. There have been huge controversies, "culture wars," in academia regarding these types of issues, for example, "literature" versus "cultural studies." Opponents of changing the canon tend to follow a binary between "high" and "low" culture and confine the purpose of academic knowledge to the former, with the added twist that the high end of culture is identified with Anglo-/Eurocentric, androcentric knowledge.

3. As things stand, over ten years after I accepted another job, no Latino/a faculty have been hired in philosophy nor have the areas of specialization I developed and represented been the subject of a philosophy search.

4. Friedrich Nietzsche, *On the Genealogy of Morals*, Part III, section 12; Michel Foucault, *The Archeology of Knowledge*, trans. A. M. Sheridan Smith (New York: Pantheon, 1971), pp. 88–195 and 118–25.

5. For a philosophical analysis of the kind of decentering of subject positions that I believe is needed to attend to subaltern differences, see my "Cultural Alterity: Cross-Cultural Communication and Feminist Thought in North-South Dialogue," *Hypatia* 13:2 (1998), 53–72. Special issue on multicultural and postcolonial feminisms edited by Sandra Harding and Uma Narayan.

6. For information see http://philosophy.rutgers.edu/events/summer-institute.

7. For information see http://rockethics.psu.edu/education/piksi/.

8. I was also a guest participant (representing the fields of Continental philosophy and Feminist Theory) in the Rutgers summer institute in 1995.

CHAPTER FOUR

PHILOSOPHICAL CANONS
AND PHILOSOPHICAL TRADITIONS

The Case of Latin American Philosophy

Jorge J. E. Gracia

Philosophers are not often attracted by questions concerning the philosophical canon, how it is formed, and how it functions. In recent years, however, with a growing awareness of works by female and minority philosophers, some of these questions have received more attention in the United States.[1] There also has been a growing, although still limited when compared with other philosophical topics, interest in philosophical historiography and this in turn has led to the discussion of the canon of the discipline.[2]

In the past it was assumed that the canon of philosophy reflected not only what has been more influential but also what is best in the history of philosophy. What survived did so because it has permanent value for humanity, and because it has made a real contribution in the human struggle for excellence and truth. But these assumptions have come under fire, particularly in the second half of the twentieth century, and the voices of the excluded have endeavored to show that truth, perennial value, historical impact, or originality have not always been the determining factors in what has come to be regarded as the Western philosophical canon.[3] The controversy has taken many turns. Some have to do with a general approach to canon formation and the factors that influence it; others are more focused on the exclusion of particular groups of philosophers and texts from the canon.

In this chapter, I address both a general and a specific question related to this topic. The general question concerns how the canon is established and the specific one asks for the reasons why Latin American philosophy in particular is generally excluded from both the canon of Western philosophy and the general world philosophy canon as these are understood in the United States. The second question serves to illustrate the problems with the first and provides an answer to it. I argue that various theories that purport to account for canon formation and the exclusion of certain philosophers from the Western canon in particular fail to do justice to the situation because they ignore the role of tradition in this process. More specifically, I illustrate how tradition accounts for why Latin American philosophy tends to be absent from both the Western and world philosophical canons.

Let me begin with the specific claim that Latin American philosophy in particular is generally excluded from both the canon of Western philosophy and the general world philosophy canon as these are understood in the United States. What does it mean, and how can it be supported?

LATIN AMERICAN PHILOSOPHY
AND THE PHILOSOPHICAL CANON

A philosophical canon consists in a group of philosophers and their writings that are the subject of repeated study and discussion both philosophically and historically.[4] It is important not to confuse a canon with a history of philosophy. A history of philosophy will naturally include anyone who is a philosopher and any text that is philosophical. This means that it is rather extensive. Historians will quibble here and there on whether to include an author or a text in a historical account of the philosophy of a period, for example, but most of them will try to be comprehensive and as inclusive as possible, although often they will use criteria that exclude authors and texts that other historians would like to include.

A philosophical canon is much narrower than the history of philosophy, within the parameters in question. A canon does not include every author and text that has made a philosophical contribution within these parameters. Canons are much narrower and introduce parameters of inclusion that eliminate from consideration much that is part of history. To repeat, a philosophical canon consists of the list of authors and texts that are repeatedly studied both philosophically and historically. Philosophically, these authors and texts are regarded as having produced something that has value beyond the immediate boundaries of their existence. Historically, their value is conceived to be the impact these authors and texts have had. And the history of philosophy is the source for all these authors and texts.

There are specific canons and general canons. Examples of the first are the philosophical canon specific to the Latin middle ages and the canon of Western twentieth-century articles in the analytic philosophical tradition.

Examples of more general canons are the canon of Western philosophy or even of philosophy. To find philosophical canons one need only look at histories of philosophy, reference works in philosophy, philosophical anthologies, and perhaps most important, the philosophical curriculum. Naturally there will be some differences here and there, but in general one finds considerable agreement on the list of texts and authors that are treated in histories, anthologized, and taught.

When one looks at canons, it is difficult not to notice that some authors and texts, and sometimes even entire philosophical traditions and schools, are excluded from various canons. Latin American philosophy is a good example of a philosophy systematically excluded from both the Western and world philosophical canons as these are conceived in the United States. This claim about Latin American philosophy may be easily documented by looking at histories of philosophy, reference works, anthologies, philosophical societies, evaluating tools of philosophy as a field of learning, educational programs such as the National Endowment for the Humanities (NEH) Institutes and Seminars, PhD dissertations in philosophy and common areas of specialization in the discipline, and the college curriculum (in the United States, philosophy is generally taught only at the college level).

Let me begin backward, with the college curriculum. Is Latin American philosophy part of the college philosophy curriculum in the United States? The answer is no, and the facts are quite clear. I have provided the relevant data elsewhere, so I do not repeat them here, but let me just mention that the number of college courses in Latin American philosophy is extremely small; none of them is required for majors.[5]

The number of PhD dissertations written on Latin American philosophy in graduate philosophy programs is practically nonexistent, and the number of specialists follows suit. Indeed, because the few persons interested in this field cannot find a job teaching Latin American philosophy, they usually write dissertations in other fields and keep their interest in this area on the side. A brief look at the American Philosophical Association's (APA) Jobs for Philosophers shows the lack of interest in the profession. In the past few years, there have not been more than half a dozen advertised jobs whose primary area of concentration was Latin American philosophy, and similarly few in which Latin American philosophy was mentioned as an acknowledged area of competence.

At present, there are no graduate training program in Latin American philosophy. Indeed, there are only a handful of faculty capable of directing PhD dissertations in the field, and there are no PhD programs that have Latin American philosophy as an area of strength or concentration. Suffice it to say that until summer 2005, the NEH had never offered a Summer Institute on Latin American philosophy. Whether this was because no proposals had been made, or because the ones made had not been adequate, it is a telling tale about the situation of Latin American philosophy in the United States. And yet, when the first Institute was offered in 2005, there were more than eighty applicants for only twenty-five available spaces; the Institute drew the largest number of applicants that year.[6]

The evaluating tools of philosophical subfields and program rankings generally ignore Latin American philosophy. For example, perhaps the most popular and commonly used tool of field and program evaluation, The Philosophical Gourmet Report, does not list Latin American philosophy as a field.[7] And the list of committee sub-fields of the APA ignores Latin American philosophy.

Another area to consider is philosophical societies, because these are indicators of interest in the field. There are societies now for many individual philosophers and also for general periods of the history of philosophy and subareas of philosophical study. Interestingly enough, in the 1970s a group of philosophers founded a society for the study of Latin American and Iberian philosophy and thought (SILAT: Society for Iberian and Latin American Thought). The society has been active ever since, but although it usually organizes programs at the meetings of the APA, attendance is low and it has been difficult to keep the society alive. The list of members does not go over a few dozens. Moreover, the APA itself did not have a committee for Hispanics/Latinos until the early 1990s, even though the APA's Committee on the Status of Blacks in Philosophy dates back to the 1970s.

With respect to anthologies of philosophical texts, we should consider two kinds: first, anthologies of philosophical texts from Latin America, and second, anthologies of philosophical texts in general. The number of anthologies (in English) of Latin American philosophy put together by philosophers is very limited. Risieri Frondizi and I compiled the first such anthology in the 1970s, but we could not find a publisher for it in the United States.[8] It was not until late in the 1980s that I found a publisher for a much revised version of it.[9] This was the only anthology available until a few years ago when three other anthologies appeared. One was an enlarged version of the earlier anthology, another was a new one edited by Susana Nuccetelli and Gary Seay, and a third was a very specific anthology on current issues published by Eduardo Mendieta.[10] With respect to the presence of Latin American philosophy in anthologies of philosophical texts in general, there are only a couple of the many hundreds published in the past fifty years that include anything from Latin America. Latin American philosophy tends to be excluded from both specific and general anthologies.[11]

The past fifteen years have seen the publication of a large number of reference works in philosophy. Dictionaries, encyclopedias, and other tools of philosophical research have become common, and most major presses have published versions of these. Some deal with world philosophy, whereas others concern western philosophy in particular, but very few include substantial articles on Latin American philosophy. The very large encyclopedias do include some relevant articles, particularly overall views of Latin American philosophy in general, but they seldom include significant articles on periods or philosophers from Latin America. In some cases they do not include any articles on Latin American philosophy and in others the editors include sections on authors who are not philosophers or are philosophers who work at the fringes of philosophy and are interested in marginal fields and approaches that have an exotic take on Latin American philosophy. There are two recent exceptions to this in the works. One is the effort mounted by the *Stanford Encyclopedia of Philosophy*, an online source that might eventually establish itself as the single most important reference source for philosophy. The editor recently appointed a committee, composed of Otávio Bueno, Manuel Vargas, and I, in charge of devising a substantial list of articles on Latin American philosophy. The other is the *Blackwell Companion to Latin American Philosophy*, currently under preparation under the editorship of Susana Nuccetelli, Ofelia Schutte, and Otávio Bueno.

Two kinds of histories are important for us to consider in this context: histories of Latin American philosophy and general histories of philosophy or of Western philosophy. There are no histories of Latin American philosophy in English, and only a couple in Spanish. The histories of philosophy in Latin America often include sections on Latin American philosophy, but no history of philosophy written outside Latin America ever includes sections on Latin American philosophy.

From all this it is quite clear that Latin American philosophy is not generally part of the Western philosophical canon as understood in this country. Now let me turn to some suggestions as to the causes for such an absence.

REASONS FOR THE EXCLUSION OF
LATIN AMERICAN PHILOSOPHY FROM THE CANON

One can easily think of many reasons why Latin American philosophy has been excluded from the canons of Western and world philosophy that are concordant with the traditional view of how the philosophical canon was formed and the criteria that determined it. Some of these have been actually proposed by historiographers. Rather than presenting a history of these positions, however, I approach the matter systematically, by listing the ones that seem more plausible prima facie, although none is ultimately effective.

The one that could be regarded as most radical argues that Latin American philosophy is not part of these canons because, simply put, is not original. There is nothing in it that can have a claim to novelty. Latin American philosophers have been content with repeating what other philosophers from other parts of the world, and particularly from Europe and the United States, have said and have said better. Their ideas are derivative and lack even the quality of making significant advances beyond their sources. Latin American philosophers have been content with translating other philosophers and even that has not been very well done at times. Many reasons are adduced for this lack of originality but this is not pertinent for our purposes. The important point for us is that, according to those who subscribe to this view, this lack of originality justifies the neglect of Latin American philosophy. Interestingly enough, the view that Latin American philosophy lacks originality and value has been supported by many Latin American philosophers themselves. Some of the best-known and important Latin American philosophers have echoed this devastating judgment.[12]

However, any serious student of Latin American philosophy will realize that this judgment is unwarranted. If we accept that originality in philosophy can be measured in at least two ways, by the novelty of the problems posed and by the novelty of the ideas used to deal with those problems, there is plenty we can find in Latin American philosophy to justify a positive judgment. Consider two authors, Bartolomé de Las Casas and Carlos Mariátegui. Both of these authors thought within well-established Western philosophical traditions, but both used those traditions to deal with new philosophical challenges and they modified those traditions in order to meet those challenges. The challenge faced by Las Casas was the conception of the status of the Indians and the treatment they deserved.[13] The question was new for Europe at the time and raised an issue that has acquired greater importance as time has passed. What are the duties of conquerors with respect to conquered peoples, and what are the rights of conquered peoples? Las Casas answers to these questions were developed in terms of the Aristotelian framework within which he was educated, but the conclusions he reached were quite different from those of his more orthodox Aristotelian opponents, who equated Indians with what Aristotle considered Barbarians and to whom he accorded no rights.

The case of Mariátegui is similar. The challenge that he faced concerned the socioeconomic situation of the Andean region and its original inhabitants.[14] How should the relation between original culture and imported ideologies be worked out in order to better the lot of the native population? The philosophical tradition from which he worked was Marxism, but Mariátegui modified it in substantial ways to adapt it to the situation of the Andean populations. Instead of expounding the orthodoxy worked out in Europe, he tried to adapt the principles that inspired Marx to a different situation and had no qualms about abandoning some of its linchpins.[15]

A second reason that might be given to support the exclusion of Latin American philosophy from the Western and world canons of philosophy is that it is primarily of local interest. It does not have the claim to universality that is essential to any philosophy that can be included in the general philosophical canon. It is a local philosophy, interested only in local issues and problems and adopting strategies and methodologies that are only appropriate at the local level.[16] Latin American philosophy has only an exotic interest; it is idiosyncratic; and it has little in common with Western and world philosophy.

Again, anyone familiar with the history of philosophy in Latin America can attest to the fact that there is little exoticism in it. Indeed, if anything, Latin American philosophy has been too concerned with the issues and problems it has inherited from European philosophy, and it is European philosophy that its critics take to be the model of scientific rigor and universality. So it makes little sense to argue that it is its lack of attention to universal themes and problems that can serve to exclude Latin American philosophy from the world canon of philosophy, and particularly of Western philosophy. Practically any important philosopher in Latin America has been concerned with topics of universal concern. Consider the large literature in the first half of the twentieth century in Latin America on the objectivity and subjectivity of value.[17] Or think about the beginning of the second half of the century, in which authors such as Francisco Romero and Risieri Frondizi sought to determine what is essential to humanity and the human self?[18] And what do we make of the more recent developments in the philosophy of liberation, that have found echoes in other parts of the world? There is indeed no basis for any kind of criticism of this sort. Still publishers and researchers from the United States tend to think of Latin American philosophy as exotic and find in it an essence that is idiosyncratic and particular rather than universal and of general application. Indeed, in the late 1970s, when Frondizi and I were looking for a publisher for our anthology of Latin American philosophical texts, the many rejections we received generally pointed out that we had not included texts that showed anything idiosyncratic and peculiar to Latin American philosophy.

A third reason that might be offered to explain the exclusion of Latin American philosophy from the canons of Western and world philosophy is that it has had no historical impact of any significance outside of Latin America, and even in Latin America to some extent. Latin American philosophy has always been isolated and marginal.

Thus stated, this claim has no validity, although perhaps if presented more modestly there is some validity to it. The claim as presented has no validity in that Latin American philosophy has been influential, although its influence has been in areas in which philosophy usually has very little influence, namely the social and political fabric of society. Unlike most Western philosophy, which has often distanced itself from the social and political fray to concentrate on metaphysics, epistemology, logic, and the philosophy of science, Latin American philosophy has frequently been involved in social and political issues. Its beginning marks this important dimension of it, when it served Las Casas to defend the rights of the original inhabitants of the Americas. But there were consequences, for Las Casas' tireless argumentation and defense were instrumental in bringing about changes in the laws used by Spain to govern the conquered inhabitants of the Americas.[19] Philosophy also was instrumental in the fight for independence from Spain during the late eighteenth and early nineteenth centuries. The liberators found in philosophy the ideological instruments to articulate their ideas of freedom and liberation, and later the development of laws to govern the liberated colonies.[20] And in the nineteenth century, the philosophy known as positivism became the standard bearer for the development of the newly liberated countries. Positivism was not a marginal, ivory-tower ideology, but a veritable set of ideas used to work out the organization of societies and the development of programs that ranged from politics to education. In countries such as Mexico and Brazil, for example, versions of positivism were regarded as national ideologies and went so far as to inform the mottos around which the new nations rallied.[21] All of this makes clear that Latin American philosophy cannot be considered an arm-chair philosophy without historical influence. Its influence in Latin America has been very substantial and thus throughout the region and its history.

Still one may argue that this is not enough to include this philosophy in the world philosophical cannon or even the Western philosophy canon. The argument is that, although Latin American philosophy may have had historical impact in Latin America, it has had no impact outside Latin America, and particularly in what is generally considered mainstream European philosophy. But even modified in this way the claim is false. Let me cite two examples, one early and one recent. The early example is the work of Antonio Rubio, whose *Logica mexicana* was printed and reprinted in Europe in the seventeenth century, and in fact became a textbook in many European universities. The second, more recent example, is the philosophy of liberation, which has had a substantial impact on philosophical thinking in Africa, India, and other parts of the third world. Yes, this impact illustrated by the second example is not on mainstream European philosophy, but it certainly shows that this philosophy is having considerable influence on the philosophical development in the world outside Latin America. So, it makes no sense to argue that Latin American philosophy is, or should be, excluded from the canon because it has had no historical influence outside Latin America.

In short, none of the reasons that are sometimes given to justify the exclusion of Latin American philosophy from the canons of philosophy in the West and the world as conceived in the United States is effective, although certainly they may be contributing factors to such an exclusion. What is missing then? Let me propose what I think is the most important factor: All these explanations rely on a conception of philosophy that ignores the role of tradition in the formation of any philosophical canon.

PHILOSOPHICAL CANONS AND PHILOSOPHICAL TRADITIONS

Tradition plays an important role in the establishment of philosophical canons. A philosophical canon is a list of philosophical authors and works, and such a list must be made by people, but not just anybody; the list is compiled by persons who have a say, that is, persons with authority. Only the opinion of some persons count. And who determines whose opinion counts? Certainly other persons who themselves have established authority in the field. Consider the case of art. Who determines the importance of artists and whether their work is canonical? Some will answer that it is the value of the work, but who determines the value of the work? The world is littered with works of artists who have not "made it," that is, who have not become part of the canon. Only certain artists make it to museums and to art histories. And who determines who they are? Surely museum curators, art historians, and other people who are part of the artistic establishment.[22] The curator of the Metropolitan Museum of Art has much to say about the works that the museum acquires, and having a work in the Metropolitan goes a long way toward the establishment of the artist, because other museums will imitate the Metropolitan, and there will be exhibitions of the works of the artists in question, and so on.

The case with philosophy is similar. There is an authoritative establishment, a group of persons who choose the discourse that is important and the authors to be included in dictionaries, reference works, and histories of philosophy. These persons establish the canon, although they do not do it by fiat; they have reasons, and those reasons have generally to do with what has gone on before, with credentials, and with continuity. So and so's opinion becomes important because he was a student of so and so, or worked with so and so. There are also judgments that have been made in the past and these are taken into account. This is in a sense like what happens with the Constitution and its interpretation; there is a body of judicial opinion that cannot be disregarded. An art critic cannot begin by saying that art that has made it into the canon has to be taken out from it. A judge presented with a difficult case cannot begin by ignoring past legal precedent, because a legal decision cannot make sense unless it is taken in the context of that past, of previous opinions. The same goes for philosophy. It makes no sense to say that Aristotle must be eliminated from the canon. Philosophers often complain about the views of canonical philosophers. Who has not complained about Descartes? He seems to be the whipping boy in philosophy. But can anyone be taken seriously who argues that Descartes should be taken off the canon of Western philosophy?

Philosophical canons are the result of communities of philosophers and historians of philosophy who over time have come up with a list of philosophers and texts they regard as worthy of study and discussion, although the reasons they give may vary from author to author and the list may not be exactly the same in all cases. Now, one could argue that it is merely the community of philosophers and historians of philosophy that is involved in this process and argue that it is ultimately a group of people that are responsible for the canon. But this is a mistake, in that the community is extended over time and, although their opinions might differ, there is a continuity of practices. These practices constitute the tradition that is the source of the canon. Contrary to what many believe, a tradition is not a set of beliefs passed on, because seldom in a tradition do we have the same beliefs throughout.[23] Indeed, even when the linguistic formulas passed down in the tradition are the same, their gloss and interpretation depend on persons and their circumstances. More important than the actual set of beliefs are the community of people in question and their practices, for it is that community and those practices that lend authority to certain persons within the community and justify their choices.

Naturally, when considering persons with authority, one must also take into account the all important element of descent. Pedigree is essential in authority. We come back to the point that so and so has authority because he was a student of so and so. And the opinion of so and so is important precisely because he was a student of so and so, who in turn was a student of so and so, and so on.

What we have, then, is a familial structure based not on genetic descent but on intellectual descent, on intellectual pedigree, which is in turn based on practices that have been passed down and modified within the familial context. Yes, we are still families and tribes, and there are exclusions and feuds. Humanity is fundamentally composed of communities, and philosophy is not different from other human endeavors. This explains why cultural, political, and ethnic considerations play a role in human projects, including academic ones. The philosophical canon is established within families tied by practices, that is, traditions. This explains inclusions and exclusions and it shows how difficult it is to break into a canon when one is not part of the tradition that ties the family in which authority rests.

PHILOSOPHICAL CANONS IN THE UNITED STATES

In the United States at present there are two major philosophical traditions. One is the so-called analytic tradition. This goes back to the beginning of the twentieth century and the work of G. E. Moore and Bertrand Russell in England and the members of the Vienna Circle and Ludwig Wittgenstein in the Continent. It is called analytic because of its emphasis on the method of analysis, the breaking down of complex entities, usually conceived linguistically, into more simple ones as a means of understanding and solving philosophical problems. The other major tradition is the so-called Continental tradition that goes back to the work of nineteenth- and twentieth-century phenomenologists and neo-Kantians. Its name originates in that its beginnings, in contrast with those of the analytic tradition, are primarily centered in Continental Europe and look back to authors who worked in Continental Europe. Neither of these major traditions has a set of doctrines that all its members hold; their members are mostly tied by certain practices and a genealogical intellectual chain.

These two traditions control most of the profession of philosophy in the United States: the jobs in universities, the publication venues, and the grants. But there also are other, less-powerful traditions. For example, there is Marxism, much diminished in presence and visibility after the demise of the Soviet Union, but still operative in certain circles. And Thomism continues to be promoted by the Catholic Church and the institutions it controls. There also is what is known as American philosophy, which consists mostly of philosophers interested in the thought of American philosophers of various stripes, ranging from pragmatists to process philosophers. Some of these traditions ally themselves, or even fit, within the Continental tradition, and some are divided, as happens with Thomism, which has analytic and Continental branches, depending on the philosophers and approach favored.

All these traditions have canons of authors and texts that have been worked out over a fairly long period of development, and the practitioners in the United States generally trace their intellectual ancestry to these authors and texts. Some of the practitioners are first- and second-generation students of the authors in question. For example, some of the members of the Vienna Circle settled in the United States, and they trained students who in turn trained other students, and so on. And the same can be said about the Continental tradition, in which the authors in question are European or American students of those European authors. An important factor is that analytic authors generally work in English and read primarily English texts. Continental authors read primarily German and French authors and texts. Most analysts do not know well languages other than English, and for their purposes it is English that is the important language because it is English authors or German authors translated into English that originated the tradition. Continentals know German and French but seldom do they know any other language; for them the important languages are these two because the authors that originated the tradition were German or French.

Under these conditions it becomes difficult for members of the mainstream philosophical traditions in the United States even to notice philosophers and texts that are not already part of the canon as they conceive it and particularly those who are not closely related to the philosophical community and traditions that establish the canon. First, there is the problem of language. Second, there is the already crowded canon of authors and texts and the pressure within the traditions to reexamine the canon and include authors and texts that have so far been excluded but are well placed within the tradition. Third, there is the lack of representatives in the power establishment of the traditions that have the authority to initiate changes, that would even consider marginalized members of the traditions. All this helps to understand why Latin American philosophy is not part of the canons as understood in the United States, but there are also two additional factors that I explore in the next section.

LATIN AMERICAN PHILOSOPHY AND THE WESTERN PHILOSOPHICAL TRADITION

One important factor in understanding the exclusion of Latin American philosophy from the world philosophical canon and the Western philosophical canon is that Latin America does not have a philosophical tradition of its own. Latin American philosophy is part of the overall Western philosophical tradition and breaks down into the same traditions into which this overall tradition breaks down in the United States. Latin American philosophy extends for close to five hundred years. It begins in 1550, when the first books of philosophy were published in Mexico, but its trajectory has mirrored the trajectory of European philosophy. It began with scholasticism and continued with Enlightenment thought, positivism, and the various currents that flourished in Europe in the nineteenth and twentieth centuries.

The second factor is that Latin American philosophy is part of Hispanic philosophy, and the European leader of Hispanic philosophy is Spain, which is generally excluded from the Western canon of philosophy for a variety of reasons, including the language barrier.[24] Latin American philosophy has had a close relationship to the philosophy developed in the Iberian peninsula. This begins with Counter Reformation scholasticism and the towering Spanish figures of Francisco de Vitoria and Francisco Suárez, among others, and continued following developments in the peninsula. Two interesting examples are the influence of Carl Christian Friedrich Krause, who was influential in the peninsula and became also important in Latin America. The other example is the impact of José Ortega y Gasset in Latin America, for not only did he introduce German philosophy into Latin America, but his philosophy had an extraordinary impact that is evident to this day.

The first factor is detrimental to the recognition of Latin American philosophy in the Western canon because the criteria of inclusion used are those of the Western tradition. If Latin America were not part of this tradition and had its own tradition, the canon for which it would be considered would be the world philosophical canon, and the criteria of inclusion in it would be criteria proper to the tradition to which it belonged. Consider what happens with Chinese and Japanese philosophy. There is much in those two traditions that would not be included in the world philosophical canon if the criteria used to judge them were the same used in the Western tradition. But because Chinese and Japanese philosophy are not part of the Western tradition, the criteria used to judge their inclusion or exclusion are the ones developed within the traditions of Chinese and Japanese philosophy. The West simply adopts what other traditions deem acceptable when it comes to the world philosophical canon. The case of Latin American philosophy is different, because no matter what Latin Americans think may be worthwhile, it is the judgment of authorities in the Western philosophical community that counts when it comes to canonical decisions. And because we are speaking of the canon as conceived in the United States, it is authority figures in this country that determine the inclusion or exclusion of Latin American philosophy in the canon.

The second factor is detrimental because very few Spanish philosophers make it to the Western philosophical canon. Only a few authors from the sixteenth century—Suárez and Vitoria perhaps—and Ortega y Gasset in the twentieth century are ever mentioned. Portugal, of course, has no one who is part of the canon. And it is through Spain and Portugal that Latin American philosophy is viewed. The result is that Latin American philosophy is simply ignored. Here one could mention the issue of colonialism, of which postmodernists are so fond. For Spain and Portugal have always treated Latin America as a former colony, and its inhabitants as second-class: Their thought has always been regarded as second best in the peninsula. Latin America, then, has no agents to promote it in the right circles, and who control inclusion in the canon.[25]

To conclude, I have claimed that Latin American philosophy is not part of the Western or world philosophical canon as this is conceived in the United States. Moreover, after examining various reasons that could explain such an exclusion, I suggested that one important factor generally neglected is the role of tradition in the development of any philosophical canon. Finally, I pointed out that the fact that Latin American philosophy is part of the Western philosophical tradition works against its inclusion in the canon of that tradition and of world philosophy in general, as these are conceived in the United States. For traditions are based on communities and authority and Latin American philosophers are not closely tied to the community that sets these canons in the United States and lacks champions in the authoritative philosophical establishment in the United States.

NOTES

1. See, for example, Mara Miller, "Canons and the Challenge of Gender," *The Monist* 76, 4 (1993). 208–227. This issue of the journal is devoted to canons.

2. See, for example, Jorge J. E. Gracia, *Philosophy and Its History: Issues in Philosophical Historiography* (Albany, NY: State University of New York Press, 1992), and Martin Kusch, ed., *The Sociology of Philosophical Knowledge* (Dordrecht: Kluwer, 2000).

3. See Richard Schacht, "On Philosophy's Canon," and Merold Westphal, "The Canon as Flexible, Normative Fact," both in *The Monist* 76, 4 (1993).

4. This has led some to argue that it concerns the classics. See Westphal, "The Canon."

5. For statistics, see Jorge J. E. Gracia, "Hispanics, Philosophy, and the Curriculum," *Teaching Philosophy* 22, 3 (1999), 241–48.

6. For the Institute, see the webpage: http://wings.buffalo.edu/philosophy/neh/index.htm.

7. See web page: http://www.philosophicalgourmet.com/overall.htm.

8. A Spanish version of it was published in Mexico in 1975, and reprinted in 1981, with the title, *El hombre y los valores en la filosofía latinoamericana del siglo XX* (Mexico City: Fondo de Cultura Económica).

9. Gracia, ed., *Latin-American Philosophy in the Twentieth Century: Man Values and the Search for Philosophical Identity* (Buffalo, NY: Prometheus Books, 1986).

10. Gracia and Elizabeth Millán-Zaibert, eds., *Latin-American Philosophy for the 21st Century: The Human Condition, Values, and the Search for Identity* (Buffalo, NY: Prometheus Books, 2004); Susana Nuccetelli and Gary Seay, eds, *Latin-American Philosophy: An Introduction with Readings* (Upper Saddle River, NJ: Prentice Hall, 2004), and Eduardo Mendieta, ed., *Latin-American Philosophy: Currents, Issues, Debates* (Bloomington, IN: Indiana University Press, 2003).

11. See Gracia, *Hispanic/Latino Identity: A Philosophical Perspective* (Oxford: Blackwell, 2000), chapter 7, and "Hispanics, Philosophy, and the Curriculum."

12. For a classic statement see: Augusto Salazar Bondy, *Sentido y problema del pensamiento hispano-americano*, with English translated by Donald L. Schmidt (University of Kansas Center for Latin-American Studies, 1969). For a more recent view, see Eduardo Rabossi, "History and Philosophy in the Latin American Setting: Some Disturbing Comments," in *The Role of History in Latin American Philosophy: Contemporary Perspectives*, edited by Arleen Salles and Elizabeth Millán-Zaibert (Albany, NY: State University of New York Press, 2005), pp. 57–73.

13. Bartolomé de Las Casas, *In Defense of the Indians*, translated by Stafford Poole (Dekalb, IL: Northern Illinois University Press, 1992).

14. Carlos Mariátegui, *Seven Interpretative Essays on Peruvian Reality*, translated by Marjory Urquidi (Austin, TX: University of Texas Press, 1971).

15. See Ofelia Schutte, *Cultural Identity and Social Liberation in Latin-American Thought* (Albany, NY: State University of New York Press, 1993). This interpretation has recently been challenged by Renzo Llorente, in "The *Amauta*'s Ambivalence: Mariátegui on Race," in Gracia and Diego Von Vacano, eds., *Forging People: Race, Ethnicity, and Nationality in Hispanic American and Latino/a Thought*, in preparation.

16. Leopoldo Zea is sometimes cited as being responsible for this local, culturalist view of philosophy in Latin America. For his view, see: "The Actual Function of Philosophy in Latin America" and "Identity: A Latin-American Philosophical Problem," in Gracia, and Millán-Zaibert, eds., *Latin-American Philosophy*, pp. 357–68 and 369–78.

17. See Gracia and Millán-Zaibert, eds., *Latin-American Philosophy*, pp. 161–219.

18. See: Francisco Romero, *Theory of Man*, translated by William Cooper (Berkeley, CA: University of California Press, 1964) and Risieri Frondizi, *The Nature of the Self* (Carbondale, IL: Southern Illinois University Press, 1971).

19. Las Casas, *In Defense of the Indians*.

20. See Gracia and Millán-Zaibert, eds., *Latin-American Philosophy*, pp. 61–75 and 233–56.

21. See Leopoldo Zea, *Positivism in Mexico* (Austin, TX: University of Texas Press, 1974).

22. For a defense of the institutional theory of art, see: George Dickie, *Art and the Aesthetic: An Institutional Analysis* (Ithaca, NY: Cornell University Press, 1974). The art canon is discussed by several authors in the issue of *The Monist* cited earlier.

23. For arguments in support of this conception of tradition, see Gracia, *Old Wine in New Skins: The Role of Tradition in Communication, Knowledge, and Group Identity*, The Aquinas Lecture (Milwaukee, WI: Marquette University Press, 2003).

24. I develop this argument in *Hispanic/Latino Identity*, chapter 4.

25. This situation calls for both further reflection and some initiatives. I have taken some initian steps in both directions in Gracia, *Latinos in America: Philosophy and Social Identity* (Oxford: Blackwell, 2008), pp. 173–84.

CHAPTER FIVE

METAPHILOSOPHICAL INTERNALISM
AND THE POSSIBILITY OF A DISTINCTIVE
LATIN AMERICAN PHILOSOPHY

Jesús H. Aguilar

On the face of it, the possibility of a distinctive Latin American philosophy seems to be almost too obvious for anyone to have any serious doubts about its existence. After all, we recognize the existence of many other philosophies whose accompanying adjectives point to regions of the world that are thought to capture distinctive types of philosophy. For instance, who would seriously question the existence of Greek philosophy, French philosophy, or German philosophy? Why then should the case of Latin American philosophy be any different? If the sole presence of thinkers who have produced philosophical ideas in regions like Ancient Greece or France, or who have articulated their philosophical thoughts in languages like German is enough to prove the existence of their philosophies, then the possibility of a distinctive Latin American philosophy is guaranteed by the presence of thinkers in Latin America whose philosophical ideas have been articulated in the dominant languages of this region. It would seem then that the question about the possibility of a distinctive Latin American philosophy has a positive and definitive answer.

Unfortunately, the situation is far more complicated than what this type of answer suggests. Like several other metaphilosophical proposals based on what can be called "externalist" approaches that try to justify the existence of a distinctive type of philosophy by appealing to things that lie outside the content and practice of philosophy, the externalist justification for the existence of Latin American philosophy faces serious challenges. Two challenges in particular stand out: First, it seems relatively easy to produce counterexamples to whatever external property is singled out to justify the existence of a distinctive type of philosophy. Second, it appears arbitrary to use an external property to account for the philosophical content and practice that gives rise to a distinctive type of philosophy. Let us illustrate these two general challenges to metaphilosophical externalism by considering the case for a Latin American philosophy justified on the basis of an externalist property like its relationship to a particular geographical region and to the main languages spoken there.[1]

If being produced in Latin America or written in one of its major languages is a necessary condition for a philosophical work to belong to Latin American philosophy, then any work by a Latin American philosopher produced in a different region of the world and in a different language than Spanish and Portuguese is not part of Latin American philosophy. For instance, if such philosophical work happens to be produced in Spain or written in Quechua, this eliminates such work from being part of Latin American philosophy. But this is counterintuitive. It is hard to see why such works lose their right to count as part of a Latin American philosophy due to something as arbitrary as the place where the work is produced or the practice of favoring two languages in a notoriously multilingual region of the world. Alternatively, if the proposal is that such an externalist condition is only sufficient to make a philosophical work count as Latin American, then any work produced in this region and written in its dominant languages would count as belonging to this type of philosophy. Again, this is counterintuitive. For instance, this condition would make an American philosopher who is a native English speaker temporarily working in Brazil and who writes a single book on logic in Portuguese a Latin American philosopher.[2]

When faced with such counterexamples the externalist metaphilosopher is typically inclined to either enrich the relevant external properties or weaken the corresponding externalist criterion, for instance, by dropping the demand for necessary and sufficient external conditions and appealing to relational properties like family resemblances.[3] Despite these efforts to improve the case for a metaphilosophical externalism, the most significant challenge remains. This fundamental challenge consists in accounting for the alleged direct contribution of an externalist property to the specific content and practice of a type of philosophy such that it becomes a distinctive philosophy *because* of that property. For no matter how enriched or nuanced is the relevant external property, unless one explains convincingly its role in determining the content and practice of a philosophy, such an external property remains only a rather arbitrary classificatory tool serving the purposes of explanatory goals outside philosophy.[4] Furthermore, unless such determination bears directly on the explanatory virtues of a philosophical idea or theory, the strong possibility remains that the externalist move amounts to little more than an anecdotal way to classify philosophies.[5]

Because the previous challenges apply to all metaphilosophical externalist efforts, the supporter of an externalist way to justify the existence of a distinctive Latin American philosophy may find some comfort in the realization that these are also challenges to the existence of far less polemical cases like Classical Greek, French, or German philosophies. The problem with this comforting defensive position is that if those are serious challenges little is done in the way of answering them by simply pointing to other cases that share the same difficulties. The fact that the full force of the establishment and tradition backs the existence of these philosophies is not a positive argument that would ground their alleged existence. It seems then that the challenge involved in establishing the ontological credentials of a distinctive philosophy based solely on externalist features is not unique to Latin American philosophy but is a pervasive problem shared by all philosophies justified on purely externalist grounds.

Evidently the explanatory merits of each metaphilosophical externalist effort to account for the existence of a particular type of philosophy need to be assessed by reviewing each case separately. Nonetheless, if one is skeptical toward such externalist efforts on the general grounds that no external property can justifiably determine in the relevant way the content and practice of a philosophy, then there is the alternative option of moving in the opposite direction, namely, toward metaphilosophical internalism.

A general rule in philosophy is that for every externalism there is a conceptually possible internalism. The present debate concerning the existence of philosophies grounded on external features is no exception to this rule. In fact, time-honored philosophical classifications, such as Platonism, Rationalism, or Marxism, typically find their justification as distinctive kinds of philosophy precisely in this internalist way. That is, these different types of philosophy justify their distinctiveness in the particular philosophical theories or methods embraced by their practitioners and not in features like the place or time in which they lived. Hence, the independent existence of different types of philosophy would be justified insofar as such internal philosophical features are real and distinctive enough to warrant a particular classification.

The question then arises whether we can employ a similar internalist strategy to justify the existence of something like a Latin American philosophy or for that matter any philosophy that is traditionally classified by referring to a region, a language, or an era. In the remaining part of this chapter, I explore this possibility. I propose that there is a very suggestive way to accomplish this apparently impossible feat, namely, to internalize external properties in order to distinguish a distinctive type of philosophy. This proposal can be generalized to deal with any philosophy that follows a pattern of justification initially based on an external property. After all, if this strategy works in the case of Latin American philosophy we can reasonably assume that less polemical cases would have an easier time to find their corresponding internalist justifications grounded on the internalization of external properties. However, in this chapter my main focus of attention will be on the possibility of a distinctive Latin American philosophy

Before articulating this alternative proposal it is useful to revisit briefly some traditional objections raised against the use of a metaphilosophical internalist approach to the existence of a philosophy and in particular of a distinctive Latin American philosophy. This way we can see how metaphilosophical internalism deals with the issue of establishing a distinctive philosophy and why traditional internalist versions fall short of the required goal of making sense of something like a distinctive Latin American philosophy.

THE TRADITIONAL METAPHILOSOPHICAL INTERNALIST STRATEGY AND ITS PROBLEMS

One traditional strategy to justify from an internalist metaphilosophical perspective the existence of a distinctive type of philosophy is to look for philosophical facts that could be used in much the same way in which scientific facts are used to establish the methodological autonomy of the different natural sciences. Normally, the autonomy of a science is supported by the existence of a set of factual predicates that cannot be reduced to another set of factual predicates associated with a different science.[6] For instance, in the case of biology an alleged biological fact about an organism could be characterized as an allegedly true statement about this organism that employs the sort of predicates that typically distinguish biology and that cannot be expressed by using the predicates of another science. The equivalent metaphilosophical internalist suggestion is to try to find something analogous within philosophy like some facts that are describable by using the typical predicates of a distinctive type of philosophy. In this way, the suggestion is that the autonomy of such philosophy is guaranteed insofar as its predicates are not reducible to the predicates of another type of philosophy or to a set of nonphilosophical predicates.

What these alleged philosophical facts happen to be is something that inevitably would give rise to fundamental disagreements among the practitioners of philosophy. Nevertheless, at first sight the present internalist suggestion looks promising since it is hard to imagine a philosophy that does not argue for some philosophical set of facts. Consider the large number of statements of the following type that fill philosophical works: The world is made of events and states; an artwork is the result of an artist's hypothetical intentions; minds are indivisible; human freedom is incompatible with God's omniscience; a life without examination is not worth living; slavery is an affront to human dignity; and so on. Not only are philosophical works filled with such factual statements but they and the arguments supporting them are grouped by their salient predicates that in turn can serve classificatory purposes. These classifications range from the identification of a theory as part of a philosophical subdiscipline like metaphysics and logic to the more specific identification related to an account about a particular philosophical issue within those subdisciplines.

If we then try to use this internalist strategy in the case of philosophies that are identified in terms of world regions or languages, a crucial step that needs to be taken consists in finding the alleged philosophical facts that correlate with such properties. That is, the success or failure of this strategy would depend on the existence of philosophical facts that share a property corresponding to some geographical, linguistic or cultural feature. Then, it would be possible to link their relevant statements in terms of a set of predicates that are unique to a type of philosophy. However, the traditional problem with this strategy is that it is very hard to think of a single external property that can be used in the required internalist way.

Consider the case of Latin American philosophy. The suggestion is that there must be at least one property that a whole set of philosophical facts share such that they can be grouped as belonging to a category that is justifiably recognized as Latin American. Nevertheless, the enormous difficulty that this suggestion faces is that there does not seem to be a single property that satisfies such requirement. Note again that pointing to the fact that the relevant philosophical factual statements are produced in Latin America or by the use of Spanish and Portuguese languages would not satisfy this internalist criterion because being Latin American or speaking Spanish are not philosophical predicates.[7] Thus, the traditional problem faced by this internalist strategy boils down to the extreme difficulty of finding a single property that satisfies this internalist criterion.

Another traditional metaphilosophical internalist proposal looks for inspiration not so much in the direction of the natural sciences but in the direction of philosophy itself and the apparently successful cases of classification based on a set of internal properties that emerge from the use of a particular philosophical method. The proposal is that the internalist way of trying to make sense of a distinctive philosophy should not be in terms of the identification of a shared property amongst a set of alleged philosophical facts but rather in terms of the identification of a distinctive philosophical method employed to uncover and theorize about them. In other words, the correct analogy here would be with philosophical methods such as Phenomenology or Philosophical Analysis and not with the strategies to establish the autonomy of scientific disciplines. This proposal would then explain the otherwise notorious absence of alleged philosophical facts in the case of Latin American philosophy because a method is actually the instrument by which such alleged facts are uncovered. This sort of internalist strategy has been more popular than the previous one amongst philosophers who have defended the idea of a distinctive Latin American philosophical method.[8]

Unfortunately, if we look again to Latin American philosophy as a case study of the efforts by an internalist metaphilosophy to justify the existence of a distinctive philosophy, this second methodological internalist strategy also faces serious problems. For what is this philosophical method that is distinctive in the case of Latin American philosophy? What method did philosophers like Andres Bello, José Vasconcelos, or José Carlos Mariátegui use that happens to be distinctive enough to identify it as characteristic of Latin American philosophy? Moreover, what method unites all of these practitioners of philosophy in a way that can be recognized as homogeneous to Latin American philosophers and different from other philosophical traditions? None, it seems. Instead, it appears that every single philosopher working in Latin America has employed a philosophical methodology that is already in place. That is, a methodology that has nothing particularly Latin American about it. Moreover, even if one were to find a philosopher whose method is impossible to place inside one of the recognized philosophical methodologies, why would this exceptional case exhibit a method that distinguishes the whole of Latin American philosophy? So, the prospects of justifying the reality of a Latin American philosophy in this second internalist methodological sense are not very promising.[9]

If neither the philosophical content understood in terms of factual statements present in Latin American philosophical works, nor the philosophical method employed by philosophers from Latin America seems to exhibit a viable internalist feature that would justify the distinctiveness needed to identify Latin American philosophy, should we abandon the internalist approach to this issue? I do not think so. There is a promising third internalist alternative based on a notion that sits between philosophical facts and methods and that is potentially capable of internalizing crucial externalist features.

STYLE AND THE PROCESS OF PROPERTY INTERNALIZATION

The previous internalist metaphilosophical proposals find their inspiration from analogous classificatory strategies used in the natural sciences and in some philosophical methodologies associated with schools of thought.

However, we have seen the serious difficulties associated with these internalist metaphilosophical efforts. Fortunately, there is another source of metaphilosophical inspiration found in the way in which artworks are classified by appealing to artistic styles. Despite the fact that there are many competing accounts about the nature of artistic style they tend to agree on the set of fundamental features that distinguishes an artistic style. It is by examining these features that we will recognize a unique process of internalization of external properties that can potentially be extended to our metaphilosophical quest. Let us first identify the set of fundamental features typically associated with artistic styles and then see how they can be applied to the metaphilosophical internalist effort to justify the existence of something like a distinctive Latin American philosophy.

There is a fundamental sense in which a style is the way in which certain things are executed and how this way determines particular features of such performances and their consequences. Hence, there is an inextricable connection between the existence of a style and the presence of a human action. Although not all actions and their consequences exhibit a style, strictly speaking only such agential products are capable of exhibiting styles. So, even when styles are sometimes attributed to persons or natural objects these attributions are either parasitic on the presence of agency or simply metaphorical.

The connection between a style and a way things are done suggests a strong link between style and method. In other words, it is tempting to propose that if a style is recognizable as a way things are done then we are essentially referring to a sort of methodology. This proposal is supported by the fact that styles and methods share several important features. For instance, a style shares with a method its essentially public nature because at least in principle a style can be employed more than once and by more than a single individual.[10] Even when the appearance of a new style is a truly creative event, once a style becomes established it also becomes a path for others to use. Thus, like in the case of methods styles can be followed, copied, and learned.

Nevertheless, a style cannot simply be reduced to a methodology.[11] For a style is not simply a recipe or algorithm that if followed will produce something necessarily belonging to a given style. That is, in contrast to methodology and despite its public character, a style can become the singular expression of a group or an individual so that it is practically impossible to adopt it unless quite stringent conditions are satisfied.[12] The reason for higher standards of satisfaction in using a style as opposed to a method, is that styles often are the result of exceptional conditions satisfied by exceptionally creative individuals who themselves may not even know how they are capable of expressing such distinctive style or how to teach others to do so. A consequence of this connection between a style and its use is that often it appears to be impossible to codify a given style into something that if learned can be applied to produce things exhibiting that style. However, the most prominent difference between a style and a method is found in the role that content plays in style. To see this let us consider that traditional and often abused distinction between form and content and how it relates to style.

Since talking about a style is essentially talking about the way something is done a traditional understanding of style stresses its formal or structural aspects. From this traditional perspective it is quite natural to see style as presupposing the distinction between form and content, where style is thought to fall on the side of the formal part of this relationship. Hence, a formalist understanding of style as a sort of methodology suggests the existence of a relationship between style and content similar to the one traditionally associated with form and content. This leads to the popular proposal that allows for a single style to express different contents and a single content to be expressed by different styles.

And yet we must be careful with this formalist way of understanding style for it seriously misses a crucial aspect of style's relationship with content. The crucial aspect that is missed by a purely formalistic approach to style is that it ignores the constitutive role that content often plays in style. When considering the presence of a style in an action or an object, besides its formal aspects it also is evident that the content is as relevant as the form. In fact, it is possible to say that sometimes what distinguishes a style is the subject matter or content. As Nelson Goodman puts it when speaking about a writer's style: "Some differences in style consist entirely of differences in what is said. Suppose one historian writes in terms of military conflicts, another in terms of social changes; or suppose one biographer stresses public careers, another personalities."[13] Thus, in Goodman's example, by emphasizing different contents these writers would exhibit different styles. The same can be said about practically all cases involving style since most involve some type of content.

Going beyond its relationship to methodology, a style also permits overlap and subdivisions that are quite useful in understanding the things that one may want to classify and explain by appealing to it. For instance, despite clear differences in architectural styles between say the Romanesque and the Gothic it is possible to encounter works of art that share features of both styles in a harmonious and aesthetically successful way. Similarly, although the musical styles of the last compositions of Beethoven and those of Schubert are significantly different, it is customary to subsume them under the early Romantic style. In this way, the use of styles as ways to categorize things typically reveals a complex and dynamic network of relationships in which the style itself is seen as easily branching into subdivisions or as belonging to a larger stylistic category. But, perhaps the clearest expression of the essentially relational nature of style is the fact that the attribution of a style is always done having in mind another contrasting style. This suggests that stylistic properties are essentially nonatomistic for apparently they cannot exist in complete isolation from other stylistic properties.

One last salient feature of style incorporates some of the previously mentioned features in a way that emphasizes the use of style not just as a tool to categorize actions and things but actually as a strategy to produce them. This feature consists in the intentional character of style whose appearance in a performance or an object reveals the essentially agential nature of style. That is, the active production of objects guided by a style or demanding the creation of a new style is explicitly or implicitly an intentional activity. It is an explicit intentional activity whenever agents consciously use or create a style as the guiding principle for their performance. Correspondingly, it would be an implicit intentional activity if the best way to account for such performance involves the attribution of a style whether or not their authors are conscious of using it.[14] Either way, a style exhibits the presence of an intentional activity identifiable in terms of that style.

All these characteristics of style provide us with the conceptual tools to make sense of the process whereby some properties become built-in stylistic elements. This process is accomplished in a straightforward way by the stylistic contribution to their respective artworks of properties like a painter's favored shapes and subjects, a writer's choice of words and topics, or a musician's preferred harmonies and textures. However, an equivalent process also can be accomplished in a less direct way by the participation of properties that begin as external elements in the context of creation and later become constitutive stylistic features of an artwork, such as its belonging to a historical period, its being produced in a geographic location, or its articulation by the use of a particular language. Such an alternative process is indirect because initially the relevant properties exist independently of the object of creation and have no evident connection to the intentional artistic outcome of that process. Nevertheless, these same external properties are later recognized as necessary items in the characterization of some stylistic elements or patterns to a point in which the very style is often identified with them.

Consider the case of Japanese or French styles of gardening. These styles can be traced back to Japan and France because these regions of the world were their birth places. However, by alluding to such geographical regions one also is pointing to the particular features that distinguish these places in terms of their causal contribution to the emergence of those particular styles. That is, by identifying a style of gardening as Japanese or

French one also is linking this style to a set of causes that gave rise to it. For instance, these regions' typical weather, their common plants and soils, and the cultural inclinations of their inhabitants toward things like spaces and colors. In this way, the identification of these two gardening styles by appealing to an external property like their place of origin allows for the recognition of specific stylistic features directly related to the process whereby such styles came to be. Furthermore, once their distinctive styles of gardening become established by the complete internalization of the relevant external properties, then it is perfectly possible to emancipate such properties from their external roots and find gardens in other regions of the world exhibiting such styles and being the products of gardeners that are neither Japanese nor French.

Consequently, the process of internalization of external properties is the result of a successful combination of etiological factors that give rise to a semantic distinction signaling the existence of a unique style. For once an external property is identified in terms of its causal contribution to a recognizable stylistic pattern this property becomes part of the internal set of features that identify a distinctive style. In fact, often the style itself will be baptized by referring to such external property. So, ideally at least, for each semantic identification of a style based on an external property there is an etiological story that roots such identification in terms of its causal contribution to the corresponding style. It is safe to assume that in most cases where a style is identified by a name that refers to an external property the process of internalization has been successfully completed.[15]

PHILOSOPHICAL STYLES AND THE POSSIBILITY
OF LATIN AMERICAN PHILOSOPHY

The idea of employing a notion like style outside its traditional sphere of application within the arts has an important precedent in the work of social scientists like Karl Mannheim.[16] According to this approach, there are recognizable patterns distinguishing distinctive ways of generating ideas in terms of styles of thought that resemble what occurs within the arts. Mannheim and his followers essentially used the notion of style to uncover patterns of thought that were the direct result of the historical conditions that gave rise to particular scientific theories.[17] In stressing the quest for the historical roots of such styles of thought Mannheim and his followers were only indirectly concerned with the more general issue that has guided our metaphilosophical quest about the possibility of internalizing stylistic properties. Although locating the historical roots of a style is a way to locate some properties that contribute to the process of internalization of external properties, not all such properties are historical or even social. As we saw with the case of a Japanese or French style of gardening, despite important contributions by historical events that led to the emergence of styles of gardening in Japan and France, there were other equally significant elements involved in their appearance such as the typical weather patterns and particular ecological niches of these regions.

Other social scientists have also used the notion of style in order to illuminate the particular contributions of individuals or schools of thought within their corresponding discipline. For instance, Peter Gay uses style to distinguish within historiography the particular modes of expression favored by someone like Edward Gibbon and not by Thomas Macaulay, or modes of expression favored by Leopold von Ranke and not by Jacob Burckhardt.[18] In fact, this is the type of approach that has been explored by the few philosophers who have looked in the direction of style to try to identify a distinctive prose that corresponds to philosophy vis-à-vis other types of prose used outside philosophy,[19] or to distinguish within philosophy different methodologies, understood in the internalist sense, that separate, say, the style of Plato from Aristotle, or the style employed by practitioners of phenomenology from other philosophical schools.[20] Again, despite the explanatory benefits of using style in this way, this metaphilosophical approach does not address the possibility of justifying the existence of a distinctive type of philosophy by the internalization of external properties.

However, we are now in a position to conclude this examination by using the previous analysis of style to justify the existence of a distinctive type of philosophy based on the internalization of external properties. Given our particular metaphilosophical purposes, the main suggestion arising from such an analysis is that for a distinctive philosophy to exist it is a sufficient condition that it has the capacity to exhibit a philosophical style that can be identified by referring to something like a region or language of the world where such style was born or is typically practiced. Whenever this condition is satisfied we are in front of a truly distinctive philosophy anchored in some originally external feature that continues to identify or describe it. The previous discussion singled out some specific conditions involved in the process of internalization of relevant external properties leading to a distinctive style. Such a process of internalization can also be seen in the case of philosophical style. Let us then conclude this metaphilosophical exploration by considering the possibility of a distinctive Latin American philosophy as an illustration of this strategy. So, what sort of conditions would need to be satisfied for a philosophical style to count as Latin American and thereby justify the independent reality of that type of philosophy? Here are the necessary conditions that follow from our previous analysis.

First, in order to begin making sense of a Latin American philosophy in terms of a distinctive philosophical style there would have to be a way of doing such philosophy that is recognizable in its salient products, namely, its typical methods, central theories, and main ideas. Such recognition has to be public in that this philosophical style would be recognizable by philosophers outside its traditional sphere of influence. Also, at least in principle, such style would have to be capable of being learned and copied.

Second, a Latin American philosophical style would have to be anchored in the history, culture, geography, and languages of Latin America in the sense that it would trace back its origins and context of creation to this region and its people. However, once the style is established, it also should at least in principle become independent of its practitioner's country of origin and even language of choice. Clearly, if the continued presence of the etiological connection to features that are only available in the region and culture distinctive of Latin America turns out to be a necessary condition for the production of key ideas and theories, then it is to be expected that this last condition can hardly be met. Thus, much like trying to start a French or Japanese garden in the Arctic tundra or in the Amazon basin, the possibility of exporting this style of philosophy to other regions of the world would be miniscule. Nonetheless, in a purely conceptual way a thorough internalization of the relevant external properties allows for this possibility.

Third, a Latin American philosophical style would very likely overlap with other philosophical styles and in turn would be able to accommodate subdivisions that could be recognized as possessing the general features that distinguish a Latin American philosophical style—subdivisions such as Mexican or Argentinean. Moreover, in the case of a Latin American philosophical style, a network of stylistic influences also must be present, at the very least in terms of contrasts with other philosophical styles.

Fourth, the identification of an independent Latin American style of doing philosophy would permit a conscious choice of that style by some of its practitioners in ways that previously might have been only unconscious. This would open up an explicit agenda in terms of an intentional effort to promote the practice of this philosophical style.

Therefore, in the same way in which an analogous case can be made that there is a Latin American style of literature, painting, music, or architecture insofar as all these styles satisfy their equivalent conditions, arguably if a Latin American philosophical style satisfies these four conditions we are in a position to justify its legitimate distinctiveness.

Nevertheless, even if one agrees that from an internalist perspective this is a promising way of understanding the possibility of a distinctive Latin American philosophy, it crucially remains to be shown that indeed there is a style of philosophy that satisfies these conditions. Because we are dealing with what is ultimately an empirical investigation, it is possible that nothing is ever found that justifies from this internalist perspective the existence of a truly independent Latin American philosophy. Perhaps once we painstakingly review the specific philosophical products that are associated with this alleged style all that is uncovered is a set of external properties that fall short of being internalized in the required way. Then if we want to talk about a Latin American philosophy we will have to resort to externalism, with all their explanatory weaknesses. But, precisely because this is a question to be settled by a careful review of the available evidence, despite such potentially negative outcome nothing precludes the future materialization of a philosophical style that is uniquely Latin American in the internalist sense articulated in this chapter.

ACKNOWLEDGMENTS

I thank David Suits, Susana Nuccetelli, and Sheryl T. Ross for valuable comments on a previous draft of this chapter.

NOTES

1. In his *Hispanic/Latino Identity*, Jorge Gracia (2000) provides an illuminating account of the two major types of externalist approaches that exist among Latin American philosophers under the categories of "culturalists" and "critics." See pp. 133–40. Gracia's own account is an externalist approach that looks towards historical events as the key elements in providing the basis for a distinctive type of Latin American philosophy. See also note 3.

2. Famously, this was the case with W. O. Quine's *O Sentido da Nova Lógica* (1996) a book that was written and published in Portuguese in 1944 when Quine was temporarily living in Brazil. Although such a book satisfies the mentioned externalist sufficient conditions, this would be hardly considered sufficient to count Quine and his philosophical work as Latin American.

3. In the case of Latin American philosophy possibly the most influential recent externalist account that follows this strategy is provided by Jorge Gracia (2000). Although discussing the possibility of "Hispanic philosophy" (pp. 70–87), Gracia's basic suggestion is that what leads to the significant objections against externalism based on counterexamples results from its traditional commitment to necessary and sufficient conditions that allegedly distinguish something like a Latin American philosophy. Gracia's alternative externalist suggestion is to move in the direction of weaker requirements like historical relationships and family resemblances to account for the relevant relational properties that would justify membership inside the open ended category of Latin American philosophy. See also (Gracia, 2000) pp. 130–158.

4. These interests would typically be related to historical, sociological, and even political agendas.

5. This potential arbitrariness gives rise to the possibility of an unbounded and gratuitous use of a classification: What stops anyone from proposing the existence

of Main Street philosophy? The whole agenda of externalist metaphilosophical proposals can be seen as an effort to deal with this central worry.

6. This characterization of the autonomy of a science is roughly based on
Jerry Fodor's influential account of how to identify non-basic sciences (1974).

7. An alternative articulation of this problem is that precisely what is at
stake is the effort by defenders of an internalist strategy to make predicates like
Latin American ones that are philosophically relevant. Later I try to explain how
this can potentially be done by using a different internalist strategy.

8. This metaphilosophical approach has been particularly fertile among Latin
American philosophers who not only have proposed the existence of a unique Latin
American perspective capable of uncovering alleged philosophical facts but also the
existence of more regional perspectives such as a Mexican, Panamanian, or Bolivian
allegedly capable of doing as much. See Schwartzmann (1950), Gaos (1952), Ramos
(1963), and in particular the essays contained in Zea's anthology (1968).

9. This absence of anything resembling a method unique and distinctive of
Latin American philosophy has often been noticed by those who search in vain for
such internalist methodology. Addressing a similar question concerning the possibility of a Hispanic-American philosophy, here is one of those deeply honest passages
that capture such frustration written by Augusto Salazar Bondy (1969):

> To review the process of Hispanic American philosophy is to relate the
> passing of Western philosophy *through* our countries, or to narrate Euro-
> pean philosophy *in* Hispanic America. It is not to tell the history of a
> natural philosophy *of* Hispanic America. In our historical process there
> are Cartesians, Krausists, Spencerians, Bergsonians and other European
> "*isms*." But this is all; there are no creative figures to found and nurture
> their own peculiar tradition, nor native philosophic "*isms*." We search for
> the original contributions of our countries in answer to the Western chal-
> lenge—or to that of other cultures—and we do not find them. At least we
> find nothing substantial, worthy of a positive historical appraisal. No one,
> I believe, can give testimony to its existence if he is moderately strict in
> his judgment. (p. 388)

Reprinted in Gracia, J. and Millán-Zaibert, E., eds. (2004).

10. This is a key feature that has been used to distinguish talking about
individual style from a shared style by several individuals. See Wollheim (1987).
For the purposes of this chapter I have ignored this distinction; most of the things
said here about style relate more to a generic way of understanding style than to
individual styles.

11. Perhaps an elaborate reductive analysis of style could ultimately perform
such reduction but only after taking into account the obstacles to be mentioned. This
reductive analysis is tempting for reasons that are independent of the ones related
to this chapter's particular goals. Nonetheless, even if such reduction is possible
the main metaphilosophical considerations developed here will remain essentially
unchanged. Thus, for present purposes I continue to assume a nonreductive relationship between method and style.

12. In the case of individual styles associated with individual creators, this stringent condition can go as far as strict identity. From this extreme perspective what would count in the more generic understanding of style as a case of inspiration may be treated as something closer to a case of plagiarism or forgery.

13. Nelson Goodman (1975), "The Status of Style," *Critical Inquiry* 1: 799–811; quoted on p. 801.

14. This feature of the use or creation of styles has led to the debate about the need to employ real or postulated authorial intentions whenever a stylistic property is found in an object or performance. See Jenefer M. Robinson, (1985), "Style and Personality in the Literary Work," *The Philosophical Review* 64: 227–47; pp. 233–42.

15. Nevertheless, it is always possible that an alleged distinctive style cannot pass the test of locating the relevant causal roots that give weight to its distinctiveness in terms of an external property. In this case, the accusation of arbitrariness is hard to avoid and the corresponding style identification loses its raison d'être.

16. See Mannheim (1982).

17. A very interesting historical account of the development of scientific styles of thought within the German genetics community inspired directly by Mannheim's work is Jonathan Harwood's *Styles of Scientific Thought* (1993).

18. See Peter Gay (1988), *Style in History* New York: Norton & Company.

19. R. G. Collingwood's *An Essay on Philosophical Method* (1933) and Brand Blanshard's *On Philosophical Style* (1954) are good examples of this strategy. See Ross (1998) and Van Eck, Caroline et al., eds. (1995) for more recent examples.

20. Beret Lang's anthology *Philosophical Style* (1980) is a good source for this type of metaphilosophical efforts.

PART II

RACISM, THE ACADEMY, AND THE
PRACTICE OF PHILOSOPHY

CHAPTER SIX

ON THE POLITICS
OF PROFESSIONAL PHILOSOPHY

The Plight of the African American Philosopher

John H. McClendon III

Given the hegemony of academic racism and political ideology as the context for African American philosophers' status and their corresponding philosophical inquiry, the guiding focus of this chapter centers on three pivotal concerns. First, I address how the exclusion of African American philosophers from the white academy is a matter of institutionalized racism as an ancillary dimension of the professionalization of philosophy.[1]

Second, in conjunction with exploring exclusion, I explore how the professionalization of philosophy is a class phenomena rooted in bourgeois social division of labor, which concerns the nature of mental labor as a professional pursuit and how power rather than academic competency is the foremost principle. Hence, the process of professionalization and the practice of exclusion, both due to power relations of class domination and racial subordination, require that I attend to the matter of the great majority of African American philosophers being relegated to the institutional network of Historically Black Colleges and Universities (HBCU). It is not a matter of happenstance that nearly all African American philosophers before the 1970s are linked to the HBCU context. This connection is manifested either in enrollment as students or employment as faculty. Generally, the evidence points to the fact that most African American philosophers assumed both capacities.[2]

Third, the HBCU context and its attendant intellectual culture subsequently influenced the substantive nature of African American philosophical inquiry as an academic pursuit. More concretely, I inspect the manner in which African American philosophers address the problems associated with the criteria of professional (academic) philosophy of teaching, research, and service. I contend that a nagging tension emerges between how to meet the expectations surrounding the curriculum of professional philosophy and addressing the constellation of problems affixed to confronting racism.[3]

PROFESSIONAL PHILOSOPHY AND ACADEMIC RACISM

My central thesis is that the history of the professionalization of philosophy, not unlike other disciplines in the white academy, is firmly rooted in an institutionalized form of academic racism. By institutionalized racism I mean, not just the attitude or belief that there exist inferior and superior races but more importantly behavior and institutions that give material support to such attitudes and beliefs by the actual suppression of the supposed inferior group. Thus, academic racism is the practice associated with the complex of institutions such as colleges and universities, including the posture of the American Philosophical Association (APA), which work together and assert institutional power by erecting standards that under the guise of professionalization were historically racist in nature and still today remain de facto racist prescriptions.[4]

I argue that institutionalized racism and political ideology are closely entwined in the history of professional philosophy and these conditions are pivotal in interpreting the plight of African American philosophers. I submit that by uncovering how institutional racism and political ideology have had an impact on African American philosophers, we can in part explain, among other social indicators, why today the negligible amount of approximately 1 percent of all professional philosophers in the United States are African American. Moreover, I contend that academic racism and political ideology are keys to why philosophical issues and topics pertaining to African Americans are afforded miniscule consideration among the professional philosophy establishment. From a professional career standpoint, such consideration is deemed the hallmark of serious (academic) attention and scholarly recognition.[5]

When I speak of the politics of professional philosophy and the plight of the African American philosopher, it should be transparent to the reader that this chapter challenges the notion that professional philosophy (especially in light of claims about its universal and abstract character) stands above the "mundane" empirical conditions of political interests and the material reality of racism. At root, institutionalized racism is a political relationship, which is embedded in the history of professional philosophy.

Consequently, the presence of racism within professional philosophy, with few exceptions, has continued to remain a neglected topic.[6]

By politics I mean the exercise of power, whereby the use of the electoral or judicial process constitutes just one of several modes of operation. The designation and appointment of those that hold decision-making power in the profession need not (and generally do not) take into account the interests of African Americans. In fact, such appointments are usually determined without input from academics representative of African Americans. More often than not when Black faculty members are hired, the ruling principle is the perceived interests of philosophy departments as determined by white members of the respective departments. Given the pervasive character of racism in the academy (with philosophy departments especially in mind) the decisions rendered are not thought of as racist; rather, they are justified as democratic because the white majority rules. Here we have a vicious circularity wherein the majority consists of the very same white scholars who serve as power brokers under institutionalized racism and the minority consists of the few African Americans in the discipline. The apparent democratic process in essence upholds the racist status quo.[7]

There is a significant distinction between the specialization of knowledge and the professionalization of scholarship. The former is a manifestation of the objective dialectical development of knowledge and the latter is a specific characteristic of bourgeois modes of development within the framework of formal academic pursuit. The logic of the development of the former as substantive knowledge is one wherein the complexity of knowledge is the upshot of two poles, where on the one hand we have what Lenin refers to as the inexhaustibility of matter (the concrete motion, change, and development of the material world) and on the other hand, its gnoseological counterpart—the successive approximation of knowledge (comprehension) of this process.[8]

The professionalization of scholarship is rooted in the bourgeois imperative to provide a measure for determining who is considered to be "knowledgeable" or certified with some degree of mastery in a specialized field of knowledge. Here we have a social division of labor (within the orbit of mental labor) wherein certification is the formal recognition of mastery. This formal recognition need not include substantive content in knowledge, that is, you may have a degree or certificate without actually obtaining mastery (qualification) in a particular field of study. In turn, one can have mastery in a field of knowledge without certification. In other words, nonprofessional philosophers or autodidacts can be competent philosophers without a professional portfolio.[9]

The antithesis of professionalization and specialization is an expression of the contradiction between form and content. Formal recognition (legitimacy) is the ticket one must have to enter the academy. Yet in reality one can be qualified without certification and certified without qualification. But given the imperatives of a capitalist job market, it is clear that certification is operative as a process of elimination, which is quite political in character. With certification, there is an essential power relationship wherein those that grant certification have power over those that lack this power. Additionally, the former have the power to determine the very criteria for certification as well as have the power of granting legitimacy to what passes as philosophical inquiry. From an institutional standpoint, African American philosophers have historically (and in contemporary times) generally lacked such power in professional philosophy, whereas white philosophers tend to monopolize the position of power brokers. I contend that the paucity of professional African American philosophers is directly proportional to the power of African Americans in the profession.[10]

The professional necessity for certification and the reality that there are competent nonprofessional philosophers results in what I call the certification–qualification antithesis. In light of the history of academic racism and the exclusion of African Americans from the academy and professional philosophy, professionalization has had a disproportionate impact vis-à-vis the small number of African American philosophers in the profession along with the omission of nonprofessional African American philosophers from scholarly discussion in the academy. To the extent that nonprofessional African American philosophers are seriously studied it usually is due to the efforts of African American philosophers and scholars.[11]

In fact, at other times I have argued that nonacademic Black philosophers have garnered more attention in the historical account of contemporary African American philosophers than have academic/professional philosophers. Historically, within the dominant Euro-American philosophical tradition, the prevailing influence of autodidacts or amateurs in the academy declined in direct correspondence with the rise of professionalization. However, the structural configuration of African American intellectual culture (both inside and outside of the HBCU) allowed for nonacademic philosophers to maintain a receptive audience in the African American community.[12]

The process of professionalization of scholarship is materialized in definitive structures whereby the process of legitimization is delegated to specified institutions as sanctioning bodies for certification. Colleges, universities, scholarly journals, standardized curriculum, and the evaluation of the merits of various forms of scholarship fall under the auspices of designated professionals and professional associations. Thus, professional philosophers maintain an elevated intellectual status due to having acquired legitimacy within the academy.[13]

Furthermore, racism elevates the position and legitimacy of white philosophers (over and above philosophers of color) not to mention that it gives priority to their research agendas, which often become the norm and standard of the academy. The particular interests of white philosophers assume the form of universality and hence we have what is in actuality none other than a false universality.[14]

Bourgeois political ideology and interests play no small part in providing the ethos of professional philosophy's orientation. Where professional philosophy is viewed as free of political encumbrances, we have the conflation of the specialization of knowledge with the professionalization of scholarship. The outcome of professionalization serves the dominant political interests under the camouflage of value-free and ideologically neutral inquiry. This permits not only that bourgeois philosophy functions as the standard for professional philosophy but also for racism to exist in a benign mode and as a covert operation.[15]

The "Color Line" as W. E. B. Du Bois so fittingly called Jim Crow is generally thought of in terms of the institutionalized exclusion of African Americans in the participation of white society at all levels. Du Bois profoundly understood that the Color Line was more than a matter of Black exclusion; he conceived the Color Line as a vital aspect of international white supremacy. Hence imperialism, colonialism, and segregation were dimensions of white dominance and all were expressions of the Color Line. White supremacy subsequently not only sanctioned the oppression African Americans via Southern segregation but also included the segregated practices of the North. Segregated practices took place at northern public and private elementary and high schools as well as with higher educational bodies. In both the North and the South, the foundations of the Color Line were tied directly to unequal power relationships, which in turn facilitated the racial oppression and capitalist exploitation of African Americans. The plight of the Black scholar derived from the general condition of white supremacy.[16]

One indicator of the status of African American scholars is that by 1936 there were only three Black PhD's serving on the faculty of white colleges in the North. Resistance to Black philosophers (and Black scholars more generally) as teachers of white students had a rather long history and remains a tenaciously held norm. Top administrators at the most prestigious institutions openly practice racial discrimination against Black scholars. We witness two glaring examples with the historian/sociologist W. E. B. Du Bois and philosopher Albert M. Dunham.

The holder of a doctorate from Harvard, when Du Bois was a member on the faculty of the University of Pennsylvania, he was forbidden from teaching classes and only allowed to do research on his project, *The Philadelphia Negro*. Du Bois reports, "I was nominated to the unusual status of 'assistant' instructor. Even at that there must have been some opposition, for the invitation was not particularly cordial. I was offered a salary of $900 for a period limited to one year. I was given no real academic standing, no office at the University, no official recognition of any kind; my name was eventually omitted from the catalogue; I had no contact with students, and very little with members of the faculty, even in my own department."[17]

The set of circumstances that Dunham faced accentuates the painful reality and personal dimension of denied opportunity. After having previously studied at Harvard with Alfred North Whitehead and at Chicago with George Herbert Mead, Dunham received his doctorate from the University of Chicago in 1933. Among his published works is the collaborative effort on the book, *George Herbert Mead: The Philosophy of the Act*. At that time, many considered Dunham to be one of the most promising among African American philosophers to rise in the profession. In fact, he was the only African American philosopher to have studied with the two aforesaid prominent philosophers and he was also very well received by the philosophy faculty at Chicago.[18]

In due course, he was even assigned to teach a summer class in the philosophy department of his alma mater. The appointment was to be a gateway to becoming a full-fledged member of the philosophy faculty. However, more than half of the students dropped the class when they discovered that their professor was a Black man. Although the administration managed to gather enough students to continue the class, the idea of Dunham joining the Chicago faculty, in light of student response, was quickly abandoned. Later, Alain Locke recruited Dunham to teach at Howard University. Those who knew him, including his sister Katherine (the renowned dancer), believed that the racial restrictions that were imposed on him with regard to the possibility of teaching at white institutions was the cause for his affliction with depression. Sadly, we discover that by 1949 and after many years of mental illness, Dunham died in a psychiatric institution.[19]

Although the Color Line as a system of oppression ostensibly involves the exclusion of Black people from white institutions, exclusionary practices and policies do not exhaust the manifold dimension of oppression under white supremacy or for that matter do inclusionary actions (in response to exclusion) in themselves undermine the substantive character of the Color Line. We must be cognizant of the conditional proposition, namely that if the inclusion of African American individuals into various institutions and organizations does not change the balance of power relationship central to white supremacist oppression then the Color Line remains intact despite the occasional appearance that the line had been broken by the entrance of individuals into white academic organizations.[20]

For instance, as early as 1879, the American Social Science Association had individual presentations from African American leaders such as Frederick Douglass, Richard T. Greener, and Booker T. Washington. In turn, philosopher Alexander Crummell, classicist William H. Crogman, educational administrator Booker T. Washington, philosopher Joseph C. Price, and college president Richard R. Wright addressed the National Education Association during the period from 1880 to 1896. Additionally, such organizations as the American Academy of Political and Social Science had African American members. The philosopher/theologian John W. E. Bowen held membership in the Institute of Sacred Literature and even reviewed applicants for the group. William S. Scarborough belonged to both the Modern Language Association and the American Philological Society. (Prior to Scarborough, the philosopher Richard T. Greener became the first African American to join this association.) Despite these breakthroughs, Jim Crow was alive and well. In terms of the white academy's oppressive relationship to the great number of African Americans, exclusion and powerlessness remained a constant factor.[21]

Furthermore, although Phi Beta Kappa allowed certain individual African Americans who were students at white institutions to join its ranks, nevertheless, throughout the later half of the nineteenth century and beyond the first half of the twentieth century, Phi Beta Kappa did not allow affiliates of its organization to be established on the HBCU campuses. The year before the historic Brown Decision, which is to say in 1953, Fisk and Howard universities were finally granted chapters. The institutional character of the Color Line takes priority over the position of individual African Americans. Thus, the wholesale exclusion of the HBCU follows from this principle. The Color Line marks a relation of institutional subordination as an expression of the power exercised by institutionalized racism.[22]

The view that individual inclusion marks the end of the Color Line is based on what I call the Jackie Robinson/Branch Rickey thesis. It is the presumptive view is that racism is primarily an attitude (or belief) based on bias and stereotyping and that these can be surmounted only by the particular actions and behavior on the part of Black people toward white racist treatment. Rather than confront and resist racist practices, African Americans must be willing to accept white racist abuse until the racists come to realize that there are no fundamental differences between African Americans and themselves and ultimately accept Black people into their organizations. In effect, Black individuals should become martyrs for the cause of breaking the Color Line.[23]

With this thesis, what we have in effect is the notion that racism is a moral problem rooted in ignorance. The moral principle ancillary with racism is that the differential treatment afforded to African Americans on the part of whites leads directly to Black people experiencing harm. One practical consequence of this conception of racism is that when Black people are actually confronted with white racism there is an expectation that they should respond in a passive manner. This thesis upholds the erroneous view that Black passive behavior toward white racism facilitates the gradual trans-formation of white stereotypical thinking and thus racist practices.

The question before us becomes, why is it presumed that passive behavior and gradualism are the most practical approaches for address-ing racism? It follows from the perspective that stereotypical constructions ultimately emerge from whites not knowing the true character of Black people. Given this consideration, it will take a substantial amount of time for whites to become educated and hence truly know the real character of Black people. Additionally, because whites are ignorant of their racism, they also are unaware of their unethical conduct as racists, that is, whites are not aware of the harm inflicted on African Americans. The substance of racism is manifestly an ethical contradiction based on a lack of knowledge. When this moral contradiction comes to the forefront, it is thought it will have an epistemological result; namely racism becomes an ungrounded belief that is ethically reprehensible to whites. At the heart of this idealist thesis regarding white ignorance, morality, and Black passive behavior is a definite view of Black inclusion. In other words, Black inclusion is predicated on white approval and acceptance and not through Black resistance to white racism; not to mention the quest for the power to enact institutional trans-formation. The telling result is that the Robinson/Rickey thesis rather than overcoming the Color Line (as a form of institutionalized racism) actually affirms institutionalized racism by not resisting its practical and material expressions as well as confronting its institutional power base.[24]

Given the power dimension of the Color Line, it was fairly inevitable that African Americans were afforded limited chances to pursue graduate study in any field of endeavor. Hence, as among other disciplines, philosophy historically had a small pool of African Americans with graduate degrees and particularly holders of the doctorate. The professionalization of philosophy and its ancillary Color Line (throughout most of the twentieth century) also meant that the vast majority of African American philosophers, with graduate degrees, were excluded from or had restricted participation in the white academy and its auxiliary professional organizations.[25]

Academic racism meant that African American philosophers were receiving their terminal degrees from white institutions and under the supervision of white philosophers and hence gained their legitimacy as philosophers from within the white academy. (With regard to the HBCU, no institution offers the PhD degree in philosophy.) Nevertheless, African American philosophers were not included as faculty on the very same white campuses. Nearly twenty years after the Dunham affair with the University of Chicago, Broadus Butler faced the same predicament as his predecessor.

Harris reports, "Broadus N. Butler who applied for a teaching position at a predominately white university after completing requirements for [his] doctorate degree in 1952 at the University of Michigan, learned that his advisers accompanying letter to a reference stated '. . . you get [a] philosopher, but of course, a Negro,' and the one-line response, 'Why don't you go to where you'll be among your own kind.' "[26]

A member of the esteemed Tuskegee Airmen during World War II, Butler ultimately managed to become administrator of the graduate division in the Liberal Arts College at Wayne State University, where he also was assistant to the dean. However, for the majority of his forty-year career, Butler remained among "his own kind" at the HBCU. Butler was dean at Talladega College, dean of liberal arts at Texas Southern University, provost and vice president for academic affairs at the University of the District of Columbia, and president of Dillard University.[27]

In concert with this exclusion from the white academy and its auxiliary associations, most African American scholars were constrained to teaching at the HBCU right up until the 1970s. In its most substantive feature, institutional racism is an exercise in power whereby the putative inferior races are relegated to a position of powerlessness. Consequently, although select individual Black people at white schools were admitted into Phi Beta Kappa or eventually were given the opportunity to teach at white colleges, this did not alter the general status of the immense majority of African American students and academics. Thus we discover that exclusion from the white academy became the plight for most African American philosophers.[28]

In 1945, for instance, Provost Edgar S. Furniss of Yale admitted in a letter to Yale's President Charles Seymour that racist exclusion of qualified Black applicants had willfully taken place for a number of years. In fact, the first African American to receive a PhD in philosophy, from a university in the United States, was Thomas Nelson Baker from Yale (1903). Yet given Yale's willful discriminatory practices, it is no accident that after Baker earned his doctorate, there would not be another PhD in philosophy until 1946 when George D. Kelsey earned his degree. Subsequently, it was nearly twenty years after Kelsey that Joyce Mitchell Cook received her degree in philosophy from Yale in 1965.[29]

When Cook gained her degree, she became the very first African American woman to earn the PhD in philosophy. Consequently, Yale was not alone, in terms of professional philosophy, in its discrimination against

Black women in philosophy. The current statistics, with respect to African American women as professional philosophers, dramatically exhibits the power of this institutional legacy. African American philosopher Kathryn Gines reported that in 2007 only 112 of the 11,000 members were African American and only twenty of this group were women.[30]

HISTORICAL CONSIDERATIONS:
BEFORE AND AFTER THE COLOR LINE

In the nineteenth century, among the Black scholars who entered the white academy two were philosophers namely Patrick Francis Healy and Richard T. Greener. More is said about them later. During the nineteenth century, among the less than handful African American scholars able to teach at predominantly white institutions were Charles L. Reason, George B. Vashon, and William G. Allen. New York Central College hired Reason to serve on the faculty when it opened its doors in 1849. Vashon and Allen joined him on the Central College faculty; hence only one institution hired the only three Black scholars in white academia before 1860. All three scholars were classically trained and this is of significance to our later discussion on the professionalization of philosophy. I must note that Oberlin College had previously admitted African American students and in fact Vashon was Oberlin's first Black graduate. However, unlike Central's policy on hiring Black faculty, Oberlin did not have Black faculty for more than one hundred years after its founding.[31]

This period under discussion was before Jim Crow was the rule of the land for all Black people, when slavery was the substance of institutional racism and Jim Crow was the formal structure that was attendant with the lives of so-called free Black people. As several scholars noted, "Jim Crow" began in the ante-bellum North, which is long before the Plessy Supreme Court decision of 1896, which established the "separate but equal doctrine" as the overriding principle of segregation or the Mississippi state constitution of 1890 that paved the way for individual states to legally uphold segregation.[32]

Slavery absolutely denied educational opportunities to African Americans and antebellum Jim Crow restricted the opportunities afforded to "free" Black folk in terms of becoming students and teachers in the United States educational system. Therefore, prior to 1840, approximately no more than fifteen Black students attended white colleges. Given the racist obstacles to acquiring an education, African Americans, in some instances, were forced to leave the United States to study and teach abroad. For example, Alexander Crummell, one of the first African American academic philosophers and founder of the American Negro Academy, went to England after being

refused admission to a white institution. Crummell studied with the Cambridge Platonist William Whewell and graduated from Cambridge University
in 1853. Convinced there was virtually no chance for African Americans to
progress in the United States, he migrated to Africa and became professor
of mental and moral philosophy in Liberia.[33]

In addition to Crummell, Patrick Francis Healy went abroad to study
and earned a doctorate in philosophy from the University of Louvain in
1865. Healy was the singular African American with a PhD to teach philosophy at white institutions before the twentieth century. The son of a
slaveholder and his slave mistress, Healy taught philosophy at Holy Cross,
St. Joseph (Philadelphia), and Georgetown. He later became the president
of Georgetown in 1874 making him the first African American to head a
white higher educational institution. An ordained Catholic priest, as with
most of his siblings, Healy was an active participant in the Catholic Church.
In no small measure, Healy's phenotype, he could pass for white, facilitated
his rise in the white Academy.[34]

The other African American to teach philosophy at a white school
in the nineteenth century was Richard T. Greener. The first Black graduate of Harvard, Greener was professor of mental and moral philosophy at
the University of South Carolina (USC) in 1873. How could this bastion
of segregation in the 1950s and 1960s have a Black person teaching philosophy? Well, the emergence of Reconstruction politics led to high Black
enrollment and white flight at USC. With the overthrow of Reconstruction,
Green left South Carolina. He later became the dean of Howard University
Law School and also served as U.S. diplomat to Vladivostok (Russia).[35]

However, even after slavery and primarily due to the impact of the
Color Line, very little happened both in terms of quantitative and qualitative change regarding the Black presence in the white academy. R. B.
Atwood, H. S. Smith, and Catherine O. Vaughan, scholars from the HBCU
Kentucky State University, carried out a survey and published their find-
ings "Negro Teachers in Northern Colleges and Universities in the United
States" in the fall 1949 issue of The Journal of Negro Education. The historical
record indicates that as late as 1949 there were seven Black philosophers on
white campuses and only four of them taught in the capacity of regular as
opposed to visiting faculty at white institutions. Cornelius Golightly joined
the philosophy faculty at Olivet College in 1945. Hence, he became the
first Black philosopher, in the twentieth century, hired as regular faculty in
a philosophy department. The Rosenwald Fund offered to pay Cornelius
Golightly's salary if the college would hire him. Olivet followed in suit and
employed Cornelius Golightly as well as his wife Catherine Golightly Cater
in the English Department. As one scholar notes, Golightly's hiring was a
precursor to Affirmative Action.[36]

After Golightly was hired at Olivet College, Forrest Oran Wiggins became a faculty member in the Department of Philosophy at University of Minnesota in 1946 and Francis Monroe Hammond joined the Philosophy Department at Seton Hall in the same year. William T. Fontaine entered the philosophy faculty at the University of Pennsylvania as a lecturer in 1947 and thereafter was promoted to assistant professor in 1949.[37]

Three other Black philosophers taught at white institutions at this time; they were not tenure-track hires but rather held visiting appointments. Alain Locke was the first Black Rhodes Scholar, first African American to receive the PhD in philosophy from Harvard and Howard University Chair of Philosophy, and coveted several visiting positions. They were appointments with Occidental College in summer 1944, University of Wisconsin in 1945–1946, New School of Social Research in spring 1947, and City College of New York in 1948–1949. Eugene C. Holmes, also from Howard and would subsequently follow Locke as Chair of the philosophy department, had a visiting position at the City College of New York in summer 1945.[38]

The other philosopher was George D. Kelsey. It is correctly noted in the Atwood et al. report that he taught at Andover Newton Theological Seminary in summer 1944. Kelsey is listed by Atwood et al. under the classification of religion and although it is accurate that he taught religion, nevertheless, he earned his doctorate in philosophy from Yale in 1946. Kelsey taught both religion and philosophy throughtout his career and he spent ten years doing so at Morehouse College. When he taught at Morehouse, Kelsey was the director of the School of Religion as well as visiting lecturer at Gammon Theological Seminary. Kelsey was a key mentor to Martin Luther King Jr. during King's undergraduate years at Morehouse. Kelsey later taught at the white institution, Drew University in New Jersey from 1950 to 1976.[39]

All of the above African American philosophers either were students at the HBCU or taught in those institutions before moving on to white campuses. The HBCU was the institutional foundation and context for what emerged as African American intellectual culture. By African American intellectual culture, I do not mean a monolithic philosophical tradition or intellectual standpoint. Rather it is the prevailing ethos affixed to the common experiences surrounding the HBCU. It is the distinctive intellectual history of the HBCU, along with the corresponding struggle to survive in light of institutionalized racism, which essentially grounds the formation of African American intellectual culture. It is within the context of African American intellectual culture then that there is a wide range of ideological perspectives and philosophical viewpoints, which on a number of occasions find themselves at odds and with severe conflicts about the direction of the African American community and education at colleges and universities.[40]

THE HBCU CONTEXT AND AFRICAN AMERICAN
PHILOSOPHICAL INQUIRY

I now investigate how the criteria of teaching, research, and service central to professional philosophy takes concrete form as philosophical inquiry within the context of the HBCU. One of the implications is the fact that service was frequently expressed as contributions to campus and community life where racism was the dominant concern. The HBCU are located in Black communities and historically faced the same racist problems of the broader community. For instance, when Richard I. McKinney assumed the presidency of Storer College in West Virginia, he became the first Black president of an institution founded on the idea of education for Black people. Yet white paternalism, on the part of its white founder, held sway from the very beginning and thus Black faculty and an African American president were very long in the making. Moreover, when McKinney arrived to take over as head of Storer, the KKK burned a cross in his yard. The general lesson here is that the HBCU as an off-shoot of the Color Line were not ivory towers removed from the dangers and indignities of racism. Hence, the immediacy of the material reality of racism was part and parcel of the HBCU life. Most African American philosophers were committed to the practical application of philosophical principles to the problems confronting the Black community.[41]

As president of Philander Smith College, African American philosopher Marquis Lafayette Harris developed "A Social Philosophy for the Negro," which he based on his assessment of the desired role for the college-educated African American. Harris asked:

> Does the average college-educated Negro concern himself very much about how he spends his time or how thorough he may be in positively desirable habits? Does he think in terms of the place of the Negro in the American social order, and how he may somehow contribute an idea or action towards betterment of the group? . . . Can he let pass acts of social and economic discrimination which characterize the condition of the vast majority of the members of his group? Does he realize that poverty and exploitation have their roots in class distinction rather than race distinction?[42]

Harris' last question about the class disposition of Black poverty should not lead the reader to think that he is suggesting a critique of capitalism as the grounds of racism or that proletarian class struggle is the road to Black liberation. For Harris concludes, "You may say I criticized the Negro too severely. I answer by saying that, in the main, leadership in its most useful aspects such as cooperatives, politics, and general social movements tend to come from the non-college people. It is such misfortune that has caused the ranks of blind Americanize communism to swell with members of our racial group."[43]

The anti-communist thrust of Harris' thesis develops as a full-blown political position among several African American philosophers in the wake of the Cold War and McCarthyism. More on that point shortly. What we have in Harris' philosophy of education is an instance of Du Bois' notion of the "Talented Tenth." However, Harris views the Talented Tenth's leadership role as more desirable than having the grassroots Black community in the vanguard of the African American struggle. Harris' position belies his commitment to the African American masses and their struggle and boldly demonstrates his petite bourgeois class allegiance.[44]

With regard to research, I explore how philosophers grappled with political/social philosophy and ethics and hence elaborated on issues relating to African American political, social and cultural life. Although there was not a single philosophy journal devoted to African American issues (that is until Percy Johnston published, *Afro-American Journal of Philosophy* in 1982–1983), African American philosophers published in Black scholarly journals such as the *Journal of Religious Thought*, *Phylon*, *Journal of Negro Education*, *Journal of Negro History*, and *Freedomways*. Popular journals such as the *Crisis*, *Opportunity*, and the *Negro Digest/Black World* were also venues to publish works around the Black experience.

On the one hand, this inquiry often was done in connection to investigating the oppressive character of institutional racism. On the other hand, a strong interest on the part of African American philosophers to prove their intellectual worth along the lines of the dominant intellectual ethos was directly expressed in terms of duplicating the hegemonic trends in professional philosophy. This generally took the form of research questions surrounding the relationship between religion and science as well as teaching courses in philosophy that followed the standardized (prevailing) curriculum of academic philosophy at white colleges and universities.[45]

The institutional power of the white academy had an impact on African American (specifically HBCU) intellectual culture wherein philosophy courses within the HBCU realm more often than not assumed a mimetic character. E. Franklin Frazier's criticism of the mimetic nature of African American intellectuals is quite telling in its summation of the particular role of African American philosophers. Frazier asserts:

> We have no philosophers or thinkers who command the respect
> of the intellectual community at large. I'm not talking about the
> few teachers of philosophy who have read Hegel or Kant or James

and memorize their thoughts. I am talking about men who have reflected upon the fundamental problems which have always concerned philosophers such as the nature of human knowledge and the meanings or the lack of the meaning of human existence. We have no philosophers who have dealt with these and other problems from the standpoint of the Negro's unique experience in this world.[46]

One important confirmation of Frazier's criticism comes by way of the fact that most African Americans philosophers did not engage in preparing dissertation topics on African American issues and problems. First to do so was Carlton Lee's dissertation on at the University of Chicago in 1951. Not until the 1970s, after the emergence of the Black Studies movement, did African Americans more generally start to write on Black topics.

Most followed the road of Wayman Bernard McLaughlin; he earned his PhD in 1958 from Boston University with the dissertation topic, *The Relation between Hegel and Kierkegaard*. An undergraduate student of Richard McKinney at Virginia Union, McLaughlin taught at four of the HBCU. His first stop was at his alma mater Virginia Union where he taught courses in philosophy and psychology from 1958 until 1959. From 1959 until 1962, he worked at Grambling State University as the coordinator of the Humanities Program where he developed and taught philosophy and humanities courses. In 1962, he moved to North Carolina to work at Winston-Salem State Teaching College (later Winston-Salem State University). From 1962 until 1967, he worked in the Department of Social Sciences at Winston-Salem State developing and teaching philosophy and humanities courses. As a testament to his outstanding teaching abilities, in his final year at Winston Salem State, he was selected as Teacher of the Year. And finally—beginning in 1967—McLaughlin taught at North Carolina A & T State University as a philosophy and humanities professor. For thirty-five years, McLaughlin was the only philosopher at the university.[47]

A friend and classmate of Martin Luther King Jr. at Boston University, McLaughlin and King, in conjunction with other African American graduate students, organized a philosophical club called the Dialectical Society. According to Taylor Branch:

Graduate students interested in philosophy or religion gathered one evening a week to share a potluck supper and a rarefied discussion about God or knowledge. One student read a formal paper, and the others then jumped in to criticize or support it. The club lasted throughout King's student life in Boston, becoming so popular that white students dropped in occasionally and Professor DeWolf once delivered the paper for discussion. A rather stiff decorum prevailed early in the evening, as pipe smoke and abstract jargon mingled in the air, but the hard core of participants usually settled into a bull session late at night.[48]

According to Branch there was relatively little discussion about racism and other political matters. "At the Dialectical Society," Branch claims, "discussions of politics were largely confined to the issue of whether it was wise for them to choose 'race-related' topics for papers, theses, and doctoral dissertations. King concurred with the general consensus that to do so might cheapen their work in the eyes of influential Negroes as well as whites."[49]

All of the above indicate that African American philosophers were ostensibly caught in the web of contradiction and dilemma. They felt compelled to stay in concert with the mainstream (white philosophers') research agenda in professional philosophy and at the same time try and figure out how to engage philosophically in confronting racism, which oppressed and exploited the general community of African Americans and intervened in the day to day campus and intellectual life of the HBCU. Philosopher Charles Leander Hill described the dilemma of Black intellectuals in terms of "In a Helluva Shape." Ironically, when Hill attempted to publish his critique of this dilemma in 1954/1955, the publisher rejected his manuscript as unacceptable to white people's sensibilities.[50]

In concert with the selection of dissertation topics, the dominant view at HBCU was that teaching philosophy had to follow suit with the direction of the white academy. This is best demonstrated with Howard University, which arguably had the most prestigious philosophy department among the HBCU. In reflecting back on his undergraduate training, during the 1950s, in philosophy at Howard, William R. Jones reported:

> The issues that the faculty in philosophy at Howard was dealing with at that time were not focusing on oppression per se, but it was more classical philosophy and the like. Alain Locke had done some work on cultural pluralism and so forth, and McAllister did some courses on ethics, but McAllister taught logic, and so forth, so my introduction was basically to logic, logical positivism, and so forth. Keep in mind that Holmes also identified himself at that time as a Marxist so I got a little splattering of that. But the main impact from McAllister and Holmes was to solidify philosophy as an appropriate and useful pursuit for African Americans interested in the struggle. They didn't themselves focus on that particular issue, but I did begin to see how I could take these kinds of tools and skills and develop an arsenal against oppression.[51]

Jones conveyed to me that when students at Howard demanded Black authors be included in a survey course on the humanities, the inclusion was made when it was determined that an Ivy League school allowed for Black authors in the syllabus. Clearly, we can observe from Jones' account that despite the fact that Holmes' research focused on a wide range of topics relating to African American issues and problems, nevertheless he was inclined to follow the same direction as we discovered with McLaughlin and King in terms of their selections for dissertation topics.[52]

I think that because Frazier also was a faculty member of Howard during this stipulated period, then perhaps at the core of Frazier's criticism were generalizations based on (but not limited to) personal experiences at Howard as well as rooted in his teaching practices and intimate knowledge of the HBCU intellectual scene. The Howard experience began when Frazier was as an undergraduate student and continued through the years during his status as a faculty member. Such experiences no doubt served to be a rich reservoir for reflection on the mimetic nature of African American intellectual culture.[53]

In conclusion, I have provided a historical overview of how the professionalization of philosophy has had its own distinctive impact on African American philosophers and their plight. The results of this professionalization are quite pervasive today as we enter into the twenty-first century. Although no longer restricted to the HBCU context, the fact remains that institutional racism plays a prominent part in the present status of African American philosophers as they constitute approximately just 1 percent of the profession. Institutional power is primarily in the hands of white professional philosophers. Thus institutional racism in the form of academic racism is very much alive and well today.

NOTES

1. Robert Bruce Slater, "The Blacks Who First Entered the World of White Higher Education" *The Journal of Blacks in Higher Education*, No. 4. (Summer 1994). "Talented Black Scholars Whom No White University Would Hire" *The Journal of Blacks in Higher Education* (Winter 2003/2004) pp. 110–115. Ironically, whereas Kuklick in his "Philosophy and Inclusion in the United States" (2006) brings to our attention that presently "White men still dominated it [professional philosophy]" and "a Black presence was miniscule" as well as he states that "various minority voices did add to a professional cacophony and confusion" (p. 176), he gives no substantive treatment to African American philosophers and racism in an article focused primarily on inclusion. Bruce Kuklick, "Philosophy and Inclusion in the United States" David Hollinger, ed., *The Humanities and the Dynamics of Inclusion since World War II* (Baltimore: Johns Hopkins University Press, 2006) p. 176.

2. I have written a number of articles on individual philosophers in the HBCU context. For representative cases see John H. McClendon, "Charles Leander Hill: Philosopher and Theologian" *A.M.E. Church Review* v. CXIX n. 390 (April–June, 2003) pp. 81–105, John H. McClendon, "My Tribute to a Teacher, Mentor,

Philosopher and Friend: Dr. Francis A. Thomas (March 16, 1913 to September 17, 2001)" *American Philosophical Association Newsletter on Philosophy and the Black Experience* v. 3, n. 1 (Fall 2003) and John H. McClendon, "Eugene C. Holmes: A Commentary on a Black Marxist Philosopher" in Leonard Harris, ed., *Philosophy Born in Struggle* (Dubuque: Kendall/Hunt, 1983) pp. 37–50. For other essays dealing with Black philosophers at HBCU, see George Yancey, "Gilbert Haven Jones as a Early Black Philosopher and Educator" *American Philosophical Association Newsletter on Philosophy and the Black Experience* v. 2, n. 2 (Spring 2003). Leonard Harris, "The Ontology of Marc M. Moreland" *New England Journal of Black Studies* v. 4 (Fall 1984) pp. 55–62. Eugene C. Holmes, "Alain Locke—Philosopher, Critic, Spokesman" *Journal of Philosophy* v. 54, n. 4 (February 14, 1957) pp. 113–18. On the general question of academic racism consult, Michael R. Winston, "Through the Back Door: Academic Racism and the American Negro in Historical Perspective" *DÆDALUS* (Summer 1971) pp. 678–719.

   3. John H. McClendon, "The African American Philosopher and Academic Philosophy: On the Problem of Historical Interpretation" *American Philosophical Association Newsletter on Philosophy and the Black Experience* (Fall 2004). St. Clair Drake, "The Black University in the American Social Order" in *DÆDALUS* (Summer 1971) pp. 833–97.

   4. When William R. Jones was collecting data, in the early 1970s, for the Committee on Blacks of Philosophy of the APA, he discovered that there were only 23 African American philosophers. See William R. Jones, "Crisis in Philosophy: The Black Presence" Report of the Subcommittee on the Participation of Blacks in Philosophy, *Proceedings and Addresses of the American Philosophical Association* v. XLVII (1973–74) and this report also appears in *Radical Philosophers' News Journal* (August 1974).

   5. For a handling of political ideology and its impact on professional philosophy in the United States read John Ryder, *Interpreting America: Russian and Soviet Studies of the History of American Thought* (Nashville: Vanderbilt University Press, 1999). On institutionalized racism consult Camara Phyllis Jones, "Confronting Institutionalized Racism" *Phylon* V.50, n. 1/2 (2002) pp. 722.

   6. John H. McClendon, "The Afro-American Philosopher and the Philosophy of the Black Experience: A. Bibliographical Essay on a Neglected Topic in Both Philosophy and Black Studies" v. 7, n. 4 Sage Relation Abstracts (November, 1982) pp. 1–53. One of the rare instances in history of U.S. philosophy where Euro-American philosophers openly address the issue of racism is the work of Josiah Royce. See his *The American Race Problem, Provincialism and Other Questions* (New York: Macmillan, 1908). Also read Shannon Sullivan, "Whiteness as Wise Provincialism: Royce and the Rehabilitation of a Racial Category" *Transactions of the Charles S. Peirce Society: A Quarterly Journal in American Philosophy* v. 44, n. 2 (Spring 2008) pp. 236–62 and Jacquelyn Ann Kegley, "Is a Coherent Racial Identity Essential to Genuine Individuals and Communities? Josiah Royce on Race" *Journal of Speculative Philosophy*, v. 19, n. 3 (2005) pp. 216–28.

   7. Stikker states "The American Philosophical Association recently disclosed that over the past five years only 1.1 percent of all American PhDs in philosophy were awarded to Africans or African Americans, exactly the same percentage as in

1980. Moreover, philosophy continues to be one of the disciplines in the academy in which African Americans are least represented. I challenge any one to offer publicly a nonracist explanation for this condition." Kenneth Stikker, "An Outline of Methodological Afrocentrism, with Particular Application to the Thought of W. E. B. Du Bois" *Journal of Speculative Philosophy* v. 22, n.1 (2008) p. 40.

8. v. I. Lenin, *Materialism and Empirio-Criticism* in Lenin Collected Works (Moscow: Progress Publishers, 1973) pp. 131–43. Theodore Oizerman, *Problems of The History of Philosophy* (Moscow: Progress Publishers, 1973).

9. Douglas Mann astutely argues, "[T]he professionalization of philosophy in universities, a professionalization that has significantly tied the discipline to corporatist . . . interests that have served to denude philosophy of a vital, critical role as the center of social, political, and cultural debate and critique." Douglas Mann, "Forgetting the Lessons of History: The Fate of Philosophy in the 20th Century" http://home.comcast.net/~crapsonline/Library/fateofphilosopyprint.htm [access February 2009]. For an example of an autodidactic philosopher of crucial import see Ralph Dumain, http://www.autodidactproject.org/my/leftout.html

10. Kenneth Stikker, "An Outline of Methodological Afrocentrism, with Particular Application to the Thought of W. E. B. Du Bois" *Journal of Speculative Philosophy* v. 22, n.1 (2008) p. 40. William R. Jones, "Crisis in Philosophy: The Black Presence" Report of the Subcommittee on the Participation of Blacks in Philosophy, *Proceedings and Addresses of the American Philosophical Association* v. XLVII (1973–74) Leonard Harris "Philosophy in Black and White" *Proceedings and Addresses of the American Philosophical Association*, Vol. 51, No. 3 (February 1978).

11. Among philosophers without portfolio are Hubert Harrison, Robert T. Browne, James Boggs, and C. L. R. James. Consult Jeffrey Perry, *Hubert Harrison: The Voice of Harlem Radicalism, 1883–1918* (New York: Columbia University, 2009). Robert Fikes, "Postscript to The Triumph of Robert T. Browne: The Mystery of Space" *American Philosophical Association Newsletter on Philosophy and the Black Experience* v. 6, n. 2 (Fall 2007). Xavier Nicholas."Questions of the American Revolution: Conversations with James Boggs" *IBW Black-World-View* vol. 1, no. 1 (March 1976). John H. McClendon, *C.L.R. James's Notes on Dialectics: Left Hegelianism or Marxism-Leninism?* (Lanham: Lexington Books, 2005).

12. John H. McClendon, "The African American Philosopher and Academic Philosophy: On the Problem of Historical Interpretation" *American Philosophical Association Newsletter on Philosophy and the Black Experience* (Fall 2004). For insight into the professionalization of philosophy and academic certification read, chapters 3 and 4, "Graduate Schools and Professionalization" and "The Personnel of American Philosophy" in C. Wright Mills, *Sociology and Pragmatism: The Higher Learning in America* (New York: Oxford University Press, 1966). On the decline of amateur philosophers see Bruce Kuklick, *A History of Philosophy in America, 1720–2000* (New York: Oxford University Press, 2001) pp. 107–10. For an important contribution concerning the autodidact as philosopher by an autodidact of immeasurable value, consult Ralph Dumain at http://www.autodidactproject.org/my/leftout.html.

13. Leonard Harris, " 'Believe it or Not' or The Ku Klux Klan and American Philosophy Exposed" *American Philosophical Association Newsletter on Philosophy and the Black Experience* (Fall 1995).

14. Jones exposes the nature of this false universality in William R. Jones, "The Legitimacy and Necessity of Black Philosophy: Some Preliminary Considerations" *The Philosophical Forum* v. 9, n.2&3 (Winter-Spring 1977–78). On professionalization and academic legitimacy read, Bruce Kuklick, *A History of Philosophy in America, 1720–2000* (New York: Oxford University Press, 2001) pp. 201–42. Unlike the Jones' article, the Kuklick account fails to address racism in the field of philosophy and is silent about African American philosophers in the profession.

15. Lucius Outlaw, "The Deafening Silence of the Guiding Light: American Philosophy and the Problem of the Color Line" *Quest: An African Journal of Philosophy* v. 1, n. 1 (1987). John McCumber, *Time in the Ditch: American Philosophy and the McCarthy Era* (Evanston: Northwestern University Press, 2001). Bruce Kuklick, *A History of Philosophy in America, 1720–2000* (New York: Oxford University Press, 2001) pp. 20–242.

16. Du Bois states in "The Forethought" of *The Souls*, "Herein lie buried many things which if read with patience may show the strange meaning of being Black here in the dawning of the Twentieth century. This meaning is not without interest to you, Gentle Reader; for the problem of the Twentieth century is the problem of the color-line." W. E. B. Du Bois, *The Souls of Black Folk* (Chicago: A. C. McClurg, 1903). On segregation and Southern Black education, read James D. Anderson, *The Education of Blacks in the South, 1860–1935* (Chapel Hill: University of North Carolina Press, 1988). Also consult Rufus Clement, "The Historical Development of Higher Education for Negro American" *Journal of Negro Education* v. 35 (Fall 1966) and Rayford W. Logan, "The Evolution of Private Colleges for Negroes" *Journal of Negro Education* v. 27, n. 3 (Summer 1958) pp. 213–20. Lucius Outlaw, "The Deafening Silence of the Guiding Light: American Philosophy and the Problem of the Color Line" *Quest: An African Journal of Philosophy* v. 1, n. 1 (1987).

17. W. E. B. Dubois, The Autobiography of W. E. B. Dubois: A Soliloquy on Viewing My Life from the Last Decade of Its First Century (New York: International Publishers, 1968) p. 194.

18. Dunham was listed as a member of the APA in 1933, 1934, 1935 as a philosophy faculty member at Howard University. See APA members list of the *Proceedings and Addresses of the American Philosophical Association*. W. Morris with John M. Brewster, Albert M. Dunham and David Miller, eds., *The Philosophy of the Act* (Chicago: University of Chicago, 1938).

19. On Dunham's racist treatment at the University of Chicago, see chapter 2 of Joyce Aschenbrenner, *Katherine Dunham: Dancing a Life* (Urbana: University of Illinois, 2002). On Locke's hiring Dunham, consult Eugene C. Holmes, "Alain Leroy Locke: A Sketch," *The Phylon Quarterly*, v. 20, n.1 (first quarter, 1959) p. 83.

20. Jonathan Scott Holloway, "The Black Scholar, the Humanities, and the Politics of Racial Knowledge Since 1945" in David Hollinger, ed., *The Humanities and the Dynamics of Inclusion Since World War Two* (Baltimore: The Johns Hopkins University Press, 2006) pp. 217–46.

21. Alfred A. Moss Jr., *The American Negro Academy* (Baton Rouge: Louisiana State University Press, 1981) pp. 15–17. John Hope Franklin, *The Color Line: Legacy for the Twenty First Century* (Columbia: University of Missouri Press, 1993). While Greener was the first African American in the American Philological Society and Scarborough the second, the first Black member was Edward Wilmot Blyden. Blyden

who lived from 1832 to 1912 was from St. Thomas. For reference to this history read, Michele Valerie Ronnick, "Three Nineteenth Century Classicists of African Descent" *Scholia* v. 6 (1997) pp. 11–18.

22. "Phi Beta Kappa and HBCUs: The Least-Favored Universities" No. 16 *The Journal of Blacks in Higher Education* (Summer 1997), pp. 16–17. "More Than a Century after Its Founding, Spelman College Is Awarded a Phi Beta Kappa Membership" *The Journal of Blacks in Higher Education* No. 18 (Winter 1997–1998), p. 71. Ronald Roach, "Extending Their Reach" *Black Issues in Higher Education* Vol. 19, n. 17; pp. 20–25. (October 10, 2002). "When Will Phi Beta Kappa Repeal Its Rules of Race?" *The Journal of Blacks in Higher Education* No. 26 (Winter 1999–2000), pp. 55–57. Caldwell Titcomb, "The Earliest Black Members of Phi Beta Kappa" *The Journal of Blacks in Higher Education*, No. 33 (Autumn 2001), pp. 92–93.

23. Prior to the Robinson and Rickey, we find that in 1938 Clark Griffith stated, "A lone Negro in the game will face caustic comments. He will be made the target of cruel, filthy epithets. Of course, I know the time will come when the ice will have to be broken. Both by the organized game and by the colored player who is willing to volunteer and thus become a sort of martyr to the cause." The quote can be found in Jules Tygiel, "Jackie Robinson: A Lone Negro in Major League Baseball" in Patrick B. Miller and David K. Wiggins, ed., *Sport and the Color Line* (New York: Routledge, 2004) p. 167.

24. For an article sympathetic with the Robinson/Rickey thesis read Peter Golenbock, "Men of Conscience" in Joseph Dorinson and Joram Warmund, ed., *Jackie Robinson: Race, Sports, and the American Dream* (Armonk, New York: M. E. Sharpe, Inc., 1999) pp. 13–21.

25. Lucius Outlaw, "The Deafening Silence of the Guiding Light: American Philosophy and the Problem of the Color Line" *Quest: An African Journal of Philosophy* v. 1, n. 1 (1987). Harry Washington Greene, *Holders of Doctorates Among American Negroes* (Boston: Meador Publishing Company, 1946). Michael R. Winston, "Through the Back Door: Academic Racism and the American Negro in Historical Perspective" *DÆDALUS* (Summer 1971) pp. 678–719

26. Leonard Harris, *Philosophy Born of Struggle* (Dubuque: Kendall/Hunt, 1983) p. ix.

27. See "UDC Official Broadus N. Butler, 75, Dies" *The Washington Post* (January 15, 1996) p. B. 04. "In Memoriam: Broadus N. Butler" *Water Highlights: DC Water Resource Center Washington, College of Life Sciences, University of District of Columbia* v. 16, n. 1 (Winter 1996).

28. For an example of penetrating examination of academic racism in other disciplines besides philosophy, read Robert V. Guthrie, *Even the Rat White: a Historical View of Psychology* (Boston: Pearson Education, Inc., 2004) and James Blackwell, and Morris Janowitz, eds., *Black Sociologists: Historical and Contemporary* (Chicago: University of Chicago Press, 1974). For a general and interdisciplinary focus on academic racism read, David G. Du Bois, "Racism in Academia" *The Journal of Blacks in Higher Education* No. 2 (Winter 1993–1994), p. 90. I. A. Newby, *Jim Crow's Defense: Anti-Negro Thought in America* (Baton Rouge: Louisiana State University, 1965).

29. On Cook consult chapter 13, 'Joyce Mitchell Cook' in George Yancy, ed., *African American Philosophers* (New York: Routledge, 1998). For an article on racism at Yale see, Garry L. Reeder, "The History of Blacks at Yale University" *The*

Journal of Blacks in Higher Education, No. 26. (Winter 1999–2000). For Baker see George Yancy, "On the Power of Black Aesthetic Ideals: Thomas Nelson Baker as Teacher and Philosopher" *A.M.E. Church Review* (October–December 2001). On Kelsey, consult the "Biography of George D. Kelsey" in the *George D. Kelsey Papers, 1932–1996 Finding Aid*, Drew University Library. Besides Baker and Kelsey, another African American philosopher to her and a doctorate from Yale was Richard I. McKinney. McKinney received his degree in 1942, however in religious education and went on to serve as Chair of the Department of Philosophy and the Division of Humanities at Morgan State University. See John H. McClendon, "Dr. Richard Ishmael McKinney: Historical Summation on the Life of a Pioneering African American Philosopher" v. 5, n. 2, *American Philosophical Association Newsletter on Philosophy and the Black Experience* (Spring 2006).

30. For Gines' statement read, "New Networking Group for Black Women in Philosophy" *The Journal of Blacks in Higher Education* (February 1, 2007). Also consult, Robin Wilson, "Black Women Seek a Role in Philosophy" *The Chronicle of Higher Education* (Diversity in Academe Section) v. 54, Issue 5, p. B4. On the contemporary plight of women of color in professional philosophy read Zack's "Introduction" in Naomi Zack, ed., *Women of Color and Philosophy* (Malden: Blackwell Publishers, 2000) pp. 1–21.

31. Central College also had open admission inclusive of Black and women students. John H. McClendon III, "Charles L. Reason" *Blackpast.org Online Encyclopedia*. Anthony R. Mayo, "Charles Lewis Reason,"\ *Negro History Bulletin* 5 (June 1942):212–15; Scott W. Williams, "Charles L. Reason African American Mathematician, 1818–1893," http://www.math.buffalo.edu/mad/special/reason_charles_1.html. For the biographical details and information on Vashon read Paul N. D. Thornell, "The Absent Ones and the Providers: A Biography of the Vashons," *Journal of Negro History*, v. 83, n.4 (1998). Christopher T. Blue, "George B. Vashon (1824–1878) *Blackpast.org Online Encyclopedia*. Glen McClish, "William G. Allen's 'Orators and Oratory' Inventional Amalgamation, Pathos, and the Characterization of Violence in African American Abolitionist Rhetoric" *Rhetoric Society Quarterly* v. 35, n. 1 (Winter 2005) pp. 47–52. Richard J.M. Blackett, "William G. Allen: The Forgotten Professor." *Civil War History* v. 26 (March, 1980): 38–52. On Oberlin see James Oliver Horton, "Black Education at Oberlin College: A Controversial Commitment" *The Journal of Negro Education* v. 54, n. 4. (Autumn, 1985).

32. C. Vann Woodward, *The Strange Career of Jim Crow* (New York: Oxford University press, 1955). Leon Litwack, *North of Slavery: The Negro in the Free States, 1790–1860* (Chicago: University of Chicago Press, 1961). Barbara Fields, "Slavery, Race, and Ideology in the United States of America" *New Left Review* (May/June, 1990).

33. On the issue of fifteen Black students at white colleges before 1840 see John E. Fleming, *The Lengthening Shadow of Slavery* (Washington D.C.: Howard University Press, 1974) p. 30. Also consult, "The Earliest Black Graduates of the Nation's Highest-Ranked Liberal Arts Colleges" *The Journal of Blacks in Higher Education*, No. 38. (Winter 2002–2003). Wilson J. Moses, *Alexander Crummell: A Study of Civilization and Discontent* (New York: Oxford University Press, 1989). C. R. Stockton, "The Integration of Cambridge: Alexander Crummell as Undergraduate,

1849–1853." *Integrated Education* (Winter 1979). Gregory Rigsby, *Alexander Crummell: Pioneer in the Nineteenth-Century Pan-African Thought.* (New York: Greenwood Press, 1987). Alfred A. Moss, Jr., Leon Litwack and August Meier, eds., *"Alexander Crummell: Black Nationalist and Apostle of Western Civilization,"* in Black Leaders of the Nineteenth Century (Urbana: University of Illinois Press, 1988, pp. 237–51).

34. James O'Toole, *Passing for White: Race, Religion, and the Healy Family, 1820–1920* (Amherst: University of Massachusetts Press, 2002). Albert S. Foley, *Dream of an Outcaste: Patrick F. Healy* (Tuscaloosa: Portals Press, 1989). Cyprian Davis, *The History of Black Catholics in the United States* (New York: Crossroad, 1990). "Patrick Francis Healy Inaugurated," American Memory Project, Library of Congress, http://memory.loc.gov/ammem/today/jul31.html [access 2008].

35. "Richard T. Greener: The First Black Harvard College Graduate" in Werner Sollors, Caldwell Titcomb, Thomas A. Underwood, Randall Kennedy, eds., *Blacks at Harvard* (New York: NYU Press, 1993) pp. 37–58. Allison Blakely, "Richard T. Greener and The Talented Tenth's Dilemma" *Journal of Negro History* v. 59 (October, 1974) pp. 305–21. Michael Mounter, "Richard Theodore Greener and the African American Individual in a Black and White World" in James Lowell Underwood and W. Lewis Burke, Jr., eds., *At Freedom's Door: African American Founding Fathers and Lawyers in Reconstruction South Carolina* (Columbia: University of South Carolina Press, 2000) pp. 130–65.

36. R. B. Atwood, H. S. Smith, and Catherine O. Vaughan, "Negro Teachers in Northern Colleges and Universities in the United States" *The Journal of Negro Education*, V.18, n. 4. (Autumn, 1949). Also consult, Horace Mann Bond, "The Evaluation and Present Status of Negro Higher and Professional Education in the United States" *The Journal of Negro Education* v. 17, n. 3 (Summer 1948) pp. 224–235. On Golightly see Richard B. Angell, "Cornelius L. Golightly 1917–1976" *Proceedings and Addresses of the American Philosophical Association*, v. 49 (1975–1976), pp. 158–59. Gilbert A. Belles, "The College Faculty, the Negro Scholar, and Rosenwald Fund" *The Journal of Negro History* v. 54, n.4 (October 1969). Reginald Wilson, "Why the Shortage of Black Professors? Slack Enforcement," *The Journal of Blacks in Higher Education*, No. 1. (Autumn, 1993). Shawn Woodhouse, "The Historical Development of Affirmative Action: an Aggregated Analysis" *The Western Journal Black Studies* v. 26, 2002. On Catherine Golightly Cater, see the *Althea Catherine Cater Papers, 1917–2001* in the North Dakota State University Archives http://www.lib.ndsu.nodak.edu/archives/collections/CatherineCaterPapers.htm [accessed February 2008]. Prior to Golightly, Allison Davis was hired at the University of Chicago in 1942 due to the intervention of the Rosenwald Fund. Consult, Gilbert A. Belles, "The College Faculty, the Negro Scholar, and Rosenwald Fund" *The Journal of Negro History* v. 54, n.4 (October 1969) p. 384.

37. Forrest O. Wiggins received his bachelor's degree in 1928 from Butler University and in the following year earned a certificate in French from the Sorbonne. He received his master's and later the PhD (1938) in philosophy from University of Wisconsin. For Wiggins see John H. McClendon, "Forrest O. Wiggins (1907–1982)" *Blackpast.org Online Encyclopedia*. Clark Johnson, "Biographical Sketch of Forrest Oran Wiggins" in the Forrest Oran Wiggins Papers, University of Minnesota Archives. Francis M. Hammond received the bachelor's degree from Xavier

University (New Orleans), the master's from the University of Louvain, and doctorate in philosophy from University of Laval (Canada) in 1943. On Hammond as first
African American professor at Seton Hall see Alan Delozier, "History of Seton Hall"
http://events.shu.edu/150/history.html#1916. Hammond was the only person to chair
both the Psychology and Philosophy Departments at Seton Hall. Consult "The Dr.
Francis Monroe Hammond Collection of Social Sciences at Seton Hall University"
http://library.shu.edu/libnews/n20021107.htm. Fontaine earned the BA from Lincoln
University, did graduate work at Harvard University, Chicago and Pennsylvania Universities. He obtained the PhD in philosophy from the University of Pennsylvania in
1936. On Fontaine see, Rhonda Williams, "Dr. William Thomas Valeria Fontaine"
http://www.upenn.edu/VPGE/FontaineBio.html [access 2008]. James Ross, "William
T. Fontaine (1909–1968) APA *Proceedings and Addresses* v. 43 (1969–1970). Bruce
Kuklick, *Black Philosopher, White Academy: The Career of William Fontaine* (Philadelphia: University of Pennsylvania Press, 2008).

    38. For Locke and Holmes teaching at white institutions see R. B. Atwood, H.
S. Smith, and Catherine O. Vaughan, "Negro Teachers in Northern Colleges" p. 566.

    39. Atwood et al. actually identify seven people as philosophers. However, my
reported seven differ from their lineup. I do not include John Lovell, from Howard
University, for the year (1948–1949) at Pascadena City College. Lovell taught English and earned is doctorate in that discipline. And as discussed in the text, Kelsey
was a philosopher and theologian. R. B. Atwood, H. S. Smith, and Catherine O.
Vaughan, "Negro Teachers in Northern Colleges" p. 566; For Kelsey's influence on
King see the "Introduction" to Clayborne Carson, ed., The Papers of Martin Luther
King Jr., v. 1 (Berkeley: University of California Press, 1992) pp. 42–46. Atwood et
al. correctly note Abram Harris was an economist, however he was actually hired
as a member of the philosophy department at the University of Chicago. On Harris
read Jonathan Holloway, Confronting the Veil (Chapel Hill: University of North
Carolina press, 2002) pp. 200–02 and William Darity's "Introduction: The Odyssey of
Abram Harris from Howard to Chicago" in William Darity Jr., ed., Race, Radicalism
and Reform: Selected Papers, Abram Harris (New Brunswick: Transaction, 1989).

    40. Mack H. Jones, *"The Responsibility of the Black College to the Black Com-
munity: Then and Now"* in *DÆDALUS* (Summer 1971) pp. 732–44.

    41. John H. McClendon, "Dr. Richard Ishmael McKinney: Historical Summa-
tion on the Life of a Pioneering African American Philosopher" *American Philosophical Association Newsletter on Philosophy and the Black Experience* v. 5, n. 2 (Spring
2006) p. 2.

    42. M. Lafayette Harris, *The Voice in the Wilderness* (Boston: The Christopher
Publishing House, 1941) pp. 16–17.

    43. M. Lafayette Harris, *The Voice in the Wilderness* (Boston: The Christopher
Publishing House, 1941) p. 21.

    44. I address the issue of anti-Communism, McCarthyism and Cold War for
African American philosophers in John H. McClendon, "The African American
Philosopher: The Missing Chapter in McCumber on McCarthyism" *Cultural Logic*
(2008).

    45. The mimetic character of teaching philosophy also had a contradictory
side. While trying to keep in sync with the white schools and scholars, nonetheless,

African American philosophers developed their own teaching strategies and textbooks. For instance, Charles Leander Hill found the existing textbooks for the introduction to the history of philosophy quite insufficient and thus developed his own textbook. See Charles L. Hill, *A Short History of Modern Philosophy: From the Renaissance to Hegel* (Boston: Meador Publishing Company, 1951).

46. E. Franklin Frazier, "The Failure of the Negro Intellectual" *Negro Digest* v. 11, n. 4 (February, 1962) pp. 31–32.

47. All of the material on McLaughlin comes from an unpublished paper/ lecture of the philosopher, Dr. Stephen Ferguson at North Carolina A & T. I want to thank Dr. Ferguson for sharing his research and insights on McLaughlin and the connection to the HBCU context.

48. Taylor Branch, *Parting the Waters: America during the King Years, 1954– 1963* (New York: Simon & Schuster, 1988) p. 93.

49. Branch, *Parting the Waters: America during the King Years, 1954–1963* (New York: Simon & Schuster, 1988) p. 93.

50. Read the Hill correspondence dated 11/29/54, 12/17/54, 12/22/54, 2/22/55, and 2/25/55 in Folder 34, Charles Leander Hill Papers, Wilberforce University Archives. More will be said about the Hill manuscript later. Of course, the condition of contradiction and dilemma is not limited to African American philosophers. W. E. B. Du Bois paved the way for this discussion of the dilemma in *The Souls of Black Folk* (1903). Also see James Weldon Johnson, "The Dilemma of the Negro Author" *American Mercury* v. 60 (December, 1928) pp. 477–81 and John Hope Franklin, "The Dilemma of the Negro Scholar" in Herbert Hill, ed., *Soon One Morning: New Writing by American Negroes, 1940–1962* (New York: Knopf, 1963).

51. The citation is taken from the transcript of George Yancy's interview of William R. Jones. I want to thank both Drs. Yancy and Jones for permission to use this interview.

52. Phone interview with Dr. William R. Jones with the author on February 15, 2009.

53. For a bibliography of Holmes' works see John H. McClendon, "Eugene C. Holmes: A Commentary on a Black Marxist Philosopher" in Leonard Harris, ed., *Philosophy Born in Struggle* (Dubuque: Kendall/Hunt, 1983) pp. 49–50.

CHAPTER SEVEN

MIGRANT, MIGRA, MONGREL

The Latin American Dishwasher, Busboy, and Colored/Ethnic/Diversity (Philosophy) Hire

Eduardo Mendieta

HOW PLATO GOT HIS FIRST TEACHING JOB AND PEIRCE LOST HIS

José Ortega y Gasset, the famous twentieth-century Spanish philosopher, claimed that "we are our circumstances," by which he meant that we are our historical worlds. We are, but only within specific historical contexts. This is surely true of philosophers, who not only think in response to canons that have been historically formed, but also to their specific times, in which they face both institutional challenges as well as support. The sophists made their living by charging for their lessons—a point that Plato mentions repeatedly in his dialogues. Socrates could engage Athenians in the agora thanks partly to the generosity of wealthy benefactors, some of whom many considered to be the source of the downfall of Athens. Plato was wealthy enough to establish the Academy, which later Platonist continued to endow it in such a way that it could be self-supporting. Augustine was a bishop, and Aquinas taught at a major university that had been established by the Church. Although it took several years, Kant did land a teaching position that allowed him to make a decent living, even if he still had to teach about forty hours a week (more than most tenured professors today). Hegel also paid his dues as a private teacher, until he was appointed to a prized chair at the University of Berlin. Heidegger, in turn, had to rush into print his *Sein und Zeit* so that he could be considered for what we could call a "tenure-track job." His political entanglements with the Nazi Party led to his banishment from the university, until the 1950s. But not all such stories went so happily, or benignly. Boethius, one of the most important Christian neo-Platonists, a beneficiary of the Church, was arrested and executed on trumped up charges. Charles Sanders Peirce was fired from his teaching job at Johns Hopkins, for "sexual inpropriaties," and died in penury in Milford, Pennsylvania, miles from New York. The last years of his life he was able to continue some of his philosophical work thanks to a fund set up by William James. Walter Benjamin was never able to land a teaching position, partly because his *Habilitation* was not accepted. He lived from his pen and the generous support of the Institute for Social Research, which by the mid-1930s had already moved to New York. Ernst Bloch, a fellow German, Jewish, Marxist philosopher, was kept by his wife, while he toiled away on his magnus opus, *The Principle of Hope*, which he wrote in German in the United States, but which was only published after the end of the war. The rise of so-called analytic philosophy in the United States, as has been well-documented by many, was directly related to the massive immigration of European exiles. As we get closer to the present, we have the stories of Foucault's appointment to the *Collège de France*, where he lectured until the end of his life, and Habermas' return to Frankfurt, to teach in the department where Horkheimer and Adorno had taught until their own deaths, after returning from the Californian exile. Rorty's departure from Princeton University to the University of Virginia marked not just a geographical move, but also a philosophical statement, one that was emphatically reaffirmed when he moved to Stanford University to take an appointment as professor emeritus of comparative literature. All of these stories, whether of success or failure, forced exile or voluntary emigration, riches to poor or poor to riches, of official acknowledgment or professional obscurity, are indicative of the degree to which philosophers are implicated in the lives of the institutions that allow them to teach, to think, and to write. In the following, I combine autobiographical reflections with some comments on the function of race and ethnicity in the U.S. academy. Although I am convinced that these reflections also can be points of departure for insights about the future of "American" philosophy and the role of "ethnic" philosophy in the U.S. academy, I postpone extrapolating these insights until the future. For the moment, I can only refer readers to two indispensable books that are in line with my own approach: George Yancy's *Philosophy in Multiple Voices* and Jorge J. E. Gracia's *Latinos in America*.[1]

HOW I BECAME LATIN AMERICAN. THEN HISPANIC, AND THEN DISCOVERED I WAS LATINO

I could begin these semiautobiographical reflections with the statement: "I embody the massive demographic transformation of the United States in the last two decades." And although such a statement would not be inaccurate, the fact is that statistics conceal the details that are significant to individuals. According to the U.S. Census Bureau, the Latino population in the United States has grown at approximately four times the national average of 13 percent since the 1990s.[2] In the last decade of the twentieth century, the Latino population grew 57.9 percent, and the largest ratio of growth was in Central and South American Latinos. Most of them are younger than the general population. They have gathered in western and southern states, but they also amount to the largest ethnic minorities in New York, Los Angeles, Houston, and Chicago. Still, of the approximately 36 million Latinos in the United States, about 59 percent are of Mexican origin, whereas almost 10 percent are Puertorican, and 3.5 percent are Cuban. The remaining percent is made up of Central, South American, and Caribbean Latinos. On May 1, 2008, the U.S. Census issued a press release stating that as of 2008 the "Hispanic" population had reached 45 million, or 15.1 percent of the U.S. population. These trends have now been confirmed by the 2010 census. There are now 50.5 million Hispanics in the United States, 16.3 percent of the total population. The Hispanic population grew by 15.2 million, which is a 43 percent growth, amounting for more than half of the growth of the total population in the United States.[3]

I belong, however, to the fastest growing group of Latinos, namely those who are gathered under the rubric of "Other Hispanic." I also belong to a rather unusual group of Latinos. I emigrated to the United States in 1979, before the large wave of Central and South American immigrants who had left their homes due to civil wars in their countries (Nicaragua, El Salvador, Costa Rica, Guatemala, to mention the most notable). I grew up in central New Jersey, about thirty miles from New York, but in a region that did not have large numbers of Latinos. I was one of a handful of Latinos in Passaic High School, where the largest groups were blacks and whites. In fact, I grew up in a section of New Jersey were Spanish rarely was heard, except when you went to ethnic restaurants, and people disapproved of hearing Spanish spoken. Moreover, one of the most noticeable indicators of the growth of the Latino population in the United States is the attitude toward Spanish. From my high school education, through college, to my PhD studies, I lived through a shift in the way in which Spanish has gained symbolic capital. Even as the Latino population constitutes the fourth largest

Spanish-speaking collective, after Mexico, Spain, and Colombia, many non-Latinos are opting to learn Spanish as a second language.

Not unlike immigrants from Europe, one of my first discoveries was that I was a Latin American, among other Latin Americans. In high school we were an inconspicuous minority, but we knew each other by our accents, when we spoke up in class. We related, however, as Colombians, Chileans, Salvadoreans, Guatemalans, and Puerto Ricans. We declared our nationalities to each other, as well as others. Among ourselves, however, we recognized each other's nationality by the kind of Spanish we spoke, and by our racial composition. Although we were Latin Americans, and had specific nationalities, we also were evidently more or less mestizo, more or less *indian* (I use the Spanish term, and not the ones that have become acceptable, Native American or indigenous, because the later two are so distinctly North American, and also because I want to flag the derogatory connotation implied in the Spanish term), more or less mulatto. Different Latin American nationalities have different percentages of racial mixtures. These racial mixtures sometimes are proportionally represented in the immigrant from each country, but most often than not, they are skewed by the racial tensions and prejudices in their countries of origin. Thus, although most Mexican migrants tend to be mestizo, a large number of other Central Americans tend to be more "indian." Large numbers of Guatemalan and Salvadoreans Latinos have "indian" roots. Similarly, some other Latin American nations have larger proportions of mulattos, such as Caribbean Latinos, that is to say Puerto Ricans and Dominicans. Cubans, on the other hand, although Caribbean, have been integrated in to the United States in what can be called a two-tier racialized integration. The post-Cuban revolution, first wave of immigrants, was predominantly made up of what we call "whites." After the Mariel Boat Lift of 1980, Cuban exiles and refugees, collectively known as Marielitos, tended to be mostly mulattos. Similar tensions have arisen among Puerto Ricans and Dominicans, where the former tend to be more mixed with Spanish and Indian, than with blacks.

The point that I am trying to make is that over the past two decades, Latin American emigration to the United States has brought new racial tensions as well as destabilized others. The long established U.S. bipolar racial matrix has been destabilized by a large and growing ethnic minority that is racially heterogeneous, and that only can be approximately categorized as multipolar (indian, mestizo, black, mulatto, and "white"). It was, however, in the context of the United States that we discovered that we were Latin Americans, who spoke Spanish in different accents, with different speeds and slang (to the point that when, as a teenager, I tried to speak with some Mexicans and Salvadoreans in Spanish, I could hardly understand them), and who also have many different racial backgrounds. Ethnically, we were almost alike. Racially, we were diverse. Nationally, we also hailed from very different contexts and circumstances; some of us came from war torn countries, others from economies stalled in the eighteenth century, with its deep economic rifts among classes, others came from countries trying to escape their national histories of racism. But as I noted already, statistics paint with broad brush what calls for detail and minutia.

I immigrated to the United States because my mother had immigrated here, in the early 1970s, when Latin Americans were just beginning to be an issue for the U.S. government. Although my mother came to the United States in search of a better life, it cannot be said that she was escaping war, poverty, or racism. She was a strong-willed, entrepreneurial, determined, independent woman in an age and society when women were expected to be abnegating, submissive, and ever patient. We moved to the United States when my mother had obtained her own citizenship, and thus could claim us. In contrast to most Latin Americans who immigrated to the United States, then, I came "legally." When I landed at JFK, I had a green card, which about five years later I traded for my U.S. naturalization and a U.S. passport. Although I have only an approximate sense of what it may mean to live as an "illegal alien," in the United States, I do have an intimate awareness that having "papers" gave me a different sense of being and growing up in the United States. Growing up in and around immigrant communities one becomes aware of the continuous threat of the *Migra* (the term used in Spanish to refer to the Immigration Police, who do "raids" and "round-ups" of so-called illegal aliens). This ominous and relentless threat manifested itself in an unmitigated fear of "Anglos" or officers of the state, but also acted as a deterrent to engage in any kind of civic activity, either on behalf of oneself or others. There would be families in which some would have documents and others not, and some would be caught and sent back. I know that growing up without these fears must have been a tremendous bonus. And that growing up with them, must have been a tremendous burden, perhaps even a deforming one. In retrospect, the subsequent level of civic engagement on the part of many Latino communities is admirable considering their histories of suspicion of anything having to do with the government. Yet, as a "Latino" I knew that I appeared in the eyes of others as a potential, if not de facto, "illegal alien." And I have been treated as such on many occasions.

Similarly, although I have "indian," but no "black," blood in my family background, and my father being the son of Spanish immigrants to Colombia, I cannot say that I embody the typical Latin American immigrant. My mother is very fair, my brother looks northern European, but I look more like a swarthy Italian or Spaniard from Andalusia. Still, as I graduated from high school and went on to college, part of my "assimilation" into

U.S. society was to learn to live with its enduring and relentless racism. It is unsettling to live in a society that must continuously place you within a hierarchy of race. You must continuously pass racial purity tests. You must be surveyed, measured, chromatically indexed, physiognomically categorized, and your accent must be carefully distinguished and geographically mapped. The occasions are innumerable, and they continue to this day, even after I have spent close to three-fourths of my life in the United States, when perfect strangers, or individuals I have just met, will say something to the effect: "You don't look Hispanic, but your accent sounds Spanish," "You look Latino, but you don't speak like one," "You speak English very well, but you have an accent," "Where have you been, you looked so tanned." I appear as a conundrum to many of my fellow U.S. citizens. My racial and national background confounds them, and destabilizes their panoptic racial gaze. Racism operates by making everything visible, surveyable, manageable, without those who are seen, surveyed and managed being able to turn back and say: "But your categories, your expectations, your ideas about me are wrong." As a mongrel, I am visible, but not legible. Illegibility instigates either incomprehensibility or the urge to communicate so as to understand.

Many, most Latin Americans, arrived to the United States as nominal citizens of their Latin American nations, but with very strong senses of patriotism. But over the years, the decades, we learned to identify and be identified as "Latinos." We learned this, because the mainstream society lumped us together under a bureaucratic label created for the purposes of the Census, but also because we came to recognize the similarities and kinship notwithstanding the differences in nationalities, ways we spoke Spanish, and worship our gods. In the same way that I have been witness to the increase acceptance and valorization of Spanish, I also have witnessed the slow process of the reinscription and resignification of the term*Hispanic*. It would be appropriate to note that the label is entirely misleading and one has to wonder how it came to be suggested and accepted at all. In both English and Spanish, *Hispanic* makes reference to Spain and the Iberian Peninsula. It throws such a large semantic net that Spaniards and Portuguese persons qualify as Hispanic. For many, if not most, Latin Americans and Latinos, this is adding insult to injury. Evidently, Latino also is not a perfect label, but no label is. Yet, it at least localizes the history and geography of the Latin American experience that is the background against which we must make sense of the Latino experience in the United States. It has been the protestation of Latinos over the past two decades, as well as the contribution of many scholars, that has forced the U.S. Census Bureau to change its terminology, and as of 2003, it started using "Hispanic" and "Latino" interchangeably, with the one, one hopes, of facing out "Hispanic."[4]

This process of the resignification, resemantization, and appropriation of a bureaucratic label from below, is what I call the "making of a new people."[5] There are no "Latinos" outside the United States. There are Latin Americans, or Mexicans, or Nicaraguans, or Cubans, etc., but not "Latinos." *Latinos* is a term, a label, a self-description that has as its point of reference a social, political, racial, cultural, and linguistic reality that is *sui generis* U.S. grounded. It is more appropriately a political and cultural tool, than an ethnic designator. Its acceptance and appropriation by Latinos marks a new stage of political and social maturity of both Latinos and the wider U.S. citizenry. For in accepting and appropriating the label, Latinos position themselves vis-à-vis a sociopolitical and cultural reality that they claim, and that they in turn allow to claim them. To be recognized and to allow oneself to be recognized with any such label is to enter into the "space of reasons"—to use that felicitous expression popularized by Bob Brandom—of U.S. citizenship, demographic politics, and civil rights discourse. I call this and similar processes of appropriation, pedagogy of the citizenry by the citizenry. As Latin Americans became Hispanic, and then Latino, they were educated in the ways of U.S. ethnic, racial, and cultural politics. But by the same token, the process of negotiation and resignification, actively pursued from below, from the ground up by civic groups, has educated the wider polity to learn to recognized differences in their specific difference, and not in terms of a proforma label that perfunctorily signals difference without acknowledging it as such. It is for this reason that I think we must talk about the "making of a new people." On the one hand, "Latinos" are autochthonous to the United States, in the sense I elaborated above, that they refer to a specifically U.S. reality. On the other hand, through a dual pedagogy of the citizenry, U.S. citizens in general have learned and are learning to recognize that race does not exist just in two, but in a spectrum in which neither "white" nor "black" exist pure, and that social equity requires that we acknowledge the weight of history.[6]

ETHNORACIAL LABELS, AFFIRMATIVE ACTION, AND SO-CALLED "BADGES OF INFERIORITY"

Although I grew up with an intense sense of being Latin American, and then eventually, as I went through college, of being really "Latino," predominantly because of the way wider society related to me and I in turn related to it, I have little, if any, experience that this label mattered to how institutions saw me. It is for the sake of institutions being "able to see you" that labels such as "black," "Latino," "white," "woman," and so on, are used. Yet, how they are used with respect to "you," remains a mystery. In high school, as I noted, I was one of a handful of recent immigrants who took advantage of the English as a second language programs available. When I went to college, in the early 1980s, at Rutgers University, I must have checked the "Hispanic" box, but once I was in college, at no point was I addressed institutionally with this label. Rutgers is a large state university, which at the time that I entered it was divided into colleges, each with its own administration, name and culture. With the exception of one occasion, which I will discuss momentarily, I was never addressed by anyone in the administration, teaching staff, or faculty as a "Hispanic." If there were any such programs, I was neither aware of them, nor made aware of them. None of my teachers talked about my being Hispanic, nor what this may have meant for me, in my career, needs, interests, and so on. Although I had a couple of outstanding mentors, neither of whom happened to be in philosophy, they never addressed my "minority" ethnic status. This may have been a blessing in disguise. In retrospect, I think my mentors did not know what being "Hispanic" meant. There was one instance when I was indeed addressed as a "minority," during my Rutgers years, and that was when I was invited to be a member of a select group of "minority" students who would apply, or would receive, Bell Laboratories scholarships, which would pay for the last two years of college and would guarantee either an internship or entry-level job at Bell Labs. Up through my second year of college I was registered as a math major with a minor in philosophy. I was a good student, or had the grades they were looking for. A dozen or so of us visited the Bell Laboratories. I distinctly remember that one of the things they were working on at the time was missile guidance, or what in the 1990s would be known as "smart bombs." After my visit, I must have decided that this was not for me, and neither was "math." I was particularly interested in fusion or plasma physics. I came to realize that the prospects of work after college for a physics-math major in the private sector, or the education sector were slim, and I would end up working for the government, in some nuclear weapons program. I flipped my major and minor and decided to focus on philosophy. I find it ironic that the one time my ethnic label got me attention from some agency or institution was in order to work on behalf of something that today I find even more abhorrent than back then, when I only had a mere intuition of what missile guidance turned out to be.

Yet, it was my college years that taught me to see myself, to identify, as a "Latino." It was during these years that I got very involved with student activism. I became a member of CISPES (Committee in Solidarity with the People of El Salvador), The Peace Center (an anti-nukes and in general peace network), and of course, the Divestment from South African student movement. I also was one of the editors of the politics and culture student newspaper, *The Livingston Medium* (where I published reviews of

Foucault, the Smiths, satires as well as exposés of professors doing military and CIA-funded research). Toward the end of my college years, the group of student activists with whom I organized many activities decided that we had done enough "single-issue" politics and we needed a nationwide student organization and network. My friends and I spent a year visiting campuses across the country making contact with local student groups. In 1987, we hosted what we hoped would turn out to be a new "Port Huron" and the revival of a quasi-Students for a Democratic Society (SDS). Needless to say, it did not turn out that way. Yet, these years of student activism constituted my schooling into ethnic politics. As someone who spoke Spanish, and had a better sense of Latin American culture, I became the default contact or liaison person when dealing with issues relating to our activism around Latin America. I met refugees from El Salvador, Guatemala, and Nicaragua, and translated for them or drove them from and to the local churches that were giving them sanctuary.

Eventually, I would form part of a "Witness for Peace" delegation to Nicaragua, to monitor the coming elections that resulted in the Sandinistas being voted out of government. My visit to Nicaragua was one of the most sobering and profoundly educational experiences I have ever had. We visited farms and villages that were continuously raided by the "Contras," Reagan's so-called "freedom fighters." We stayed in private homes, and were able to get a sense of the daily preoccupations and rhythms of the Nicaraguan people. I distinctly remember that the few dollars that I could afford to bring and that we were allowed to bring had made me a millionaire in Nicaragua. A couple of hundred dollars turned into cases of Nicaraguan pesos. Collectively, we figured we could buy a farm and set up a school—we were that naïve and utopian. We were hopeful that the Sadinistas, who had done so much for Nicaragua, despite a decade of waged war by the United States, would win the elections. But we were realistic enough to see the exhaustion of the people and could hear between the lines of what people said that if the Sadinistas stayed in government, the U.S.-backed war would rage on. The Sadinistas did not lose; rather, the United States won a dirty, illegal, and unconstitutional war. This is what we came to say a few months later after we watched the results on television. The Nicaraguan people did not vote against the Sandinistas, they voted for peace with and from the United States. These years of activism around Central America, specifically, constituted my "university learning" in racial and ethnic identity politics. I came to recognize two basic facts: as a citizen of the United States I had a unique advantage. As a citizen I had the right and duty to demonstrate, challenge, denounce the policies of my "government." This much I had learned from SDS, the Port Huron document, and the many years of activism against Apartheid and the deployment of nuclear weapons in Europe.

But as a "Latin American" I had a specific duty to take advantage of my contingently given, but indispensable skills: I spoke Spanish, and had an insider's view on many aspects of Latin American culture. I came to recognize that these two facts, these two lessons, taught me to think of my "Latin American" background not as a handicap, something that I had to supersede and overcome, but rather something that was a strength, an asset, even a virtue. But this asset, this strength, this advantage made sense only in conjunction with my being a U.S. citizen. I was a U.S. citizen, who was of Latin American background, and I was a Latin American who had a privilege and a duty. This is how I learned that I was a "Latino," someone with a specific ethnic and racial background who can make claims on the wider U.S. citizenry, and who in turn can be claimed by that very citizenry, as I was when as a student activist I was called on by duty and outrage to work on behalf of better university provisions for women on our campus, and for the divestment of our university from South Africa.

My experience of "ethnic" or "identity politics," thus has been from the side of what it encouraged or commanded me to do vis-à-vis the wider polity. Identity politics is indeed one way of being politicized, of being taught about the rights and duties of citizenship. It also is one way of being educated about one's social singularity, and thus, of being educated about the different histories that each individual brings to the public agora, that are both burdens and strengths, and that invariably enrich our wider self-understanding. What I have subsequently come to realize is that my "Latino" identity does not just link me to a past, to a history, to a particular memory, but also, and perhaps most importantly, to a future, to a project, to what is not yet. When I claim that "I am Latino," and when I fill out a box in any official form that says "Hispanic," I am de facto making a prospective, future oriented claim. I am positioning myself in a particular way to a political futurity. Looking back on my student years at Rutgers, I can say that it was my fellow students who politicized me. It was through them that I learned to see my unique social position. Perhaps the university administration had some use for my "Hispanic" label when it used it as part of a statistic that it sent to Trenton. But at no point did I receive an iota of direct benefit from such statistical appreciation. Even my teachers failed to register the ways in which my "Latino" identity could have been an asset, or something that I should affirm positively. For instance, I was never told that there may be scholarships for graduate school specifically ear-marked for "Hispanics," or that I should use my native Spanish as an asset. No one among my teachers offered to help me write a graduate school application, or what graduate schools to apply to, or what a kind of writing sample to submit. In fact, in one case, I was asked by one of my recommenders to draft the letter of recommendation that I had asked them to send on my behalf! I don't begrudge them for this. In retrospect, I think they simply did not know what kinds of things to do, to recommend. They were absolutely outstanding teachers and mentors, but poor advisors. And I would not change anything if I had a chance to re-live it, except perhaps the bit about how to write excellent or approximately good long papers (which given my interests was an indispensable skill, and one that given my recently acquired English, was sorely lacking). I do have regrets and begrudgements, but against Rutgers as a state university. In the five years I was there (I took one extra year to finish because of all my activism and extracurricular activities), I did not have one minority faculty member teach me. Not one African American, not one Hispanic or Latino, not one Native American. I did have a Japanese-American teacher, who taught religion. He was one of my favorite teachers because he introduced me to Rosmerary Ruether's and Dietrich Bonhoeffer's works. Only in hindsight can I honestly express both astonishment and regret at this fact. It was only when I got to graduate school, a theological school with a long history of involvement with the Black Church and social justice, that I had my first black and Latin American teachers.

It was only after my master of arts in systematic theology at Union Theological Seminary that my identity as "Latino" came to mean anything in terms of institutional support. I should note that I decided to pursue a degree in theology because I wanted to study liberation theology, something that I knew a lot about because of the role of many catholic priests in the Nicaraguan revolution, and the many Jesuit institutions throughout Central and South America that worked on behalf of the poor and social transformation. My work with CISPES had exposed me to the work of the Ecclesiastical Base Communities, some of which I had visited myself. Ernesto Cardenal had taken Paulo Freire's pedagogy of liberation and applied it to the gospels. I had studied enough liberation theology and seen how it was a form of praxis before it was a form of teaching. I also recognized that it was one of the most important intellectual, theological and philosophical movements to emerge from Latin America. Liberation theology had become a worldwide movement. As a Colombian, I also knew about Camilo Torres, the Catholic priest who joined the guerillas to fight on behalf of the poor, and who is famous for the pronouncement that "If Jesus were alive today, he would be a guerrillero." Union Theological Seminary had one of the most outstanding faculties in the country for studying liberation theology. James H. Cone, the father of "black liberation theology"; James Melvin Washington, the editor of Martin Luther King's writings; Beverly Harrison, a pioneering feminist theologian; Cornel West, who called for a "prophetic pragmatism"; and a rotating chair that was occupied each year by a different Latin American, African, Asian or European theologian. Unfortunately,

Cornel West left for Princeton at the time, and Union Theological Seminary was going through major financial problems during the early 1990s. Needless to say, I did not receive any special help or attention because I was "Latino" at Union. While I was at Union, however, I did get to study with Richard J. Bernstein at the New School, a school I knew a lot from having studied the origins of SDS and from having followed the careers of many refugee German philosophers of the Nazi years. It was Dick Bernstein who recruited me to the New School, and made sure I got the best financial package that the school could offer at the time. But, as far as I remember, while I am sure that Dick mentioned my ethnic background in his letter of recommendation, I received fellowships that were generically named "Presidential" and "Dean's" fellowships. I had also applied to Harvard Theological Seminary, where I wanted to do a doctorate in theology, a ThD, with a focus on liberation theology and Habermas' theory of communicative action (the Fiorenzas were teaching at that time at Harvard). I chose the New School, although the financial package I got offered by Harvard was larger.

Still, it was during my years at Union that I was able to benefit directly and explicitly from my "Latino" identity. I learned, on my own, of the Hispanic Scholarship Fund, which gives scholarships, then of up to $1,500, to Latino or Hispanic students in postgraduate education. I applied on several occasions, and on each I was awarded up to $1,500, which for a self-supporting graduate student was like mana from the sky. I bought my first laptop with one of these grants, the laptop on which I wrote my dissertation, and on which I edited my first three books. The others I used to pay for my German language classes. It was these classes that allowed me to apply and receive a German Academic Exchange Service (DAAD) scholarship to continue my studies in Germany, Freiburg to be specific. Eventually, my intense work in German allowed me to apply for another DAAD scholarship, this time to work in Frankfurt on my dissertation. As a graduate student I was a beneficiary of support from the New School, a school known for its commitment to minorities, and specifically from the German government (the DAAD) and a Hispanic foundation that is financed by Latino benefactors. My experiences in Germany, during the almost two years I lived there as a graduate student, confirmed my insights about being a Latino. I discovered that I could move between worlds and groups: the European, the United States, and the Latin American. I could speak Spanish to the Latin Americans and Spaniards, English to the U.S. students, and German to the Japanese, Danish, Italian, or German students I met. The non-U.S. students accepted me, and even sought me out, with what appeared to be greater ease and comfort, because I was not a complete "American." And my Latin American and Spanish friends sought me out because I was Latin American, even if when I spoke Spanish I already spoke it with a "Gringo" accent. Even my German professors, specifically Karl-Otto Apel and Jürgen Habermas, appreciated immediately this uniqueness about me. I could converse with them in English or German, but I also could give them insight into what the Spanish and Latin American students were writing or saying. Being of the "United States" but not from it, being "American" but "Latin American" made me uniquely interesting, safer, and perhaps less unlikable or more difficult to assimilate than other "U.S." or "American" students. I do not know whether these experiences and attitudes would have translated similarly in France, or Italy, or even England. But I know that my being "Latino" was an incredibly positive aspect of my U.S. ethnic identity in Germany and later when I went to lecture in Spain, Mexico, Colombia, and Brazil. I also know that my "Latino" identity was one of the specific reasons why I was invited to teach graduate seminars at the European Humanities University in Minsk, Belarus, where I taught seminars on globalization, postcolonialism, and border theory.

While I was in Germany, writing my dissertation, editing and translating a book, an administrator at the New School who took care of graduate students wrote to me to alert me of a doctoral fellowship that involved teaching and possibly a future tenure position. This was the James Irvine Scholar Fellowship, which is funded by the James Irvine Foundation, a foundation that has its mission "to expand opportunity for the people of California to participate in a vibrant, successful and inclusive society." As the Web site of the foundation makes explicit, in order to pursue its mission, it has been guided by the following goals:

1. Advance the educational and economic prospects of low-income Californians to share in and create California's prosperity;

2. Engage a broad cross-section of Californians in the civic and cultural life of their communities and the state;

3. Enhance mutual understanding and communication among diverse racial, ethnic, and socioeconomic groups; and

4. Enrich the state's intellectual and creative environment.[7]

The fellowship was a residence fellowship, being offered at the University of San Francisco (USF). I applied, was interviewed over the phone across the Atlantic, and soon found myself on a eleven-hour flight from Frankfurt to San Francisco. The James Irvine Fellowship allowed me to finish my dissertation, but it also allowed me to acquire some experience in teaching, and above all, it exposed me to a teaching environment and colleagues who were both welcoming and nurturing.

Teaching at USF was one of the most gratifying experiences of my life. It was there that I learned I could be an inspirational and efficacious teacher, and that I also could be a great mentor. USF is a Jesuit University, located in the heart of one of the most diverse and progressive cities in the world. Yet, the university had a problem attracting and retaining minority faculty. When I arrived, there were a handful of minority professors, albeit more than I had been exposed to at any other school since. The Irvine Fellowship program had been won by the university precisely to diversify its faculty, which was already growing very senior, and to bring in young, highly qualified minority scholars who could or would want to stay on as members of the faculty. I was one of the first such fellows. I was neither the first nor the last to leave. Yet, I must say that the program brought to the university energetic, highly qualified, and productive minority scholars. The James Irvine program and the university were competing with an almost impossible housing market in San Francisco, a critical lack of qualified minority faculty across the nation, and what appeared to be an unbridgeable chasm between two cultures within the university (the senior, less-diverse faculty, and the younger, more-diverse faculty). Nonetheless, the seven years (1994–2001) I taught at USF were some of my most productive. I also learned that when a group of administrators and faculty work together to address a problem, they can succeed. USF faced a crisis, a potentially embarrassing one giving the university's avowed mission to nourish and serve a racially and ethnically diverse community. It set out to fix this problem and got a program in place, funded from a variety of sources, but mostly from a private foundation. As one of the early fellows, I participated in the selection of later Irvine Scholars. As such I was privy to discussions in which faculty would reject the offer from the dean's office for an Irvine Scholar because of putative holes in certain areas of the curriculum, or because they could not get assurances that this new fellow would count against their future hires. I have heard similar arguments in which a highly qualified minority faculty is not courted because the faculty felt that they were not getting a "free hire," but a Trojan horse. Still, the administration at USF was determined and adamant. The faculty had to be more ethnically diverse, and they had to attract younger faculty. The deans, and in particular Dean Marin, who is one of the most distinguish Latino scholars and social scientists in the United States, had a vision about where the university should be in a decade, two decades. Faculty had a narrow horizon, one that was ideological, self-serving, and hypocritical. I say self-serving and hypocritical because although they argued about the integrity of the curriculum, and serving the students, few of them took initiatives to improve their teaching, to offer new courses, to mentor more closely students, to engage in the student activities that better prepare students for the world and postgraduate work.

I have seen the same modus operandi at large state universities, where I also heard arguments about "minority" hires along the same lines. Yet, for us Irvine Scholars, our minority status was not a "badge of inferiority"—to use that most-telling formulation by Justice Clarence Thomas—but rather "badges of excellence." We were by far better educated, we had published more, had more experience with the contemporary academic world, we were better connected and informed about what was going on in our respective disciplines. We all took very seriously the mission of the Irvine Foundation and the university: We saw ourselves as scholars who were working toward a more just and representative society. We took extremely seriously our task of being both role models and mentors. For this reason, we also were on every imaginable committee: governance, curriculum development, and so on. Our status as "minority" scholars, thus, turned into a special job. One that no average, nonethnic faculty has to do, is expected to do, or will ever have to do.

DISHWASHER. BUSBOY. GARDENER. CUSTODIAN: THE MEXICAN HANDYMEN IN ACADEMIA

There are now more than 34 million Latinos of Mexican descent in the United States, which is why we see them practically everywhere. Throughout California they are day laborers, fruit pickers, gardeners, and Taqueria servers. In New York, they are the crews that keep up the immaculate lawns on Long Island, and the kitchen crews of most restaurants in Manhattan. In Chicago, they work the warehouses, and the O'Hare Airport food outlets. I have worked next to some such Mexicans, and I have been to their homeland. They are hard workers, patient, demurring, humble, loyal, and frugal. They are everywhere, but they hardly murmur, except when they become the explicit target of policies and legislation that try to punish them for their industriousness and entrepreneurship. I have nothing but admiration for the Mexican people, and like to think of Mexico as my second *Patria* (fatherland), the oldest nation on this continent, a people made of many peoples, many peoples who are the trace of our American history. Thus, when I say that we ethnic, minority, racial hires are like the Mexican handymen of the U.S. academy, I mean that as an encomium to Mexicans, and as a slight to the U.S. academy. In the United States, Mexicans are hired because they are cheap, pliable, demurring, and obedient. And because they are not U.S. citizens (although most are), they are owed no loyalty. They can be fired at will, and many employers actually abuse them and rob them of their earned salaries. They are in, but they can be put "out" speedily and without regrets. Surreptitiously, they are hired, and with the same bad faith, they are sent away, seen as a nuisance and an embarrassment. Americans want a Mexican to take care of their children, to make their food, to roll their burritos, to cut their lawns, to replace their roofs, to teach and prepare their children for a racially and ethnically diverse society, but they can't tolerate them, and are not willing to extend civic friendship and loyalty to them. They are never an asset, a resource, a cultural advantage to be recognized and celebrated. They are indispensable and yet totally disposable. Such is the situation of the minority hire.

I left USF because I could not afford a house even within a reasonable commuting distance of the university, and because I wanted to mentor a new generation of ethnically and racially diverse and sensitive PhDs. I was recruited to one of the best philosophy programs in the United States, at the State University of New York, Stony Brook. I was hired under a short-lived initiative launched by the then president of the university. The "presidential hires" were to be outstanding minority scholars who would diversify the faculty while enhancing their scholarly profile. I was recruited by Kelly Oliver, who subsequently left to take up an endowed chair at a private university, as one faculty among several who would make the program the best in the country on race, gender, and ethnic philosophy, while enhancing its strengths in Continental, political, and social philosophy, with a focus on critical theory, deconstruction, and postmodernism. I would bring to the program: Latin American philosophy, Frankfurt School, postcolonial and globalization theory, and a focus on ethics and political philosophy. But, my line would be funded directly by the president, and not by the College of Arts and Sciences. I would be a freebie. Later I found out that some of my colleagues did not like this arrangement, again for the reasons I discussed earlier.

Our department had twenty-six lines, but we are down to twenty-two. In terms of gender, race, and ethnicity, we have one of the most diverse departments among similar top programs in the United States. Tellingly, the faculty who have added to the program's racial diversity have been hired within the last decade or so. Most of the faculty, however, have been in the department since the program's launching in the early 1970s. Several of them are about to or will be retiring shortly. Sine I arrived at Stony Brook in 2001, I have been on many provostial and presidential committees that draw on my "ethnic" status. I have been asked to mentor other minority faculty. I am the *de facto* department's representative to the Turner Fellowship, a state-funded program that used to bring minority graduate students to the program (in 2006 the wording of the fellowship was changed for fear that it would be litigated against. Now, it is a program serving "deserving" populations, whereas before it targeted blacks, Native Americans, and Hispanics).

Every recruitment cycle requires that we identify potential Turner Fellows. Since I arrived, I have been the one to advise, mentor, and recruit such potential graduate students. I have served on several of the graduate program committees that select the incoming pool of graduate students. On all the occasions, I have served on this committee, the committee's goals have been to get the students with the highest Graduate Record Examinations, grade point averages (GPAs), and the ones who have the strongest letters, from reputable scholars. Invariably, we end up competing for the same graduate recruits with schools such as Penn State, Northwestern, DePaul, and Chicago, some of which can offer better stipends. In short, and in my view in a grimly ironic way, selecting the future philosophy PhDs is boiled down to a number-crunching exercise. Never, however, have I heard any of my colleagues argue that we should use one of our allocated recruitment lines to bring in a student who is a minority. We leave that for the Turner, from which at most we will get two lines. Thus, by default, we use the Turner as our means of keeping a modicum of racial and ethnic diversity. But this is a default mode. It is not proactive, nor does it acknowledge that our program is biased toward nonminority students. The fact is that the Turner has turned into a device that allows us to bring mostly "international" minorities. Most of the present Turners are either foreign born, or of Latin American descent, and most of them come from South America (we have more Argentians than any other nationality among our "Latinos"). We have no Mexicans, no Cubans, no Puerto Ricans, and only one Native American. We do have two black students, and until about 2010, we had three. But one of them does not qualify as a U.S. black, for she is of Caribbean origin. I have advocated that we be more proactive in recruiting black graduate students, as well as Mexicans. But I have not made any headway. On several occasions, I have identified such candidates and mentored them in their applications, but my colleagues have turned them down. I have written to members of the committee pointing out the embarrassing statistics of our recruitment, and called their practices racists. I have pointed out that since its inception, our program has only graduated two black PhDs, out of 170 some odd PhDs, and those were from the early 1980s and not within the past two decades. (This is based on statistics officially kept by the university.) A bad move, because you don't want to call avowed liberals racists. They take it very personally, even if their actions prove that they are perpetuating racist policies. They hide behind the shield of scores, GPAs, and the scholarly interests of the faculty. If we were able to recruit more minorities, however, I fear that they would flounder. For the most part, our faculty is very disengaged with mentoring. Since 2001, at Stony Brook, I can count on my hands the number of times I have seen some faculty. Our department is located on an L-shaped hall. Most of the year this hall is empty of faculty, except for the four or five who come on a regular basis to work at their offices, hold office hours, and to meet with graduate students. Our colloquia rarely are attended by more than three faculty, almost always the same guilty parties. Most of our dissertation committees are made up of a handful of faculty. Three faculty alone have almost 90 percent of the dissertations (I am one of them). In the seven years I have been to the Turner dinners (which welcomes and celebrates the accomplishment of our minority alumni), I have only seen one faculty from my department, although I know some of them have been invited. In any event, I am sanguine enough to both know and recognize that these conditions are typical of most graduate programs in philosophy, especially for those with very senior faculty.

I am trying to be dispassionate and objective and thus hope that what I take to be the mere statement of the facts does not sounds like either bragging or complaining. I was hired as a "presidential" appointment, as a "highly qualified" minority. I was one of a few of such hires. Some have already left the university. I almost did. Why? The university and my department have not been the most hospitable of places for us. We are required to do an inordinate amount of work. We are on every imaginable committee. We chair searches. We chair dissertation committees. We do administrative work. We double as experts in our fields, but we are also the obliging and indispensable ethnic representatives at every level of the university. Stony Book University is a major state university, with one of the most diverse student bodies in the country. Yet, its faculty is aged, and aging. The budget is at the mercy of Albany, and the discretion of the president. Since 2001, my college of arts and sciences has lost more faculty than it has been able to replace. Between 2001 and 2004 we were unable to hire due to budget cuts. Then we had a hiring freeze between 2004 and 2006. Since then we have hired three new faculty to replace the ones we have lost to departures and retirements. One of the them we were only able to hire through a special program financed from Albany, SUNY Central, that allows us to hire highly qualified minorities. In these austere times, in which public university budgets are being slashed, hiring minorities has become highly contentious, and some may even say "a luxury."

Stony Brook has one of the least ethnically and racially diverse faculties I have ever met or worked with, and also one of the least welcoming I have had to interact with. And there is no initiative or strategy to remedy the situation. Although New York and specifically Manhattan, which is fifty or so miles from our campus, have the largest Latino populations, we have few Latino faculty, and those we do have we keep losing. Like San Francisco, we also have one of the most expensive real estate markets in the country. And the commute from the boroughs is punishing (a mere forty-five miles away, yet about one hour and forty-five minutes by train, one way). The environs, which are highly gentrified, also are not welcoming to racial minorities.

I think, in retrospect, that my department and my university got a bargain when it hired me as a minority hire. Since 2001, I have served on every major committee and subcommittee of the department, on occasions, serving on three and four simultaneously: the history exam, the placement, the colloquium, and two hiring committees. I have lead into expansion and repute the master of arts program that we offer at Manhattan. I advise and mentor students who have never taken one of my seminars and whose work I do not know. Yet, I am also a visible "Latino" scholar who has added substantively to the strengths of the department. I know for a fact that my publication record was key in placing our department among the most productive in the nation, according to a new federal ranking.

Yet, I have been very cheap. I have been like one of those Mexicans that we see toiling quietly in our kitchens, gardens, farms, restaurants, warehouses, and schools. Without question, I have been a beneficiary of affirmative action. I have benefited immensely from ethnically targeted fellowships and hiring initiatives. I would not be who I am today without such funding opportunities. Along the way, however, I have also been the fortunate receiver of gratuitous, generous, and disinterested mentorship from other minority scholars, and more so than from nonethnic minorities. Jorge J.E. Gracia and Linda Martín Alcoff, two highly prominent Latino philosophers and scholars, have mentored me, although they had no direct links to me. Nancy Tuana was another early mentor, someone who also was equally generous with her advice, and who did so voluntarily and without reward or institutional acknowledgment. Their example has inspired me to reciprocate, which is why I end up writing an average of three letters a year for tenure and promotion for other minority and nonminority scholars.

Meanwhile, nonethnic or nonraced faculty have never offered their mentorship, help or advice (with the exception of Tuana). They have hardly offered their welcome. At best, they have made me feel tolerated, but at worst, unwelcome and guilty. Yet, their department and their university have benefited immensely from their "Latino" faculty. I have suffered both overt and covert racism, tolerably subtle and snarlingly blatant. But I have had comrades, colleagues, and friends, who have been there to support, encourage and offer most welcome advice. Mostly, they have been fellow "minority" colleagues. The racist culture of the American academy is evident by the statistics, but it is also palpable in our meetings, where absurdly we retreat into the high school habits of congregating by race. If my experience can lead to a moral it may be that racially and ethnically targeted programs, fellowships, and funding are indispensable, and very much still needed, but it also should be said that the culture of philosophy departments has to change, and that has to begin from the top of the colleges, with the deans, who must force faculty members to engage in critical self-analysis of their recruitment policies, and not to think of race and ethnicity as either potential freebies, or burdens, but as major concerns for the future vibrancy, competency, effectiveness, attractiveness, and fairness of their respective educational institutions.

I close by quoting one of the most moving sentences I have ever read in a book. Charles Mills writes in the acknowledgment section of his book, *The Racial Contract*, "A beneficiary of affirmative action, I would not be in the American academy today were it not for the struggles of black Americans."[8] I share Mills' gratitude, and like him, I also feel an intellectual and existential loyalty to that tradition. When I claim my "Latino" identity, I am also positioning myself in relation to this long struggle for social justice and racial equity. The Latino quest, which is just beginning, for full citizenship is but an extension of that long political and philosophical tradition that African American's pioneered. We are brothers in that struggle.

NOTES

1. George Yancy, *Philosophy in Multiple Voices* (Lanham, MD: Rowman & Littlefield, 2008), and Jorge J. E. Gracia, *Latinos in America: Philosophy and Social Identity* (Malden, MA: Blackwell Publishing, 2008).

2. All of the following statistics come from U.S. Census Bureau, *The Hispanic Population. Census 2000 Brief.*

3. I developed a more in-depth analysis of this process than somewhere I called "Latinization" of the United States. See "La Latinización de "América": Los Latinos en los Estados Unidos y la Creación de un nuevo Pueblo" in Francisco Colom, ed. *Relatos de Nación: La construcción de las identidades nacionales en el mundo hispánico* (Madrid and Frankfurt am Main: Iberoamericana and Vervuert, 2005): pp. 975–998.

4. I offered a more in-depth discussion of these issues in my essay on Gracia's book *Hispanic/Identity Identity: A philosophical Perspective* (Malden, MA: Blackwell, 2000), in "The 'Second Reconquista,' or Why should a 'Hispanic' become a Philosopher?: On Jorge Gracia's Hispanic/Latino Identity: A Philosophical Perspective." in *Philosophy and Social Criticism*, Vol. 27, No. 2, pp. 11–19.

5. See my "The Making of New Peoples: Hispanizing Race" in Jorge J. E. Gracia and Pablo de Greiff, eds., *Hispanics/Latinos in the United States: Ethnicity, Race, and Rights* (New York: Routledge, 2000), pp. 45–59.

6. See "Becoming Citizens, Becoming Hispanics" in David Batstone and Eduardo Mendieta, eds. *The Good Citizen* (New York: Routledge, 1999), pp. 113–131.

7. These are statements that can be found on the foundation's Web site: http://www.irvine.org/about_irvine/mission.shtml. Accessed Monday, August 4, 2008.

8. Charles W. Mills, *The Racial Contract* (Ithaca and London: Cornell University Press, 1997), p. xii.

CHAPTER EIGHT

WHY ARE HISPANIC PHILOSOPHERS MARGINALIZED IN THE AMERICAN PHILOSOPHICAL COMMUNITY?

<hr>

Gregory Fernando Pappas

Hispanic philosophers suffer from marginalization. I have experienced this in my own career and in the lives of the few Hispanic graduate students whom I have directed. Here is what a female Hispanic graduate student had to say when I asked her about her own experiences:

> Being Hispanic in philosophy is not easy. Having a Spanish last name, an accent and being brown doesn't seem to go down easy for other philosophers or students. It's almost as though we have to prove that we're profound/smart enough to be in the club, whereas if I were white and had a beard I would at least look the part.

There is, however, almost nothing written about this problem. One important exception is the last chapter of Jorge Gracia's book *Hispanic Identity*, titled "Foreigners in our Own Land: Hispanics in American Philosophy."[1] Gracia's focus in that chapter is the situation of Hispanics in American philosophy but it also is one of the most critical assessments of the American Philosophical Association (APA) that I have read. According to Gracia, the problem of marginalization of Hispanics is just one of many in the American philosophical community, a "community" that lacks unity and where philosophy is "too often practiced for reasons which have nothing to do with philosophy: power and immortality."[2] One may question Gracia's pessimistic view of the APA, but why has Gracia's sharp and provocative criticism about the entire philosophical community in the United States been largely ignored? Is it because it comes from a Hispanic?

In this chapter, my starting point is Gracia's provocative answers to the question posed in the title. My goal is to continue the inquiry started by Gracia by adding my own experiences and providing a more systematic analysis of the complexity of the problem, as well as suggest some possible ways to deal with it.

MARGINALIZATION AS A PROBLEMATIC EXPERIENCE

Before addressing the marginalization of Hispanics in the United States and evaluating Gracia's account, let me first lay out three of my working assumptions about marginalization in general.

1. *Marginalization is not always negative, problematic, or something that must be eliminated.* The marginalization caused by racism, oppression, slavery, or sexism usually is an integral part of these moral evils but there is marginalization that is morally permissible or even good for those that are marginalized. There are many groups that I belong to for which I am glad to be marginalized. Marginalization may even be a necessary experience of those moral revolutionaries who go against the mainstream or the established moral codes of conduct of a society. In this chapter, I do not attempt to reach some rule or criteria about when marginalization is or is not morally worrisome. I prefer to be a contextualist with respect to it.[3] In my view, it depends on the particular situation whether to experience oneself as "invisible," "unimportant," "not invited," "neglected," or "ignored" is a moral and social problem requiring amelioration. For the purposes of this chapter, I take for granted that the instances of marginalization under discussion are serious problems affecting Hispanics and the community of philosophers.

2. *Marginalization experienced is a matter of degree.* This is true not only in terms of how marginalized a person or group is but also in terms of how morally harmful, problematic, or denigrating is the situation. For example, the marginalization experienced by Hispanics in the philosophical community may be, in comparison, not as bad as the one experienced by Hispanics in other social contexts or in society at large. According to my Hispanic graduate student, despite her experience of marginalization, "the philosophy group (white males included) has been the group of people that have accepted me the most aside from my personal friends." On the other hand, there may be other social contexts in which Hispanics have a better experience than in philosophy. For instance, I have been told that Hispanics are better accepted in the community of musicians.

3. *Marginalization is ultimately grounded on immediate and personal experiences.* This assumption requires explanation. Gracia begins "Foreigners in

our Own Land: Hispanics in American Philosophy" by providing different statistics that are alarming, including (a) "the APA did not have a committee devoted to Hispanic issues until 1991. . . . By contrast, the Committee for Blacks in Philosophy has been in existence since [1973]"[4]; (b) "the percentage of Hispanic graduate students in philosophy is 3.8 percent"[5]; (c) The number of PhDs in philosophy awarded to Hispanics since 1974 is the lowest of any discipline except for English; (d) "there are only half a dozen Hispanics who have become established philosophers [i.e., full professors] in the United States,"[6] and most of these philosophers have little or nothing to do with Hispanic issues (as their specialty); (e) the philosophy curriculum, journals, and encyclopedias of philosophy in this country ignore the history of Hispanic philosophy. In summary, Gracia says, it is "quite clear how invisible and unimportant Hispanics still are in the American Philosophical establishment."[7]

Although Gracia presents these statistics, this is hardly the starting point in his own inquiry. The statistics provide further evidence that there is a problem, but the inquiry into these numbers was something that Gracia investigated after first experiencing marginalization as something immediate and personal in his own life. Gracia is one of the few established Hispanic philosophers in our profession and has been a member of the APA for many years. His personal stories about how he has experienced marginalization are in a certain sense primary. It is because we (Hispanics in philosophy) experience marginalization that we may inquiry into numbers. We do not begin our inquiries with a general quest for a predetermined quota for Hispanics or with a preconceived notion of the degree of attention Hispanic issues and philosophers should have in our profession. We engage in inquiries about our marginalization because, to speak crudely, we first "feel" a problem in our everyday interaction within the community of philosophers.[8] The rock-bottom fact is that many of us "feel" marginalized. The experience of marginalization has been described in different ways. It is the experience of feeling "invisible," "unimportant," "alien," "within the boundaries," or "not invited to the table." We (the marginalized) could, of course, be mistaken about what we feel or our feelings may be found out to be pathological, but none of this makes them less real and serious while we are having these experiences. On the other hand, if no Hispanic ever experienced marginalization in our profession, that would be sufficient grounds to be suspicious about the "reality" of the problem. This "empirical" starting point and understanding of the problem is not without difficulties.

A common difficulty about marginalization as a communal problem is that the majority or mainstream may never experience the problem, at least not in the same immediate and evident way that it is present in the everyday life of the marginalized. There is, in other words, an experiential–phenomenological gap between people that belong to the same community. Although marginalization of Hispanics can be a shared problem that we have as a community, it only affects in an immediate and obvious way those who are marginalized. This last gap is a challenge. How can we make mainstream philosophers aware that there is a problem if they do not experience it and may even find comfortable the status quo of the philosophical community? This is where the numbers presented by Gracia may be important. The statistics are important because we want to convince others that there is a problem that requires further inquiry. At the very least, the search for statistical evidence may allow us to convince others that our "feelings" of marginalization are not spurious or pathological.

One could, of course, raise some skepticism about my analysis so far, for it assumes that we can all come to some minimum agreement about what counts as evidence of marginalization as a problem. Moreover, Hispanics may argue that no matter how convincing or alarming the numbers may seem on paper, those in the mainstream will never understand or do anything about it because they are not experiencing it. There is some truth in these responses, but they only point to practical challenges and do not undermine my analysis of the problem of marginalization. They show why marginalization as a communal problem is usually so difficult to ameliorate. I am, however, not ready to give up hope. Historically, there have been similar problems in many communities where the kind of experiential gap mentioned before has not meant a totally unbreachable gap. Even though masters do not experience being a slave, can they not *imagine* what it is like? This last challenge seriously underestimates our empathetic capacity to understand someone else's pains and sufferings. Is it so hard to imagine how others feel when they are marginalized? It is not as if marginalization is a rare type of experience that only a few have ever experienced. In fact, given the many changing and complex communal relations most people get to experience since an early age, it is unlikely that one has not experienced to some degree, and at some point, a bit of marginalization. Many people remember, for example, that classroom or that particular group of friends growing up with in which they felt at times somewhat neglected, invisible, at the fringes, or not "cool" enough to be taken seriously. In any case, why assume that those in the mainstream must, strictly speaking, experience marginalization in the same way as those that are marginalized in order to experienced it as a shared communal problem?

GRACIAS' ACCOUNT OF HISPANIC MARGINALIZATION

In *Hispanic Identity*, Gracia considers different possible explanations for the marginalization of Hispanics in philosophy. Is it our socio-economical status? Is it a language barrier? Cultural differences? Lack of intelligence? He finds none of these possible explanations convincing. Instead, he thinks the answer cannot be pursued without also considering how prone to alienation is our American philosophical community, which he describes as a dysfunctional and changing community centered on the APA. This last institution, as well as the community which it serves, is far from ideal. It is not true that the philosophical community in the United States is centered on the pursuit of wisdom. Philosophical activity in the APA is "a field of competition" where the central quest is "for power and intellectual immortality."[9] The activities of philosophers in America, such as attending conferences, publishing and creating philosophy journals, are mostly about the "power to impose and disseminate one's view."[10]

Neither has there been historically much "unity" in the philosophical community. "The schizophrenic world of contemporary American philosophy" is grounded on the long-standing political tensions between analytic versus the continental philosophers. In recent years, things have gotten worse because there has been a proliferation of new philosophical families and traditions, contributing to further seclusion and isolation of all of its constitutive groups. In our "community," typecasting, censure, political monopolization, exclusion, and isolation are among the many means that have been used to relegate many philosophers to a marginal role. Gracia adds that, "[t]he situation is particularly bad for those who do not belong in any established family, for they are attacked from all sides."[11] Gracia's focus is the situation of Hispanics in the American philosophical community, and the report is not good. Our invisibility is worst than that of blacks and Asians. Why are Hispanics so marginalized? Gracia presents an interesting hypothesis: We are perceived as foreigners. Our "issues and thought are regarded as belonging to a different, non-American culture."[12] In this way, our community resembles the nonphilosophical world. "We are, as a group, alienated and marginalized; that we are considered foreign; and that we are stereotyped in various pernicious ways."[13]

Gracias' hypothesis has been made about Hispanics outside of our particular academic community. Why do Hispanics continue to be experienced as foreigners in the United States? Gracia does not elaborate but he makes reference to the book *Ethnic Labels* by Suzanne Oboler. Oboler explains how and why "people of Latin American descent in the United States have long been perceived homogeneously as "foreign" to the image of "being American."[14] Since the nineteenth century, a series of events have fostered in the United States a national identity based in part in racialized perceptions of all Hispanic groups in and outside the United States. The confusion of race with nationality was the basis of the conception of "foreign others" that both at home and in the hemisphere justified expansionist actions and helped with the problem of national integration. As a result, in the twentieth century, "the community of Americans came to be imagined as white, protestant, and Anglo-Saxon"[15] despite the long-established presence and citizenship of many non-whites. Oboler acknowledges that, as a result of this misidentification, blacks as well as Hispanics have been marginalized—but in different and important ways. The exclusion of African Americans is rooted in slavery. The Civil Rights movement of the 1960s was important in order to get the community of Americans to recognize the rights of blacks but there was never a doubt that they were not "alien," because their birthplace was the United States. In other words, "the exclusion of blacks has not been couched in distortion steaming from xenophobic portrayal of them as foreign born."[16] In summary, blacks and Hispanics have been excluded for similar but also for different reasons. They are both near or outside the boundaries of the imagined national community because they both have the "wrong" color but Hispanics also are "foreign."

The perception of Hispanics in the United States as "foreign," even if unjustified, is not totally groundless in the case of those Hispanics that came recently or that have kept close family and cultural ties to nations in Latin America. For at least there is some "outside reference" in terms of which we could appeal in order to make some sense of the prejudice. It gets more absurd in the cases of Hispanic populations that are native to the United States, as for example those in the south of Texas and California.

If Gracia is correct, then this "foreign" prejudice is so powerful and pervasive that it even affects our philosophical community. I have no reason to doubt Gracia's "foreign" hypothesis. I do, however, have doubts that it adequately captures or explains the full complexity of the problem. I want to supplement his account by suggesting other implicated causes of the problem, and in the last section propose some suggestions about what can be done to ameliorate the problem in light of my analysis.

THE PROBLEMATIC SITUATION OF HISPANICS IN THE U.S. PHILOSOPHICAL COMMUNITY

Gracia's diagnosis of the situation of Hispanics can actually be subjected to two different interpretations. One is that we experience ourselves as marginalized (and sometimes even invisible or alienated) because the mainstream philosophical community excludes us based consciously or unconsciously on the prejudice that we are Hispanics and therefore "foreign" in race or nationality. This would seem to make prejudice the cause of the problem. Another interpretation is that the racism or prejudice against us as "foreign" is just a convenient means used by those in power to perpetuate their status. These two interpretations are not incompatible. It could be that the marginalization of Hispanics is in some instances a consequence of a dominant power group or structure that has clever ways to perpetuate their status quo, and in others it is just simply a consequence of a prejudice or stereotype of Hispanics as "foreign." The first makes the problem of marginalization at bottom political (i.e., the result of power conflict). The second makes the problem of marginalization a matter of a prejudice and ignorance. Shortly, I suggest how best to incorporate these two diagnoses and avoid reductionism in dealing with the problem. For now, I want to continue to explore other factors not mentioned by Gracia that may add to the complexity of the problem.

There are other facts of the situation in the community of philosophers here and abroad that can make someone question Gracia's assessment of the problem. For comparison, I highlight the marginalization of two other groups of philosophers in order to examine how their situation correlates with Gracia's hypothesis. One of them is the marginalization of "American philosophers" in the United States, and the other one is the marginalization of Hispanic philosophers in Latin America.

By "American philosophers" I mean those philosophy scholars (like myself) who have made their specialty the study and further development of the thought of the classical American philosophers (including Charles Peirce, William James, and John Dewey). Here are some facts. You can easily get a PhD in philosophy in America without knowing anything about the American philosophical tradition. Most new PhDs in philosophy know a lot more about the analytic and continental traditions than about the classical American tradition. If they heard about Peirce, James, or Dewey, it is only because some continental figure (e.g., Habermas) or some analytic philosophers (Davidson, Quine) have mentioned them as an influence or have acknowledged a historical connection. Very few students in philosophy are encouraged to study classical American figures. They have no incentive to do so because it is not trendy or mainstream (i.e., neither analytic nor continental). Today to work in the American philosophical tradition is usually regarded as an exercise in historical curiosity or equivalent to the study of the history of philosophy. For sure, it is not regarded as something that has any significant philosophical relevance to the "serious" or "cutting-edge" issues that concern the most recent "stars" or "big-shot" philosophers. Prospective PhDs in philosophy are discouraged from specializing in American philosophy simply because there are hardly any job openings in this area. The majority of philosophy departments in the United States do not even have one scholar specializing in the classical American tradition and, more importantly, they do not care that they do not. There are only two journals in the nation that would publish anything in this area. Furthermore, at a more direct or social level specialists in American philosophy experience marginalization in the APA. The Society for the Advancement of American Philosophy (SAAP) had to be created many years ago in order to counteract the alienation and invisibility felt by many American philosophy scholars in the APA.

As a member of both groups, I must confess that the marginalization of Hispanic philosophers is worse than the marginalization of American philosophers, but this is a difference of degree that should not be surprising. What is surprising, or at least in need of an explanation, is why American philosophers are marginalized in America *at all*. This puzzle does not fit very well with Gracia's hypothesis that we have been considering. You would think that if the U.S. philosophical community is prone to exclude and marginalize what it perceives as "nationally foreign," then it welcomes better what is not foreign and is "native," such as its homegrown philosophy. However, my personal experience and the evidence just discussed suggest that they do not. What do we make of this inconsistency? Perhaps the main reason behind the marginalization of these two different groups is just different, but this comparison does show how complex are the causes of marginalization. Certainly, it makes me doubt seriously that if we could somehow tomorrow remove the "foreign" prejudice against Hispanic philosophy and philosophers it would remove their marginalization. If the "national" philosophy is marginalized, then changing the dominant image of what is "American" to include Hispanic Americans may be insufficient. Although I do not deny the role that race and nationality plays in marginalization within our philosophical community, it seems that it is not the whole story. I suggest that perhaps the reasons for exclusion and marginalization of Hispanics in philosophy also has something to do with having certain preconceptions of what is or is not good philosophy and a good philosopher, so that any philosophy or philosopher that does not meet these preconceptions or standards can be ignored and excluded. Here are some possible prejudices that may operate in this way in our philosophical community:

Professional Prejudice

Good philosophy and philosophers are determined by their current reputation or status in philosophy as a "profession." The *professionalization* of philosophy as a discipline is a recent phenomenon. It means that, in some respect, we are not any different from bankers and lawyers. To "succeed" in a profession requires that we have more than the required licenses, memberships, and specialization. It also requires that we pay attention to the current and latest rankings, trends, and reputation. (Is this why the Leiter Report has become so important?) Professionalism, however, cannot be separated from the institutions that ground and sustain our profession.

Our universities compete for better rankings and reputation from national magazines. We learn early on in our profession the importance of choosing the "best" universities from which to get a degree and at which to teach. Hence, if someone wants to "succeed" in philosophy as a profession he or she must keep up with the most recent implicit or explicit "standards" in the profession. The upshot of all this is that the "successful" philosopher not only needs to know whom and what to seek (philosophers, journals, associations) but also whom to ignore, avoid, or exclude. In other words, "success" in our profession requires that we learn to contribute to marginalization. At this point in time, it is unwise to associate with American philosophers and Hispanic philosophers if we want to be "successful."

Eurocentric Prejudice

Good philosophies and philosophers come from or have their roots in European philosophical traditions (e.g., England, Germany, or France). This prejudice is deep and functions differently depending on who are the marginalized. Hispanic and American philosophy are, for some people, considered marginal or secondary to the more serious philosophical traditions. For they are both only indirectly or remotely connected (historically, ethnically) to "The source" of all good and serious philosophy. This is the appropriate place to bring up the second marginalized group for comparision: Hispanic philosophers in Latin America. There has been plenty of testimony about their similar experiences of marginalization. In a recent paper, Carlos Pereda, former president of the Mexican philosophical association, says "We are invisible: this melancholic assertion alludes to the"'non-place' that we occupy as Latin American philosophers or, in general, as philosophers in the Spanish or Portuguese languages. We tend to survive as mere ghosts, teaching courses and writing texts, perhaps some memorable ones, which, however, seldom spark anybody's interest."[17] Among the causes of invisibility, Pereda mentions the "colonial mentality" or the inferiority complex that has remained in Latin America; but this is another name or manifestation of what I have called the "European prejudice."

Prejudice About the Nature of Philosophy

Good or serious philosophy and philosophers are only those who are concerned with certain topics or problems and philosophize with certain methods or styles. Philosophers have preconceptions about the nature of good philosophy that are independent from their views about their profession or the national origins of a philosophy. For some people, American philosophers and Hispanic philosophers are not concerned with "serious" philosophical problems, or do not follow the methods that are at the very heart of serious philosophical inquiry. Of the three prejudices presented, this one seems harder to support in relation to the groups that we have described as marginalized. There is plenty of diversity in problems and methods among their members. Nevertheless, it is an important complement of this prejudice to assume a stereotype that homogenizes what these groups of philosophers do. For example, there is the one that American philosophers are just concerned with the history of philosophy (i.e., getting right what Dewey and James actually said and when). They have nothing to contribute to serious "cutting-edge" philosophy. In the case of Hispanic philosophers, the stereotype seems to be that they are just philosophers concerned with the problems of their community and not with the universal problems of philosophy.

If I am right that some of the prejudices disccussed here contribute to the marginalization of Hispanics in the philosophical community, then the situation is more complex than suggested by Gracia. The "foreign prejudice" is only one among several prejudices that keep Hispanics marginalized. Suppose we add all of the prejudices to a fuller diagnosis of the problem, even then we would only be scratching the surface. Is the problem of marginalization of Hispanics just a matter of prejudice? Or is the core really a political power issue (e.g., because white male Anglo-Saxon philosophers dominate our community)? To what extent is it also a problem about systematic and institutional ways of excluding individuals based on perceived differences? In any case, what follows from marginalization conceived as caused by prejudices in terms of ways to effectively ameliorate the problem? These all are important issues that I cannot fully consider here but that are key to finding out what needs to be done.

Before concluding with some positive suggestions or proposals that are implied in this inquiry, I add one more consideration that, although adding complexity to an already difficult problem, also opens up a promising handle and new possibilities for inquiry. Marginalization sometimes functions as a habit. I agree with John Dewey (and the pragmatist tradition) about the importance of habits. It may be worthwhile to think of the problem of marginalization of Hispanics in philosophy also a problem at the level of habits. First a word about what I mean by "habits."

Habit is an organism's subconscious predisposition to transact with others in particular ways. They are constitutive of a self, but of a self that cannot be separated from its environment. Habits cover not only the ordinary way of doing things, but a broad spectrum of tendencies and dispositions, dominant ways of acting, ways or modes of response, abilities, attitudes, sensitivities, accessibilities, predilections, and aversions. "Habits are the fibre of character, but there are habits of desire and imagination as well as of outer action" (LW 9:187). When one develops a habit, what one has acquired is not a possession within the confines of a self but a *way of interacting* within a social and natural environment. Habits permit the everyday unreflective flow of action. Since habits are allocated in both individuals and the world in which they live, a change in a self cannot be separated from changes in the environment. In fact, they are mutually dependant. The habits of the self are more likely to be changed by indirect means (i.e., changing the environment or social interactions that it is a part of and sustains the habits of the self). As Shannon Sullivan explains:

> A person cannot merely intellectualize a change of habit by telling herself that she will no longer think or behave in particular ways. The key to transformation is to find a way of disrupting a habit through environmental change and then hope that the changed environment will help produced an improved habit in its place.[18]

How can the notion of "habit" be useful to an inquiry about the problem of marginalization of Hispanics? If all of the prejudices (including the foreign prejudice) mentioned here function at the level of habits, then the problem is not simply a matter of ignorance about American history or Hispanics. To correct the "foreign prejudice" may require more than argumentation. It may require disrupting habits of the imagination. Isn't what needs to be changed the dominant and habitual *image* of Americans? The way in which people habitually imagine and define their national community changes and is reinforced in the popular mind by institutions and the media (including TV and Hollywood). If this is correct, then we should engage in criticism of the institutions and media that reinforce the habits and the narrow images of America.

We must also consider seriously the possibility that the privileged position of a few and the marginalization of other groups in our philosophical communities may be an environmentally constituted habit. Marginalization, priviledge, exclusion, and racism are things that often function in an "invisible" way (especially to the ones that are privileged). This is only because habits are the things we do without thinking. Philosophers are always concerned with ideas that are the object of their conscious attention or reflection, but they participate-interact with other philosophers in nonconscious habitual ways. Today, there may well be plenty of conscious and deliberate efforts by some philosophers in the APA to exclude and make invisible other philosophers. I doubt, however, that most philosophers in the APA that enjoy the priviledge to be part of the mainstream would openly proclaim that they purposely or actively exclude others or attempt to make them invisible. Indeed, many would openly deny that they believe that any of the above prejudices actually contribute to the marginalization of Hispanics. This does not mean, however, that they do not contribute to the experience of marginalization of others. To find out if we contribute to the problem of marginalization, it is not enough to run an introspective search into what we believe or discern our conscious intentions to be. Just as important is to address the issue of how we actually transact with others when we attend an APA meeting as well as the character of our participations in the community (e.g., referring journals, reviewing books, conducting interviews).

CONCLUSION: HOW TO INQUIRE INTO THE PROBLEM OF MARGINALIZATION OF HISPANICS?

What I have presented is a preliminary and tentative analysis of the problem, one that supplements and advances the inquiry started by Jorge Gracia. There clearly is much work to be done. Although I do not offer *the* solution to the problem of marginalization of Hispanics, my analysis has some important positive implications about how to continue to inquire into the problem and how to search for its amelioration. In conclusion, then, I offer the following important observations:

1. We must avoid reductionism and oversimplification in any inquiry into the problem of marginalization. The difficulty with marginalization is that it usually is experienced as a problem with a plurality and unique set of causes or factors, where none is reducible to the other but coexist in an "organic" relation to each other. Although I have no reason to doubt that there is a "foreign prejudice" against Hispanics, there are other prejudices that contribute to the marginalization of Hispanics, including the "professional prejudice," the "Eurocentric prejudice," and the "prejudice about the nature of philosophy." Furthermore, we must be careful not to reduce marginalization to a problem centered on prejudices, as if it is merely a problem of ignorance, or a matter of changing peoples beliefs ("their minds"). Beyond or besides educating people, we may have to bring about more fundamental changes in political relationships, economic resources, institutions, and the environment. This is not to say that a prejudice is (or that prejudices are) only a consequence or a by product of any of the other factors, as if to ameliorate the problem of marginalization we can just put our efforts in changing these basic factors.

We must avoid the tendency (temptation) to reduce the problem either to a problem of individual psychology or to a social, economical, or political problem. Instead, marginalization is a problem that must be engaged at *all* ends of the spectrum of factors that can be distinguished by reflection. A complex "organic" problem requires an intelligent organic approach.[19] That is, it requires not only that we ameliorate the problem from all sides, but that we are alert to how one side affects, sustains, and nourishes the other.

2. Oversimplification is avoided and inquiry seems effective if we take seriously how habits operate in our everyday experience. The immediate association or perception that many have in our community of Hispanics as "foreign" is something that has deep historical roots outside the philosophical community and does not always operate as a belief or proposition; it operates as the product of a nonconscious habit. Habits are hard but not impossible to change or control. They must be subjected to reflection, criticism, and conscious influence but we also must not be naïve to think that we can directly, and by a single act of fiat change our habits. Making those who are unconsciously excluding or enjoying priviledge aware of what they are doing (i.e., the object of conscious reflection) is certainly a step in the right direction, but we also must not delude ourselves in thinking that it is sufficient. Becoming aware of what we are doing is not always sufficient to change what we are doing. Perhaps some indirect strategies where we change the environments that "feed" our habits of perceptions and association is required to change how Hispanics are perceived in the philosophical community. The way to combat marginalization is not just by direct argumentation or information; we must find ways to impact unconscious habits by means that engage people's imaginations, perhaps via literature, art, and film.

3. The problem of marginalization of Hispanics is grounded on concrete problematic experiences. Any empirical inquiry into the causes of marginalization must begin with and take seriously the experience of marginalization, instead of an a priori search and application of a predetermined, theoretical criterion of marginalization. This experiential approach is not without difficulties. I have only mentioned a few here but more should be investigated. Although marginalization of Hispanics can be said to be a problem of the philosophical community as a whole, we must be attentive to the "experiential gap" mentioned between the marginalized and the ones doing the marginalizing. We must find ways to narrow this gap so that most people in the philosophical community become aware and concerned about marginalization as a shared problem that requires amelioration. Ideally, this would require an open dialogue where the marginalized share their experiences and the rest of the community is receptive and empathetic. I am not naïve enough to think that this will happen any time soon. There may well be political and institutional obstacles that must be removed before we can even dream of having such a dialogue. Meanwhile, it is important that Hispanics bring all of the evidence we can gather to provoke criticism, reflection, and more dialogue within the APA. We need to find ways to convince others that there is a problem that requires further inquiry.

NOTES

1. Jorge J.E. Gracia, *Hispanic/Latino Identity: A Philosophical Perspective*, (Malden, Mass: Blackwell Publishers, 2000), pp. 159–188.

2. Gracia, p. 175.

3. For more on what it means to be a contextualist about judgment see my *John Dewey's Ethics: Democracy as Experience* (Indiana University Press, 2008).

4. Gracia, p. 162. I thank George Yancy for the correction.

5. Gracia, p. 160.

6. Gracia, p. 161.

7. Gracia, p. 162.

8. Philosophical support for this view of inquiry can be found in the writings of Charles Peirce and John Dewey.

9. Gracia, p. 171.

10. Gracia, p. 175.

11. Gracia, p. 173.

12. Gracia, p. 159.

13. Gracia, p. 167.

14. Suzanne Oboler *Ethnic Labels, Latino Lives: Identity and the Politics of (Re) Presentation in the United States* (Minneapolis: University of Minnesota Press, 1995), p. 18.

15. Oboler, p.19.

16. Oboler, p. 32.

17. Carlos Pereda, "Latin American Philosophy: Some Vices" *Journal of Speculative Philosophy*, Vol. 20, 3, p. 192.

18. Shannon Sullivan, *Revealing Whiteness: The Unconscious Habits of Racial Privilege* (Bloomington, IN: Indiana University Press, 2006), p. 9.

19. For more about this general approach to social problems see my "The Role of the Philosopher in the Pragmatic Approach to Racism" in *Pragmatism and the Problems of Race* edited by Bill E. Lawson and Donald F. Koch, Indiana University Press (2004).

CHAPTER NINE

PHILOSOPHICAL PLAYA HATIN'

Race, Respect, and the Philosophy Game

Bill E. Lawson

There is a saying commonly expressed in the black American community: "Don't hate the playa, hate the game." There are some people out there who are just "haters." We all know someone who is a "hater." In fact you may be a "hater" yourself. What is a hater? A hater is a person who dislikes or feels resentment when another person has some success. "Hatin'" also takes place when one person does well in a certain endeavor and another person begins to discount the accomplishment or disparage the person. Hatin' is not uncommon. People in nearly all walks of life "hate" at some point. There are always people who we think do not deserve their success and we think it is our job to remind them. Although most people will not admit to hatin', in moments of self-reflection we must admit that we all have "hated." I must admit that *hater* is not a term that one finds used in academic discourse or writing. One will never find the term used as I use it here in works of academic philosophical writings. This may reflect the efforts of many philosophers to maintain the "purity" of philosophical discourse. Although philosophers may not use the word, they often practice the deed. They hate. In fact, there are some people in the academy who "hate" on philosophers of color. Truth must be told and this chapter is about hatin' or more specifically philosophical playa hatin'.

DEFINING TERMS

The terms *player* and *game* need explanation here. The term *player* denotes someone who participates or is skilled in some game. A *game* is seen as

181

any competitive endeavor. When there are situations where we have winners and losers, we have both players and a game. In this sense, the game
analogy is used to cover many of our life experiences. Thus, players can be
found in many areas of social endeavors, sports, politics, entertainment, and
the academy. Michael Jordan, Cheryl Miller, Barack Obama, Condoleezza
Rice, Will Smith, Vanessa Williams, Cornel West, and Anita Allen all are
examples of players in some of life's games. They have been successful in
their chosen fields of endeavor. In street parlance, the term is *playa*. In this
arena, the term *playa* often has a sexual connotation denoting someone who
is into and very successful at sexual conquests. But the term also is used
to denote someone who is successful in his or her social endeavors. Here,
I need to make some additional comments because one of my graduate
students accused me of doing what old people often do; they misuse words
that younger people understand in a particular way. My graduate student
claimed that my use of persons like West, Rice, and Obama as playas was
a misuse of the term. It would be like a father trying to be hip saying to
his son, "You're my Shorty." The father over heard the son use the term
in a conversation and decided to show how hip he had become. Of course,
the father's use of the term is off the mark. The father meant that the son
was someone special to him. The term has a number of street meanings but
let me cite two of the most common: a *shorty* is a cute young woman or
someone who is new to a street hustle or game. The father's use of the term
given these meanings is actually misused. If we accept the student's claim,
then "playa" has a class-specific meaning and being a "playa" means not
being in the mainstream. Street hustlers, pimps, and other denizens of the
street could be players but not mainstream figures. Although I understand
my student's concerns, I see no reason to limit the use of the terms *player*
or *playa* to a particular socioeconomic group or specific social endeavors. I
am using the terms *player* and *playa* as synonyms. Whereas the term *playa*
may be part of the current colloquial black lexicon, the term *player* has a
long history in the black community. Heavyweight champion Jack Johnson
was a *player* or *playa* in and out of the boxing ring.

Here, I use the game and playa analogy to explore the relationship
between non-white and white players in the academic game. Working in
the academy is playing a game. There are skills that have to be learned and
there are winners and losers (as shown in Table 9.1).

In this sense, being in the academy is playing the career game. There
are star players and there are supporting players. The "game" is an endeavor
that a person participates in and where one can be a winner or a loser. The
individuals cited previously (i.e., Obama, Rice, West, et al.) all are winners
in their professional areas. They play their particular games well and are successful. There are all types of games. Being successful in the academic arena

Table 9.1. Winners and Losers in the Academy Game

Winners	Losers
Tenured	Untenured and let go with no job prospects
Writer of well-respected articles	Writer of mediocre articles
Respected in area of specialization	Not known after years in the profession
Teaching at a major prestigious research institution	Teaching at a small nonprestigious teaching college after many years

is being able to play the scholarship, research, publication, and personality game well enough to be a winner in the academy. In the street life there is a certain amount of respect players in the game show each other. You respect the player's abilities and achievements. Many scholars of color do not feel that their white counterparts respect them. The rules of the academic game are fairly clear. You publish in respected journals, write books that add to the knowledge of your area of specialization, and give presentations at noteworthy places. In the endm you should have name recognition among your peers and hopefully their respect.

RACISM IN THE ACADEMY

When scholars of color come into the academic game, they appreciate that the playing field is not level. The field is tilted; "tinged" with racism. They hope that if they publish in the right journals, become tenured, and have name recognition in their area of specialization, the players in the academic game will show them some respect. It is the lack of respect that often makes playing the game so difficult. It is hoped that your fellow players will respect you and treat you with respect. Those persons, in this case white philosophers who are colleagues, who dislike the accomplishments of minority philosophers and minorities in the academy, more generally, are guilty of "playa hatin'." How often have we heard our white colleagues comment negatively about the success of their non-white colleagues? "The study of race or the black experience in philosophy is not really doing philosophy." This is hatin'.

A classic example may be the experience of Cornel West at Harvard. The word on the street is that Harvard president Lawrence Summers rebuked West's work for lack of academic rigor. Although there may have been other concerns, West's work with members of the hip-hop community was not seen as the type of scholarship worthy of a senior Harvard professor.

Even those philosophers at prestigious universities are suspect, particularly if they work in areas of race or Africana philosophy. The black philosopher's work, no matter how highly regarded it may be outside of the philosophical circle, is never seen as having philosophical merit. It often is questioned as to whether the work is even philosophy.

West felt that he was not respected or being respected by Harvard's president. Consider the reasons that West may have felt disrespected.

1. Disrespected as a scholar

2. Disrespected as a black man

3. Disrespected as a scholar doing research on the black experience

4. Disrespected as a university professor

5. Disrespected as a person

Players want respect from other players. West felt he had been a faithful player and should have garnered the respect of his white colleagues in the academy. What behavior or attitudes should/could have been shown West to "assure" him that the president's comments were not a sign of disrespect? This is a difficult question because showing respect may be more complicated than we think. Knowing when one has been shown respect may be just as problematic.

What does it mean to be respected when one is a member of a group that is in the minority in the academy? Although the concept of respect has been the focus of a great deal of philosophical debate, what it means to respect another person is still unclear. This is particularly true when we consider the type of respect that should be accorded members of groups, for example, black men, white women, and black women,[1] that have been thought of as not full members of the human community. Stephen Darwall's insightful article "Two Kinds of Respect"[2] is somewhat helpful here:

> The appeal to respect also figures in much of recent discussion of more specific moral problems such as racism and sexism. For example, it is argued that various ways of regarding and behaving towards others, and social arrangements which encourage those ways, are inconsistent with the respect to which all persons are entitled.[3]

Fortunately, some philosophers have turned their attention to respect in this area. Darwall again:

> The claim that all persons are entitled to respect just by virtue of being persons may not seem wholly unproblematic, however. How

could respect be something which is due to all persons? Do we not also think that persons can either deserve or fail to deserve our respect? Is the moralist who claims that all persons are entitled to respect advocating that we give up this idea? Questions of this sort should call into question just what respect itself is.[4]

Questions like the ones above should indicate that our understanding of respect still needs some work. This is particularly true when we consider the respect that should be accorded persons of color in the academy. Darwall wants to show the relationship between respect and self-respect. I only focus on the manner in which lack of respect can be shown to persons of color as persons.

Darwall thinks that there are two interrelated conceptions of respect that often are combined. The two different ways in which a person may be respected provide but one instance of a more general difference between two attitudes that are both termed *respect*.[5] These are recognition respect and appraisal respect. Recognition respect is "a kind of respect which can have any number of different sorts of things as its object and which consists, most generally, in a disposition to weigh appropriately in one's deliberations some feature of the thing in question and act accordingly."[6] Examples of such objects, according to Darwall, are the law, a person's feelings, social institutions, and the social roles person occupy. This kind of respect consists in giving appropriate consideration or recognition to some feature of the object:[7]

> Persons can be the object of recognition respect. Indeed, it is just this sort of respect which is said to be owed to all persons. To say that persons as such are entitled to respect is to say that they are entitled to have other persons take seriously and weigh appropriately the fact that they are persons in deliberating about what to do. Such respect is recognition respect; but what it requires as appropriate is not a matter of general agreement, this is just the question of what our moral obligations or duties to other persons consists in. The crucial point is that to conceive of all persons as entitled to respect is to have some consideration of what sort of consideration the fact of being a person requires.[8]

A person may not only be the object of recognition respect as a person but as a person occupying a particular social role. To fail to take seriously the person as the presented self in one's responses to the person is to fail to give the person recognition respect as that presented self or in that role.[9]

Darwall argues that there is a close relationship between recognition respect and appraisal respect. Appraisal respect consists in a positive appraisal of a person, or his or her qualities:[10]

Typically, when we speak of someone as meriting or deserving our respect, it is appraisal respect that we have in mind. We mean that the person is such as to merit our positive appraisal on the appropriate grounds. It is true that in order to indicate or express such respect, certain behavior from us will be appropriate. But unlike recognition respect, appraisal respect does not itself consist in that behavior or in judgment that is appropriate. Rather, it consists in the appraisal itself.[11]

It is recognition respect and appraisal respect given to persons that is the major focus of Darwall's article. He thinks that there is a connection between our appraisal respect and our recognition respect in that the characteristic we deem important in persons qua persons can impact on our appraisal of persons. In his example of the tennis player, Darwall notes that the tennis player can be respected for his or her backhand and yet not be respected as a person because he or she appears to exhibit a lack of the characteristics that we think worthy of respect as a person. For example, the player exhibits a bad attitude toward other players on and off the court and other persons in general:

> Which Features of persons are properly regarded as features of their character and hence as appropriate grounds for appraisal respect? Being resolute and being honest are character traits. Being prone to sneeze in the presence of pepper is not. But there are difficult cases as well. How about being irascible? Or being good natured? Or prudent? Discerning? Sensitive?[12]

Darwall adds, "The notion of character (whether of persons or other things) seems to involve the idea of relatively long-term dispositions. But not all long-term dispositions of persons are held to be part of their characters. The question then becomes, which such dispositions constitute character?"[13]

Darwall thinks that the Kantian conception of the person as a moral agent is the basis for appraisal respect. He argues:

> If the appropriate conception of the person which is relevant to appraisal respect is that of a moral agent, then one would expect our notion of character to be likewise ties to such a conception. I think that this is indeed the case. The dispositions which constitute character (at least as it is relevant to appraisal respect) are dispositional to act for certain reasons, that is to act, and in acting to have certain reasons for acting. For example, honesty is a disposition to do what ones takes to be honest partly for the reason that it is

what honesty requires. Aristotle's theory of virtue and Kant's theory of the moral worth of actions both stress that what is appropriate to the assessment of persons is not merely what they do, but as importantly, their reasons for doing it.[14]

The respected person must have the ability to act for the right reasons. What is referred to here is not a disposition to act for any particular reason, but rather the higher-level disposition to act on what one takes to be the best reasons whatever they may be. Thus, the conception of character that is relevant to appraisal respect includes both rather more specific dispositions to act for certain reasons and the higher-level disposition to do that which one takes to be supported by the best reasons.[15] First, Darwall notes that we can have a positive appraisal for a person not grounded in our respect for him or her as a person. The person we need for a bank job may exhibit character traits that make him or her a good accomplice.[16] Second, he notes that appraisal respect admits of degrees:

Appraisal respect is something which one may have or fail to have for someone, and it is an attitude which admits of degree. One may respect someone more than someone else. When we speak of having respect for someone what is implied is an appraisal of him as satisfactory with respect to the appropriate grounds. Many attitudes have this sort of structure. We speak alternatively of liking or not liking things as well as of liking something more than something else.[17]

Darwall thinks, "Appraisal respect is an attitude of positive appraisal of a person either judged as a person or as engaged in some more specific pursuit."[18] He argues that there is a difference between recognition respect and appraisal respect in that recognition respect is to give appropriate weight to the fact that the person is a person in our deliberations. Following Kant, Darwall thinks, "Recognition respect for persons, then, is identical with recognition respect for the moral requirements that are placed on one by the existence of other persons."[19] The difference between recognition respect and appraisal respect is that recognition respect does not admit of degrees. For example, he maintains:

What sense can be given, however, to degree of recognition respect? For example, a person might think that we should have more respect for people's feelings than for social conventions. Presumably what such a person thinks is that we ought to weight other people's feelings more heavily than we do considerations of social conventions.

Insofar as we can give a sense to have more recognition respect for one thing than another it involves a disposition to take certain considerations as more weighty than others in deciding how to act. There is, of course, a kind of appraisal involved here. But it is not an appraisal of a person as such, but of the weight that some fact or feature ought to have in one's deliberations about what to do, and if all persons as such should be treated equally, there can be no degrees of recognition respect for them, although one may be a greater or lesser respecter of persons.[20]

It is the very important fact that one is a person with certain natural abilities that we should accord him or her with recognition respect. According to Darwall, the distinction between appraisal and recognition respect allows us to see why there is "no puzzle at all in thinking both that all persons are entitled to respect just by virtue of their being persons and that persons are deserving of more or less respect by virtue of their personal characteristics."[21]

To highlight the connection between recognition respect and appraisal respect, Darwall notes that we connect a person's ability to exhibit the appropriate objects of recognition (behavior) for recognition respect in our appraisal of that person. This connects the person's character with our appraisal. Important for our discussion of playa hatin' is his next comment:

The only beings who are appropriate objects of appraisal respect are those who are capable of acting for reasons and hence capable of conceiving of various facts as meriting more or less consideration in deliberation. Once again, so much is entailed by the account of character. Because of the particular sorts of reasons which are relevant to our assessment of character, we many say that the only beings who are appropriate objects of appraisal respect are those who are themselves capable of recognition respect, that is of acting deliberately.[22]

Darwall notes that one can have both appraisal and recognition respect for oneself. This is self-respect. Thus, West's leaving Harvard shows that he is self-respecting in that he did not want to be shown disrespect as a person nor as a black man.

Is this the end of the story? Unfortunately not! Laurence Thomas presents us with other considerations regarding respect in his article "Moral Equality and Natural Inferiority."[23] Thomas writes: "I wish to raise a question in moral psychology concerning the wherewithal it takes to have moral respect for a group of people deemed to be substantially inferior intellectually in virtue of their group membership—say, race or gender."[24] Thomas correctly notes that hardly anyone would accept the claim that some people are intellectually inferior. He says:

> The issue of whether considerable intellectual inferiority on the part of a group is a significant barrier to having moral respect for them is nicely raised in Kant's work. As is well known, Kant made unequivocally clear in his anthropological writings that he took blacks to be quite inferior intellectually.[25]

There have been attempts to show that Kant's moral theory is not touched by his racist anthropology.[26]

> It is the view that individuals are worthy of moral respect in virtue of their personhood (and therefore regardless of their intellectual inferiority) that is invoked to maintain that the intellectually inferior do not present a problem when it comes to the matter of being shown moral respect.[27]

Thomas thinks that showing respect for the intellectually inferior is more difficult than often imagined, if the inferiority is great enough.[28] Thomas' aim in the article is neither to show that Kant nor his moral theory were racist, but to point out that his theory does not do all one might want it to do.

Thomas' work is in moral psychology. He argues that even if Kant is correct that we should treat persons with moral respect, there is a serious problem when a group is deemed intellectually inferior and this inferiority is unequivocal and ineliminable. The intellectual inferiority is a part of their character. It is something that sets them apart from other "normal" persons. Our appraisal of them will be different than our appraisal of persons with normal intelligence. No matter what they do they will not be evaluated in the same manner as a "normal" person. Thomas thinks that this is not as much of a problem in a society (world scenario [WS]2) where the inferiority was randomly scattered among persons (Betas) who cannot be identified by their phenotype. Although it may be difficult if the intellectual inferiority is great, people will be disposed to act with regard and consideration because they can always say there for but the grace of God go I. The situation is different in a society (WS1) where the inferiority is connected with and identified with a particular group (Omegas) with its racial phenotype. In this case if the inferiority is severe enough, Thomas thinks that it will be very difficult if not impossible for members of the intellectually superior group (non-Omegas) to know what it would mean to show respect for members

of the intellectually inferior group (Omegas). This is particularly true if it
appears that members of the intellectually inferior group are incapable of
being seen as persons who can have ends. If this is true of a group, then
knowing how to show them respect becomes difficult. If Darwall is correct,
we draw our appraisal respect from our recognition respect. Our recognition
respect will draw our attention to the features or characteristics that should
be considered for appraisal of the person. In this regard, a person must be
able to be "capable of acting for reasons and hence capable of conceiving
of various facts as meriting more or less consideration in deliberation." This
would leave out those persons who are so intellectually inferior that they
cannot act using higher-order reasoning. They cannot even see "themselves
as Legislators of universal moral law or members of the Kingdom of Ends."

A rather lengthy quote may help to highlight Thomas' point. Thomas
thinks that the analogy between two types of automobiles can help us see
the problem more clearly. A Mercedes-Benz and a Ford Pinto are both cars
but they are evaluated differently:

> A Ford Pinto has much less horsepower than a Mercedes-Benz
> that has, say, 500 horsepower. Let us suppose that a Pinto in good
> condition is a 200-horsepower car. A defective Mercedes may actu-
> ally be capable of only 200 horsepower, and so be equivalent in
> horsepower to a Pinto. In that case both cars lack 500 horsepower.
> But it is only the Mercedes and not the Pinto-that lacks what it
> ought to have or would have if it were as it should be. A Ford
> Pinto lacks 500 horsepower; and this lack is not a defect on its part.
> Instead, that is precisely the way that it should be. So a Pinto's
> lack of 500 horsepower accords with its constitutional make-up. A
> Ford Pinto is simply not in the same league as a Mercedes Benz,
> though both are indisputably cars. It is not possible for an informed
> person to expect a non-defective Ford Pinto to perform like a
> non-defective Mercedes-Benz. In (WS2), the Betas who are vastly
> deficient intellectually are rather like a defective Mercedes-Benz,
> whereas in (WS1), the vastly deficient intellectually, namely the
> Omegas, are rather like a Ford Pinto. Notwithstanding the fact that
> non-Omegas recognize that Omegas are persons, the non-Omegas
> view the difference between themselves and Omegas in accordance
> with the sharp reality that distinguishes the two groups. The his-
> tory of the world shows that viewing someone as a human being
> does not require putting her or him on the same plane as oneself
> either morally or intellectually. It is clear that Kant thought that
> blacks were persons. However, in Kant's day this did not settle as
> much as one might suppose in terms of moral expectations. For

Kant the idea of a person had to be necessarily a normative one, in that he could not have thought that everyone who is called a person (such as the mentally unstable) possesses all the qualities of personhood that a person would have were her or his development as it should be. Thus, he could consistently think that blacks are persons without thinking that they possess the wherewithal to follow the moral law as whites do.[29]

Thomas notes that Kantians might argue that it is difficult but not impossible to treat those persons deemed morally inferior with the same respect given to the nonintellectually inferior. The difficulty, however, is something we are less obligated to do:

> Kant's theory does not say that it will be equally easy to respect all individuals in virtue of their personhood. With perfect consistency, Kant could have held that respecting the moral personhood of blacks requires more concentration or more reminders around the home or whatever than does respecting the moral personhood of white Europeans, but that blacks are owed such respect nonetheless.[30]

The problem is that if members of a group are so intellectually inferior that they have no respect for themselves, they do not understand what one is doing, when shown respect they do not act appropriately, and the entire group is constitutionally incapable of reciprocating by doing likewise, what it means to respect them will be problematic.[31] For these reasons, Thomas thinks there will be a reluctance to show members of the intellectually inferior group moral respect. Even if we want to be a good Kantian, Thomas thinks that the failure to reciprocate appropriately by the intellectually inferior will lead to resentment that is understandable. Darwall would have to agree that a lack of intelligence would be a fact in our deliberations about how to recognize persons and how to appraise their actions. If intelligence is connected to character, then lack of intelligence will impact on character. If intelligence is a character trait, it must be taken into account in both our recognition of personhood and our appraisal of persons.

This appears to be Kant's position. Although he had little to no interaction with blacks his respect for their intelligence and their personhood was low because they were blacks. He writes in "On the use of Teleological Principles in Philosophy":

> In Sprengel's Contributions, Fifth Part, pp. 287–92, a knowledgeable man states, in opposition to Ramsay's desire to make use of all Negro slaves as free workers, that, among the many thousand freed Negros

that one meets in America and England, he is acquainted with no instance in which anyone of them has ever pursued an occupation that one can really call work. To the contrary, he says that when such slaves get their freedom they immediately give up the easy work they had previously been forced to do as slaves in order to become hawkers, miserable innkeepers, livery stable workers, always going fishing or hunting, or, in one word, petty hustlers. One also finds exactly the same pattern of behavior in the gypsies among us.[32]

Kant seems to think that blacks were so intellectually inferior that they could not be persons with ends of their own. Once set free from the forced labor of slavery they would become idle. How does one respect someone who is so intellectually inferior that none of our standard conceptions of morality and standards of behavior means anything to him or her? If our appraisal of a person is connected to our recognition of that person as a person, the person having a lack of intelligence will impact on our recognition respect and our appraisal of that person's actions and behavior, especially if the intellect is very low to none at all.

As noted, Thomas' aim in his paper is to show that the use of Kant may not give one what one wants when it comes to respecting persons who are deemed radically different. My use of Thomas is to highlight the manner in which racism and racist practices have fostered in the minds of many whites and some blacks that blacks cannot be appraised in the same manner as whites because they are morally and intellectually inferior. Although both black and white activists have consistently challenged this position, the idea that blacks are intellectually inferior still haunts the achievements of black scholars.

Thomas' paper points out how deeply we have been impacted by Kant; that is, the belief that we can respect a person no matter how little regard we have for him or her as a person. The fact that the being is a person means that there should be some minimal recognition respect given. We can admit to degrees of appraisal respect but as long as the person is a physical person we should and can show recognition respect. Thomas forces us to rethink this Kantian point. If he is correct that persons can be off the moral radar and thus not worthy of moral respect, at that point it becomes less clear how to treat that "object." In this case, they are not worthy of recognition or appraisal respect. This also seems to raise questions about the role of empathy in the treatment of persons. If whites cannot recognize blacks as "normal" persons and if the intellectual acumen of blacks is so much lower, it will be difficult if not impossible to empathize with them. Historically the debates between Frederick Douglass and Martin Delaney highlight this concern. Douglass thought that whites could come to respect blacks through moral suasion. Delaney thought that whites saw blacks as irredeemably other. In this context, whites could never look at blacks and say, "There but for the grace of God go I." Whites could never see blacks as their intellectual or moral equals.

Two points should be made here: First, if Thomas is correct then given the history of racism in this country respect for a black person is different than respect for a white person. The same recognition respect is missing because of how blacks have been characterized as morally and intellectually inferior. Second, this means that appraisal respect will be different given one's racial identification. To this end, I list some of the comments that point to philosophical playa hatin' or lack of appraisal respect connected closely to lack of recognition respect. Let me note that there can be both hatin' comments and hatin' environments. You can be in the presence of a hater; you may be in a hater filled environment. You may be hated or "hated on" for any of the following reasons:

- If they think your salary is too high

- If they think your work is mediocre at best

- If you are expected to teach about race, African American philosophy, or Africana philosophy just because you are black

- If they do not send students to study with you

- If they think your dissertation director wrote your dissertation

- If your work is published in a top-tier journal and it is stated that even good journals make mistakes

- If you feel that your promotion dossier has to be much better than the young white male philosopher who just got tenure

- If you feel that your vote does not count in department decisions

- If you feel alienated from your department

- If you have ever been to the APA Eastern meeting and the words of Du Bois come to mind: "only dogged strength keeps his or her soul from being torn asunder"

- If you are a black woman and your professor or colleagues feel they can make improper sexual remarks to you or about you— both haters and sexual harassers

- If you work in Africana philosophy and your colleagues claim not to know what you do

- If there is resentment that you could move to another university and most of your colleagues cannot

- If some of your colleagues feel or even voice that the only reason you have a job is because you are a member of a ethnic, racial, or sexual minority

- If you are the last to know about major changes in the department

- If your colleagues think you work outside of "traditional" philosophy is not acceptable or not philosophy

- If it is claimed that you work on race because you could not do "real" philosophy

- If they think you could be doing "real" philosophy instead of working on issues of race and racism

These are examples of the lack of respect shown scholars of color and the African American experience. As noted here it makes the game difficult to play. Respecting other players is a basic attitude one should have in almost any game. Unfortunately, the academic black philosopher understands that the lack of respect shown him or her is connected to the lack of respect shown black people in general. The race game is the big game given the history of racism in the United States. For a black person to win, he or she must negotiate what it means for black people to be successful in their chosen endeavor, particularly when their success requires them to compete with whites. Here I need to state some primary assumptions that I will not argue for, but will take for granted that most readers will understand why there is no need to do so. The basic assumptions of this chapter are:

- Racism is still a factor in the lives of all persons in the United States.

- The academy is not race-neutral.

- In the academy, the same white racism that exists in America, in general, exists.

- American racism, in regard to black Americans, is the belief that blacks are morally and intellectually inferior to whites and that blacks should not get any thing that appears to be better than what a white person has. It also is the belief that any success that comes to a black person is not deserved.

- The hate shown philosophers of color is directly related to the lack of respect and regard given to blacks generally.

With this understanding of white American racism, the discipline of philosophy has the same problems with racism, as does the rest of American society. It often is thought that persons working in the academy are not like the rest of American society, that they, professors, are learned and use reason to access the world. This turns out not to be true. They are subject to the same racism and racist beliefs that the rest of the so-called unlearned hold. These attitudes might be expected given that we live in a society that postulates that whites can be race neutral. What this means is that white people are capable of transcending race in a manner that black people are not. This may explain why black judges and predominantly black juries are viewed as suspect when the defendant is black. Whites do not want an all black jury because they think the jury will be biased against the white person because of black anger at white racism in the United States. However, white judges and juries can sit in judgment on cases that involved any racial or ethnic person. Whites are believed to have the natural ability to be race neutral. This line of reasoning seems to hold that black minds have been poisoned against whites. But there is never the belief that white minds have been poisoned against blacks. Given the history of a deep and profound racial consciousness, it is said that whites have not been impacted. When race comes into the room, logic goes out the window!

At this point someone might say: "Hold on playa, you might be right that blacks are not respected in the same manner that whites are, but 'to hate' really means to envy another person." The hater is really envious of the player. My comments here are brief. I contend that envy also is what white philosophers feel toward successful black scholars. In the case of West, I suggest that some whites feel that his public acclaim is not deserved because he is black and, according to them, his work is not that good. The lack of respect for him as a black man impacts on the appraisal of the quality of his work. In this case, envy is connected to a lack of recognition respect. Here, I must admit that in this manner the envy that some black scholars have in regard to the success of some of their white colleagues is envy. The envy is engendered by the belief that the success of some of our white colleagues is to the result of their being white rather than the quality of their work. Racism can engender hatin' on all sides of the racial spectrum. This is why recognition respect is so important. A person's standing in the profession and the person's view of him or herself as a person with ends is connected to his or her being recognized as a moral and intellectual equal. This means that even self-respecting blacks have problems getting appraisal respect from their white colleagues.

Perhaps, the example of Bernard Boxill will help here. There is probably no philosopher that would claim that Boxill is not a very good philosopher. He has published in some of the top philosophical journals. His work on race, racism, and affirmative action is thought to be excellent across the board. Yet we find very little reference to his work in the works of white philosophers who write about social and political themes. It is not that his work is just about race, it is about the major themes in ethics, and social and political philosophy, which means his insights are important to our understanding of how race can be used to understand these issues. What can be the reasons for the lack of attention to Boxill's work?

Like law professor Derrick Bell,[33] I agree that racism is an inherent aspect of the lives of all Americans. I am claiming that racism is a fact of life for blacks in and out of the academy. More specifically, I argue that the racism endemic to American society is found in the academy. Racism in the United States impacts how black philosophers are viewed in the academy. Blacks often are not seen as the type of individuals who can do philosophy well. If they work on issues of race they are not doing serious philosophy. Then again, if they work outside of race they are not taken to be serious scholars in other areas of philosophy. In either case, they lose. What African American philosopher has name recognition in metaphysics, epistemology, logic, and philosophy of mind? No matter how good their work is, they are not seen as major players in these areas. This can change. Philosophers can work on making the relationships between players more respectful even if they cannot change the attitudes of persons outside of the academy or even lessen societal racism. They must work to understand the importance of what philosopher Irving Thalberg identified as *visceral racism*.[34]

HATE THE GAME

Let me be clear at this point: I am not claiming that all philosophers playa hate. It is true that most blacks working in the discipline of philosophy owe a great debt of gratitude to a particular white philosopher who worked with him or her. These philosophers are to be thanked for their concern and efforts. There have been challenges to the game made by white philosophers like Nelson Goodman and Morton White who were friends of black philosopher William Fontaine. Paul Ziff, Ernst Manasse, John Dolan, and Irving Thalberg Jr. also come to mind. There are, however, white philosophers who hate on black philosophers and will never try to change the game. It is to those philosophers that this chapter is addressed.

Philosophers of color have been faithful to philosophy even when philosophy has not been faithful to them. We recruit young scholars of color to attend graduate school and study philosophy because we respect the discipline of philosophy and recognize that we still need to dispel the myth of black intellectual inferiority. One can look at these times like the early years of school desegregation when blacks sent their children into hostile schools even with the knowledge that the trek would be full of haters (persons who had no respect for blacks). We are still sending our children out to integrate schools, only this time it is in graduate departments both as graduate students and new professors. Just like the black students who integrated elementary, and high schools in the 1960s, we are integrating philosophy departments in the new millennium.

CHANGING THE GAME

These ruminations and reflections have been gathered from conversations and discussions over twenty years in the profession. This is not the rant of an angry black man. That some white philosophers will find these claims overblown may explain why many philosophers of color feel alienated from their departments. It also points to the lack of respect given to black people in general when they give negative testimony about their experiences with whites. It will be claimed that blacks really do not have a clear picture of race relations. They just cannot understand the *love* shown by whites toward blacks. Again, when race comes in the room, logic goes out the window. In this regard, white colleagues must come to grips with their own understandings and feelings about race and what racial distinctions mean in their evaluations of other persons. This is difficult and disturbing work. How this work should be done has to be left to the persons committed to changing the manner in which race and radical distinctions play a role in philosophy and the academy. Our colleagues are not idiots. They are trained to solve problems. Like most people they will work to solve a problem if they think that it is important. If they think that racism in the profession is a problem, they will begin to work with their own and their colleague's racism and sexism. No person of color can force them to work to change the game or their attitudes. If they think that blacks are indeed inferior intellectually, then they will feel no compulsion to change the game. However, if there are white philosophers who are passionate about the elimination of disrespectful practices in philosophy, they could start by reading renowned historian John Hope Franklin's "The Dilemma of the American Negro Scholar."[35] Franklin notes that the black scholar who wants to be respected as a scholar understands that his or her respect is tied to the respect that other blacks in the country receive. It has been a truism that a black person being respected in one arena of social interaction gives us no hint of how he or she will be respect in others. However, respect must begin at home. Philosophers across the racial spectrum must work together to make race and racism less of a factor in the lives of scholars of color. They must start in their own departments. It will take time given the history of racism in both America and the academy.

BACK ON THE BLOCK

Players know that some games have a built in bias toward certain players. It is understood that these games are difficult to win if you stand in certain relationship to other players. That's just the nature of the game. If you play, you play with the knowledge that the game may be stacked against you. Betting games in Las Vegas are examples of games with a bias slanted to the casino. If you play and lose you should not hate the casino. You should hate the game you played, poker. In the United States, racism has always been in the game and if you try to be successful in any endeavor that pits whites against blacks you should understand that the game has a racial bias tilted toward whites. Because of this we can imagine white philosophers saying to their colleagues of color: "Don't hate the playa, hate the game."[36]

NOTES

1. Reitumetse Mabokela and Anna L. Green, *Sisters in the Academy* Stylus Publishing (April 2001).

2. Stephen L. Darwall "Two Kinds of Respect" *Ethics*, vol. 88, No. 1 (Oct., 1977), pp. 36–49.

    3. Ibid., p. 36.

    4. Ibid., p. 37.

    5. Ibid., p. 38.

    6. Ibid., p. 38.

    7. Ibid., p. 38.

    8. Ibid., p. 38.

    9. Ibid., p. 38.

  10. Ibid., p. 39.

  11. Ibid., p. 39.

  12. Ibid., p. 42.

  13. Ibid., p. 42.

  14. Ibid., p. 43.

  15. Ibid., p. 44.

  16. Ibid., p. 44.

  17. Ibid., p. 44.

  18. Ibid., p. 44.

  19. Ibid., p. 45.

  20. Ibid., p. 46.

  21. Ibid., p. 46.

  22. Ibid., p. 46.

23. Laurence Thomas, "Moral Equality and Natural Inferiority" *Social Theory and Practice*, vol. 31, No. 3 (July 2005), pp. 379–404.

  24. Ibid., p. 379.

  25. Ibid., p. 379.

26. Ibid., p. 379.

27. Ibid., p. 380.

28. Ibid., p. 380.

29. Ibid., p. 393.

30. Ibid., p. 393.

31. Ibid., p. 395.

32. Immanuel Kant, "On the Use of Teleological Principles in Philosophy" (1788) reprinted in Robert Bernasconi ed *Race* Blackwell, 2001, pp. 37–56.

33. Derrick Bell, *Faces at the Bottom of the Well: The Permanence of Racism* Basic Books, 1993

34. Irving Thalberg, "Visceral Racism" *The Monist* 56, no.1 (1972): 43–63.

35. John Hope Franklin (1972). 'The Dilemma of the American Negro Scholar,' in: Herbert Hill. (ed.), *Soon One Morning: New Writings by American Negroes, 1940–1962* (New York: Knopf, 1963), pp.

36. This paper benefited from discussions with Samaiyah Jones-Scott, William Allen, Tina Botts, Tim Golden, Michael Burroughs, Cigdem Yazici, Twana Adams, Donald Baker, Laurence Thomas, Renée Sanders-Lawson, Brian Henderson, and George Yancy.

PART III

GENDER, ETHNICITY, AND RACE

CHAPTER TEN

TOWARD A PLACE WHERE I CAN
BRING ALL OF ME

Identity Formation and Philosophy

Jacqueline Scott

In this chapter, I discuss the peril and promise of identity formation for female African American philosophers. More specifically, because one generally does not see "black woman" and "philosopher" as intersecting identities, attempts to embody such an identity hold both perils and promises. Because it is not a ready-made category, one is forced to create and maintain it in the face of, at worst, hostility or, at best, indifference. This lack of fixity can simultaneously hold the promise of creating one's own identity as one sees fit, and the peril of feeling identityless or schizophrenic. The issues of identity, identity politics, and subjectivity as they intersect with issues of race and gender identities have begun to be addressed in philosophy. Linda Alcoff, among others, has written in this area, and this chapter is a further contribution in terms of the identities of black, woman, and philosopher. Alcoff contends:

> Although subjectivist approaches have important advantages in accounting for how race works, they have been underdeveloped in the recent theoretical literature, even while there are many first-person memoirs and rich descriptions of racial experience that might be tapped for theoretical analysis.[1]

This chapter attempts to marry theory with accounts of my own experiences.

I argue that the creation and embodiment of such a hybrid identity potentially allows for a healthier type of subject formation which in turn could allow for the possibility of creating more vibrant, elastic communities that openly and lovingly reflect the complex identities of their members. Not only would this change the way we in philosophy think about issues such as race, subjectivity, and identity, but it also might change the philosophers who carry out such investigations.

PERIL: PHILOSOPHY, IDENTITY, AND HOMELESSNESS

I fell in love with philosophy soon after being introduced to it. I would like to say that I got to know it after an extended courtship and only after careful consideration did I consent to enter into a long-term relationship. Yes, that is what I would like to say. The truth of the matter is that only after reading part of Plato's *Republic* in a seminar my freshman year in college was I completely swept away by this *thing* (after all, it seemed to be much more than a mere area of study—let along an academic discipline).[2] I fell in love with philosophy because of its emphasis on reason, wisdom, and the promise of enlightenment. It asks fundamental questions about those very things we have always assumed to be obviously true, and in philosophy the search for the answer is more interesting and important than the answer itself.

Of course, philosophy and I were soon to hit a rough spot in our relationship because I had taken a part of it and assumed it duly represented the whole of it. I was completely taken with a type of philosophy that has been characterized as "the art of living."[3] Alexander Nehamas helpfully characterizes this type of philosophy as one that entails making conscious decisions about practicing a meaningful life—and in this sense it involves both theorizing and practicing what it means for a particular individual to live well. In engaging in these activities, one may of course take a more passive approach and borrow wholly or in part from the theories and practices of others (one might argue that this is what one does in adhering to a particular religion or philosophy). At the other extreme, one might take a more active approach and work on wholly creating one's approach or consciously quilting together a combination of others' practices and theories with one's own. The dictum that guides this type of philosophy is Socrates' (via Plato): "The unexamined life is not worth living."[4] As Nehamas points out, although one might associate this philosophy most closely with the Greeks, there have been well-known philosophers throughout the history of philosophy who have exemplified this type of philosophy (e.g., Montaigne, Nietzsche, and Foucault).

The love of this kind of philosophy helped to bring out a kernel of myself that I had previously failed to recognize fully. Looking back, I realize that I had worked actively to create a meaningful life. In part, I had done this because I had never felt as though someone had laid a template for a particular life in front of me. Since an early age, I felt like an outsider to the various communities I belonged (my family, school, and grandmother's church). Part of this had to do with the fact that I was a black girl living in a predominantly white upper middle-class suburb and attending a college preparatory school. I was just not around many people who looked—or acted—like me.[5] I am certain that many philosophers also would describe themselves as feeling like outsiders because of their temperaments (there is a reason that history is marked by attempts to silence, control, or kill philosophers. We really are an annoying disruptive bunch!). The combination of my race and gender has further exacerbated these feelings of marginalization.

In many ways, I *did* fit into my school and home communities, but I was just "different" enough to find myself thinking about both who I was (such that I was so different from those around me) and what I wanted to be (to avoid necessarily becoming more "similar" in order to fit in). During my freshman year at Spelman College (a historically black college for women), I had a crisis in terms of my identity. I had chosen (with mild trepidation) to attend a black college for women so that for once I could be in the majority in terms of race and gender, and yet, during my first semester I felt more on the "outside" than I did at my predominantly white high school. Others likened me to an Oreo (black on the outside and white on the inside) and in many ways, I agreed with them—I did not know what it meant for me to call myself a black woman. I certainly identified as one, but that identity was not very well-thought out and so it felt very thin to me.

That first semester, my philosophy class was the only one that really proved a challenge to me. I diligently did the reading, came to class prepared to discuss the plot of Book I of the *Republic*, and the professor quickly pushed me to move beyond my plot summary to probe the foundational issues and questions. I was at a loss for words, but loved the fact that mere memorization was insufficient. Instead, delving into the theories beyond the surface of the text was more highly valued. Philosophy had claimed me. I became friends with another student who also was intrigued by this class and we spent two hours over dinner and then another few hours in the hallway of our dorm trying to come up with a definition of the Idea of Beauty. The next day we presented our definition to our professor who encouraged us to become philosophy majors (while also telling us how esoteric and difficult the discipline is). So not only was I in love, but by the start of my sophomore year I had pledged a good portion of the rest of my undergraduate program to my new love.

Then I quickly experienced dissonance between my lived life in philosophy and the rest of my life. There were no black women teaching, writing, or appearing in the philosophy I read. Other students and some professors at Spelman told me that black people do not do philosophy or that philosophy is a white person's discipline. By doing philosophy, according to this thinking, I was endangering my authentic black self. At the same time, in developing my philosophical self, my life felt more full, meaningful, joyful—more complete. My identity as a philosopher brought out a kernel of power, a feeling of "me-ness" as well as a love, affirmation and celebration of my powers. It allowed me to fell in love with myself. I saw myself reified in philosophy. It was puzzling that the philosophy that had allowed me to feel this way also supposedly rendered me an inauthentic black woman.

Moreover, it seemed to me that it is black women (and black folks in general) who *should* be engaging in the philosophical enterprise. Philosophy, as I understood it then, is generally characterized by concerns about formulating what it means to "live well" outside of commonly accepted categories, questioning accepted beliefs, and, following Socrates, aiming to be a gadfly and physician to the culture. These actions also are found in African American cultures—particularly in their relationships to the larger American culture. Because of this congruity, and because of the support of friends at Spelman and other local colleges as well as my parents I decided to stick with my decision to major in philosophy.

During my senior year, I decided to make Friedrich Nietzsche the subject of my senior thesis. He was the first philosopher I read who questioned the basic assumptions and values of traditional philosophy, and did so from the perspective of wanting to heal the culture and the discipline. Moreover, the perspective from which he wrote was as a marginalized insider to both the culture and the discipline.[6] I was intrigued by his approach and found his style of writing to be both humorous and enlightening, but Nietzsche did not fill me with the wonder and sense of majesty that Plato, Aristotle, Kant, and Rousseau did. He left me thinking hard about whether or not I agreed with him and with little satisfaction as to what a type of philosophy might succeed his criticisms. Also during my senior year I took a class called "African Philosophy" with Lucius Outlaw.[7] In this course, the readings and discussions had a similar effect on me as did reading Nietzsche: They both pushed me to examine the assumptions and values of traditional philosophy as practiced in the United States. Although this was exciting, it also was very unsettling. Nevertheless, in my applications to doctoral programs in philosophy, I stated that I was primarily interested in ancient political philosophy. Upon my acceptance at Stanford, I had assumed that I had "done away" with Nietzsche altogether. I looked upon him as a childish interest and not as a serious philosopher.

In my first few years of graduate school, I suffered from all sorts of crises of confidence. They were due at least in part to my own perfectionist personality, but also partly due to studying philosophy, for the first time, in a group comprised largely of whites and men who asked me to justify my presence there. To be clear, this questioning was neither overt nor malicious, and my discomfort with the discipline probably had more to do with the type of philosophy that was emphasized than anything approaching racism or sexism. I found myself uninterested in the specialized forms of analytic philosophy that I studied during my first two years (philosophy of language, mind, etc.). I had difficulties in connecting the philosophy that I had come to love during my undergraduate studies with the philosophy I was now studying. This disconnect was not solely due to the necessary specialization and rigor one encounters at the graduate level. Contemporary analytic philosophy is not primarily focused on philosophy as the art of living. Once again my interests were on the margin of philosophy.

I found myself turning back to Nietzsche in whose writings I had discerned similar criticisms and concerns about philosophy and the culture to those I was experiencing. I also found his arguments about the necessity of actively forming one's own identity by establishing the values that render one's life meaningful to be instructive to me personally. Although I do not think that all philosophy must directly involve the art of living, I do think that the overemphasis on several narrowly construed areas of philosophy has meant that other types of philosophy have suffered from neglect. As an undergraduate it was the art of living that drew me into philosophy and lit a fire in my belly, and it was that fire that fuelled me and that I hoped to transfer as a spark in the bellies of my students.

In the end then, in terms of my relationship with philosophy, we had once again come to a stage of *détente*. Although I had come to a fuller understanding of the object of my affections, and although some of this new information gave me pause, I remained in love and it continued to help make my life meaningful—even if so many others did not understand the attraction. As I was coming to embody the part of my identity labeled "philosophy professor" and feeling self-assured about it, I also experienced numerous incidents that served to remind me that I was a curiosity in philosophy.[8] Perhaps most interesting to me about being a curiosity is that I go along in my life feeling how lucky I am to be paid to do something that I love—philosophy seems like a natural fit for me. At the same time, I regularly have experiences that disrupt this feeling of naturalness and serve to remind me just how "unnatural" most people regard my race, gender, and the combination of the two in philosophy.

1. When I was applying for my first tenure-track position, during the campus visit, my host for the day (a white male professor in the department) picked me up at my hotel and took me out to dinner.

He told me that he was going to take me to a place he thought that I would like, a "real authentic breakfast joint." The place turned out to be a black-owned diner, not close to the university, and whose customers were largely black and working class. The food was fine, but nothing special, and he was very intent on knowing my reaction to the place. Did he take all job candidates there? Is this where he thought I would be most comfortable (where the real me would fit in best)?

2. During my final year in graduate school, I was chatting with one of the first-year graduate students who I had helped recruit into the department. She came from a working-class background and she and I bonded over our feelings of displacement in philosophy. I was going through my mail and remarking about how the private school I attended for high school wanted me to donate money, and I was laughing about how little of my graduate student stipend I could afford to give to the well-endowed school. She asked me about the school and then remarked how hard it must have been for me to go to that school in the wealthy suburb from "my neighborhood." In actuality, my childhood neighborhood was not all that different from that of the school's, but my friend had assumed that I had grown up in a predominantly black poor/working-class neighborhood. I gently corrected her misperception and wondered to myself from where she had derived this assumption? Had I somehow misled her?

3. While an untenured faculty member, I was sitting in my office, and one of my older white colleagues knocked on the door and asked me to help him with a student. This student had been having trouble in his class because of her verbally abusive and controlling boyfriend who also was in the class. The boyfriend continually talked to her in the class and would not "let" her drop it. My colleague asked me to accompany him to his office where the student had "snuck" away from her boyfriend and come for help in extricating herself from the situation. I followed my colleague to his office and spoke with the student (a black woman) who was there. I was not sure what my colleague thought I could do, but I recommended that she go to the university health center to speak to a mental health counselor and that she call a hotline for victims of abuse to help her. After she left, my colleague thanked me profusely for helping because he did not know how to handle the situation, but had sought me out because he thought I would "know how to deal with her."

4. One of the other mothers in my son's kindergarten class and I would often chat after dropping off our kids. We would walk for a block or so together before going our separate ways. I had told her that I was a philosophy professor and that I was trying to finish a book on Nietzsche. She was taking a few graduate courses and so we would commiserate about writing. Lately she regularly asks me how my dissertation is going. I used to correct her that it was not a dissertation but a book manuscript, but then a few weeks later she would make the same mistake. In many ways it does not matter at all that she forgets that I already have my doctorate, but I do wonder why she cannot seem to remember that fact about me. She seems to remember so many other facts about me, why doesn't this one stay in her head? Is it due to a faulty memory or cognitive dissonance? This sort of thing happens just often enough that it is hard to believe that most of these people just forget that I have my doctorate.

Can it really be that they *do* not remember or is it that they *cannot* remember—that they cannot keep this seeming contradiction in their heads? One generally learns, and remembers, by associating a new bit of information with previous information. What if the new bit of information is so different that "it does not compute"—it does not "fit" into the factual picture and so it is lost or forgotten. Nietzsche describes the phenomenon in this way:

> Ultimately, nobody can get more out of things, including books, than he already knows. For what one lacks access to from experience one will have no ear. Now let us imagine an extreme case: that a book speaks of nothing but events that lie altogether beyond the possibility of frequent or even rare experience—that it is the first language for a new series of experiences. In that case, simply nothing will be heard, but there will be the acoustic illusion that where nothing is heard, nothing is there.[9]

In this quote, I take Nietzsche to be describing his own experience in writing about a type of philosophy that in his view is meant to be fundamentally different from traditional philosophy and thus no one was able to understand his writings. Although I think there might have been all sorts of reasons why no one was buying Nietzsche's books beyond the fact of their "originality," I do think that in the quote he offers an interesting insight. The cognitive dissonance he describes here ("For what one lacks access to from experience one will have no ear"), seems to explain the description of my experiences.

If most people have not met a black women philosophy professor before (it is an event that "lie[s] altogether beyond the possibility of frequent or even rare experience"), then the combination of traits is not "heard" and so often the professor part of my identity disappears ("the acoustic illusion that where nothing is heard, nothing is there"). Similarly, the fact that I am a black woman who grew up in an upper middle-class neighborhood also is not heard and so one might substitute the fact that better fits into their own experiences. As a result, I am looked at and listened to, but not seen or heard.

These types of "acoustic illusory" experiences apply not only to the fact that I am a philosophy professor. I am also married to a white, Jewish man and we have two biological sons. Additionally, before getting married I converted to Judaism. When I am out with our kids and without my husband, even though my sons are forever calling me "Mommy," people often assume that I am their babysitter. I think that because I am darker skinned than my children, these people assume that the kids are white (or not black) and so I could not be their mother. When we attend services in new synagogues, people tend to stare at me throughout the service. They cannot seem to make sense of the fact that a black women stands before them in a prayer shawl and yarmulke and prays in Hebrew. Even when I look at them, they continue to stare at me and often do not respond when I nod or say Shabbat Shalom (a traditional greeting on the Sabbath day).

This actually became a weekly source of humor for me during the year after I converted to Judaism and before we got married. I was living without my fiancé (now husband) in Memphis, Tennessee and I was a member of a synagogue there. I attended services almost every Saturday morning. The first few weeks, many of the congregants stared quite openly at me, but after a while, they came to know me and would treat me like other members. Many of these people were very kind and invited me to their homes for holiday meals and to serve on committees in the synagogue. A critical mass of older white people, however, stared at me throughout my year there. They would react with surprise when I said Shabbat Shalom, and would mumble an automatic response—and this would happen every Saturday. After awhile, my presence certainly could not have been a surprise, but it did seem to put them in a mental state called aporia, and in this state one suffers from a cognitive dissonance brought on by seemingly inconsistent ideas.

In philosophy such a state of aporia, although deemed necessary for ridding one of contradictory or illogical concepts, must be "overcome" by using reason to arrive at logically consistent conclusions. It seemed that this critical mass of congregants in Memphis were unable to make rational sense of the juxtaposition (at least in their minds) between my race and religious identity (and perhaps also my gender in that, unlike most of the other women in the congregation, I wore a yarmulke and prayer shawl).

In many ways, my identity as a philosopher has exacerbated these fissures between my social identities and my lived identity. In my saner moments, my lived identity as a female, black philosopher is almost seamless. It makes perfect sense to me because my life is meaningful and it is a meaningfulness that helps me to affirm life in general. I also like to think that this meaningfulness allows me to successfully aid others (family, children, friends, and students) in creating meaningful lives of their own.[10] In terms of my life within the profession as well as in terms of my life as it relates to philosophical doctrines, these aspects of my identity make for a fractured, irrational, impure, and nonsensical self. Just as I started out falling in love with a philosophy that heralds a rational, universal, and unconditional conception of truth, I have found that the person I have become does not coincide with the right, true best self that is derived from this conception of the truth. In short, philosophy tells me (and this is generally reinforced by regular encounters with the outside world) that I am irrational because my various identities do not cohere.

Although this is the general view of traditional philosophy, there are more contemporary movements that call into question this view of a singular true, healthy subject. In particular, recently, in both continental and analytic circles, philosophers have interrogated this view as it pertains particularly to individual racial identities.[11] It is beyond the scope of this chapter to engage this literature fully, and for my purposes here I focus on Alcoff's writings on these matters.

One might contend that philosophy specializes in analyzing and theorizing the profound and fundamental problems that affect our lives and at the same time resist empirical measurement. It would then seem that philosophy is an appropriate discipline to take up issues involving contemporary conceptions of racialized identities. It has generally been accepted that races do not exist as biologically/genetically based entities.[12] To varying degrees, they are understood to be socially created entities and they also play a significant role (along with other visible and "acknowledged identities") in our relationship to the world as well as in our interior life. Alcoff writes:

> Thus our "visible" and acknowledged identity affects our relations in the world, which in turn affects our interior life, that is, our lived experience or subjectivity. If social identities such as race and gender are fundamental in this way to one's experiences, then it only makes sense to say they are fundamental to the self. . . . There are two aspects of selves that are involved in social identity. By

the term identity, one mainly thinks about how we are socially located in public, what is on our identification papers, how we must identify ourselves on Census and application forms and in the everyday interpolations of social interaction. This *public identity* is our socially perceived self within the systems of perception and classification and the networks of community in which we live. But there is also a *lived subjectivity* that is not always perfectly mapped onto our socially perceived self, and that can be experienced and conceptualized differently. By the term subjectivity, then, I mean to refer to who *we* understand ourselves to be, how we experience being ourselves, and the range of reflective and other activities that can be included under the rubric of our "agency."[13]

Here Alcoff helpfully makes the logical connection between identity and subjectivity, and the way that they inform one another. In relating my own identity formation above, I hope that I have exemplified the ways in which there can be problematic fissures between one's public identity and one's lived subjectivity. In order to explain the importance of identity in what I have called here the art of living, Alcoff quotes Charles Taylor:

My identity is defined by the commitments and identifications which provide the frame or horizon within which I can try to determine from case to case what is good, or valuable, or ought to be done, or what I endorse or oppose. In other words, it is the horizon within which I am capable of taking a stand.[14]

In short, we forge our identities by making commitments, and identifying with, various communities that, in turn, we use to aid us in creating values and meaning in our lives. Given the importance of the self, values and meaningful lives in philosophy, one can now see why I contend that philosophy should take up racialized identities as legitimate objects of study.

In the history of philosophy, some have argued, philosophers not only focused on races as legitimate objects of study but in fact, they might be credited with creating the modern conception of races that has become so problematic.[15] In her book, *Visible Identities*, Alcoff helpfully traces various conceptions of the self through various phases and schools of philosophical thought.[16] In general, the healthy modern self is seen as one that is able to attain autonomy by being able to disengage from the surrounding culture as well as one's own desires so that one can engage in rational judgment that is not unduly influenced by the passions or outside influences. Rationality and critical distancing are important attributes of such a self. In particular, Alcoff points out that this view assumes that "the traditions of one's culture may have been arrived at rationally, or they may be irrational and based on desire."[17] In short, one only legitimately adopts or identifies with cultural traditions because one has found them to be rational. Does a critical distance mean that one adopts a generally held view of this cultural identity in order to assess one's own attachment? If not then upon distancing oneself from one's identity, what perspective does one adopt? What is one to do, if one cannot find one's attachment to a cultural identity to be rational (according to cultural norms of rationality)—largely because the culture has deemed this identity to be irrational? Is it possible to have a rational attachment to an irrational identity?

Looking at the history of philosophy then, the self either is pure, rational, coherent and unified and is therefore healthy, or it is fractured, constituted by an external philosophy (or Other) and is therefore pathological.[18] As a result, philosophy tends to view identities (e.g., racial and gender) in this way:

1. Identities are artificial and oppressive constraints on the natural indeterminacy of the self.

2. Identities are the product of oppressive practices such as self-disciplining mechanisms, and the desire for their "affirmation" is a manifestation of a repetition–compulsion complex.

3. Identities are pathological and unproductive, even doomed, responses to lack or ego dysfunction and instability.

4. Identities are never accurate representations.

5. Identities are manifestations of a primary alienation in which categories are imposed from without.[19]

My own experience in philosophy exemplifies many of the downsides to such a view of the self. If I am to enact these views in terms of my self-conception as a philosopher, then my gender and racial identities are problematic. Of course those in philosophy recognize that these aspects of my identity are in some sense unavoidable but my attachment to them is seen as foreign to philosophy. In particular, my desire to re-think philosophical generalizations about human psychology, behavior, and the concomitant best practices based on them in light of specific gender or racial identities is at best suspect and at worst "pathological and unproductive." Although it might be fine for me to live my life as a black woman and have those identities form a large part of my self-conception, when I try to combine these identities with my philosophical theoretical work, at least in the shadow of the prevailing views in the history of philosophy as well as in those of contemporary philosophy (although that is more true for race than for gender), it does not work.

In this sense, there is peril for women and people of color in engaging in philosophical practices, but also in becoming full-fledged practitioners of the discipline. At times, I feel that as an academic, I am homeless. The discipline in which I house myself does not want all of me to settle in and fully join the community. Although aspects of it claim to yield insights into the art of living, these insights generally do not accept as legitimate or healthy aspects of myself that I consider to be fundamental. In order to be a fully legitimate philosophical self, I must be unified and coherent. The self that I am and want to bring to philosophy is not this—it is multifarious, impure, continually in flux and so disjointed that it often is deemed incoherent by others (and often by me).

Healthy theoretical conceptions of the art of living then for me are not based solely on this legitimate philosophical self. This might be one of the reasons that the numbers of women and people of color are so small in the discipline. It is not solely due to a past history of overt exclusion. It might also be the case that in both theory and practice philosophy does not seem to be a good "home" for those populations (as well as others). The perception might be that in order to enter and feel welcome in this well-established home (and thanks to Kant, firmly placed on a solid foundation), one has to either leave out those "secondary" qualities that are not seen as legitimate aspects of one's self or bring in one's full self and contend with the feeling of either being, at worst, schizophrenic, or at best, identity-less. How might philosophy learn to speak to the practice of forging one's identity as black women (engaging in an art of living that involves those types of embodiment) as well as to theorizing about selves and identities that resist the ready-categorization and the fixity demanded by most philosophical conceptions of the self? The good news is that a way of approaching an answer to this question already resides within philosophy itself.

THE PROMISE OF PHILOSOPHY

To some degree, philosophy has always been a schizophrenic discipline. Although there were early claims to a teleological and steady progress toward universal and unconditional conceptions of Truth, there have also always been counter-claims that question the ability to attain such Truths, the value of such Truths, as well as the wisdom of placing such a high valuation on a perfection that is ultimately unattainable. In this way, philosophy already had within it many of the tools for diagnosing and addressing the peril I described in the previous section. In order to demonstrate this promise in philosophy for healing itself, I want to examine further the ways in which some in philosophy are using the discipline to theorize about healthier racial identities. These approaches to racial identities are a way of beginning to address some of the philosophical "problems" about my own racial identity I discussed above.

Alcoff describes her project in *Visible Identities* in this way:

> This book offers a sustained defense of identity as an epistemically salient and ontologically real entity. . . . The road to freedom from the capriciousness of arbitrary identity designations lies not, . . . in the attempt at a speedy dissolution of identity . . . but through a careful exploration of identity, which can reveal its influence on what we can see and know, as well as its context dependence and its complex and fluid nature. . . . This book, then, explores race and gender as visible identities and seeks to uncover some of the mechanisms by which they are identified, enacted, and reproduced. In one sense, my aim is to try to make identities more visible, to bring them from their hiding places where they can elicit shame and obscure power. But my approach does not assume that there are ahistorical, transcultural truths about identities. My question is, rather, how are racial and gendered identities operating here, now? What is the best descriptive account of their current operations? How do they relate to their subjectivity, lived experience, and what a given individual can see and know? And what are the implications of a fuller understanding of these identities on political practice?[20]

Alcoff then wants to use traditional philosophical tools (analyzing whether something is "an epistemically salient and ontologically real entity") and goals ("freedom from the capriciousness of arbitrary identity designations") in order to bring about "the implications of a fuller understanding of these identities on political practice," as well as broaden our understanding of how these identities operate at both the theoretical and practical levels. One of her goals is to reveal the ways in which we tend to group disparate racial and gender markers into a unitary identity, and then correlate this identity with a "rational capacity, epistemic reliability, moral condition, and, of course, aesthetic value."[21] Moreover, she claims that we tend to take this correlation to be reliable and depend on it as we negotiate our world. This dependence is particularly evident, Alcoff argues, when we find ourselves unable to read definitively racial and gender markers (or when we cannot "see" or "find" them). In this case, we find ourselves at a loss about how to deal with that person.[22] I argue that this case is precisely what happens when people stare at me in synagogue or when they stare at me and my children after they understand that I am their mother. As Alcoff contends, if we in academia can reveal the ways in which we racialize people and in particular the role individuals play in creating and perpetuating identity categories, then the closer we might come to reducing or ending the racism and racist practices that often accompany these acts of valorization through racialization.[23]

A result of such a project might be a re-thinking of the way in which we not only think about racial identities but also the values that we place on them. As I argued elsewhere, I think that we should move away from racial designations that are "monolithically thick" and thus affect individuals in every realm of their existence and do not allow for diversity or variation.[24] Arguments by Alcoff, among others, might move us toward racial identities that are "multifariously thin."[25] By this I mean to indicate one's race would not determine most aspects of one's life and there would be more diversity within as well as between races. So my blackness would not necessarily "determine" or allow someone else to predict the race of my life partner, my class status, what my children might look like, nor my religion. It would also allow for me to be "authentically" black *and* Jewish, and for my children to be *both* black *and* white without *having* to choose one race over the other.

The fact that the monolithically thick or pure conception of race still prevails struck me in a recent incident. A few months ago, I went alone to a YMCA to update our family membership by adding our youngest son to it. The young white man behind the counter was a recent hire and did not know how to work the computer system very well. As a result, he regularly consulted another employee (a young black woman) for help. Apparently, the Y was collecting racial statistics because the man asked the woman how to skip the racial identity step. He murmured to her (seemingly avoiding eye contact with me) that he wanted to enter "not applicable" as my son's race. Either she did not hear him, knew that was not an option, or thought that adding in the response was necessary because she looked at me and told him to type in "B" (presumably for "black"). Note that she did not ask me for either my son's racial identity or mine, and instead, she assumed *his* race based on how *I* look.

For many people, this might be an accurate way of predicting another's race. In this case, in some ways, it is not. My son is 3.5 years old and if asked I am not sure he would offer any type of racial identity. As far as I know, no one has told him what race he is, and depending on who is with him, people seem to assign various racial identities to him. When he is with his white Irish nanny, many assume that he is her son and the same goes for my husband. When my son is with me, often they do not assume I am his mother. When he is with his slightly darker-skinned and darker-haired brother, people often assume he is some type of racial mix, but they are not sure what that mix is. When I fill out forms for both sons, if possible, I check both the black/African American and the white/Caucasian boxes. So what race *is* he?

I suppose that I could have spoken up and "corrected" the woman, but what is the correct answer? I could at least have asked the man to enter both a B and a W, but would that have been possible or just caused more frustration on the part of the new employee? Yes, race is important, but in this case it did not seem all that important. I suppose my son's race might have had an affect on the formulation for the allocation of funds—and then it would have been important for the Y. It just did not seem important for me or my son at the moment, plus I just wanted to get back to preparing for my graduate seminar. I also found myself laughing at how much the scene reminded me of the experiences of immigrants at Ellis Island.

My point here is to indicate the ways in which we traditionally think and use race are often laughably inaccurate or nonsensical. To be clear, traditionally racial designations have always been inaccurate or nonsensical to varying degrees, but given the increasing complexity of our social identities and our increasing insistence that racial and ethnic labels reflect these identities, our traditional labels more often seem wholly inadequate.[26]

Paul C. Taylor asks those in academia: "What if those of us concerned with intellectual race work took the complexity of race not as an incentive for disavowal and negation but as a challenge to our ability to creatively and productively engage with, which is to say to re-create, the world?"[27] Alcoff argues that accepting this challenge also entails thinking "creatively [about] and productively engag[ing] with" philosophical conceptions of the self. Again, the reconceptualization of the self does not necessarily entail that one leave philosophy altogether. One need only look to the history of philosophy in order witness the fissures in *the* philosophical conception of the self.[28]

The Hermeneutic approach calls into question this claim about the necessity of assuming a critical distance (e.g., Cartesian doubting). Instead it calls for the ability to imagine a self that is multifarious and questions the ability or wisdom of adopting an "objective" perspective from which one could evaluate cultural identities as well as one's attachment to them.[29] In the Hegelian tradition, the self only becomes autonomous after it has engaged with another self, but at the same time the self only fully comes into being by dominating and overcoming the Other. Also the engagement with the Other is seen as only temporary.[30]

Aspects of the discipline are also moving toward changes that might allow for more multifarious and fractured senses of an authentic self. Alcoff cautions us against a subject that is so nomadic as to be seemingly free of any communal attachments altogether. Her concern is that such a subject would seem to represent "an absence of identity rather than a multiply entangled and engaged identity."[31] Although we might not find a home in the traditionally conceived philosophical self, being completely homeless does not seem like a viable option either. Alcoff contends that she has found peace by "no longer seeking some permanent home onshore. What I seek is no longer a home, but perhaps a lighthouse that might illuminate this place in which I live, for myself as much as others."[32] I read this as her call for philosophical enlightenment—as a call for philosophical investigations that might shed a light on her own complex racial identity (white and Latina)—and the self that is attached to it.

I wonder if such an investigation might actually change the way in which we view our philosophical home. Perhaps we will come to realize that as opposed to situating our discipline in a singular permanent house with a solid foundation (and the conception of a self that goes along with it), that we re-think what having a home and being homeless might mean. Nietzsche, in his attempts to distance himself, and any future like-minded souls, from his nationalistic racist culture (as well as the philosophy on which it was founded), considered homelessness a badge of honor.

> We who are homeless.—Among Europeans today there is no lack of those who are entitled to call themselves homeless in a distinctive and honorable sense: it is to them that I especially commend my secret wisdom and gaya scienza. For their fate is hard, their hopes uncertain; it is quite a feat to devise some comfort for them—but what avail? We children of the future, how could we be at home in this today? We feel disfavor for all ideals that might lead one to feel at home even in this fragile, broken time of transition; for its "realities," we do not believe that they will last. The ice that supports people today has become very thin; the wind that brings the thaw is blowing; we ourselves who are homeless constitute the force that breaks open ice and other too thin "realities." . . . We who are homeless are too manifold and mixed racially in our descent, being "modern men," and consequently do not feel tempted to participate in the mendacious racial self-admiration and racial indecency that parades in German today. . . . No, you know better than that my friends! The hidden Yes in you is stronger than all Nos and Maybes that afflict you and your age like a disease; and when you have to embark on the sea, you emigrants, you, too, are compelled by this by—a faith![33]

He called on his fellow homeless ones to recognize the creaky foundation on which we all rest, to be the "wind" that will break open the "ice" that constitutes the foundation, and to revel in their own "manifold and mixed" nature. While this destruction will imperil them because it will render them literally homeless, the promise of their complex and modern selves will aid them in embarking out to sea and with an affirmative ("the hidden Yes") "faith" they might yet create a meaningful life.

In my view, this active, affirmative creation would mean re-thinking what it means to have a home. In a novel, Barbara Kingsolver describes an alternate way of thinking about "home."

> "The greatest honor you can give a house is to let it fall back down into the ground," he said. "That's where everything comes from in the first place."

> I looked at him, surprised. "But then you've lost your house."

> "Not if you know how to build another one. All those great pueblos like at Kinishba—people lived in them awhile, and then they'd move on. Just leave them standing. Maybe go to a place with better water, or something." . . .

> Loyd rubbed his hand thoughtfully over my palm. Finally he said, "The important thing isn't the house. It's the ability to make it. You carry that in your brain and in your hands, wherever you go. Anglos are like turtles, if they go someplace they have to carry the whole house along in their damn Winnesotas."

> "We're like coyotes," he said. "Get to a good place, turn around three times in the grass, and you're home. Once you know how, you can always do that, no matter what. You won't forget."[34]

In this dialogue, Loyd, a Native American man, discusses his conception of home with a Latina named Codi. Loyd argues that he learned from his Pueblo ancestors that a house that rests on a solid foundation and resists destruction is not necessarily synonymous with a feeling of being at home. In his view, "home" means that you "have the ability to make" a structure in which you, family and friends can reside, and that you can rebuild it when circumstances, or you, dictate. This structure need not be literal—just as a coyote builds a metaphorical home by turning "around three times in the grass." What then might be the conception of the self that underlies such a conception of home? What type(s) of philosophy might one need in order to formalize that self-conception? Would it mean that we might place less importance on the self or selves we count as "authentic and healthy," and instead value more the skills in one's brain and body (individual and communal) to make a self or selves?[35]

TOWARD A PLACE WHERE I CAN BRING ALL OF ME HOME

In this section, to push this argument further, I ruminate and speculate about how capitalizing on these promising aspects of philosophy might affect philosophy as a discipline as well as those who engage in it. If we take seriously the challenges to the traditional conceptions of the self in the history of philosophy, and combine them with contemporary challenges leveled by those within the discipline, perhaps we will be steering toward a discipline that is more promising and welcoming for women, people of color, and others who have felt alienated by it. This means that philosophers will need to do a better job of recognizing, analyzing, and theorizing about the lived experiences of people outside of those practicing traditional academic philosophy.[36] We need to conceive of a philosophy that is in the service of life—in the service of the complex, multifarious, incoherent lives most people really live, and we need to convey this in both our research and teaching.

And so my relationship with philosophy continues. I do not even want to contemplate who I might become without it. Yet, philosophy is not perfect and I hope that both of us will continue to evolve and grow as we move forward in the future. As in any healthy relationship, I do not want to change philosophy completely (I do not want it to become psychology, literature or physics), but I do hope that I can help it to mediate "with [its] worst self/On behalf of [its] better selves"—just as it has done with me. At the same time, I often get frustrated "having to remind [it]/To breathe/Before [it] suffocate[s]/[I]ts own fool self."[37]

NOTES

1. Linda Alcoff, *Visible Identities* (New York: Oxford University Press, 2006), p. 184.

2. I have recounted some of these aspects of my autobiography in another essay, "Into the Crucible: My Art of Living," in *Philosophy, Feminism and Faith*, Ruth E. Groenhout and Marya Bowers, editors (Bloomington, IN: Indiana University Press, 2003), pp. 120–39.

3. Alexander Nehamas, *The Art of Living* (Berkeley: University of California Press, 1998).

4. Plato, *Apology* (38a).

5. As I discuss in later sections of this chapter, so much of our visual racial and gender identity has a large impact on how we (and others) view ourselves, our life chances, and what constitutes a meaningful life.

6. "[O]ne has hitherto never doubted or hesitated in the slightest degree in supposing the 'good man' to be of greater value than the 'evil,' of greater value in the sense of furthering the advancement and prosperity of man in general (the

future of man included). . . . What if a symptom of regression were inherent in the 'good,' likewise a danger, a seduction, a poison, a narcotic, through which the present was possibly living *at the expense of the future?* . . . So that precisely morality was the danger of dangers?" (Friedrich Nietzsche, *On the Genealogy of Morals*, Walter Kaufmann, transl. (New York: The Modern Library, 1968), Preface 6.

7. At the time (1988–1989), Outlaw was a visiting professor at Spelman. Although I did not know it then, he was, and remains, one of the preeminent scholars in the field of Africana philosophy.

8. As of January 2009 the count of black women philosophers (those with PhDs) was approximately 30 (of about 10,000 philosophers in North America). Kathryn Gines at The Pennsylvania State University has formed an organization called the Collegium of Black Women Philosophers whose goal is to increase the number of black women in philosophy and provide a network of support for its members.

9. Friedrich Nietzsche, *Ecce Homo*, Walter Kaufmann, transl. (New York: The Modern Library, 1968), "Why I Write Such Good Books."

10. I might even go so far as to say that this ability to affirm my own life also helps me and others to forge communities that in turn aid their constituents in creating collective meaningful, affirmative lives.

11. Kwame Anthony Appiah, *The Ethics of Identity* (Princeton, NY: Princeton University Press, 2005); Paul Taylor, *Race: A Philosophical Introduction* (Cambridge: Polity Press, 2004); Anna Stubblefied, *Ethics Along the Color Line* (Ithaca, NY: Cornell University Press, 2005).

12. See for example Charles Mills, *Blackness Visible* (Ithaca, NY: Cornell University Press, 1998) and Lucius Outlaw, *On Race and Philosophy* (New York: Routledge, 1996).

13. Alcoff, *Visible Identities*, pp. 92–93.

14. Charles Taylor, *Sources of the Self: The Making of Modern Identity* (Cambridge, MA: Harvard University Press, 1989), p. 27.

15. See Michael Banton, *Racial Theories* (Cambridge: Cambridge University Press, 1987); Robert Bernasconi and Tommy L. Lott, ed., *The Idea of Race* (Indianapolis, IN: Hackett Publishing Company, Inc., 2000); Robert Bernasconi, ed., *Race* (Oxford: Blackwell, 2000); Emmanuel Eze, ed., *Race and the Enlightenment* (Oxford: Blackwell, 1997); Charles Mills, *The Racial Contract* (Ithaca: Cornell University Press, 1997).

16. See Alcoff, *Visible Identities*, Chapter 3.

17. Ibid., p. 53.

18. Ibid., p. 268.

19. Ibid., p. 80.

20. Ibid., pp. 5, 8.

21. Ibid., p. 191.

22. Ibid., pp. 191–93.

23. Ibid., p. 194.

24. "It is 'thick' in the sense of its profound effects on individuals, groups and the country in virtually every realm of existence. It is 'monolithic' in that within individual races, the concept does not allow for diversity or variation. In other words, a race is a discrete undifferentiated whole into which one is born, and because of

one's 'blood' one is in general consigned to that racial designation for life. In some sense, one is born into a racialized culture and its attendant values, and one is therefore provided with the values that might help one to organize a meaningfully ordered life-world, to borrow Outlaw's terminology. At the same time, due to internal and external pressures, one is expected, and punished for failing, to accept these 'life-world' values based on one's perceived racial identity" (Jacqueline Scott, "The Price of the Ticket: A Genealogy and Revaluation of Race," in *Critical Affinities: Nietzsche and African American Thought*, Jacqueline Scott and Todd Franklin, eds. (Albany, NY: SUNY Press, 2006), p. 161.)

25. "'Multifarious' in the sense that individual races would allow for more diversity within themselves as well as between themselves and other races. It would be 'thin' in that one's racial identity would not determine virtually every aspect of one's life. This 'impurity'-based model of race would more readily reflect the multi- and inter-cultural nature of our world where race is less construed solely based on similarity of appearance, and more on the multiple communities and cultures in which individuals live and create life-worlds. In this world, the purity-based model of race fails to play the legitimating role it played in the past. One would not *have* to primarily identify oneself according to race—it would be one identity among many. Race would be less a noun than an adjective; less essentially constitutive than existentially reflective" (Jacqueline Scott, "The Price of the Ticket: A Genealogy and Revaluation of Race," in *Critical Affinities: Nietzsche and African American Thought*, Jacqueline Scott and Todd Franklin, eds. (Albany, NY: SUNY Press, 2006), p. 164. See also Kwame Anthony Appiah, *The Ethics of Identity* (Princeton, NY: Princeton University Press, 2005); Paul Taylor, "Ecce Negro: How To Become a Race Theorist" in *Critical Affinities: Nietzsche and African American Thought*, Jacqueline Scott and Todd Franklin, eds. (Albany, NY: SUNY Press, 2006); Lani Guinier and Gerald Torres, *Miner's Canary* (Cambridge, MA: Harvard University Press, 2002).

26. Paul Taylor provides a telling example of these types of inadequacies in his essay "Ecce Negro: How To Become a Race Theorist" in *Critical Affinities: Nietzsche and African American Thought*, Jacqueline Scott and Todd Franklin, eds. (Albany, NY: SUNY Press, 2006), pp. 109–110.

27. Taylor, "Ecce Negro," p. 110.

28. For example, see Alcoff, *Visible Identities*, pp. 109–12, 82–83, and 270.

29. Ibid., p. 56.

30. Ibid., pp. 75–58.

31. Ibid., p. 277.

32. Ibid., p. 284.

33. Friedrich Nietzsche, *The Gay Science*, Walter Kaufman, transl. (New York: Vintage Books, 1974), 377.

34. Barbara Kingsolver, *Animal Dreams* (New York: HarperCollins, 1990), pp. 242–43

35. Anthony Appiah, *Cosmopolitanism: Ethics in a World of Strangers* (New York: W.W. Norton & Company, 2006), pp. 33–34, 37, 52.

36. Anthony Appiah, "The New Philosophy," *New York Times*, 9 December 2007.

37. Donna Kate Rushin, "The Bridge Poem," in *This Bridge Called My Back: Writings By Radical Women of Color*, Cherríe Moraga and Gloria Anzaldúa, eds. (Latham, NY: Kitchen Table, Women of Color Press, 1983), p. xxii.

CHAPTER ELEVEN

RE-READING PLATO'S *SYMPOSIUM*
THROUGH THE LENS OF A BLACK WOMAN

Donna-Dale Marcano

Plato's *Symposium* is well known for its conversation on Eros and in particular the speech of Diotima that chronicles the role of Eros in the pursuit of wisdom and ultimately the pursuit of philosophy. However, a less-discussed but much more interesting conversation takes place between Socrates and the young Alcibiades. In the light of Socrates' re-telling of Diotima's narrative about the journey of the soul from seeing beautiful things to Beauty Itself, the drunken, angry, philosophically incapable Alcibiades represents the failed journey of someone in pursuit of Socrates qua philosophy. This chapter explores Alcibiades' pursuit of Socrates and thus philosophy as a symbol of the "outsiders" relationship to philosophy. In particular, I link the character and experience of Alcibiades with the character and experience of Black women as they attempt to negotiate philosophy within the context and viewpoint of philosophy's tenuous relationship with them.

When it comes to reading Plato's various dialogues, the *Symposium* has always occupied a special place in my heart. Diotima's speech, generally regarded as the most important section of the dialogue, seemed to speak to me of the lofty journey to philosophical wisdom all through the fundamental emotion of love. It was this speech (along with the *Republic*) that found its way in most philosophical anthologies of classic works. Imagine my surprise, when, at this stage of my career and in the midst of teaching an Introduction to Philosophy class, I found that the figure that appeared most compelling to me was Alcibiades. This attraction to Alcibiades and the subsequent desire to link black women's experience with such a figure may appear at first incongruous, if not an oxymoron of sorts. Why not, one may ask, seek an experience for black women through Diotima, the

225

lone woman's voice inserted into the corpus that is the Platonic dialogues? I contend that the role of Diotima may indeed be significant in considering the role of the "feminine" in philosophy; however Diotima is at best a figure that can represent "woman" or the "feminine" in the abstract. Her presence, we can hope, hints at the equality of soul for philosophically inclined men and women that the story of the ideal state in the *Republic* suggests; a figure of the capacity for understanding possible in women (or at least Greek women). Nonetheless, this abstraction and thus capacity cannot be traced easily to all women if we are to take seriously the discourses of race and gender, both hidden and explicit, in which black women, because of their race and gender, are least likely to be considered the conveyors of philosophical wisdom. I argue then that given the standard and canonical representation of Socrates as the philosopher *par excellence*, the figure of Alcibiades represents a direct contrast; and, that this contrast, expressed through the person of Alcibiades, best captures the intensely conflictual, yet erotic relationship of philosophy to black women who have been historically excluded from the life of the mind and hence from what is considered the expression of fundamental philosophical imagination. Indeed, the figure of Alcibiades represents both the tragic outsider relationship to philosophy that black women philosophers, like myself, may experience and a powerful critique of philosophy's own self-imagination originating from the depiction of Socrates as the model for philosophical life.

Alcibiades has long been considered, along with characters such as Thrasymachus, a "bad boy" of Platonic dialogues. For this reason and others, few philosophical writings on Socrates or Plato take up his speech as a significant critical response to Socrates' presence as *"the* philosopher" and to philosophy itself. Alcibiades is the character who *cannot* fulfill the journey and promise of the philosophical enterprise. The historical facts of the life of Alcibiades themselves provide another reason to consider Alcibiades a "bad boy" and, most importantly for the purposes of this chapter, antiphilosophical. A member of an elite and prominent family, Alcibiades is often regarded as having set his sights on political power and fame. Saved by Socrates on the battlefield, he later became known as a brilliant but traitorous politician who played all sides in the conflict between Sparta and Athens. In the *Symposium*, Alcibiades is most notably regarded as the most handsome young admirer of Socrates.

The *Symposium*, of course, begins with the young Apollodorus who declared himself as living an aimless and worthless life until meeting Socrates and with whom he has since understood the value of philosophy through his constant companionship with Socrates.[1] It is thus fitting then that the dialogue ends with another young companion of Socrates' whose relationship to Socrates and thus philosophy both praises the philosophical life as

Socrates himself embodies it and yet nonetheless is incapable of fulfilling his desire for Socrates and philosophy.

Alcibiades enters what turns out to be an all day fete just after Socrates offers a retelling of Diotima's story of Eros as a powerful workmate in the ascent to the Beautiful Itself—"the absolute, unmixed and unpolluted by human flesh or colors or any other great nonsense of mortality."[2] Socrates finishes the story with his own praise for the power and courage of Love to the loud applause of his companions. Alcibiades enters the party "very drunk and very loud," half-carried by some friends and demanding to know the whereabouts of the host, Agathon.[3] And it is at the sight of Socrates and a well-placed encouragement from Erixyimachus that Alcibiades details his tragic pursuit of Socrates in an encomium that turns out to be as much a critique of Socrates as it is an obvious expression of praise.

Alcibiades begins his alleged encomium with what he deems as an appropriate image of Socrates which he claims to "aim at the truth."[4] Socrates, he says, looks like a statue of Silennus, a reputed follower of Dionysus, who was said to be a great wine consumer (a drunk in our terms today) and who often was carried by his Satyrs, themselves figures of voracious appetites and who appeared in imagery as holding large erections.[5] One story of Silenus claims that he was captured by a King for his drunken prophesies and shared with that King the philosophy that "the best thing for man is not to be born and if born should die as soon as possible."[6] The statues of Silenus, as Alcibiades describes them, are found in any Athenian shop and are hollow but contain in the insides tiny statues of gods. However, Alcibiades notes that he is not merely looking at resemblances in appearance between Socrates and Silenus as well as the Satryrs but that Socrates bears resemblance to their impudent, contemptuous, and vile attitudes toward life and the living.[7] Alcibiades's description of Socrates is quite interesting because throughout the Platonic dialogues and including Alcibiades' own details of Socrates, Socrates succumbs to neither wine nor sexual appetite and is impervious to extreme weather conditions. And yet, these are the very contradictions that Alcibiades claims Socrates embodies.

Alcibiades charges Socrates with living his whole life as one big game of irony.[8] It is a game of incongruity in which Socrates both "follows beautiful boys in a perpetual daze" and yet can care less "whether a person is beautiful, rich, or famous."[9] Socrates can drink the best of them under the table and yet no one has ever seen him drunk.[10] Alcibiades recounts that Socrates saved his life on the battlefield and was a brave and alert soldier yet, he is also known for standing on the battlefield in one spot from one morning to the next contemplating a problem.[11]

Socrates claims ignorance and yet he somehow inspires Alcibiades to take account of the condition of his soul and the lack in his life. Thus,

Alcibiades bemoans that Socrates traps him, makes his political career seem a waste of time and in the process inspires the feeling that his life is not worth living, a life as miserable as a slave's.[12] In his desperation to become the best man he can be, Alcibiades offers his body, his mind, his belongings to Socrates in the hopes that this lover and teacher of wisdom would help him. Yet, Socrates rebuffs the student companionship of Alcibiades in a flair of the ironic by remarking that Alcibiades' ability to see his (Socrates') beauty of the soul is a sign that Alcibiades already accomplished more than he thinks only to also add that the exchange of favors between them would be like exchanging bronze for gold: "You seem to me to want more than your proper share: you offer me the merest appearance of beauty, and in return you want the thing itself, 'gold in exchange for bronze.'"[13]

Reduced to the mere appearance of beauty by Socrates, Alcibiades' tale of rejection by Socrates is nevertheless infused with his desire not merely for Socrates but for philosophy. Alcibiades' admission of his many attempts to seduce Socrates can be easily dismissed as a performance of the pursuit of the mere physical appearance of Eros. But such a dismissal quickly overlooks the real intensity of Eros that Alcibiades claims Socrates inspires, the love for philosophy. Prior to the detailing of the seduction of Socrates, Alcibiades proclaims that he will discuss Socrates' greatest accomplishment in the presence of those who suffered the same pain as one might discuss a snake bite in the company of those who have been bitten. What is Socrates' proudest accomplishment? It is that the heart of Alcibiades was bitten by philosophy:

> Well, something much more than a snake bite has bitten me in my most sensitive part—I mean my heart, or my soul, or whatever you want to call it, which has been struck and bitten by philosophy, whose grip on young and eager souls is much more vicious than a viper's and makes them do the most amazing things.[14]

Describing the guests at the table, including Socrates, as having all "shared in the madness, the Bacchic frenzy of philosophy," he goes on to detail his humiliating tale of pursuit of and rejection by Socrates.[15] Here, Alcibiades conveys the spirit of philosophy as associated with Eros in all its sensuality, a frenzied and gripping love with a Dionysian character. Alcibiades, in effect, describes his relationship to Socrates and thus philosophy with all the intensity and drunkenness associated with falling and being in love—something that Socrates himself never appears to do but nonetheless inspires. Socrates, then, inspires love but does not love. That august teacher has moved beyond the loving of persons or things or situations: Socrates exhibits love only for the transcendent. Alcibiades fails in his attempt to be a lover of Socrates and philosophy because his love is particularized, contextualized, erotic in its sensuality. He sees no difference between love of wisdom in its transcendence and love of wisdom in the finitude of being human or loving a human. What is bitten? Is it his heart or soul? It makes no difference; they are indistinguishable.

But Alcibiades is left only with shame. He is not only left with the shame of never accomplishing the seduction of Socrates, but more importantly he is left with the shame of failing to fulfill the path of philosophic wisdom. What is his failure, his sin? Alcibiades admits that Socrates is like a Siren, his words like melodies with the capacity to possess, to reveal, to be divine.[16] He states that Socrates has the ability to "make me stay by his side till I die."[17] Nonetheless, despite the overwhelming magnetic pull of Socrates and the promise of philosophy, Alcibiades states:

> Socrates is the only man in the world who has made me feel shame. . . . Yes, he makes me feel ashamed: I know perfectly well that I can't prove he's wrong when he tells me what I should do; yet, the moment I leave his side, I go back to my old ways: I cave into my desire to please the crowd. My whole life has become one constant effort to escape from him and keep away but when I see him, I feel deeply ashamed, because I'm doing nothing about my way of life, though I have already agreed with him that I should. Sometimes believe me, I think I would be happier if he were dead. And yet I know that if he dies I'll be even more miserable. I can't live with him, and I can't live without him![19]

This passage articulates the failure of Alcibiades to conform to the expectation of what it means to be a philosopher. It is self-accusatory. Alcibiades himself portrays what he believes to be the distinction between the desires of the philosopher and his own desires. He desires to please the crowd, a character trait that philosophers, through the representation or myth of Socrates, disavow with self-congratulatory pride. This is, in fact, the passage one would point to in order to highlight who is *not* the philosopher.

Yet, remember, Alcibiades also states that Socrates is "impudent, contemptuous, and vile," and it is this aspect of Socrates which Alcibiades claims to give witness in his speech.[19] How should we understand Alcibiades' claim as witness to the contemptuous, impudent, and vile nature of Socrates even as he speaks in the midst of what appears to be a flagrantly self-accusatory tale of failure to what amounts to becoming a better person? Indeed, it is not merely a tale of failure but an admission of refusal as Alcibiades just seconds earlier states, "So I refuse to listen to him; I stop my ears and tear myself away from him."[20] Alcibiades intentionally refuses Socrates *and* philosophy; so are his words a sign that he rightfully comprehends that he is not good enough for philosophy?

In addition to this question we should ask, to what exactly does Alcibiades see himself as a witness? What should we make of this particular witness whose story of suffering and rejection ends the *Symposium* in contrast to the apparent ease of the young Apollodorus who begins the *Symposium*? Or should we ask ourselves to what extent does the figure of Alcibiades show how philosophy fails some of us?

Drew Hyland has argued, against traditional readings of Platonism, that the story told by Diotima, and which is taken to narrate the ascent to philosophical wisdom, is really a story of the fully tragic dimension of the human situation.[21] A traditional interpretation offers the ascent from beautiful bodies to Beauty Itself as the force of Eros that enables the future philosopher to move from the particular to the transcendent at which point the particular is understood as mere appearance and inferior to true knowledge. This is a prelude to the famous divided line of the *Republic* in which lower levels of thinking are rejected as one moves to the forms. In an overall philosophical project that aims to undo the emphasis on the achievement of transcendence in Platonism as it has been established, Hyland contends that Diotima's speech shows the paradoxical nature of human erotic striving:

> Eros's parentage, according to Diotima, shows that there is something paradoxical about it; it is at once incomplete and overfull, the true child of Poros and Penia. That paradoxical character does not deny but rather makes it possible that human erotic striving could be, on the one hand, fated to fail, yet on the other hand, a revelation of the nobility of human aspiration; in a word, genuinely tragic. Not only are humans fated to a condition of incompleteness that they never fully overcome, not only are they therefore fated to aspire toward a goal to which they are doomed to fail, but this aspiration, notwithstanding its fated failure, nevertheless can, in the striving, ennoble human being. The portrayal of Eros in the Symposium therefore sets out in full richness the potentially tragic character of the human situation.[22]

Elsewhere, Hyland describes this tragic dimension of the human condition as incompleteness, a recognition thereof, and a striving to overcome it.[23] If Hyland is right, then I contend it is through the figure of Alcibiades that we most clearly find the expression of the tragic and very human relationship to philosophy.

With this in mind, we can now reconsider the accusations Alcibiades levels against himself in the face of his relationship to Socrates. What then, could it mean that he "desires to please the crowd?" Could it be more than a trivial disposition? Does it mean that one can easily be marked as anti-philosophical? I think the answer is no. Suppose instead we take Alcibiades' desire to please the crowd as an intimation that he not only loves but desires to be loved: That Alcibiades understands that loving and being loved is part of what it means to be engaged and committed to a community of peers. The desire to be loved may well not have been explicitly articulated in the story of Diotima but to assume that Eros works only if one plays the position of the lover neglects that the desire, in its lack, wants something back. If one hopes to love and gain wisdom then this relationship includes being loved by wisdom. The hope is that wisdom reveals itself to you. Indeed, Alcibiades' desire to be loved by Socrates and others can be contrasted to Socrates' apparent pursuit of young boys only to never love them. In this context, Socrates does not desire to be loved. Indeed, Socrates admits in the "*Lysis* that unlike the two young friends, Lysis and Menexenus, *he has never had a friend.*"[24] One can imagine Socrates constantly in the presence of his peers, engaging in discussions around truth, virtue, and piety, and in the midst of these wise interrogations and discussions, he has not once experienced the love of a friend (or a lover for that matter). Socrates has not once experienced the desire to love someone or to be loved.[25]

I believe that this little irony is not lost on Alcibiades. In what often is taken as high praise of Socrates, Alcibiades states that Socrates is unique and cannot be compared with another human. Although we can compare one great orator with another or one person with another, Socrates stands alone:

> There is parallel for everyone—everyone else, that is. But this man here is so bizarre, his ways and his ideas are so unusual, that search as you might you'll never find anyone else, alive or dead, who's even remotely like him. The best you can do is *not* to compare him to anything human, but to liken him, as I do, to Silenus and the satyrs, and the same goes for his ideas and arguments.[26] (italics added)

In a twist of irony, Alcibiades shows how Socrates defies humanness, and thus the very incompleteness, recognition, and striving that constitutes the tragic nature of Eros even as it pursues wisdom. More importantly, I suggest that Socrates himself not only defies the finitude of humanness but refuses it. It is this refusal to which Alcibiades points in aiming at the truth of Socrates. Socrates is neither just beyond the mere human nor is he the best human; he is *bizarre*. He not only refuses the particular desire of

Alcibiades but also the desire to be loved. Socrates misses or at least refuses to admit that Alcibiades' pursuit of him is not merely the particular pursuit of physical Eros but that Eros in its multiple manifestations provides meaning in and through the particular even as it attempts more and strives to be more—to stand in one's particularity, finding resources there through and from which one pursues a broader relationship to philosophy. Alcibiades is witness, then, to Socrates' own refusal to be human. If being a philosopher means denying or refusing your particular and concrete being-in-the-world, then Alcibiades' self-accusation is a full admission of his refusal to follow this model. Therefore, we can say it is not Alcibiades that fails philosophy but that philosophy fails Alcibiades.

Does philosophy fail some of us then? Yes! It fails those of us who understand that we are particularly situated. We are particularly situated in our desires, in our communities, in our race, in our genders, in our loves. For this, black women's intellectual work that engages their racialized and gendered perspectives and which aims to take account of the social and political contexts in which these perspectives take shape often are viewed as so particular as to be of no philosophical value. Such a viewpoint retains Socratic pretensions to be wholly transcendent, above the realm of human beings who desire and live in and among communities, and who desire and live within particular political contexts with political aims and visions. Additionally, such a viewpoint refuses, as Socrates did, to recognize its own incompleteness and the necessity of striving as what is indeed the truly philosophical nature of the human condition. Indeed, the very presence of a black woman in a room of predominantly white male philosophers suggests a specificity that challenges the pretensions of universality and transcendence that have been ascribed to those white males bodies. We can even say that the presence of black female bodies are mistakenly presumed to be anti-philosophical.

More, however, can be said about black women's relationship to philosophy through the figure of Alcibiades. Similar to the situation of Alcibiades in which we can't live with it and we can't live without it, ours is indeed a conflictual relationship to the discipline as it has come to represent itself. Our experiences are frequently marked, if not marked daily by this conflict that is deeply rooted in Eros. Relationships involve knowing and being known by one's lover; but philosophy refuses to know us as its lover.

This was brought home to me as I walked into that Introduction to Philosophy class and many others, consisting in my case of mostly young white boys, and realized that their ability to take up the position of the philosopher occurred with relative ease. Whether they accept or reject philosophy they are able to articulate their positions as knowers. But then again, they also are known by philosophy.

It is by no accident, I think, that Alcibiades often is portrayed only as a sexual suitor whom Socrates rightfully rejects. Alcibiades conveys the discomfort, the conflict, and the push and pull of understanding one's self in relation to philosophy as it is theorized and most importantly as it is lived. He reveals the "outsider" relationship. His refusal to pursue only the transcendent without the particular, without the physical, without appearance has deemed him an incapable critic of Socrates. Just like Alcibiades, however, black women's relationship to philosophy as "outsiders" allows us to grasp the greatness of philosophy as well as it failures. Indeed, I advocate that we enter the scene just like Alcibiades, raucous, loud and drunk with wine and Eros so that our presence can never be forgotten or lost even if suppressed.

ACKNOWLEDGMENTS

This chapter was originally presented at the First Collegium of Black Women Philosophers at Vanderbilt University, October 2007. It is dedicated to those women at our first meeting together.

NOTES

1. *Symposium*, 173. All line references to the *Symposium* are taken from the translation in *Classics of Western Philosophy* 6th edition; ed. Steven M. Cahn (Indiannapolis: Hackett Publishing, 2002)
2. 211e2
3. 212d6
4. 215b
5. "Silenus," *Wikepedia, the Free Enclycopedia*. October 8, 2007. http:// en.wikepedia.org/wik/Silenus.
6. Ibid.
7. 215b9
8. 216d18
9. 216d-e
10. 220a4
11. 220c-d
12. 216a
13. 218e
14. 218a4
15. 218a4
16. 215c-d
17. 216b1
18. 216b3-c
19. 215b11
20. 216a9

21. Drew A. Hyland, *Finitude and Transcendence in the Platonic Dialogues* (Albany: State University of New York Press, 1995), p. 122

22. Hyland, *Finitude and Transcendence in the Platonic Dialogues*, p. 122.

23. Drew A. Hyland, *Questioning Platonism: Continental Interpretations of Plato* (Albany: State University of New York Press, 2004), p. 145.

24. Drew A. Hyland, *Plato and the Question of Beauty*, Bloomington, IN: Indiana University Press, 2008. Hyland argues that Alcibiades may represent a Platonic criticism of Socrates because Socrates "does not adequately love the human, that his enourmous eros is directed more or less exclusively on what he takes to be the divine, the forms," p. 110.

25. We know, of course, that Socrates has been loved. After all, Plato, and the many others in the *Apology*, showed concern for Socrates' life.

26. 221d

CHAPTER TWELVE

DEFENDING GENDER
AND ETHNIC PHILOSOPHIES

Oscar R. Martí

Everyone who works in an "ethnic" philosophy—black, Chicano, Latin American, and so forth—is familiar with the blank stares or dismissive smiles from colleagues when we talk about our fields. This also holds true for people who do gender, although they also might get other reactions. Asian scholars seem to be in a relatively safe position (Indian or Chinese philosophy carries a limited respect in the West) depite the perception that these philosophies are tainted with "all that flapdoodle which blows out of the East like a breath from the plague."[1]

Such reactions seem anachronistic when one considers the magnitude of the social and political changes that occurred in the United States this past half-century, changes that had an influence on the development of those philosophic movements whose object was to study the presuppositions and implications of gender or race.[2] These fields of inquiry were forged out of relentless philosophical probing and from an incisive application of critical reasoning and philosophical analysis to those circumstances and beliefs that fostered gender, ethnic, and racial biases. Unlike the nineteenth-century romantics, who invoked feelings as explanations, contemporary philosophers who study gender and ethnicity have kept themselves within the confines of rationality and logic. In a way, their work is no different from that of conventional philosophers; it just happens that they engage in issues of time and place, and try to understand human diversity, personal or social identity, or even to conceptualize the characteristics of gender, ethnicity, cultures, race, or nationality.

Coming from philosophers, this reaction of indifference or even antagonism is surprising. Rather than welcoming efforts to apply philosophic methods to new areas as genuine philosophic practices, many have instead denied it legitimacy and treated gender and ethnicity philosophers as illegal alien workers. Although in some cases, this attitude could be due to biases—and thus beyond rational discourse—the behavior can be explained as a result of some serious rational concerns. Here, I address some of these concerns philosophically. Four arguments suggest themselves. Philosophers who deal with issues of gender and ethnicity are not doing legitimate philosophical practices because of the following four arguments:

1. They are insincere or opportunistic people who use philosophy to propagate a political agenda;

2. Their philosophies are full of defective arguments;

3. Their methods are not traditional forms of philosophizing;

4. Their philosophies go against the grain of good philosophy.

Many critics have expressed views similar to these arguments. Are these arguments sound or plausible? Or are they invalid, fallacious, or implausible? And if the latter, what would constitute a reasonable counterargument? My strategy is to understand them, assess their worth, and give some possible counterarguments. Here I offer nothing new. My goal is modest: I want to state and challenge some unstated assumptions in a debate that has been going on for a long time.

Argument 1, that philosophers who deal with issues of gender and ethnicity are not doing philosophy because they are insincere and opportunistic or because their motives are bad or because they are motivated by politics, is an *ad hominem* fallacy. People might be sincere or insincere when they argue, but these are rhetorical considerations irrelevant to the logical worth of an argument (whether they are valid or fallacious, plausible or unlikely). Debaters question the sincerity of an argument in order to persuade the listener of its invalidity or implausibility without adducing proofs. The same applies to motives: Motives for formulating an argument are independent of the logical worth of that argument. People have all kinds of motives for offering arguments, some good and some bad; everyone is more or less sincere in offering these arguments; and every one has a political agenda. People might be insincere or ill-willing yet offer very sound logical arguments; and morally good, sincere people might offer us very poor ones. Evaluating a motive or determining sincerity is a psychological or a sociological question. But whether the argument itself is good or bad, that's a matter of logic. In order to show that ethnic philosophies are not legitimate, reasons other than bad motives must be produced.

A caveat is in order: Pointing out the logical weakness of the first argument is not a defense of ethnic and gender philosophies. It is only a logical evaluation of the criticism, and of limited scope. I cannot accuse critics of being racist or biased, for then I also would be incurring the same kind of fallacy—evaluating the critics' arguments in terms of their personal motives. Furthermore, there is no law that forbids disliking people, although there are directives that forbid limiting or denying economic or social opportunities to people just because you dislike them. Such actions are called biases, in our case racism or sexism. The same holds for what some philosophers do. Conventional wisdom tells us that biases are not, in a normal sense, reasoned out arguments, but symptoms of irrational preferences.[3] In present company, they merit little space, other than to remind ourselves that they do exist.

Argument 1 might be interpreted to mean that gender and ethnicity arguments are morally suspect because the intentions of its proponents are morally suspect. In some moral theories, intentions can matter—both to the proponents and of the critics. Argument 1 then becomes a question of morality, with two groups arguing for different takes on what is and what is not moral. In this kind of dispute, both sides would be called to justify their moral stands, and they must do it in a morally neutral way, that is, without assuming the superiority of one particular set of moral beliefs (their own) over another. This is difficult because what people see "clearly" or "is generally believed," and so on, are but expressions of their own group's mores. So interpreted, Argument 1 has lost its edge as a criticism given that gender and ethnicity philosophers are arguing about choices between competing ethical, social, or political theories, which is a perfectly legitimate philosophical practice.

Argument 2 seems to be another rhetorical move: belittling ethnic and gender philosophies because its practitioners present us with defective arguments. In a way, the criticism embodies a reasonable request: Any philosophical position is and should always be open to criticism. This is a rule of inquiry. Any form of gender and ethnic philosophies should be critically examined. And they will probably be found wanting. But by itself, that is not a sufficient reason to belittle these views or seek to exclude them from the corpus of philosophy. Applying the same rule of inquiry to any philosophical idea—traditional or mainstream—also will show it wanting. The *Republic* and *The Critique* are full of bad arguments, but no one is calling them illegitimate philosophical works. To look for flaws is a part of normal philosophical practice. If one excluded every flawed argument from the corpus of philosophy, there might be very little philosophy left and, most of it very uninteresting if not truly worthless.

I suppose it might be possible to rank philosophical arguments, from indispensable to worthless, provided that the criteria for worth and their

relative weights be clearly specified and mutually agreed on. Else, such ranking would be a statement of personal preference, useful for some purposes and
useless for others. But like morally neutral arguments, that kind of ranking
might prove to be a difficult to deliver promissory note.

Argument 3 seems to be more substantial: Gender and ethnicity philosophers do not focus on the traditional philosophical themes of philosophy,
like the nature of truth, beauty, goodness, or justice, and so on. These themes
have been a philosophical staple for a long time. They have attracted many
to the profession and produced an impressive literature, so impressive that
it has been used to define the cultural character of Western civilization,
and even to mark its ethnic borders. By creating newer philosophic themes,
gender and ethnicity philosophers are perceived as abandoning a "noble"
philosophical tradition and sapping the energy and intelligence of its readers
in pursuit of frivolous (nontraditional) matters.

Traditional philosophical questions are no doubt important, but so are
many others. First, dealing with one kind of question does not, of necessity,
erase the others. In the past, interest in some traditional questions have
crested and ebbed and crested again. Second, there was always a first time
for every philosophical idea introduced, and that new idea did not supplant,
exclude, or remove from the corpus the previous tradition. Rather, it added
another theme. It happens that this is the case of some questions about
ethnicity, identity, gender, and the like. Finally, there is nothing new about
philosophizing about gender roles, about ethnicity, about identity, and so on,
that can't be found in Plato's *Republic* or Aristotle's *Politics*.

Argument 3 admits of another interpretation: These new philosophies
are challenging the traditional ways of doing philosophy. It is true that
some gender and ethnicity philosophers do challenge the mainstream—say
analytic philosophy, foundationalism, pragmatism, Thomism, utilitarian-
ism, rationalism, and so forth. That might be a bad thing, if the challenge
brings about some philosophical turpitude—but that requires proof. What
is wrong with challenging a philosophical view? Argument 2 issued a challenge. Challenging philosophical views is part of doing philosophy. It was
done by Aristotle, Thomists, pragmatists, and the like. Now that they are
well entrenched, are they to dispense the same acrimonious reception to
challenges they received when they were challenging the themes of their
day? I suppose that gender and ethnicity philosophers have nothing about
which to complain, for acrimony has been a part of the philosophical patrimony. And, because of philosophical commitments, gender and ethnicity
philosophers will probably break away from the tradition.

A third interpretation of Argument 3 could be that only traditional
forms of philosophizing are valuable. Why? Traditional philosophy might be
deemed valuable depending on reasons that have to be spelled out; but one

of the reasons cannot be that they are traditional or mainstream. Neither can be a claim to endurance: Traditional philosophy should endure because it has endured or survived. There are all kinds of things that although they have survived, I still would not want to see their continuance: bigotry, poverty, war. Furthermore, that something has survived is not a guarantee that it will continue to be or do so.

This criticism misrepresents the very tradition that it upholds. What is this philosophical tradition and why is it so valuable? Western philosophy has been doing a lot of things during the past 2,500 years, some of it quite odd. It has tried to prove the existence of a God, and to challenge any such proof; it has tried to show that the moral worth of an action lies in the consequences and not in the motive and also that it is in the motives, not in the consequences where moral worth resides; and that the mind is a material substance, a mental substance, or a linguistic construct; that there is and that there isn't a free will, and so on. As a matter of fact, what an examination of the tradition shows is an enormous diversity of philosophical views and a continuous dissent among its practitioners. Adding to this tradition an inquiry into the nature and function of gender and ethnicity would hardly diminish the field's reputation.

Finally, the third argument could be construed as a request that gender and ethnicity philosophers articulate more clearly the worth of the fields they are establishing. This is an important request and one that I think all philosophers should comply with. After all, nonphilosophers criticize philosophy for sapping the energy and intelligence of the young by steering them toward problems that have not been solved for centuries and which, even if they could be solved, would not bring about world peace, an end of famine, or a cure for cancer. And how is this self-evaluation to be carried out? It stands to reason that well-entrenched philosophers mentor the newcomers. Critics of gender and ethnic philosophies are in the enviable position of showing gender and ethnicity philosophers how to justify our field. I suppose that once shown the "proper" way, "problematic philosophers" will rise to the occasion and give a good account of their field's worth.

Repeating an earlier caveat, challenging Argument 3 is not a justification of gender and ethnicity as legitimate philosophy—only a deflation of criticisms. Yet, there is value in this criticism: Gender and ethnicity, just like any other philosophy, should show its intrinsic worth. Specifying how this can be done, however, remains a task for all philosophers, not just for the new arrivals.

Argument 4, asserting that these philosophers are going against the grain of good philosophy, is ambiguous. What is meant by (a) *going against the grain* of (b) *good philosophy*? The phrase "going against the grain" suggests that gender and ethnicity philosophers are going against philosophical tradition.

The phrase "good philosophy" now adds a new dimension to the criticism. It is a request for an evaluation of the philosophical practice, of how well philosophers ply their trade. Although there is no universal agreement about what philosophy *is*, and some about what it is *about*, there is consensus about *how* it should be done well: Good philosophy should be clear, reasonable, and logical; it should be free to question everything; and it should be articulated in a language. What is unintelligible, intrinsically obscure or purposely vague; what takes everything for granted and refuses to question anything; what is unutterable and cannot be discussed in any language—that is considered bad philosophy. Some might even refuse to call it philosophy.[4] These desiderata are not so much a question of taste as a question of necessity. They are rules of thumb that emerge from the practice of philosophizing. Illogical or obscure language generates frustration rather than a response; taking things for granted thwarts discourse; and what's ineffable fails to elicit a dialogue. Curiously, even the violation of these desiderata creates philosophical discussions: in clarifying the illogical or obscure; in challenging skeptical apathy; or in speculating about what could or should have been said.

Most gender and ethnicity philosophers conform to these criteria. Many make their case clearly, reasonably, logically, although some also include a dose of activism and political advocacy. Most gender and ethnicity philosophers question assumptions about gender and race, about the social and political thinking that makes up the status quo, about the cherished beliefs of many. It is in fulfilling the traditional role of philosophical gadflies that they reap irritation instead of admiration and vituperations in lieu of thanks. Although there are some who make claims to gender and ethnic ineffability,[5] most show elegance, expressiveness, and eloquence that indicate a mastery of the language.

Unfortunately, to these desiderata about the practice of good philosophy other requirements have been added, not because of need but because of an unjustified conviction that one way of looking at the world is better than another:

1. There can be only one (or a very few) good ways of doing philosophy.

2. The good philosopher must have a commitment to the Truth.

3. The good philosopher searches for the most general truths about the world, for some kind of universal truths.

At first sight, these requirements seem reasonable, that is, until they are challenged, which is precisely what a good philosophical practice is supposed to do. What is wrong with asserting that there's but only one, or a very few, good ways of philosophizing (read: positivism, philosophical analysis, critical theory) and conversely, that not all ways of philosophizing are good, or that most others are very bad? As an opinion about philosophy, nothing. This belief has been at the core of considerable philosophical creativity and generated much good and bad philosophy. And it has kept the riff-raff away. However, as a criterion for evaluating a practice as being good philosophy, it is problematic: (a) that not all philosophical views can be good because there can be only one or a very few ways of doing good philosophy, begs the question; (b) it doesn't tell what good philosophy looks like, which was the problem with Argument 3; (c) it leaves unquestioned whether some specific type of philosophy is good. And leaving things unquestioned would be, in principle, bad philosophy.

The second condition for doing good philosophy is that philosophy is, seeks, or somehow should love the truth. A commitment to the truth also sounds good, but it is not very helpful as a condition for doing good philosophy because of fundamental philosophical disagreements not about what is to count as true or whether and how one should love the truth, but about what truth is. Is it an undefined primitive, an arbitrary sentential value, the coherence with or correspondence of sentences with facts, or what works? These are good questions, but to presume a commitment to the truth so one can come to an agreement about what truth is, is to stack the deck, especially when many discount as mere appearances what just as many call reality. This does not mean a turn toward subjectivism or an abandonment of the truth; just that truth is an object and a goal of philosophical speculation, and not a presupposition about good philosophy. You can't have it both ways.

Sincerity, as demanded by the proponents of the first argument, is not a good substitute either—that whatever I am asserting is not aimed at facetiousness or hypocrisy but because I believe this is the way things are. Aside from the moral baggage it carries, sincerity presupposes that in order to do philosophy, we should all believe in a number of facts and adhere to a similar conception of truth, else one is being insincere. Such requirement forces philosophers to accept unquestioned assumptions and prevents them from considering counterfactuals. That would be a pity because being the devil's advocate or considering what is true false and what is false true has generated much philosophical discourse, good and bad. So, for the time being, the requirement that philosophical discourse should be sincere or true is best dropped out. One has to be satisfied with just considering all possible worlds, or just assuming that all philosophical statements, including this one, are hypothetical, convenient fictions, speculation, or true lies.

The third condition has to do with searching for general or universal truths. Nothing is wrong with that either. This is in part due to a need to be more efficient and more economical with our time and resources. It is rooted in everyday experience and in scientific practice where instead of examining items one at a time, the investigator looks at the class to which they belong and hopes that what is peculiar to each individual is also peculiar to the group. It is a labor- and time-saving strategy that helps the investigator to spend more time on what is important in an investigation. This strategy was imported to philosophy from mathematics, and applied to concepts, removing empirical constraints, and elevating generalizations to the ontological level of universal truths: Everything is One, if you ignore the difference. Determining the scope, usefulness, and validity of this search for universal truths has been a major theme in Western philosophy. It tempts us, however, to downplay the influence of details, the particulars, the accidents, and the individual. As philosophies frame their thoughts in more general and abstract terms, they become more inclusive, and by using formal tools, give the appearance of greater rigor and closeness to the nature of things. They also give the appearance that philosophy is not about particular things or about particular facts and if, somehow, philosophers stray into factual territory, they do it only as embodiment of larger truths. Why? Because particulars are less inclusive (that's true); less rigorous (incorrect); or depart from the true nature of things (debatable). And this last condition is regarded as a reason for denying legitimacy to gender and ethnicity philosophy. Argument 4 could be reformulated as follows:

Ethnic philosophers are not engaged in legitimate ways of philosophizing because

> 4_a they concentrate on the inessential or accidental, on the particulars instead of the universal qualities of human relations—on gender and ethnicity instead of Man and his place in Nature—and consequently bring disunity and create conflicts.

Argument 4_a rests on a mistaken assumption: That all gender and ethnicity philosophers are particularists, concerned only with individual gender or ethnic identity, or with a specific group's preferences, or at worst selfishly demanding some equity only for their own group. In point of fact, aside from a common interest in gender and ethnicity issues, there seems to be little else common to the group. Its members differ in method, aims, and philosophical commitments. True, there may be some particularists among them, or some who engage in decadent or iniquitous arguments, but many fall within classical philosophical *practice*: They search for a fit between words and action; they define, and redefine, and test for conceptual adequacy; critically examine some assumptions; examine principles and test them for consistency; look for the moral, social, or political implications and test for consistency of race and gender concepts and of the epistemological, social, and political frameworks in which they are embedded. Some are not arguing for radically different universal conceptions of justice, retribution, being, and so on. Others ask for the formulation of new moral principles and for a social reconstruction. They just demand that the old distinctions be applied fairly. Although they might investigate facts, poll opinion, adduce or challenge experimental results, they are still working within a traditional philosophical frame of reference. In a way, they do the same thing other philosopher do, except for the subject matter. One might not agree with their analyses or conclusions, but must admire the adroitness with which they marshal philosophical arguments.

Some proponents of 4_a still maintain the illegitimacy of gender and ethnicity philosophies on the grounds that they are divisive and introduce conflicts at a time when philosophy should be a healer of social and political wounds. This is a different kind of criticism: That a philosophical outlook causes divisiveness is a hypothesis relating facts (social divisiveness) to a possible cause (philosophizing about gender and ethnic issues), and as such it is open to verification. Divisiveness in the form of sectarianism, racism, sexisms, and other "isms" have been around for a long time and cannot be laid at the doorsteps of gender and ethnicity philosophers. Furthermore, studying a social phenomenon is not necessarily the same as advocating it. The accusation of divisiveness is also a serious moral charge. Ours is a time of crisis, of limited resources, and philosophers should speak with one voice against injustice. Noble as it might sound, this call for unity is not too helpful for it leaves open what is to count as a unifying philosophy. Am I to agree to one kind of philosophy so as not to be divisive? Why? Because if I disagree I am being divisive? Or am I to remain silent so as not to be divisive? Silence is not necessarily a cure and is often a cause. Am I then to abstain from questioning? Wouldn't that go against the consensus that philosophy should question everything? Philosophy is by nature divisive—a gadfly—rather than a uniter.

All this assumes that gender and ethnicity philosophers can speak as a group, but are they one? A quick overview of their work shows a variety of methods, aims, voices, and often the presence of many disagreements. Such diversity militates against a common philosophy, never mind a legitimate one. The suspicion emerges that one is dealing with several philosophical approaches, each one in need of separate justification. In light of these observations, a new argument can be formulated:

> Argument 5: No blanket statement can be given about the legitimacy of gender and ethnicity discourse because it's not one but many discourses, some of which do not seem to have a place in the philosophical practice.

Argument 5 undermines our effort to even speak of the field by threatening to multiply the task of justifying these philosophies. There are several options. One is to accept the criticism. True that because there are so many philosophers discussing gender and ethnicity issues so differently, it is difficult to make blanket statements about the topic without falling into trivialities or errors. There is not much one can do about this except to be careful about what one says, look at the variety of arguments, and try to show each one to be philosophically legitimate. Proponents of this argument could counterargue that maybe all we have are people who have accidentally picked a topic, a relevant, important, or compelling topic, but one only incidental to their philosophizing; a topic that could easily be discarded as other, more relevant ones emerge. This would make all questions of gender and ethnicity, like deceitful demons or brains-in-vats arguments, devices for investigating deeper philosophical problems and not genuine philosophical fields; that perhaps, gender and ethnicity issues are meant to showcase the philosopher not create philosophies. This is an unreasonable criticism meant to devalue the subject while capitalizing on the multiplicity and diversity of its advocates. The issues discussed are no mere philosophical devices or bridges to introduce philosophical problems. They are real problems that are to be examined with the philosopher's toolkit. Although the subject is cut from a different cloth, it is cut with the same scissors.

Another alternative is to show that issues of gender and ethnicity are legitimate philosophical endeavors, that there is a place in philosophy for most gender and ethnicity arguments. Legitimacy here means conformity with practice, with what philosophers do as philosophers. That is, that all the different gender and ethnicity discourses fit in to some philosophical activity. What is this practice? And how do gender and ethnicity philosophies fit in?

The philosophical practice can be seen as a science,[6] as a literature, and as a craft; that is, as an organized form of knowledge about Reality, the self, or morality; as an expression of human concerns, attitudes, norms, or emotions; and as a series of techniques for clarification, justification or persuasion. These views are not mutually exclusive, and often a philosopher can engage in all of them without any misgivings or inconsistencies. Although they all seek to understand, they differ in important respects. The first aims at explaining and stresses truth, the second aims at expressing and stresses feeling and emotions, the third at clear reasoning and stresses the instrumentality of the discipline.

As a science, philosophy took physics as a model in form, as it laid the groundwork for understanding Reality—to ascertain the truth about some hypotheses about that fundamental structure of the world and the self. Its philosophical canon is the records of some attempts at a rational and reconstruction of the world, and evidences its progress by pointing to the development and refinement of the tools used to accomplish the task to a greater degree of satisfaction. Questions about the nature of reality gave rise to metaphysics; about how one knows that reality, to epistemology; how one should act and choose in accord with that reality, to ethics. Logic has turned out to be an invaluable tool in organizing and testing possible truths, and its enormous applicability to the empirical and mathematical sciences has tempted many to separate it from philosophy itself. According to this view, the philosopher's task is to examine concepts, propositions, or principles, test their adequacy, consistency, coherence, their presuppositions and implications, and reformulate them when found wanting. This approach has been favored by many gender and ethnicity philosophers, for instance, when they find concepts such as "Latino" or "woman" inadequate and, offer more satisfactory definitions or characterizations that will lead to a more accurate understanding of the world; or when they speculate about conceptions of human rights that applies to all; when they explore the implications of gender roles; even when they reformulate more equitable justifications for social redistribution of limited resources. Their investigations have increased in value as we tend to become less of a global village and more of a worldwide supermarket, packaging, shelving, and selling ideas under recognizable labels and priced by a common currency.

Despite its productive history, philosophy, as a science, had a very modest record of success. Not only were the fundamental questions posed more complex to answer than originally thought but even asking them turned out to be very difficult. Yet these questions seem to have endured, in part because of the intimate reactions they elicit from the questioner: Arising from wonder and anxiety, they remind us of the human condition. This has led many to suggest that the quest for Truth is beyond our reach, or even unutterable, and insist that philosophical views are but personal reactions to the absurd, expressions of individual emotions, expectations, and aspirations. To them philosophy is more like literature than science. Philosophy is written by people for people. It aims to persuade, to stimulate the imagination as well as thought, to teach about being human, and to transcend the commonplace. In this approach the histories of philosophy and of ideas change emphasis. By looking for reasons and motives, history turns from an attempt to understand how past practitioners made such howlers to a discovery of their personal reasons and motives, the problems they perceive, and the alternative methods and solutions they saw open to them. Often philosophers, either from the past or from other cultures, are read as sources of interesting ideas regardless of their truth. This conception of philosophy is partly true of some radical skeptics and nihilists, of existentialists, postmodernists, and deconstructionists. This is also true of those who see gender and ethnicity philosophies as the voice of the ethos of the people, as expressions of anger, frustration, desperation, or cries for liberation, justice, or redress.

Once it is understood that treating philosophy as literature is part of philosophical practice, it seems a truism to assert that all of philosophy is ethnic. Just like literature, that does not alienate writers from their time and place, their history and their social environment, their reasons and motives, their hopes and fears, without pretense to having or searching for universal verities, philosophy as literature does not separate the philosopher from his or her gender or ethnicity. And just as in literature, where there is no intrinsic difficulties discussing Latin American, African, Ancient Greek, British, or Feminist literatures, there should be no difficulties in conceiving of Latin American, African, or Feminist philosophies. In this sense, there is no question about the legitimacy of these philosophies. Rather, the question is about how good it is. And that's a question of standards to be negotiated.

The expressionist view of philosophy also has some shortcomings. There are as many expressions as there are expressers, and some are of two minds, making philosophical discussion difficult. Without an apparent objective criterion, it would be difficult to weed out the good from the bad philosophy. Philosophy so portrayed becomes a matter of taste, fleeting and inconsistent, subjective, like the taste for some foods. In its defense, being subjective in this sense is not necessarily the same as being arbitrary. Subjectivity here is a question of individual preferences and choices, but these choices are more often than not subject to rules and criteria that are quite compelling. Nothing is as subjective as our taste in foods; yet, we tend to conform to a very narrow spectrum of tastes and find it impossible to eat really different foods. Same with clothing. We have the freedom to dress any way we want to, but rarely do we see men in miniskirts or women with unmatched shoes. It seems almost impossible to go against our subjective tastes and we would seldom venture into the exotic. Still, many philosophers see this practice as not belonging to philosophy. They feel uneasy with such a subjective approach and express a preference for what they feel are solid methods and objective truths.

Philosophy can also be portrayed as a craft.[7] The philosopher reflects on a problem, usually in a specific area or discipline, and, in accord with some standards of rigor and a body of knowledge, evaluates the evidence, draws out presuppositions and implications, and assesses alternatives in order to provide some insight. This practice is as old as Socrates and the sophists, and includes any modern philosopher who uses his toolkit to examine anything critically. Philosophy becomes an instrument for cogent reasoning and rational living and a handmaiden to the discipline that's employing it. This instrumentalism is presupposed in critical reasoning, medical ethics, social philosophy, legal philosophy, the philosophy of science, applied logic, and so on. And this is the approach many philosophers use to deal with gender, race, or ethnicity problems—with whether, say, Affirmative Action is sexist, or with what would constitute an alternative for sexual harassment redress, and the like. And although the gender and ethnicity character is dependent on the topic under investigation—thus characterizing anyone as a gender and ethnicity philosopher, even if arguing against the field—there is another sense in which this approach is ethnic: A craft results from an individual's performance in accord with changing beliefs and standards of place and time, and accommodating to the local tastes and demands.

As a craftsman, the philosopher examines an issue and assesses it in terms of his beliefs, logical skills, values, and those of his audience and offers as a product a particularly individual argument. Thus, an ancient Greek philosopher's arguments would obviously differ from those of a medieval philosopher; so would the arguments of a seventeenth century English, French, or Spanish philosopher. And since crafts are a result of the time and the place, and because they express individual values, they are also ethnic, in the same way cooking or music is ethnic. And in a way, this is what is meant by characterizing a philosophy as British, French, Asian, and by extension, African or Latin American. Characterizing a philosophy "x" is relevant to the kinds of arguments that are used, what shared knowledge is presupposed, what rhetorical devices, with what purpose, or to what audience. To the disappointment of essentialists, it lacks a unique set of descriptive properties or essential features; to the disappointment of expressionists, it need not express a feeling or voice concerns. When investigating, for instance, the analytic-synthetic distinction or the nature of empirical knowledge, a philosopher's ethnic character can surface in the examples given (unmarried Norwegian bachelor farmers or Cuban palm trees), the use of some expository styles (the elenchus, the essay, the myth), the language used (Latin, French, or Ebonics), and so forth.

That the craft of philosophy is ethnic seems to be a truism. All philosophical activity is carried out within one or another culture. It uses language and categories that have specific cultural roots. Even the rules of logic: As rules they are chosen because they work efficiently to achieve goals valued in our culture: truth, public testability, consistency, economy of action. They would serve no useful function where these values are not operant. Again, these are not arguments in favor of giving up all objectivity or the subjectivity of truth but a reminder that it is people in an environment who try to be objective and truthful, sometimes.

Perhaps a guiding fear among well-meaning philosophers is that by allowing ethnic and gender philosophies into the canon, we might also be allowing all kinds of fads and pseudo-philosophies. Unfortunately, philosophy has a long history of dabbling into what later became fads—from phrenology to the language of God—while considering as fads that which later became part of the canon. And only the future can decide what flumdiddle is. Two equally unpleasant alternatives are open to us: Either we carefully and consciously come to an agreement about the nature, extent and demarcation of the field, and then level whatever does not fit our criteria, or we can but be tolerant and hope bad philosophies will eventually sink to the bottom while the good ones float, some despite efforts to drown them.

ACKNOWLEDGMENTS

I thank the Chicana/o Studies Department, and Professor David Rodriguez, for their academic support and continuing encouragement.

NOTES

1. Henry Miller, *Tropic of Cancer* (Paris: Grove Press, 1934), p. 191.

2. Among the specifically philosophical works are Linda Martin Alcoff, *Visible Identities: Race, Gender, and the Self* (Oxford: Oxford University Press, 2006); Anthony Appiah, *The Ethics of Identity* (Princeton: Princeton University Press, 2005); Jorge J. E. Gracia, *Latinos in America: Philosophy and Social Identity.* (Malden, MA and Oxford: Blackwell, 2008); Leonard Harris, *Racism* (New York: Humanity Books, 1999); Cornel West, *Keeping Faith: Philosophy and Race ire America* (New York: Routledge, 1994); George Yancy, *Cornel West: A Critical Reader* (Blackwell Publishing 2001). Also interesting is Linda Leung, *Virtual Ethnicity: Race, Ethnicity and the World Wide Web* (Burlington, VT: Ashgate, 2005).

3. But see D. T. Goldberg, "Racism and Rationality: The Need for a New Critique," in Harris, *Racism*, pp. 369–97.

4. Even here exceptions are always allowed: for instance Heraclitus philosophical aphorisms, G. E. Moore's assurances about the existence of an external world, or mysticism as a religious experience.

5. For instance, the radical epistemological claim that only insiders can understand the issues that concern a particular gender or ethnicity.

6. For lack of a better word, I am using the Latin term *scientia*. The term *theory* has too many connotations, some too precise, some too broad.

7. R.G. Collingwood, *Principles of Art* (Oxford: Oxford University Press, 1938), pp. 15ff.

PART IV

PHILOSOPHY AND THE GEOPOLITICS

OF KNOWLEDGE PRODUCTION

CHAPTER THIRTEEN

THINKING AT THE LIMITS OF PHILOSOPHY
AND DOING PHILOSOPHY ELSEWHERE

―――――――――――――――――――――

From Philosophy to Decolonial Thinking

Nelson Maldonado-Torres

It is no secret that philosophy is and has been one of the strongest bastions of Eurocentrism in the Western humanities up to this date. Having given up to some extent the monopoly of legitimate culture and experience, the West continues to hold on to the privilege of reason. As self-declared queen of rationality, philosophy therefore remains in a unique position of value, even though it is often marginalized within the humanities themselves, which have tended to favor the study of language, literature, and culture at large, sometimes at the expense of normative questions. But philosophy's Eurocentrism nonetheless remains central to the self-definition of the university, since the university presupposes substantive conceptions about self, knowledge, and world that have been articulated by philosophers, among others. The centrality of such ideas, however, is probably reaching an end as the university is increasingly relying on technical (not substantial) conceptions of knowledge and as it has gradually adopted corporate models for evaluating knowledge production and conceiving of financial and bureaucratic priorities. Philosophy is thus, like the rest of the humanities, in a state of crisis.

We are already familiar with some of the ways in which philosophers have handled this sort of crisis in the past century. One of the responses has been accommodation. It has been argued, for instance, that the prevalence of analytical clarity in the service of methodological rigor that is dominant in philosophy departments in the United States mirrors the privilege of

science in the university setting. This privilege and the relation of philosophy to science are at the same time linked to a political and geopolitical
reality of competition for technological advancement and the persecution
of substantive critical thinking in the Cold War.[1] One wonders if similar
adjustments will take place in face of the post-Cold War reality of unhindered transnational capitalism and the preeminence of economics and corporate models of measuring efficiency. Will the university as a whole, and
philosophy in particular, accommodate themselves to them just like they
tended to do with science? Will philosophy conform to clarifying the limits
and possibilities of economic reason within the parameters of liberal ideology and human rights discourse alone? Or, will it take refuge in its old
Eurocentrism to help the university maintain undesirable others at bay, and
to limit demands for diversity and justice at the social and cultural levels
while leaving the question of cognitive justice aside?[2] We should not forget
that the post-Cold War age of unhindered transnational capitalism is at the
same time an age of massive migratory flows from the south and the former
colonial territories to the north.

To be sure, these are not the only possibilities. Philosophers could aim
to simultaneously overcome Eurocentrism (race, excessive class difference
largely premised on race, and sexist and heteronormative bias at the social
and epistemic levels), the fixation with scientific method, and the reduction
of matters of value to efficiency and corporate criteria.[3] One place to begin
in formulating an agenda of work that aims to do this is in the realization
that these matters are more historically connected than what they appear
at first sight. Consider that colonial subjects and people of color at large
have often, if not paradigmatically, been conceived as inferior by Eurocentric
biases, which have led to a conceptualization of them as testing ground for
scientific investigation and as dispensable disorderly entities to be managed
appropriately by forms of reason that lead to apparent order and profit.
The experiences of people of color as they try to become philosophers and
participate in the field of philosophy may therefore offer good lessons about
the pitfalls and the possibilities of certain strategies to overcome philosophy's
main challenge today. It is with this hope that I offer my own personal
reflections here.

This is the story of how a colonial subject from the U.S. territory of
Puerto Rico arrived to the discipline of philosophy and how he has traveled
through philosophy and beyond it, as typically defined. The story may not
be so different from others who are in philosophy and related fields, as it
touches on aspects that are quite central to the division of knowledge in
the modern university: the division between the sciences and the humanities, the investment in the development of the former vis-à-vis the decaying
interest in the latter, and the disconnection between questions of efficiency,

questions of interpretation and value, and questions of social change or transformation. Anyone who deviates from the hegemonic form of valuation that prizes technical rationality, objective discovery, and short-term quantifiable change most often goes through a process of reflection that reveals, at least at some level, the extent and limits of modern disciplinary arrangements. My case is more peculiar, however, as in addition to these challenges, I dealt with other factors as well: Questions about power, justice, liberation, and identity very much related to my being a person of color in a colonized territory.

In my efforts to promote decolonization, I was in search of a way of thinking that combines the rigor of method, sophisticated interpretation, and ideas that help to change the world. I soon came to realize that these areas (method, interpretation, and praxis) have been separated from each other in modernity and that, by and large, academic philosophy has played a crucial role in legitimating the split. Thus, I gradually concluded that for philosophy to be useful it also had to be decolonized, even to the point of abandoning philosophy as a professional enterprise or as one's exclusive home. My conclusion was that although it may be possible to decolonize philosophy gradually from the inside, other fields are already more in tune with the imperative of decolonization and thus offer unique opportunities to use theory and philosophy for that purpose. For me, the same fundamental impetus that led me to philosophy turned me gradually to a transdisciplinary form of critical and constructive thinking more related to what we know today as ethnic and postcolonial studies. This chapter is my story of thinking at the limits of philosophy and doing philosophy from elsewhere in a path that took me from philosophy as a discipline to decolonial thinking and praxis.

PHILOSOPHY 101: REASON IN THE COLONIES

Everybody seemed curious that, after having excelled in science and mathematics for most of my life, and after doing superbly on the quantitative parts of the college board exam, I turned down an offer to study engineering in college and decided to pursue studies in the humanities and social sciences. The reason was not clear, as I had benefited enormously from special science and mathematics programs tailored for promising students in public schools. The irony is that perhaps it was in part because of such programs, in addition to my visits and participation in university settings before I had graduated from high school, that I developed the distinct impression that the investment in technology and science was taking place at the expense of sustained reflection about the meaning, the social impact, and ethics in the application of scientific and technical knowledge in general. I was thus led to the idea that I would use whatever talents I had to work on areas of substantive reflection about social issues and values rather than aspire to develop my talents in mathematics and science, even though I was more equipped for the latter than for the former. To be sure, I don't think that substantive reflection about social issues and values, and mathematics and science are by any means opposed to each other, but it was clear that they were divided in the university setting, reflecting, I believe, a hierarchy of value that was operative beyond the university itself.

After making my choice for the humanities and the social sciences, it first occurred to me that I should study psychology, but I soon changed to sociology because I was primarily interested in understanding and promoting social change and I thought that sociology would prepared me best for that. I was content with the choice, but I still had questions that required me to explore the humanities and particularly philosophy. These were questions about the meaning, value, and significance of human enterprises, including the knowledge produced in mathematics and the sciences. They were questions also not so much about how things really are in the more empirical sense of the term, but in terms of how things are constituted and how things should be in light of how we understand such constitution. I soon realized that these questions required more systematic and consistent reflection than empirical study alone, and that scientific methods and objects of investigation necessitated philosophical clarification for their proper conceptualization and use. These concerns were fundamentally philosophical, and thus it was not strange that shortly after I took my first philosophy class, I shifted to philosophy as a major.

When I shifted away from mathematics and the natural sciences toward the social sciences there was the presumption that I was abandoning my interests in exactitude and methodological precision. In turn, when I shifted from the social sciences to philosophy and the humanities, the concern was that I was leaving behind my deep interests in social change. I was even warned that gradually I could easily turn into a self-absorbed intellectualist. I discovered that such is how folks in the humanities are sometimes conceived by some of their peers in the natural and social sciences. That is unfortunately not completely misleading, at least in some cases. Needless to say, I saw my shift to philosophy differently. It was not a question of being less rigorous or socially committed, but of being precisely more rigorous—by asking questions about the conditions of possibility for subjectivity and objectivity—and more prepared to promote change—by having a better understanding of what change means and the possibilities for it, among a myriad of other fundamental questions. I never thought that this could be done through philosophy alone, so I kept studying the social sciences and followed discussions on the epistemology of mathematics and the natural sciences, in addition to also studying literature, and other fields in the humanities. But it was the study of philosophy that marked me the most, and thus, a reflection on the teaching of philosophy in Puerto Rico is in order.

In Puerto Rico, with few exceptions, students come to have a taste of philosophy only at the university level.[4] In the meantime, besides science and mathematics, they are taught Spanish, English, Western history, U.S. history, history of Puerto Rico, and Spanish and Puerto Rican literature. Teaching about the United States and Puerto Rico clearly takes a privileged position. These two areas also are taught in the most traditional ways. There is something in the material, however, that makes it impossible not to raise questions and problems. Even though the Puerto Rican is said to be the result of a most excellent mixture of different races, nobody can erase the idea that, like in virtually every other place in the Americas, this mixture took form by the forces of violence and subordination. But the issue is more complex: What you come to know is that since Puerto Rico was conquered by the Spaniards more than five hundred years ago the people of the island have always been in some form of political subordination in relation to another people. Puerto Rico is perhaps the oldest colonial territory in the Americas, if not the world. The experience of subordination becomes in this way for the Puerto Rican not some contingent result of their being, but a constitutive factor of who they are. Their lives, culture, and history are marked by the trace of the colonial, a constant intervening factor that complicates the ordinary life, the ethics, and the politics of the Puerto Rican. For this reason, the remarkable efforts to avoid the sudden emergence of an explicitly political consciousness fail, or perhaps succeed too well. In any case, politics becomes a daily business and an ordinary affair in the lives of Puerto Ricans.

A colonial configuration marks the very being of the Puerto Rican. Hyphenated beings in a hyphenated place marked by coloniality—postmodern colonials, and even one might argue, as Laó Montes suggests, postcolonial colonials or colonial postcolonials.[5] It is like this that we go to college classrooms to learn about the Greeks, the Romans, and Descartes. At the intellectual level, we do not know ourselves as Caribbean before we know ourselves as part of Western civilization and foreign grandsons of the Greeks. With the Greeks, the *paideia*, and the *polis* in one pocket and with our "jibarería criolla" in the other we walk and talk thinking that in some way at least a part of our soul would be redeemed—a most fantastic split of consciousness that ironically promises the possibility of vanquishing our several identity complexes through knowledge and the affirmation of one sole identity. In the process, a new species of the human is born: the Greekorrican, with its familiar outcome, the Eurorican. Beautiful lectures about the Enlightenment and positivism confirm the origin and the destiny of this soul. Most passionate disquisitions or even quarrels about what is philosophy and what is not, take the place of some common identity complexes.

There is something intriguing about philosophy. Even though philosophers praise the plasticity of their field—that philosophy cannot be encapsulated in a definition, that its meaning has changed through the ages, and so forth—at the same time they can become the harshest arbiters, believing that they know exactly the necessary and sufficient conditions for anything to be considered philosophy. It is as if the spirit of philosophical adventure has some very definite limits. Philosophy appears to be Janus-faced: at one moment taking the shape of radical thinking, while at another giving expression to the most regressive ultra-conservative and counter-revolutionary intellectual forces. Thus, although my philosophy training in Puerto Rico was very serious and rigorous, at the same time I could not but feel certain anxieties that characterized the field of study. The anxieties emerged whenever the absolute value of Western reason or the Western canon were put, or seemed to be put in question. The sources of the challenges were diverse: One of them was Western poststructuralism, housed mainly in literature programs, but with some representation in the department of philosophy itself. I perceived this to be largely an internal quarrel, reflective to some extent of the permanent tension between rationalism and skepticism in philosophy. My main concerns had to do with two other sources and types of anxiety: the anxiety about the relationship of philosophy and religion, and the anxiety about non-European forms of thought.

It was my struggle with religious questions that had initially led me to philosophy as an area of enquiry in my precollege days. I initially learned of philosophy through a very dear friend who had a brother and an older friend who had studied philosophy formally before. My friend, Héctor, and I used to have long conversations about faith, God, transcendence, meaning, and "the life of the spirit" in general. We were very close. In fact, both of us had declined offers to study engineering and chose to stay at the campus where the humanities and the social sciences were most central. I believe that he may have declared philosophy as a major right when he was admitted. At that time, he was also an enthusiastic reader of not only Western philosophy, but also Eastern thought, particularly Buddhist. His energy and enthusiasm were contagious, and his utmost seriousness and talent elicited a great deal of respect. At college, we continued to read and have conversations about philosophy and religious thought, Western and not. We noted a large degree of convergence between what was called philosophy and what was simply referred to as myth, doctrine, tradition, or religion. We knew that there were differences, but in some cases they were completely blurred and in some others completely subverted—as when philosophy appeared as more mythical than myth, and when religious ideas conveyed the power of rational thinking to a greater extent than philosophical opinions.

Disciplines were created to discipline, so we learned promptly that we were expected to maintain certain things apart. We also came to know that the recognition of philosophy as a separate field of enquiry greatly depended on its differentiation from religion and its gradual association with science. Thus, to combine philosophy and religious thought too closely challenged not only the self-understanding of the discipline, but also its status in the secular university and among the humanities. Although the association with science seemed to put philosophy in a high place among the humanities, the link with religion seemingly pushed it away from secular reason and thus from the boundaries of the university altogether. It should be noted that the University of Puerto Rico, like many universities in the Spanish-speaking world, poses a strong divide between academic research and confessional views to the point of being skeptical of areas such as religious studies, even though this is an established area within the secular humanities in many universities in the United States. This obviously has to do with differences in the role of religion in higher education and public life in Latin America and the United States, particularly differences between the influence of Protestant elites in higher education in the United States vis-à-vis the perception of the Catholic Church in the process of nation building in Latin America. It is also relevant to note here that Protestant churches and seminaries in Puerto Rico were introduced as part of the process of U.S. colonization, even though, in some cases, they also provided a space for the dissemination of radical thinking and resistance to colonization. As I noted before, politics takes a particularly omnipresent form in the colonies.

My friend and my resistance to think of philosophy as an area that could be limited or circumscribed to a set of ideas found in a very specific set of books written by Western authors spoke, I think, of our commitment to spiritual, epistemological, and political liberation. Also, we could not accept the proposal that the "life of the spirit," the life of the mind, and our political possibilities were all limited and disconnected from each other in the way that we were taught. We refused to accept the idea that, temporally, philosophy had undergone a linear process of separation from anything considered to be religious, and that, spatially, it had disconnected itself from everything that was non-Western. It was to a great extent this refusal and dissatisfaction that led my friend and me to take very seriously both what we were taught by our teachers, but also the areas that were banned to us by the discipline. And so, gradually, the idea that we needed philosophy, but that our path could not be completed in that discipline, became clear to us. Unfortunately, my dearest friend could not complete the path that he had set out for himself because he passed away before we finished college.

The loss had a strong impact on me. This happened while we were both in a special exchange program at Hunter College in New York where we went to study philosophy and religious thought. The exchange program in question aimed not only to allow students in Puerto Rico to complement their education abroad, but also to introduce them to New York City and, particularly, to the Puerto Rican community there. Here again, the personal, the intellectual, and the political met in intriguing ways.

I came back to Puerto Rico in a solemn spirit, but determined to continue the path that my friend and I had initiated. I worked and volunteered as a teacher in a maximum-security jail for two years while I finished college. Although matters of faith were not as central for me as before, I still considered religious thought important and difficult, if not impossible, to fully separate from philosophy. Readings in Hindu and Buddhist thought also continued, along with Christian liberation theology, which had always stimulated interest in me for its contributions to theological method, its questioning of epistemic and economic dependency, and the assertion of Latin America and the Third World as a viable locus of enunciation for theological and theoretical questions. It was interesting to me that my teachers and the field of philosophy generally speaking seemed more concerned with criticizing these areas of thinking as not philosophical enough, than in joining in and contributing to the critique of epistemological dependency, whether in philosophy or not. Indeed, for them to talk of Latin American philosophy, for instance, was almost as anathema as engaging religious thought.

It was thus that I grew as a very young intellectual: The lessons that I learned from my teachers were as fundamental to my education as the anxieties that I discovered in philosophy as a field. Philosophy provided fundamental tools to address theoretical and intellectual questions, but I found that it limited itself in reaction against the religious and that it was largely indifferent to the legacy of colonialism and Eurocentrism. Philosophy's commitment to what it considers as a universal point of view simultaneously bans religious thought, which is rendered as something particular or specific to religious creeds, and covers up epistemological colonialism, because it identifies European thought, not as a particular that has been largely imposed with the help of powerful institutions, but as the true expression of humanity's reach for the universal. Ironically, European thought itself takes the place of the dominant religious systems of old: It has a body of texts that contain or provide the lenses to produce "legitimate" knowledge and it maintains clear divides between the sacred space of Euro-versal reason and everything else. For me, it was a matter of philosophy unnecessarily limiting itself to secularizing Eurocentric lenses. This posture could satisfy neither my vast intellectual interests nor my political concerns. I longed for more.

PHILOSOPHY 102: TOWARD DECOLONIAL REASON:
VIRTUES AND LIMITS OF COMPARISON
AND INTERDISCIPLINARITY

My bachelor's degree in philosophy from the University of Puerto Rico, and my exposure to religious studies courses in New York, gave me the impetus to pursue graduate study in either modern Western thought or comparative religious and philosophical thought. Both possibilities departed from the traditional philosophy degree in that I could engage questions and authors who traveled the philosophical and religious universes without an excessive concern with maintaining them apart. My possibilities were limited to philosophy programs that were tolerant of the study of religious philosophies, and to religious studies departments with strong interests in philosophy. Because I needed a fellowship to study, my options were to a great extent limited to the United States. Many of my teachers had obtained degrees in Europe, where education was free and they just needed some support to be able to study. The younger professors, however, mainly came to the island with degrees from prestigious universities in the United States, which offered not only tuition relief but also a stipend. When I was in college, going to the United States was perceived as the main alternative for someone who wanted to pursue graduate study in the humanities abroad.

The genuine options to pursue my interests were not that many. Departments of philosophy in the United States tend to be one-sided: Most of them have a strong, almost exclusive, focus on analytic philosophy, and a few on continental philosophy. Analytic philosophy was even more restrictive than continental philosophy when it came to legislating over what is considered to be "proper" philosophizing, so I knew that departments with such a focus were not the best place for me. Continental philosophy programs were more open to the exploration of ideas that interested me, but, an unquestioned Eurocentrism seemed to prevail in their horizons and focus. Religious studies departments seemed more attractive, but most focused on theology or history (mainly history of Christianity), whereas my interests resided in the intersections between religious philosophies (Western and not) and secular thought. I discovered a few programs with such priorities and gradually realized that these programs had been created and maintained by scholars with a similar profile to mine who had escaped the prison of philosophy (and theology in some cases) and opened a niche for themselves in departments of religion or religious studies. But, because these departments were interdisciplinary, they could be in conversation with historians, anthropologists, and other specialists in religion, while focusing on philosophical and theoretical issues. Also important is that religious studies tend to embrace more fully or allow the study of non-Western thought than philosophy departments. To be sure, religious studies allows for more freedom to pursue philosophy precisely because it is formally recognized as "religious studies" and not philosophy. This categorization allows for more freedom because "religion" is not so much recognized as the site of reason, but as the place of culture, mysticism, or devotion. Also, by the twentieth century there already was a consensus that all peoples and cultures had a religious component, but not necessarily a philosophy, which is perceived as fundamentally a Western possession. Thus, philosophical explorations could take place more freely in places that are not labeled as philosophy, because they are not taken to be formally philosophy—but rather culture or thought—and therefore do not threaten the perception of a Western monopoly of reason.

I applied to programs in philosophy and religion and got accepted in both. I chose the Religious Studies Department at Brown University because it took philosophy and theory as central, while it also was comparative and interdisciplinary. One of the two main areas in the department focused on comparative religious ethics, comparative philosophy of religion and religious philosophies, and modern Western thought. I continued exploring the intersections and liminal zones between philosophy and religion, and between the West and its "others." Partly for intellectual and partly for personal reasons, I became committed to the project of comparison. Comparison facilitated a process of critical assessment of ideas and self-discovery that I believed to be essential. Coming from a small island in the Caribbean with such a long history of colonialisms and a particular fixation with its political status, I felt that I needed to lose myself in what was strange to me in order to gradually come back to the issues that were closest to me and hopefully see them in a better light. I felt that my perspectives on me and the world had been compromised and that I needed to liberate myself or to decolonize myself, as it were, by traveling to the most distant conceptual and cultural world and return without ever losing sight of my origins or my fundamental convictions and intuitions. I believed that comparison was a route to intellectual and personal decolonization.

My attention turned to two main areas: the East and West dialogue, and religious and secular existential and radical political thought. I was fascinated with parallels and differences between Greco-Roman, Christian, and European thought on the one hand, and Hindu, Buddhist, and Taoist conceptions of the world, knowledge, and values on the other. I had the idea of learning Sanskrit or another Asian language in order to be able to understand elements of Hinduism and Buddhism on their own terms. I did research on engagements of Nietzsche, Heidegger, Sartre, and other Western thinkers with Asian counterparts or with varieties of Asian philosophies in general. I was fortunate to study with specialists in these areas, and my conception of philosophy grew in important ways, but I soon knew that I was at a disadvantage if I wanted to seriously enter this field. I did not yet possess the language requirements and my dream of learning Sanskrit was gradually becoming less and less a possibility. But although the door of pursuing comparative research in Eastern and Western thought was closing, another door began to open up more firmly. That was the door of studying religious and secular existential and radical political thought. I am glad that this happened because it provided the foundation for me to discern serious problems in my early comparative project and in comparative approaches overall.

My interest in existential and radical thought was as old or more so as my interest in comparative research in Eastern and Western thought, and I was in fact more prepared to engage in it than to do the other. My early formal training in philosophy had focused on phenomenology and existential philosophy. Existential philosophy is one of those areas where one finds secular and religious thinkers, Western and not, all of them contributing in very original and profound ways to important discourse. One can legitimately study the work of Kierkegaard, Heidegger, Sartre, Keiji Nishitani, and others without having to apologize for introducing a secular or religious thinker. Existential philosophy had also been very influential in Latin America, both in its Heideggerean and Sartrean variants, so one could legitimately introduce the south and not only the east in the conversation. This becomes all the most obvious through a figure such as Frantz Fanon, who combined existential philosophy and psychoanalysis in his analysis of colonial and racial alienation and liberation in the third world. But Fanon complicates the "continental" approach in the East–West dialogue in more profound ways than by simply adding the "South." He also introduces a form of radical thought that supersedes the limits of the Christian–Marxist dialogues with which I was acquainted and with dependency theory and liberation theology in their classical formulations. Engaging Fanon led me to question the project of comparison and opened up new vistas in my conceptualization of radical decolonial thinking.

What I learned from Fanon was a conception of "decolonization as first philosophy." By this I mean that the fundamental axes of reflection about human reality are grounded in the human-to-human relation, and that the primary questions out of which philosophy itself emerges are motivated not so much by wonder in the face of nature, but by desire for inter-human contact and scandal in the face of the violation of that possibility. This means that the *telos* of thinking, if there is any, is the struggle against dehumanization, understood as the affirmation of sociality and the negation of its negation. I refer to the negation of sociality as coloniality and to its negation and overcoming as decoloniality. These are concepts that have become central in my work and the work of other scholars with whom I have been in conversations for a decade.[6] Each individual gives a particular meaning to them and uses them in different contexts and for different but also related purposes. I take coloniality to mean the systematic negation of sociality and ordinary forms of interhuman contact, particularly as they have unfolded in the over five hundred years of European expansion and the influence of its ideas of superiority and inferiority throughout the world. By the same token I take decolonization or decoloniality to mean the struggle for the restoration of healthy social bonds and intersubjective relations.

Both concepts, coloniality and decoloniality, are coextensive, by which I mean that their meaning is not limited to strict social relations. They refer to relations between anything that stands in for or is grounded on interhuman contact, such as for instance cultures or bodies of knowledge. This means that one could talk, for instance, about the coloniality and the decolonization of knowledge. More importantly, the concept of decolonization as first philosophy indicates that the enquiry about coloniality and decoloniality is more fundamental than the comparative project. That is to say, comparison among forms of thinking must be preceded by a critical examination of the way in which such differences have been constituted, particularly in relation to a hierarchical order that renders them as fundamentally equal or unequal. The main problem with the project of comparison is that it tends to equalize terms that have been produced as unequal, or render invisible the presuppositions for thinking of any two or more elements as equal or unequal. Comparison can thus easily serve the function of hiding inequality and colonial relations from view, and of delaying the engagement with the questions that challenge such relations. These questions often, if not always, shed new light on the object of comparison because one can no longer take each object as separate but as co-constitituve of each other in a system of unequal relations forged by colonialism and related forms of hierarchies.

I began to develop these ideas in my first serious encounter with Fanon in graduate school and in conversations with two teachers and mentors, both of whom have strong ties with Fanon. They are Lewis Gordon and Enrique Dussel. In addition to having a common intellectual ancestor in Fanon, Gordon, and Dussel share a deep commitment to liberation thought and with the project of "shifting the geography of reason."[7] They also approach philosophy and religious thought as historically and conceptually co-constitutive of each other, and therefore, although they recognize their differences, they also refuse to isolate one area from the other. Their combined attention to radical thought, the overcoming of Eurocentrism, and the questioning of the segregation between philosophy and religious thought matched the set of questions, interests, and concerns that I had developed since earlier on when I realized the limits to thinking created by philosophy's constitutive anxieties. It was therefore not surprising that both Gordon and Dussel did not form part of philosophy departments when I met them, even though they both have philosophy degrees.[8] This is telling, particularly considering that they both currently are the most prolific and influential Caribbean and Latin American philosophers.

The concept of decolonization as first philosophy and its strict meaning took a while to emerge, and it involved a series of conversations and collaborations with other scholars, particularly those in the Modernity/Coloniality/Decoloniality collective.[9] Those conversations began late in graduate school and continued in my first tenure track position in the Department of Religion at Duke University. I chose to become a faculty member in the Department of Religion at Duke even though I had the opportunity to return to philosophy as a professor in another university. Once again, I had chosen to continue my philosophical and theoretical explorations in a different home. I came to Duke to teach courses on critical theory of religion, religion and society, and related fields. Now, Duke's Religion Department is very different from Brown's Religious Studies Department, at least when I was there as a graduate student in the mid- and late-1990s. Duke's Religion Department is predominantly focused on history, even though some faculty are in conversation with theory. Another important difference is that Duke University has a quite conservative Divinity School, which is very strong in theology. In general, the theologians tend to take philosophy more seriously than the historians, and there was no exception here. At the same time, theology at Duke tended to be quite dogmatic, though in a particular sense that renders dogma as a tool of social critique, and very critical of anything like a "dispassionate study of religion," be it social scientific, historical, or philosophical. I felt that I had connections to both worlds, but at the same time I could not avoid but feeling mutually excluded by both factions in that, notwithstanding their differences, they complemented each other by maintaining the study of Judaism and Christianity as absolutely central in both, to the deprivation of other areas. There were important exceptions to this tendency, of course, but I still could not but begin to develop some of the feelings that I had found in philosophy before. The field had become too restrictive.

The limits that I found in religion at Duke and its unproductive dialectic with the Divinity School, which was nonetheless successful in attracting very competent students of Christianity, surpassed the particular institutional and conceptual arrangement of that department. The study of religion is premised on their being an object of study, religion, or the religious, which requires analysis, description, and explanation. One can take different approaches to this object of study, but insofar as it is the primary focus it delimits the questions that can be asked and the possibilities of analysis. So, even though religious studies is, to its credit, an interdisciplinary field, the presupposition of a coherent object of analysis both legitimizes its existence as a field and places limits on its possibilities as a form of decolonial thinking and critique. This is not too different from unidisciplinary areas like sociology, economy, or political science, all of which presuppose the existence of a coherent object of study—society, the economy, or politics—that gives credence to its particular methods. This is more or less a circular process insofar as the methods themselves are the ones that allow one to find or delimit the object of study. Ultimately, it is difficult to establish whether the object of study provides legitimacy to the field, or if it is the method that both gives credence to the field and to the presumed object of study. In short, method and object of study constitute themselves mutually, and when or where the object is not found or does not seem to provide much insight into anything, it or its significance must be invented!

The circular process in the dynamic between object and method of study affects the unidisciplinary and the interdisciplinary fields. I had been already disillusioned with comparative studies. Now I was reaching a similar point with interdisciplinary studies. The multiplicity of approaches to one object of study only allows for raising and aiming to respond only to certain kinds of questions. That is to say, even though the methods could be multiple, the questions themselves are still limited by both the methods and the object of study. I myself had learned differently in philosophy. The one important thing that attracted me to this area was that it gave primacy to the process of questioning itself, out of which one could decide to find or create objects of study. And, I was indeed at a point in my intellectual trajectory where questions, not particular methods or objects of study, were driving my scholarship. Thus, my scholarly work and my courses gradually resembled less and less what one could take as legitimate religious studies production. Also, to the extent that academic philosophy has limited its field of questions dramatically because of its Eurocentrism or its analytic framework, my scholarly work did not resemble philosophy either. It was clear at that moment that I had to navigate to a different space, and that space was Ethnic Studies.

PHILOSOPHY 103: DECOLONIAL REASON
BEYOND COMPARISON AND INTERDISCIPLINARITY

It probably sounds not only strange but also contradictory that my critiques of philosophy and religious studies as areas of study led me to Ethnic Studies. For, on the one hand, Ethnic Studies had not typically included my traditional areas of interests—philosophy and religion—and, on the other hand, its virtues presumably reside in being comparative and interdisciplinary, the very two aspects that led me away from religious studies. So how can Ethnic Studies represent a refuge or a new home? The key here is on my work on Fanon, and on the philosophical principles that I have derived from his work and from my dialogue with other Fanonians or serious Fanon scholars. I already indicated that with Fanon I learned to overcome the limits of typical comparative approaches, but I also found in him a critique of disciplinarity (both uni- and multidisciplinarity), and a lens that pointed to Ethnic Studies as a field that was founded on "decolonization as first philosophy" and that was characterized by the exercise of decolonial reason. How so?

I already commented on the way in which the idea of "decolonization as first philosophy" challenges the project of comparison and gives new meaning or direction to this task. Fanon's critique of disciplinarity is even more direct and obvious as he explicitly recommends to "leave methods to the botanists and the mathematicians."[10] By this he meant that human reality cannot be understood methodically in the way that nature and other areas that are grounded on exactitude presumably can. Fanon defended the primacy of the questioning process itself inspired by a concern for the status of human relations. This is a practical dimension of the idea of "decolonization as first philosophy": the process of questioning in regards to human dignity and human relations displaces the primacy of the object of method(s) of investigation. This imperative leads to a transdisciplinary, not to an interdisciplinary form of scholarship. And this is precisely what I discovered at the heart of Ethnic Studies.[11]

Ethnic Studies, and related fields like African American and Women Studies, all of which were born in between 1968 and 1970 as results of social pressures from below, were not primarily interested, I would argue, in creating new objects of study in existing fields or in inventing new methods—even though both of these are necessary—but in defending the centrality of certain questions and problems. The most influential figure in African American Studies, the great W. E. B. Du Bois himself, whose work preceded Fanon's and who died before African American Studies became a field in the academy, put a problem, not an object or a method, at the center of a new area of thinking. For him, it was "the problem the color-line," understood as "the relation of the darker to the lighter races of men in Asia and Africa, in America and the islands of the sea."[12] Well before area studies were born, Du Bois was already questioning the division of the world into regions to produce new objects of study. He was simultaneously questioning an understanding of Ethnic Studies as parallel to area studies in the sense that Ethnic Studies is said to focus on ethnic groups just as area studies focuses on regions.[13] Instead, Du Bois called attention first to "problems" and second to "relations" among peoples in different social positions (power) and geographical locations (spatiality). He also wanted to elucidate "meaning" as when he stated that he wished to contribute to the understanding of "the strange meaning of being black here in the dawning of the Twentieth Century."[14]

Du Bois's scholarship was driven not by any particular method or conception of the object of study, but by questions, concerns, and problems. It was his task to find the most urgent questions of the day and to try to understand them properly and find a response to them. He realized that traditional disciplines that often time relied on the apparent legitimacy of their methods to produce knowledge, were misguided by a fundamental incomprehension and perversion of the main problems of his age—and ours. When Du Bois began to write, there was a large amount of literature on the so-call "Negro problem," which was taken to be the problem of what to do with Negroes after emancipation. In this picture, the Negroes themselves represented a problem to the well-being of an honest enlightened and Christian society. Du Bois, then, gave primacy to the articulation of questions and problems through which methods and objects of study need to be continuously recreated and other times overcome through syntheses and complex forms of interrogation that cannot be circumscribed to methodological steps or rules. Otherwise, methods can participate in the fabrication of false problems that themselves become part of the real problem.

Through the lenses of Fanon and Du Bois, but also through the work of the Chicana Gloria Anzaldúa, and other figures who are central to Ethnic Studies scholarship, I arrived at an understanding of Ethnic Studies as a transdisciplinary decolonial field, rather than as comparative and interdisciplinary. Transdisciplinarity refers to the primacy of problems vis-à-vis methods, objects of study, and the comparison between different methods or between objects of study. Transdisciplinarity becomes decolonial when the problems and questions to which it gives primacy emanate from concerns about the possibilities and limits of sociality and human interaction in different contexts and situations, that is, when it is part of the exercise of decolonial reason and when it is guided by the principle of decolonization as first philosophy. Decolonial reason is itself transdisciplinary in the sense that "decolonization as first philosophy" entails, as it was stated earlier, the primacy of the questioning process. This is a questioning process about oppression, liberation, and the possibility of restoring humanity and fulfilling human potential. The questions that emerge in this process demand the exploration of multiple objects of analysis and methods, as well as their constant critique. In this sense, a transdisciplinary decolonial approach is different from disciplinary formation as it is from "traditional critical theory" that is anchored in a set of questions that for the most part derive and make sense out of the particularity of European philosophy and the European historical experience. That is, a critical theory that is not decolonial risks becoming traditional. In that sense, one can no longer be entirely satisfied with Horkheimer's separation of traditional and critical theories.[15] Sometimes the latter collapses into the former as the traditional Eurocentrism is continued through different means.

Ethnic Studies and related fields, at their best, are guided by decolonial reason and transdicsiplinarity, not comparison and interdisciplinarity. Instead of relying on the existence of supposedly coherent objects of study, it is focused on the relations among human groups, the forms of power that condition such relations, and the situations and initiatives that create the possibility for apparently singular groups to emerge in the first place. The study of singular groups, the challenges that they confront and their achievements, is always part of such an endeavor, but only within a more general understanding of a system of differentiation that always operates through relationality, never through complete isolation. The singular is always relational, as the relational or the encounter among selves or groups, is a condition of possibility for singularity. The study of the singular contributes to decolonization when it is done with an understanding of the primacy of relation. Questioning, relationality, and elucidating meaning thus appear as the central aspects of ethnic studies, at least in terms of how I approach it and try to practice it.

My voyage from philosophy as an academic field to religious studies and finally to Ethnic Studies, has not made me feel that I have betrayed philosophy, but quite the contrary. In Ethnic Studies I am constantly in conversation with colleagues and students who specialize in different areas, all of them with similar questions in mind. What unites us are the questions, not the methods, a canon, or objects of study. The voyage from philosophy to religious studies to Ethnic Studies as academic areas, has naturally also led to important shifts in my work with professional associations. In previous years, I have participated in steering committees in the American Philosophical Association (APA) and the American Academy of Religion (AAR). The APA and the AAR are perhaps the largest philosophy and religious studies associations in the world, but they are arguably driven by the same principles or ideas that I found so problematic in the fields of philosophy and religious studies. Thus, although they provide an important space for dialogues among experts in those fields, they also help to reproduce these fields' constitutive limits. And so, although I recognize the importance of these associations, I also have grown disappointed with them, which has led me to explore other spaces. Today I do most of my work in the Caribbean Philosophical Association (CPA). The CPA aims to decolonize philosophy by shifting the geography of reason. This means to create a formal space for dialogues that occur not so much with the goal of cultivating knowledge of a specific set of texts or ideas, or with the desire to compare view points, but with the transgressive intent of sharing knowledges, memories, and visions of transformation that serve to better understand the whole extent of human limits and possibilities. In short, the CPA aims to promote decolonial transdisciplinarity. That is why many of its members pursue philosophical and theoretical questions, but they do not have philosophy degrees or teach in philosophy departments. There is a philosophical Diaspora out there, and it is finding refuge outside of traditional philosophy departments and associations.

In addition to the CPA, I also have been impressed by the National Association for Ethnic Studies, and other associations or groups of activists and intellectuals in the United States and abroad who forge decolonization in different but related ways. Important tasks for the future include the formation of yet new national and international institutions that foment similar engagements with ideas, and the creation of spaces for mutual communication and exchange among the institutions and informal associations where decolonial thinking and praxis is taking place. These tasks provide a way to respond to the crisis of philosophy and the humanities with which I began this chapter. Here, decolonial thinking and praxis are offered as an alternative to Eurocentrism, scientificism, and economicism in inspiring and providing criteria of rationality for philosophical work and the humanities. The idea of decolonization as first philosophy points to the primacy of decolonial thought and action over contemplation and being. The "I think, therefore I am" turns into "I think and am in relation, therefore I decolonize."[16] Under these premises, philosophy can hardly be encapsulated in a single set of books, a single culture, or a single discipline. True philosophizing exceeds those limits, and so it will always challenge its location into a specific field, nation, or territory. And so, when it comes to philosophical thinking, many, like me, will find the best place to be is not in philosophy departments, but elsewhere.

NOTES

1. For an elaboration of some of these points see, John McCumber, *Time in the Ditch: American Philosophy and the McCarthy Era* (Evanston, Ill.: Northwestern University Press, 2001).

2. Boaventura de Sousa Santos has spelled out the question of cognitive justice in interesting and productive ways. See, for instance, Boaventura de Sousa Santos, ed., Cognitive Justice in a Global World: Prudent Knowledges for a Decent Life (Lanham, Md.: Lexington Books, 2007).

3. For a more the more complete definition of Eurocentrism that I follow here see Enrique Dussel, "The 'World-System': Europe as 'Center' and its 'Periphery' beyond Eurocentrism," in Beyond Philosophy: Ethics, History, Marxism, and Liberation Theology, ed. Eduardo Mendieta, trans. Eduardo Mendieta (Lanham, Md.:

Rowman & Littlefield, 2003), pp. 53–84; Aníbal Quijano, "Coloniality of Power, Eurocentrism, and Latin America," Nepantla: Views from South 1, no. 3 (2000): pp. 533–80.

4. The following two paragraphs and a half, including this one, appeared in longer form in Nelson Maldonado-Torres, "Latin American Thought and the Decolonization of Western Philosophy," *The American Philosophical Association Newsletter on Hispanic/Latinos Issues in Philosophy* 00, no. 1 (2000): pp. 69–72.

5. Agustín Lao Montes, "Islands at the Crossroads: Puerto Ricanness Traveling between the Translocal Nation and the Global City," in *Puerto Rican Jam: Rethinking Colonialism and Nationalism*, ed. Frances Negrón-Muntaner and Ramón Grosfoguel (Minneapolis: University of Minnesota Press, 1997), p. 174.

6. Peruvian sociologist Anibal Quijano introduces the concept of coloniality of power in different writings. Ramón Grosfoguel, Agustín Lao-Montes, Walter Mignolo, Catherine Walsh, Edgardo Lander, Santiago Castro Gómez, and María Lugones, among others have built on or enter in a critical conversation with Quijano on the idea. The notion of decoloniality has been developed in different circles, beginning with Chicana feminist figures in conversation with the work of Gloria Anzaldua such as Emma Perez, Chela Sandoval, and Laura Pérez, and more recently by the work of the Modernity/Coloniality/Decoloniality collective that includes the figures mentioned above. See Santiago Castro-Gómez and Ramón Grosfoguel, eds., *El giro decolonial: reflexiones para una diversidad epistémica más allá del capitalismo global* (Bogotá, Col.: Universidad Javeriana y Siglo del Hombre Editores, 2007); Ramón Grosfoguel, *Colonial Subjects: Puerto Ricans in a Global Perspective* (Berkeley: University of California Press, 2003); Edgardo Lander, "Eurocentrism, Modern Knowledges and the 'Natural' Order of Global Capital," trans. Mariana Past, *Nepantla: Views from South* 3, no. 2 (2002): pp. 245–68; Edgardo Lander, ed., *La colonialidad del saber: eurocentrismo y ciencias sociales: perspectivas latinoamericanas* (Caracas, Ven.: Facultad de Ciencias Económicas y Sociales (FACES-UCV); Instituto Internacional de la UNESCO para la Educación Superior en América Latina y el Caribe (IESALC), 2000); Walter Mignolo, *The Idea of Latin America* (Malden, Mass.: Blackwell, 2005); Walter Mignolo, *Local Histories/Global Designs: Coloniality, Subaltern Knowledges, and Border Thinking* (Princeton, N.J.: Princeton University Press, 2000); Emma Pérez, *The Decolonial Imaginary: Writing Chicanas into History* (Bloomington: Indiana University Press, 1999); Laura E. Pérez, *Chicana Art: The Politics of Spiritual and Aesthetic Altarities* (Durham: Duke University Press, 2007); Quijano, "Coloniality of Power," pp. 533–80; Aníbal Quijano, "Modernity, Identity, and Utopia in Latin America," in *The Postmodernism Debate in Latin America*, ed. John Beverly, Michael Arona, and José Oviedo (Durham: Duke University Press, 1995), pp. 201–16; Aníbal Quijano, " 'Raza, 'etnia, y 'nación': cuestiones abiertas," in *José Carlos Mariátegui y Europa: la otra cara del descubrimiento*, ed. Roland Forgues (Lima, Peru: Amauta, 1992), n.p; Aníbal Quijano and Immanuel Wallerstein, "Americanity as a Concept, or the Americas in the Modern World-System," *International Social Science Journal* 44 (1992): pp. 549–57; Catherine Walsh, ed., *Pensamiento crítico y matriz (de)colonial: reflexiones latinoamericanas* (Quito, Ec.: Editorial Universidad Andina Simón Bolivar, 2005).

7. The concept of "shifting the geography of reason" was coined by Lewis Gordon and by consensus made into the motto of the Caribbean Philosophical

Association. See Lewis R. Gordon, "African-American Philosophy, Race, and the Geography of Reason," in *Not Only the Master's Tools: Theoretical Explorations in African American Studies*, ed. Lewis R. Gordon and Jane Anna Gordon (Boulder, Col.: Paradigm Press, 2006), pp. 3–50; Lewis R. Gordon, "From the President of the Caribbean Philosophical Association," *Caribbean Studies* 33, no. 2 (2005): pp. xv–xxiii.

8. In 1996 Lewis Gordon taught in the Religious Studies Department and the Program in African American Studies at Brown University. Although Dussel teaches philosophy in Mexico, he was a visiting professor in the Literature Program at Duke University when I met him.

9. I already mentioned some of its key members in a previous note.

10. Frantz Fanon, *Black Skin, White Masks*, trans. Charles Lam Markmann (New York: Grove Press, 1968), 12.

11. For related conceptions of ethnic studies and accounts of trasndisciplinarity see Lewis R. Gordon, and Jane Anna Gordon, eds. *Not Only the Master's Tools: Theoretical Explorations in African American Studies* (Boulder, Co.: Paradigm Press, 2006), and Santiago Castro-Gómez, and Eduardo Mendieta, eds. *Teorías sin disciplina: latinoamericanismo, poscolonialidad, y globalización en debate* (San Francisco, University of San Francisco; and Mexico, D.F.: Editorial Miguel Angel Porrúa, 1998). I have advanced related ideas in "Toward a Critique of Continental Reason: Africana Studies and the Decolonization of Imperial Cartographies in the Americas," in *Not Only the Master's Tools: Theoretical Explorations in African-American Studies*, edited by Lewis Gordon and Jane Anna Gordon (Boulder, CO: Paradigm Press, 2006): pp. 51–84, and "Pensamento crítico desde a subalteridade: os Estudos Etnicos como ciências descoloniais ou para a transformação das humanidades e das ciências sociais no século XXI," *Afro-Asia* 34 (2006): pp. 105–29.

12. W.E.B. Du Bois, *The Souls of Black Folk (100th Anniversary Edition)* (Boulder, Col.: Paradigm Publishers, 2004), 8.

13. Immanuel Wallerstein argues universities tended to understand and legitimize the existence of ethnic studies areas by seeing them as parallel to the already existing area studies. See Immanuel Wallerstein, "The Unintended Consequences of Cold War Area Studies" in *The Cold War and the University: Toward an Intellectual History of the Postwar Years*, edited by Noam Chomsky. et al. (New York: The New Press, 1997), pp. 227–228.

14. Du Bois, The Souls of Black Folk (100th Anniversary Edition), LIII.

15. Max Horkheimer, "Traditional and Critical Theory," in Critical Theory: Selected Essays, trans. Matthew J. O'Connell (New York: Continuum, 1975), pp. 188–243.

16. For a related and complementary analysis see the analysis of Levinas, Fanon, and Dussel in Nelson Maldonado-Torres, Against War: Views from the Underside of Modernity (Durham: Duke University Press, 2008).

CHAPTER FOURTEEN

THINKING THROUGH THE AMERICAS TODAY

A *Philosophical Perspective*

Lewis R. Gordon

The "R" in "Lewis R. Gordon" stands for "Ricardo." Such is the name that rescued me when my parents attempted to name me "Lewis Calwood Gordon," . . . "Jr." My maternal great-grandmother, in the seeming wisdom of her age, intervened and insisted that "Calwood" was a terrible name and recommended, "Why not call the boy 'Ricardo'?"

WHY RICARDO?

Ricardo, as it turns out, was a Cuban man who stood up my great-grand-mother. She went to meet him at the docks where they were to elope to Cuba. Had he showed up, her next child may not have been my grand-mother, and, at least as such logic suggests, I would not have been born. So, I'm grateful that Ricardo never showed up. Yet I bear his name, which leaves me wondering what my great-grandmother may have been up to in those days after my birth, if not, at least, a practical joke.

The name Ricardo was so much a part of my childhood that Lewis did not seem to come into being until I went to college. So my childhood was laden with experiences of a skinny little boy from the Anglo-Caribbean who appears, by virtue of his middle name, to be connected to the Latin one. I have recounted in *Her Majesty's Other Children* the experience of being attacked by white and black boys as a Puerto Rican in New York City. Being taken as Hispanic ("Latino" didn't come around until the 1990s) or

271

Latin American was not the only kinds of misidentification I have received. I have been addressed as Arab, East African, North African, East Indian, Pakistani, and American Indian, depending on my weight or skin tone in a given season. My favorite example is of once being addressed in the early 1990s by a West Asian woman as someone from her village while riding on a bus in New Haven, Connecticut. I explained to her that I was born in Jamaica and grew up in the United States, in the Bronx, New York, and she promptly berated me as a liar and scoffed that I was attempting to "pass" as a black person. Although she was wrong about my attempting to pass, she was partly correct about what she saw. I am, through my maternal great-grandmother's paternal grandmother, also Tamil. Having subsequently visited India and met quite a few Tamils, I continue to be dazzled by the reach of genes across so many generations. No one sees me as an outsider in India, even when I explain I don't speak the local languages and wasn't born there. As the reader might guess, nearly all of those identities for which I have been taken are, to some degree, correct.

But back to Ricardo. Ricardo, at least by graduate school, disappeared for nearly a decade. I use the "R" in my name when stating authorship because there are several Lewis Gordons in the academy. Adding the "R" does not deter some from reversing my name and confusing me with Gordon Lewis, the famous Welsh historian of the Caribbean, and still others confuse me with "Gordon R. Lewis," a systematic theologian at Denver Seminary. I've seen the second on Google.com "image," and have often wondered if some Internet surfers think that I am that distinguished white man, about three decades my senior, sporting that wonderful smile.

Ricardo returned when I became president of the Caribbean Philosophical Association (CPA) in a profoundly welcoming way. Having a few email accounts because of the volume of mail I received, I opened a special one for CPA and used my full name. An error in the procedure led to the account addressing the receiver as "Ricardo Gordon." To this day, there are people who write letters to that account addressing Lewis Gordon and Ricardo Gordon as different people. Many seem to have thought that Ricardo was Lewis' assistant. Life takes many strange and circular paths, and perhaps these turns, errors, and acts of naming and renaming and misnaming serve purposes more fortunate, and often amusing, than accident will permit.

I am no longer president of the CPA. My last months in that role were spent, oddly enough, in the Francophone world. After our international meeting in Guadeloupe, I went to meetings in Paris, Corsica, and Montreal. In Corsica, I had the good fortune of spending time with Ghjuvanteramu Rocchi, the national poet of that "region" of France. Rocchi was very much interested in discussing the meaning of colonization today, especially with a scholar who has written on Frantz Fanon and who has traveled through and worked with other intellectuals in most of the Caribbean, parts of Central America, and some of South America. In our conversations, he raised a fascinating observation, which I call the problem of "cultural disaster."

French colonialism is very methodical. Having learned from their mistakes, the French realized that they should build up the infrastructure of their colonies/departments/regions/ territories and solidify the center, the metropole, or, simply, *Paris*, as a cultural siphon. As all flows to the center, Corsica was transformed from an island of 1 million inhabitants to 250,000; from a place in which most inhabitants spoke Corsican to one in which fewer and fewer do. The Corsican struggle now also involves the meaning of being Corsican through a Diaspora without even a linguistic relation to the land that situates their identity. An ironic dimension of the Corsican situation, perhaps like my name Ricardo, is that Ghjuvanteramu Rocchi's children, one of whom teaches Corsican in the village of his father's birth, is also Guadeloupean. The flag of Corsica has the face of a Moor, the people who ruled the island through the Middle Ages until the Genoans seized it at the dawn of the Age of Exploration and the expansion of southern Europe into the Atlantic and the New World. Corsica became whiter again, but now, as those Corsicans take flight into Frenchness and the racial matrices it offers, the preservation of the language flows from the mouths of native speakers who are black sons and a daughter of its poetic voice. (In Corsica, by the way, I am "Luigi.") Ghjuvanteramu Rocchi, his brilliant son Jean-Paul Rocchi, who is an artist and a scholar of literature in Paris, and I reflected on these issues each night, under the family's cherry tree, in the mountains, with a view of Tuscany, Sardinia, and Monte Cristo. The Terranean Sea, speckled with neighboring small islands, served as a conduit with coasts reminiscent of the Caribbean, where from some islands, others can be seen, and from still others, shores such as those of continents jot and dot the horizon. Our conversations inevitably led to thoughts about another island man, Frantz Fanon.

Among our thoughts is of how we make selections from the past. I lamented that, at least among academics in the study of politics and theories of social transformation, an intellectual's analysis of the present situation of people of color often depends on where he or she locates someone like Frantz Fanon, if, given the levels of loss literacy these days, the name is even recognized. Those who choose to entomb him in the past often attempt to do the same to the insights he offered: the futility of colorblind responses to racism; the almost foundational role of race and racism in the modern world; the radicality of colonization, so extreme that it hits even the foundations of knowledge; the futility, even absurdity, of seeking recognition from those who dominate us; the need to change both conceptual and material conditions of revolutionary movements; the need for revolution; the violent

dimensions of decolonization; the possibility of a national versus nationalist consciousness; the uselessness of the postcolonial bourgeoisie; and the
accuracy and usefulness of colonialism and neocolonialism as descriptions
of the present global situation. If those insights are all past, what, then, is
going on in the present?

Those who choose to see Fanon's thought as part of a continuum of
events, where people are engaged in an ongoing struggle of working out the
contradictions of the societies in which they live, regard Fanon's time more
as a point of departure for an analysis that speaks to us today because he
spoke to the conditions of our epoch. What those who trivialize or even
reject the insights offered by Fanon fail to consider is that we continue to
know more about him than many of his critics because the problems he
addressed were more foundational. The situation is similar for W. E. B. Du
Bois. Only historians specializing in the history of social science recall Du
Bois' U.S. colleagues in sociology at the end of the nineteenth century.
All of them white and Eurocentric, they continued to push the conditions
of Europe on the United States. The result was a failure to take seriously
how race functioned there, and for that matter, in the entire New World.
As the persistence of class and spiritual alienation led to Karl Marx, Max
Weber, and Emile Durkheim being recognized fathers of sociology, we could
add, as my colleagues Paget Henry and Nahum Chandler have argued, that
the recalcitrance of race in the modern world has led to Du Bois deserving
such credit.

The critics of Fanon's persistence are, in many ways, like the proverbial
ostrich with its head in the sand. Contemporary world events reveal so many
instances of continued strife. Look to the plight of African immigrants in
Parisian suburbs, who gave new meaning in 2006 to the expression "Paris is
burning"; think of the War on Terror inaugurated by the attacks on the Twin
Towers on 9/11/2001, at the center of which are themes straight out of the
Algerian War, but this time on a global scale; think of the infrastructural
devastation in postcolonial Africa and the consequences of recent forms of
economic control such as structural adjustment there; think of the rise of
First Peoples, often ascribed as indigenous peoples, in countries where the
age-old problem of land takes new form as such people find themselves laying
claim to territories on which there are precious resources such as oil, coal,
and uranium at a time of unprecedented demand for fuel; think, as well, of
the emergence of the postcolony. By the last, I do not mean the concept
advanced by Achille Mbebe in his book that bears that name. I see little
difference between that notion and neocolonialism, if we take time to delve
more deeply into the antimodernization legacies of colonialism in Africa,
as Olúfémi Táíwo has argued. What I mean, additionally, is the absence of
legitimacy of colonialism in the face of its continued practice. I mean the

shame of colonialism. In the early years of the twenty-first century, colonialism continues as brutal as ever. But such times permit such actions under the condition that they are not named. Thus, although Iraq and Afghanistan are exemplars of painful efforts to effect U.S. hegemony in West Asia, the absence of the use of the word "colonies," in fact the denial of it entirely, marks the postcolonial moment. The United States would never dare do what Britain, France, Spain, Germany, Holland, Portugal, and it used to do, which was to *justify* their actions in terms of colonialism. President George W. Bush could not maintain legitimacy (what little of it he had left) if, in one of his televised addresses, he had looked directly at the camera straight through to the people of the United States and declared that for their economic interests, the U.S. government was acquiring colonies where there were precious reserves of oil and other natural resources, and colonies where, if developed by the people living there, would challenge the domination of the United States in certain markets such as pharmaceuticals and information technology.

Yes, when the Rocchis and I looked at world events in summer 2008, Fanon's continued relevance was evident.

Corsica is an island with cultural (and biological) genealogies that include the North African Afro-Arabic world, the Italian Renaissance world, and modern and postmodern French society. This makes it, as we will see, quintessentially part of the Latin world, and it also exemplifies many affinities with the Latin *American* world. America, after all, emerged during the same period as the expulsion of the Moors from the Iberian peninsula and the subsequent maritime conflicts and exploitation of resources that created the Atlantic and Modern world, and just as it was the French who had formulated and lobbied for the notion of Latin America, as Walter Mignolo reminds us, it was also they who advanced the same for Corsica, whose native son, Napoleon, affected the Francophone Americas with his re-establishment of chattel slavery. (Corsicans prefer to remember the earlier national liberation Enlightenment intellectual, Pascal Paoli, whose influence, some reminded me, can be found in the progressive dimensions of the U.S. Constitution.)

I saw things in Corsica that I would probably not have seen without my experiences in the CPA. By this, I do not mean the issue of opportunity. I mean the phenomenological point about the conditions of possibility that transform things within our visual field from penumbral and overlooked phenomena to things *seen*. Although I already had the conviction that philosophers who explore problems of human reality should travel, a view that had already taken me to southern Africa and eastern Europe before my tenure with the CPA, there were so many surprising additions, from Australia to South America, that affirmed for me how small the world is and of how much we are still working out the throes of global disruptions of a prior age.

Allow me a brief history of the CPA. The association is an academic organization founded in 2003 during a meeting at the Institute for Caribbean Thought at the University of the West Indies at Mona, Jamaica. The circumstances around its birth were wonderfully poetic: A celebration of the work of George Lamming under the title, *Liberation of the Imagination*. A year earlier, at an international celebration in honor of Sylvia Wynter, titled *Seminar on the Human After Man*, several colleagues and I had discussed the need for such an organization, but it was at the Lamming meeting that we made it official after long discussions at the Mona Lodge on the UWI-Mona Campus.

The first international meeting of the CPA convened the next year in June in Barbados at the Accra Hotel. The reader could imagine what it was like to have such a gathering while looking out at the Atlantic Ocean in the direction of Ghana, where the ancestors of so many were snatched into the Middle Passage, perished at sea, and, for those who survived, brought to the New World as a stain on modernity's self-portrait. The theme we chose for the inaugural conference was *Shifting the Geography of Reason*. There were forty papers, and about eighty people attended from nearly every Caribbean country, the United States, Canada, Germany, and African countries such as Nigeria, Ethiopia, and South Africa. After the papers and discussions, which had a strong emphasis on the importance of south–south dialogue, of affirming the legitimacy of the southern hemisphere as a source of ideas as an antidote to the hegemony of the north, the organization decided to make the theme of shifting the geography of reason its motto. By the second meeting, the number of presentations grew to nearly a hundred, and nearly two hundred scholars from countries that then included Serbia, England, France, Argentina, Mexico, and Sierre Leon attended. In subsequent meetings, there were participants from every continent save Antarctica.

The formal goal of the CPA, as its Mission Statement attests, is to build a home for ideas in the Caribbean context:

> The Caribbean Philosophical Association is an organization of scholars and lay-intellectuals dedicated to the study and generation of ideas with a particular emphasis of encouraging South–South dialogue. Although the focus is on engaging philosophy that emerges in the Caribbean, membership is not limited exclusively to scholars with degrees in philosophy, and any region and historic moment is open to the exchange of ideas. In similar kind, membership in the organization is not limited to professional scholars. Any one with an interest in theoretical and philosophical work can become a member.

Finally, the Caribbean Philosophical Association is also dedicated to assisting with the development of institutions that would preserve thought in the Caribbean and facilitate the creation of new ideas.

The motto of shifting the geography of reason converges with this statement. For how reason has been mapped out across the modern world has been such that much of what the CPA does will seem strange to organizations whose goal is to affirm the hegemony of the order of things as understood in the northern countries. Such an order depends, for instance, on a divide along national and linguistic lines. A terrible consequence of this has been the great distances between the Anglophone and Latin Caribbean, despite their geographical proximity. Walter Mignolo explains, in *The Idea of Latin America*, that this development was not accidental. French intellectuals in Europe and "white" intellectuals in Hispanophone, Lusophone, and Francophone communities of South America, Central America, and the Caribbean had drawn upon a notion of a common Latin-based culture and set of languages at which French civilization stood at the center in its battle for imperial space with U.S. and British domination across the globe. As always been the case, a new name emerged out of a battle of imperial forces, and at its heart was another imperial declaration. The "Latin" in Latin America is no less imperial, in other words, than the "Anglo" in Anglo-America and the Anglo-Caribbean except for a difference in historical location. It is, after all, an Anglo-centered America that, at least militarily, dominates or exercises hegemony over the world at the beginning of the New Millennium. Given the terrible U.S. economy and the debts the United States had acquired as of the writing of this chapter, most of which is to China, the question of economic rule faces its greatest challenge. Economic rule is not identical with cultural rule, however, so even China finds itself facing the continued force of Western cultural influence: Owning much of the United States may, in the end, amount to making more of China become Chinese-American. Intellectuals from such a China should consider having a conversation with Ghjuvanteramu Rocchi in Corsica.

In the Caribbean, the geography of culture, of language and knowledge, has proven to be greater than the challenges of the sea. A book that played a major role in the formation of the CPA, through the author's bringing these issues together in a systematic work, is Paget Henry's *Caliban's Reason*. That work brought momentum to the question of Afro-Caribbean philosophy by offering a set of ideas as a home for at least a portion of this region's thought. Among discussions of the revolutionary, historicist tradition and the poetic, imaginative one, Henry includes discussions of creolization and indigeneity. That this text won the association's first Frantz Fanon Prize (by unanimous votes from a worldwide community of referees) stimulated a reflection on how linguistic gaps can be bridged in the creolized reality of the New World. Fanon was, after all, Martinican, and it was the French, as we have seen, who formulated the notion of Latin America.

The founding board of the CPA made bridging the linguistic divide a central focus of the association. So we worked to develop a system of secretaries across the various linguistic regions. One of them, Nelson Maldonado-Torres, who became president of the organization in 2008, was already working on this mandate for several years. Maldonado-Torres organized our relationship with scholars in Central America, South America, and the Latin Caribbean, as well as their relations with scholars in Europe and North America. Working with him, I participated in forums with colleagues in Costa Rica, Colombia, Mexico, and Brazil. As well, after the conference in Barbados, we decided to require our annual meetings to cross the linguistic terrains each year. The second meeting was thus held in Old San Juan, Puerto Rico, where we were generously hosted by The Centro de Estudios Avanzados de Puerto Rico y el Caribe. An institution devoted to archaeological and anthropological research, especially on the indigenous Caribbean, it turned out to be the right place for reflections on what it meant to be human in the Caribbean and what such a reflection offers the rest of the world.

It was perhaps ancestral forces at work in the selection of the Frantz Fanon Prize that year. Sibylle Fischer's *Modernity Disavowed: Haiti and the Cultures of Slavery in the Age of Revolution* and Alejandro J. De Oto's *Fanon: política del sujeto poscolonial* were winners that garnered subsequent accolades from other organizations. The significance of a book that engages the ideas that emerged out of the Haitian Revolution and a book on Fanon, and that both were Francophone topics written in English and in Spanish, exemplified the themes of creolization, geography, and language that emerge in the effort to build a home for Caribbean thought. The meeting at Puerto Rico was also marked by so many representatives of so many dimensions of thought from the "underside" of the modern world. Among many were Ramabai Espinet, the Indo-Caribbean novelist and poet; Sylvester James Gates Jr., the African American physicist who is well known for his groundbreaking work in string theory; Natalija Mićunivić, the Serbian scholar on critical theory and critic of European nationalism; Enrique Dussel, philosopher, historian, and theologian from Argentina and now an ex-patriot living in Mexico; Linda Martín Alcoff, the famed feminist philosopher, epistemologist, and proponent of Latin American philosophy; Carlos Rojas Osorio, whose work on Puerto Rican philosophy and on Hegel revealed that he and Paget Henry were ironically working together without knowledge of each other's work; and of course, Puerto Rico's Native Son, Nelson Maldonado-Torres, whose work in philosophy of liberation, marked, for example, by his groundbreaking book *Against War*, which offers a conception of decolonial ethics through a fusion of the thought of Levinas, Fanon, and Dussel, is a source of pride for us all.

The meetings that succeeded Puerto Rico at the composition of this chapter include Montreal (2006), Jamaica (2007), and Guadeloupe (2008). We met in Montreal to reach out to the Haitian and other Francophone communities and to highlight the influence of Canadian universities and their intellectuals in the Caribbean. Many participants from the local Francophone community came, especially to the screening of Kevin Pina's *Haiti: The Untold Story*, which garnered an audience of about eight hundred people, in addition to the two hundred already in attendance at the conference. The winner of the Fanon Prize that year was Walter Mignolo's *The Idea of Latin America*. Whereas the sessions in Puerto Rico were presented in Spanish and English, those in Montreal featured French and Portuguese as well. This led to a similar spectrum of presentations in Jamaica, where the winners of the Fanon Prize were Elias K. Bongmba's *Dialectics of Transformation in Africa*; Brinda Mehta's *Diasporic (Dis)Locations: Indo-Caribbean Women Writers Negotiate the Kala Pani*; and Catherine Reindhardt's *Claims to Memory: Beyond Slavery and Emancipation in the French Caribbean*. These books brought to the fore the membership's interest in the intersection of Caribbean thought with those in Africa and West Asia.

Sessions in Jamaica were presented in English, French, Portuguese, and Spanish. We often have been asked why we do not offer translators for our sessions. Many of us were trained to have some working knowledge of these languages while in graduate school, and the Africans among us learned these European languages in addition to several African ones. Although there was some protest by members who worked exclusively in the English language, we noticed that most members began to hone up on their translation and speaking skills in more than one language. It's a struggle these days, with the hegemony of English, but significant changes began to develop among the membership. More of us began to research in the different languages, which enriched our scholarship and offered a broader understanding of Africana, Afro-Latin, and Indo-Caribbean thought. An increased number of participants developed ongoing working relationships with the scholars they met in each region. Our intellectual horizon, in other words, began to expand. This was particularly evident in Guadeloupe, where we met during the terrible economic situation of a strong euro and a weak dollar for the U.S. members. A consequence of U.S. hegemony is that most Caribbean countries, and many African ones, are subject to the ebb and flow of the dollar. Meeting in places ruled by the euro or pounds posed economic challenges for an organization with many members in countries labeled "Second" and "Third" worlds. Those forces did not deter the presence of a sizeable contingent (ninety papers), however, although a good number of members from Africa could not attend that and the meeting in Jamaica because of visa difficulties from new regulations and their concomitant pressures from the U.S. government. More germane to the topic of this volume, we had implemented a new award at that meeting, the Nicolás Guillén Philosophical Literature Prize. Guillén was an Afro-Cuban poet, philosopher, and political critic. We noticed that novelists, poets, and playwrights with philosophical predilections regularly attended the meetings. We created this prize to honor their contributions. The premier winners were Wilson Harris, the famed Guyanese novelist, poet, and essayist, and Ramabai Espinet, the Trinidadian author whose poetry, novels, and essays have been the subject of many panels, articles, and other studies in the association. Subsequent winners were Edwidge Danticat, the famed Haitian writer, and Gabriel "Gabo" Garcia Marquez, the Nobel Laureate and major exemplar of magical realism. The Fanon Prize winners were Drucilla Cornell's *Moral Images of Freedom: A Future for Critical Theory* and Patricia Donatien-Yssa's *L'exorcisme de la bles: Vaincre la souffrance dans Autobiographie de ma mère de Jamaica Kincaid*. Donatien-Yssa is the only Martinican to have received the Fanon Prize thus far. An additional powerful dimension of that meeting was that Mireille Fanon-Mendes-France, Fanon's daughter, had conferred the prize. Ideas in the Caribbean were taking concrete form in these meetings, and with that, the question of philosophy itself was being reimagined, expanded, and in many cases, challenged. At the completion of this chapter, Linda Martí Alcoff's *Visible Identities*, Nigel Gibson's *Fanon and the Postcolonial Imagination*, Oscar Guardiola-Rivera, *What If Latin America Ruled the World?: How the Second World Will Take the First into the 22nd Century*, Angel Quintero Rivera's *Cuerpo y cultura: las musicas "mulatas" y la subversion de baile*, Susan Buck-Morss's *Hegel, Haiti, and Universal History*, Marilyn Nissim-Sabat's *Neither Victim nor Survivor* have been added to the list of winners of the book prize and lifetime achievement awards have been given to Enrique Dussel, Bernard Boxill, and Michel Rolph-Trouillot. Boxill's acceptance letter is worthy of a full quote here, but I will only offer the last few lines due to the limitations of space:

> Far too slowly it has dawned on me that many of these classics [of western philosophy] that I had turned to in order to make my work more "respectable" are ideal theory, which is to say, evasions of the urgent problems that first drew me to the study of political philosophy, while others actually develop the ideologies that have led to those problems. This is the lesson I have learned. We philosophers of the Third World must not get caught up in the endless debates about the details of Western political philosophy, but always keep

in mind what the whole enterprise helped to do to us. So I must end commending the Caribbean Philosophical Association which has from the first encouraged a critical attitude to Western political philosophy and urged its members to make reflection on their own experiences as the scapegoats of that philosophy the inspiration for their own philosophy.

We noticed over the years some fascinating sociological dimensions of organizing across the regional and linguistic divides. In Puerto Rico, for instance, challenges were faced at each stage of organizing the meeting, but our colleagues on the island simply accommodated us along the way by copying flyers, helping us locate housing, finding a performing artist for our fiesta, and participating in several sessions. The Centro de Estudios Avanzados de Puerto Rico y el Caribe simply opened its doors and welcomed us without charge and encouraged us at every stage of our meeting. We were similarly welcomed in Jamaica, and in Guadeloupe, the Regional General provided much support for which we are very grateful, and the same in Cartagena, Colombia.

The founding of the CPA, although having taken place in Jamaica, was in the spirit of the pan-Caribbean and by extension Pan-American. It went beyond its New World focus by reaching across the globe to participants from non-Caribbean regions. The founders were a mixed community that reflected the range of people from African to Asian; Anglophone, Francophone, and Hispanophone, and Hindi. But more: Each founding member shared the conviction that philosophical reflection has become a dangerous activity in the contemporary world. By that, we did not mean the narrow, self-absorbed practices that dominate most professional philosophical organizations. We meant *philosophy*, as it has been historically understood, where people struggled with ideas that transformed their understanding of themselves and their lives. *Philosophy*, as ideas that offered the blue print of radical social transformation in different periods of history; *philosophy*, which inspired new relationships between humanity and the cosmos and which brought to consciousness the realization of human responsibility in our struggles for freedom; *philosophy*, where ideas engaged and had an impact on world events. For us, this meant being willing to go beyond professional philosophy by examining thought where thinking became so infectious, dissent also became a dimension, and even a value, of social life. The Ghanaian philosopher Kwame Gyekye says it well in his book *Tradition and Modernity* when he writes:

> The practical concerns demonstrated not only in the philosophical arguments but also in the personal involvement of some philosophers

in sociopolitical reform programs clearly contradicts Marx's view that "Hitherto philosophers have only interpreted the world in various ways, but the real point is to change it." . . . Plato, Aristotle, Bentham, Mill, and others set themselves the task of reforming the societies in which they lived. Moreover, changing the world involves having well-defined goals, and philosophy can be of great assistance in defining and articulating those goals. (p. 23)

We are living in times bullied by enemies of thought. The United States has been stained in the new millennium, for instance, by the first eight years of its governing bodies being guided by individuals who placed a low premium on intelligence. For many, the end of the G.W. Bush administration meant the actual entry of the world's most powerful nation into the twenty-first century, although sadly hampered by much pressure from the now infamous Tea Party movement. Because thinking and dissent go together, any social order that advances rule over politics finds itself in a conflict with those who challenge it and, consequently, in a war against thinking. A longstanding feature of politics is its fragility. Rule or governing, after all, preceded politics. This is because the latter is, properly, an activity of equals. It is only where equality limits the bounds of force that speech, with its accompanying dissent, can emerge, where opposition can be discursive. Where persuasion matters, as a long, unusual line of thinkers from Aristotle to Machiavelli to Arendt to Biko knew so well, politics exists. The growth of or at least effort to spread democracy in the world, then, means, in effect, the expansion of politics in the daily lives of people. The many efforts by people all over the world to reduce the disparities in wealth and access to social resources in the middle quarters of the twentieth century were in fact increasing political participation in the lives of ordinary people. These efforts, as is well known, were brutally suppressed in many regimes well into the new millennium, many of which were able to radicalize their behavior through the right-wing expansion facilitated by the War on Terror. The word "radical" was used primarily as a slur against the left, which meant a period of solidification for the radical right. The sources of such development had roots, however, in struggles from more than a century past. The repression or counter-dialectic began, as Du Bois showed so well in his monumental *Black Reconstruction in America*, in the transmutation of slavery into its new forms by the dawn of the twentieth century. The repercussions of what happened in the United States were felt in Central and South America, Africa, and South Asia by a renewed assertion of northern imperial power, which became more arrogant near the end of the twentieth century with the fall of the Soviet Union. But this reaction was also well-aware of the danger of thought. It was thinking, matched by much chutzpah, that led to the Age of Revolution in the first place, and even though history is not short of many good intentions gone wrong, a retreat to mental indolence was hardly a better alternative.

It is no accident that academics were (and continue to be) targeted in the United States and by U.S. covert activity internationally, and by the 1990s, especially in the Anglo-Caribbean, those who persisted in cultivating thinking, of encouraging equal, democratic participation guided by reflective thought, did so at their peril. More and more, critical and creative institutions of thought, especially those in the Anglo-Caribbean, had began to fall sway to those who were dominated by "cultural criticism," where state forces and other manifestations of potentially brutal power and the management of material wealth fell to the wayside of academic analysis in favor of attacking the powerless for their lack of urbane values: The people themselves and their cultural mores became increasingly blamed for the problems of poverty and violence that besieged so many of them at the end of the twentieth century. The motto seemed to have become "Don't think," and if one must think at all, try to reduce its political potential and affirm the legitimacy of establishment and conservative institutions.

So, the appeal to datedness, which, as we saw, has been ascribed to Fanon, had infected Anglo-Caribbean intellectuals. Marx and Fanon were rejected as outdated by scholars who devoted their energy to Thomas Hobbes and Martin Heidegger, even though, as Babacar Camara pointed out in *Marxist Theory, Black/African Specificities, and Racism*, it is the former two who actually offer a theory of the social and economic order in which most human beings live in recent times. Conservative, even fascist thinkers from Europe were propped up almost as saints against anticolonialists and liberationists from the Caribbean, Central, and South America. Classic categories that effected political action in the past such as poverty and disease came upon deaf ears. Unlike colonialism, which is now permitted as long as it isn't named, poverty and racism became widely acknowledged *and permitted* since the bases of their rejection were supposedly "outdated." One is thus learning to live by a very low standard in places where inequality continues to grow.

Founding the CPA, then, with its mandate of learning through reaching across the various communities in the region and the world was a decision to defy the bullying values of imperial models of globalism, where "cosmopolitanism" is argued for, for instance, so long as it enables elites to live the same way in different places. What can be made of the globalization of more rigorous methods of enslavement as inequalities increased? What is the point of being globally located if one becomes so as a commodity for the entertainment and comfort of an elite whose distance from the suffering of the masses of humankind has increased in our age? History offers too many instances of the important role of intellectual work in the formation of human self-understanding and struggles against bondage for us to ignore the value of such work.

I have found it difficult to travel through the Caribbean, Central, and South America without thinking, ironically, of E. Franklin Frazier and Frantz Fanon. My now adding the former, especially given the terrible status of his research on black families and assimilation, may seem to many readers to be out of place. Yet it was Frazier who pursued not only questions of what was going on culturally and economically among the large African-descended populations of Salvador, Brazil, in the first half of the twentieth century, as the scholarship of Livio Sansone has shown there, but also questions of what awaited a black leadership whose main source of legitimacy was race mediation instead of the development of material capital. *Black Bourgeoisie* first came to print in France as *Bourgeoisie Noir* two years before the English edition, perhaps also prophesying or at least offering a model for some of the reflections I am offering here. That work was published in 1955, a year before the Black Writers' conference in Paris, which Fanon, a wanted man, attended, Robin Hood style, under the name of Aimé Césaire, where he met an array of black Diasporic writers who included Richard Wright and George Lamming. Although without reference to Frazier, the connection between Fanon's analysis of the postcolonial, or better, neocolonial bourgeoisie and Frazier's critique of black leadership in the United States is unmistakable. The call, from both intellectuals, for each generation to build up its nation was ignored as the incomes of black leadership grew without capital, without *wealth* and its effect of a developed black infrastructure. The consequence in North America was evident in the fact that blacks owned 5 percent of wealth in the United States in 1865 and only 1 percent at the end of the first decade of the twenty-first century. The result in Africa, as Fanon warned, was independence bereft of material support while bloated with rhetorical excess. New debts. New dependence. A continuation of what was thought of to have become past.

Fanon's emendation to Frazier's neo-Marxist analysis of the need for capital development among black ruling elites is manifold. First, Fanon, a radical democrat, was concerned about the divisive significance of nationalism in an Africa, and, by extension, South America and Caribbean, left with state borderlines that crossed ethnic ones and, as a consequence, called for the important distinction between national consciousness and nationalism. The "nation," after all, needn't be racial or ethnic, but the question of thinking beyond the specific interests of racial and ethnic groups and individual self-interests meant the articulation of a common-good understanding and accompanying of creative responses to the many social problems that beset a community literally faced with building a future without a distant past. Among the creative responses is the realization that without having an industrial base, the Marxist logic of a European working class faced its limits. In the African, and by extension Caribbean, context, the absence of large-scale production and other forms of infrastructural development meant that some form of mixed economy was needed to achieve the material conditions for the fulfillment of basic modern needs and requirements. Moreover, the uniqueness of colonial struggles meant that the logic of a proletariat leadership suffered in the reluctant need for participation of a lumpen-proletariat community. The relevance of this question of the place of the lumpen-proletariat in the logic of black emancipation continues through, among many examples, Rastafari in the Caribbean and the gangster/rude boy figure as well.

The Anglo-Caribbean leadership, as we know, went through a phase of Marxist and socialist aspirations only to be pummeled by forces from the United States and England both explicitly and covertly. In Latin America, similar tactics were brutally unleashed, especially in the 1980s. The horrid litany of death as the late Cold War played itself out in the New World became a gruesome feature of conflicts toward social change in the region, particularly in such places as Chile, El Salvador, and Colombia. In the last, where I have been spending more time recently, the effects of this brutal period are left literally on many of the women's bodies, which, marked by exaggerated buttocks and other features, have been transformed into a local understanding of what is described as drug dealers' aesthetics. That the size of Colombia's black population is only seconded by Brazil's leads to a consideration hardly discussed in international media: The majority of the people killed during the drug wars and terrorized across the Pacific coasts of Colombia were Afro-Colombians. Race and class thus come together in a perfect storm there and in much of South America.

The structural realities of the Caribbean are, however, impacted by the reality of island-nations without some form of pan-Caribbean federalism. Thus, unable to be self-sustaining, due to the absence of an industrially developed infrastructure, agricultural efforts pressed on under the heels of large corporate farming companies, and even in such lucrative areas as the pharmaceutical industries, the weight of transnational corporate giants blocked what little room was available for the development of such markets through an indigenous Caribbean base.

Latin America, especially on the South American continent, however, has the advantages of large, nearly self-sustained territories for several countries, and added to all that are the precious and nonrenewable resource of oil and the large forest reservoirs of possible botanical medicines. There is, as well, the uniqueness of historical circumstances, where the mightiest northern neighbor, the very one that undermined economies and placed dissidents under the crushing heels of repression, is enmeshed in guerilla wars in West Asia/East Africa that are taxing both its wealth and political and emotional energy. How much could the United States devote to repression in Latin America as defiance asserts itself when Chinese demand for oil to fuel its burgeoning economy continues to rise? Previous policies of neglecting African and South American oil in the hope of limiting the infrastructural development of those regions reveal their limitations.

The situation offers poetic irony as ground-level-up politics reasserted itself in South America at the dawn of the new millennium, and organizations among the indigenous populations find growing support for their struggles. President Hugo Chavez's offer to supply low-cost, subsidized oil to poor families in the northern mid-western United States in winter 2007 into 2008 is indication of a kind of witty defiance long missing from the stage of international politics. When, in his first period as prime minister of Jamaica, Michael Manley stood up against the United States, he failed to realize that he needed more to stand on than bauxite and a slim set of agreements during the Cold War. To understand Chavez and his allies, one must realize that much of Latin America has been under a form of veil in the U.S.-dominated world of Anglophone consciousness. This has been the case primarily because the lens through which Latin America is seen in the Anglophone countries has been that of poor and often illegal immigrants versus the wealthy, jet-setting populations that move, elite cosmopolitan-style, through North America, Europe, and Australia. And even the immigrant populations, many of whom go to the United States, reflect those with the means, albeit often very modest ones, of getting there. Those who stand below them do not go across the visual fields, much less the consciousness, of the north.

Reality versus misperception came to the fore during Maldonado-Torres and my visits to Mexico. The first thing that struck me when I first visited Mexico City was the scale and variety of indigenous peoples there. It reminded me of visiting South Africa and seeing the range of indigenous black peoples that so outnumbered my experience of the kinds of black people I knew in North America and the Caribbean (many of whom in the latter are also Afro-East Indian). The hundreds of kinds of indigenous peoples, and the range of Mestizos, as well as the varieties of blacks and "mulattoes" (the preferred term in some of those places), and the varieties of whites depending on which waves of migration, all walked through a robust, global world and economy on a land whose history of commerce extended thousands of years before Cortez's arrival. The many villages and small cities tell more than a tale of a vast country as one realizes that nearly anything that money could buy was found in Mexico, a world governed by resourcefulness and ongoing reflections on its own destiny. Professional intellectual meetings also revealed a world very distinct from the version presented in the United States. In the United States and Anglophone Caribbean, at least in philosophy, there has been the domination of a very conservative, avowedly apolitical conception of the field. What, as it turns out, makes its way from Mexico to the American Philosophical Association is mostly work from small institutes and think tanks that are well funded by U.S. foundations (and possibly covert governmental and corporate ones). What the *Mexican people* regard as philosophy, however, is, without question, ideas on struggle, social transformation, and liberation. It is not that they do not engage the other forms of thought such as analytical metaphysics, epistemology, and philosophy of science. There are also specialists in European Continental Philosophy, and in fact quite a few scholars could be characterized as Eurocentric. What is different is that the context of their Eurocentrism is not only Marxist, but also through the mediated understanding of home-grown, Latin American forms of Marxist and other forms of liberationist thought, especially those emerging from the cultures of First Peoples. Many Mexican students and scholars, in other words, want to see how the world appears through Mexican and other Latin American sources of interpretation. Thus, what I discovered in Maldonado-Torres's and my efforts to present Afro-Caribbean thought in the Brazilian, Colombian, Ecuadorian, and Mexican contexts were audiences hungry for thought indigenous to the region and an understanding of their relation to the global arena of other countries rife with their own internal dynamics of social struggles and change. And even more, it is clear that the *value of thought* requires very little defense among the First Peoples and indigenous populations, whose understanding of their struggle against invisibility is linked to a keen awareness of the power of symbols and how they are articulated.

Few experiences exemplified these observations more than a memorable day Maldonado-Torres and I spent with Enrique Dussel in Morelia, Mexico. A great philosopher and theologian, Dussel is also a major historian who commenced his career with a monumental historical study of Mexico, a shortened version available in English as A *History of the Church in Latin America: Colonialism to Liberation (1492–1979)*. Dussel guided us with explanations and stories about nearly every street, wall, and statue in that beautiful city. He showed us the statue of José María Teclo Morelos y Pavón, leader of the Mexican independence movement and the city's namesake. The city's indigenous name was Guayangareo. It was Vasco de Quiroga, however, the first Bishop in the region, who drew considerable discussion. He was a lawyer with a gift for learning languages. He became a priest who came to the New World to administrate the growing Spanish bureaucracy but quickly took on the cause of the Prindas people, who affectionately called him *Tata* Vasco (Father Vasco). Dussel's portrait of Vasco is indicative of Dussel's philosophy of liberation: Vasco was embroiled in dialectical struggles in the expanding Christendom over its many contradictions of conquest, colonization, enslavement, genocide, and racism in the name of salvation. This double reality is part of European modernity, where just as members of the oppressed betrayed their causes, so, too, did agents of oppression change sides, although in Dussel's formulation, the motivation was primarily ethical. The walk was not only enriched by the wealth of history Dussel offered, but also by his unveiling of a world that was hidden before us in proverbial plain sight. This was particularly evident when he discussed the statue of Miguel de Cervantes, famed author of *Don Quixote*, who was a soldier twice enslaved by the Moors. As Dussel's narrative unfolded, it was as if sunlight spread across the city to reveal its Moorish architecture. The Spaniards who founded Morelia were from a clearly Afro-Arabic civilization, which made sense if we recall their having just ended 800 years of formal colonization by the Moors for only a period of forty-nine years at the time of the city's founding in 1541.

The Afro-origins of Latin America are often discussed solely in terms of enslaved Africans brought to the Americas, but not in terms of the very hybrid cultures that initiated its conquest. The emergence of white supremacy in Latin America was a process that erased the memory of its foundations. Even the term *race* has its origins in the Iberian civilizations' conceptions of the world through the lens of their natural theology. The term is from *raza*, which referred to breeds of dogs, horses; Jews and Moors. (My placing the semicolon in the series reveals the ontological difference between our world and that of Medieval Iberia, for the comma would have been the grammatically correct punctuation of the series since the presumption was that this grouping was of similar *kinds*.) The expunging of Moorishness and, correlatively, Jewishness continued in the New World and is a central aspect of the formation of modern whiteness. I bring this up because of the discrepancy between how Latin America, and Latin American thought, is often presented in the American academy versus what I saw on the ground as an Africana philosopher there. I have argued, especially in *An Introduction to Africana Philosophy*, that the modern world has brought three dynamics to the fore in what could be called "subaltern" thought: (1) philosophical anthropology, (2) philosophies of freedom, and (3) metacritiques of reason. For many theorists, this has meant (1) identity ["What am I/What are we?"], (2) social transformation ["How should we change things?"], and (3) problems of legitimation and justification ["How do we justify our reasoning, and, indeed reason, in the first two?"]. In the United States, there tends to be a focus on the first at the expense of the others, and the communities of Latin America are often misrepresented as being far more flexible on race with regard to blacks than reality reveals. Maldonado-Torres and I observed in Latin America the two kinds of people who occupy the bottom wrung of society to be consistently black and First peoples. That isn't very different from North America. What is different, however, is the complex history of how Mediterranean whiteness organized the racial landscape, and of how the influx of Germanic peoples in the twentieth century have affected these conceptions, especially in South America. It is not that black, brown, and red are different in Latin America but that whiteness is more fluid, even though its political location is the same. It is the endurance of the former three categories, however, that led consistently to our appearance being of great interest: Our being two Afro-Caribbean men, one from the Latin Caribbean and the other from the Anglo-Caribbean, exemplifying spaces of *intellectual authority* sometimes fell on the verge of a spectacle. Embodiments of thought in the south, pretty much as in the north, was generally expected to be white. That an entire region of people has been lumped together into a new ethnic category in North America that leads to racial-ethnic misrepresentations is another observation worth considering. Latinos (the U.S. category), for instance, are structured in terms of immigration from a Latin America under a narrative that erases its demographic realities. But even more, the *immigration narrative* is also misleading since there are Latinos who are not from Latin America but are descendants of annexed regions of a pre-twentieth-century expansion of the United States. Thus, the identity question requires more to be understood; it is a question linked to the social transformation question, the teleological problematics of where the communities are trying or ought to be trying to go. That there is a symbiotic link between the first set of considerations and the second set of considerations is what is pointed out by the third: Can we really justify thinking through the travails of modern communities in purely identitarian and purely liberating terms?

In Latin America, philosophy, at least as I see it, faces the plight of Afro-South Americans, First peoples, and the broad array of Asian and European peoples who came there into a history in which ideas are formed through struggles many of which attempt to erase such difference while others fight, like the Moorish dimensions of Morelia, to appear from being hidden in daylight. Oddly enough, the missing narrative of my own middle name, which as life shows is not just a name, has added resonance when I add that my maternal great-grandmother, the woman who named me, was also of Sephardic Jewish origins. I don't recall my great-grandmother speaking Ladino, but her Jewish origins, and my mother's father's (from Jerusalem), and the reality of the Anglo-Caribbean once having been Spanish possessions, highlights this continued story of thought and appearance under the effects of *raza*.

None of what I am writing here would be strange to Fanon. He understood, as many of us should today, that no regime lasts forever; no government, no society, no one. The world is littered with the ruins of humanity's efforts at building eternal cities. Each effort to do such is premised on a failure to remember that human beings are not gods. The resources required to support eternity go beyond the capacity of the universe itself. Thus we find ourselves facing the truth of the old proverb that every dog has its day. This was evident in conversations in that small intellectual community of friends in the mountains of Corsica, away from Latin America and the Caribbean, as we looked at what was left of the empires that passed through that island nation like storms in the night. They left their mark, but life goes on with *or without* them, whether Moors, Genoans, and now French.

As we look at history, the evidence is showing that the life span of empires has been shortening as their geographic scope became global. It will be crucial, as processes of decay continue to use more resources and as compression of time and space continues as the expanding social spirit makes the globe smaller, to determine the kinds of political actions, economies, and cultural resources such regions as the Americas and Africa, to name two, and their fusion will need to address the uniqueness of the coming, global historical situation. Such understanding will require imagination of thought attuned to the challenges posed by reality. Much, to appeal to another saying that has now become proverbial, needs to be done.

WORKS CITED

Alcoff, Linda Martín. 2006. *Visible Identities: Race, Gender, and the Self*. New York: Oxford University Press.

Arendt, Hannah. 1958. *The Human Condition*. Chicago: University of Chicago Press.

Bongmba, Elias. 2006. *Dialectics of Transformation in Africa*. New York: Palgrave.

Boxill, Bernard. 2010. "Letter of Acceptance for the Frantz Fanon Lifetime Achievement Award." Caribbean Philosophical Association website: http://www.caribbeanphilosophicalassociation.org/Letter_of_Appreciation.html

Camara, Babacar. 2008. *Marxist Theory, Black/African Specificities, and Racism*. Lanham, MD: Lexington Books.

Chandler, Nahum. 2006. "The Figure of W. E. B. Du Bois as a Problem for Thought CR: *The New Centennial Review* 6, no. 3 (Winter 2006): 29–55.

Cornell, Drucilla. 2007. *Moral Images of Freedom: A Future for Critical Theory*. Landham: Rowman & Littlefield.

De Oto, Alejandro J. 2003. *Política del sujeto poscolonial*. Mexico City, Mexico: El Centro de Estudios de Asia y Africa, El Colegio de México.

Donatien-Yssa, Patricia. 2007. *L'exorcisme de la bles: vaincre la souffrance dans autobiography de ma mere de Jamaica Kincaid*. Paris: Manuscrit.

Du Bois, W.E.B. 1903. *The Souls of Black Folk: Essays and Sketches*. Chicago: A.C. McClurg & Co.

———. 1938. *Black Reconstruction in America, 1860–1880*. New York: Harcourt, Brace & Co.

Dussel, Enrique. 1981. *A History of the Church in Latin America: Colonialism to Liberation (1492–1979)*. Grand Rapids: William B. Eerdmans Publishing Co.

Fanon, Frantz. 1963. *The Wretched of the Earth*. Translated by Constance Farrington with an introduction by Jean-Paul Sartre. New York: Grove Press.

——. 1967a. *A Dying Colonialism*. Translated by Haakon Chevalier with an introduction by Adolfo Gilly. New York: Grove Weidenfeld.

——. 1967b. *Black Skin, White Masks*. Translated by Charles Lamm Markman. New York: Grove Press.

——. 1967c. *Toward the African Revolution*. Translated by Haakon Chevalier. New York: Grove Press.

Fischer, Sibylle. 2004. *Modernity Disavowed: Haiti and the Cultures of Slavery in the Age of Revolution*. Durham, NC: Duke University Press.

Frazier, E. Franklin. 1997. *Black Bourgeoisie: The Book That Brought the Shock of Self-Revelation to Black America*. New York: The Free Press. (Originally published in Paris, France, in 1955 as *Bourgeoisie Noir* for Librairie Plon, and translated into English in 1956.)

Germain, Felix. 2010. "In Search of Full Citizenship: The French West Indian Case (1948–2009), *Journal of Contemporary Thought* 32 (Winter): 99–112.

Gibson, Nigel. 2003. *Fanon: The Postcolonial Imagination*. Cambridge, UK: Polity Press.

Gordon, Jane Anna. 2010. "Degrees of Statelessness: Vulnerability and Political Capital," *Journal of Contemporary Thought* 32 (Winter): 17–40.

Gordon, Lewis R. 1997. *Her Majesty's Other Children: Sketches of Racism from a Neocolonial Age*. Landham, MD: Rowman & Littlefield.

——. 2008. *An Introduction to Africana Philosophy*. Cambridge, UK: Cambridge University Press.

Greer, Margaret R., Maureen Quilligan, and Walter D. Mignolo (eds.). 2008. *Rereading the Black Legend: The Discourses of Religious and Racial Difference in the Renaissance Empires*._Chicago, IL: University of Chicago Press.

Guardiola-Rivera, Oscar. 2010. *What If Latin America Ruled the World?: How the Second World Will Take the First into the 22nd Century*. London: Bloomsbury.

Gyekye, Kwame. 1997. *Tradition and Modernity, Philosophical Reflections on the African Experience*, New York and Oxford: Oxford University Press.

Henry, Paget. 2000. *Caliban's Reason: Introducing Afro-Caribbean Philosophy*. New York: Routledge.

Maldonado-Torres, Nelson. 2007. *Against War: Views from the Underside of Modernity*. Durham: Duke University Press.

Mbembi, Achille Mbembi. 2001. *On the Postcolony*. Berkeley, CA: University of California.

Mehta, Brinda. 2004. *Diasporic (Dis)Locations*. Kingston, JA: University of the West Indies Press.

Mignolo, Walter. 2006. *The Idea of Latin America*. Malden, MA: Blackwell Publishers.

Nissim-Sabat, Marilyn. 2009. *Neither Victim Nor Survivor: Thinking toward a New Humanity*, ed. by Carolyhn M. Cusick and Michael R. Paradiso-Michau. Lanham, MD: Lexington Books.

Reindhardt, Catherine. 2006. *Claims to Memory: Beyond Slavery and Emancipation in the French Caribbean*. New York: Berghahn Books.

Rivera, Angel Quintero. 2009. *Cuerpo y cultura: las musicas "mulatas" y la subversion del baile*. Iberoamericana / Vervuert.

Táíwo, Olúfémi. 2010. *How Europe Preempted Modernization in Africa*. Bloomington, IN: Indiana University Press.

PART V

PHILOSOPHY, LANGUAGE, AND HEGEMONY

CHAPTER FIFTEEN

THE SOCIAL ONTOLOGY OF AFRICAN AMERICAN LANGUAGE, THE POWER OF *NOMMO*, AND THE DYNAMICS OF RESISTANCE AND IDENTITY THROUGH LANGUAGE

George Yancy

It is ABSURD to assume, as has been the tendency, among a great many Western anthropologists and sociologists, that all traces of Africa were erased from the Negro's mind because he learned English. The very nature of the English the Negro spoke and still speaks drops the lie on that idea.

—LeRoi Jones

Every dialect, every language, is a way of thinking. To speak means to assume a culture.

—Frantz Fanon

The spoken word is a gesture, and its meaning, a world.

—M. Merleau-Ponty

In order to illustrate the interpenetration between life and philosophy, I wrote a short and selective philosophical autobiography exploring my philosophical development.¹ In the chapter, I consciously decided to use the language of my *nurture* (African American Language [AAL]), the linguistic expressions of my life-world, the language that helped to capture the mood and texture of what it was like for me to live within the heart of North Philadelphia, one of America's black ghettoes. After all, what other linguistic medium could I use to articulate the rhythm, the fluidity, the angst, the aesthetics of coolness, and the beauty involved in traversing those dangerous, challenging, and inviting ghetto streets? These streets were sites where style mattered; where respect was key; where blood was shed; where families were poor, weary, and often hopeless; where who you knew could save your life; and where one had to be bad, had to project that tough image in order to survive. Writing about the background of this existential space of anguish and hope, a background within which my philosophical self evolved, was no easy task. However, writing *in* the language of my nurture not only helped me to remember much of what was "forgotten," but helped me to make "inroads against the established power-lines of speech."²

After having read my chapter, a white philosopher whom I admire came up to me at an American Philosophical Association (APA) conference and told me how he really enjoyed the piece and how he had not known so many intimate details about my life. He added: "I really enjoyed it, but why did you use *that language* [meaning AAL]. You write very well [meaning in "Standard" American English: SAE]. You don't have to use that language to make your point." I listened in silence, realizing that he completely missed the point. Indeed, for him, AAL was not a viable language, not a legitimate semiotic medium through which my life-world could best be represented. Rather, in his view, the language that I chose to use was slang, an ersatz form of communication that clearly should not have been used. By using AAL I had somehow fallen from the true heights of academic professionalism and broken the norms of respectable philosophy-speak. Indeed, perhaps he thought that I was being "too black" in my speech, not white enough, not "proper" enough. As Frantz Fanon observed, "Nothing is more astonishing than to hear a black man express himself properly, for then in truth he is putting on the white world."³ Fanon's observations suggest deeper relationships that may exist between the function of language and a specifically *racialized* and racist philosophical anthropology. Again, Fanon observed:

> The Negro of the Antilles will be proportionately whiter—*that is, he will come closer to being a real human being*—in direct ratio to his mastery of the French language. I am not unaware that this is one of man's attitudes face to face with Being. A Man who has a language consequently possesses the world expressed and implied

by that language. What we are getting at becomes plain: Mastery of language affords remarkable power.[4]

Fanon's observations also contain profound implications for the specifically racial and cultural dimensions of philosophy-speak. Indeed, perhaps in the United States it is philosophy-speak that is "too white," creating a kind of dislocation for many black folk who find it necessary to speak AAL to communicate some subtle cultural experience or way of "seeing the world" philosophically. This does not mean that Anglo-American or European languages are inherently inadequate for expressing philosophical ideas per se; rather, the point is that these languages are presumed the normative media through which philosophy qua philosophy can best be engaged. It is the imperialist, and, of course, colonialist, tendency of these languages that is being rejected. Nevertheless, in my chapter, it was not I who failed philosophy, but it was SAE—that dominant, territorial, imperial medium of philosophical expression in the United States—that failed to convey the logic, the horror, the humanity, the existentially rank, the confluent, and the surreal realities embedded in my experiences in one of America's Black ghetto enclaves.

It is here that one might ask: "Are Anglo-American and European philosophical forms of discourse inadequate for re-presenting the complexity of black experiences?" After all, not any form of discursivity will do. My experiences were in excess of what SAE could capture. Some forms of knowledge become substantially truncated and distorted, indeed, erased, if not expressed through the familiar linguistic media of those who have possession of such knowledge. In a passage rich with issues concerning the lack of power and effectiveness of SAE to capture the personal identity and personal experiences of a young black boy, writer R. DeCoy asks:

> How . . . my Nigger Son, can you ever hope to express what you are, who you are or your experiences with God, in a language so limited, conceived by a people who are quite helpless in explaining themselves? How can you, my Nigger Son, find your identity, articulate your experiences, in an order of words?[5]

Regarding white philosophers (or even black ones) who simply fail to understand the importance of AAL as a rich cultural and philosophical site of expression, I believe that it is the job of knowledgeable and responsible black philosophers—at least for those who are willing to admit that they speak both the Language of Wider Communication and the powerful vernacular shaped by African retentions and African American linguistic nuances—to invite them to enter African American semiotic spaces of discursive difference and overlap. We should keep in mind that being black or African American in North America does not ipso facto mean that one is familiar with the subtle complexities and power of AAL. After all, there are black philosophers from middle-class (and lower-class) backgrounds whose linguistic assimilation of SAE, a form of cultural capital ownership and privilege, functions both as a badge of white acceptance, and an antidote for reducing white anxiety and fear. The invitation, however, should not be a plea, but an honest gesture to explore the language on its own terms. This is why it was so very important that this chapter be written unapologetically in the language of my *nurture*, the medium had to be the message. Keep in mind that an invitation is not the same as a *forced* introduction. This was the situation that blacks of African decent faced; they were forced to learn the language of the colonizer, forced to split, to multiply in so many different cultural, psychological, linguistic, and spiritual directions against their will. The fact that this chapter appears in a philosophy text invites a certain level of cultural and linguistic splitting on the part of its readers, perhaps not very different from what is required when reading Kant or Heidegger, particularly given their penchant for neologism.

Let's be honest, articles and chapters that typically appear in philosophy journals and philosophy texts, more generally, have no doubt been written in SAE and by predominantly white male philosophers, philosophers who have been trained to engage in "proper" philosophical prose. I, too, can write in this language. To write in this language is to reproduce the professional culture of philosophy, to perpetuate lines of power, and to show that you have been "properly" educated and worthy of hire. Moreover, to engage in this discourse is to *perform* linguistically before an audience of gatekeepers who probably fear too much fat in their discourse, too much play, too much signifying, too much indirection, too much ambiguity, too much vagueness, too much concrete, everyday reality. Like AAL within the larger context of SAE, by appearing in this philosophy text this chapter also enters into a space of established norms of linguistic propriety, calling into question and perhaps rupturing the authority of "Standard" philosophical prose, that *unhip* discourse of professional philosophers. Of course, having this chapter published in this text could turn out to be a curse or a blessing. Realizing the degree to which "proper" philosophical discourse is required by philosophy texts and how such discourse in turn shapes and legitimates philosophy journals, and other sites of philosophical knowledge production, many readers of this book may read the chapter with contempt. Some may approach the article as a piece of exotica. Some may even view my use of AAL as a disgraceful "Stepin Fetchit" performance that does a disservice to black philosophers who are all too eager to perform well in the presence of white power, to show the world that *we be* real philosophers because we speak the language of Mister Charlie. Then, of course, there are some philosophers who are open to creative possibilities, differences, and alternatives to hegemonic linguistic territorialism, who believe in plural experiences and multiple discourses for articulating them. When the medium is the message, one has got to get wit da medium. It will take more than this chapter to impact significantly a certain linguistic-philosophical reference point that is buttressed by so much history and power that has historically structured philosophy-speak. To best articulate that black existential space where the *real* world (not that abstract possible world) is filled with pain, struggle, blood, tears and laughter—where death follows a minute of joy, where so much is improvisatory and surreal, moving with the quickness, where the streets are hot, dangerous, and familial, where love is abundant and hate smiles in yo face, where melodic sounds fight to stay above the sounds of gunfire, where babies cry all night long, because mama done gone and hit the pipe, where a brotha gots to be down, where brothas be runnin game, talkin that talk, keepin it real, and showin much loyalty—requires fluency in the language which partly grows out of the nitty-gritty core of the epistemology and ontology of that space.

It is my contention that African American linguist Geneva Smitherman is working within the rich situated practices of Africana philosophy and should be acknowledged as such. She is self-consciously aware of the meta-reflective analysis that is necessary to make sense of what it means for black people to have forged an identity through the muck and mire of white racism. After all, black folk were deemed inherently inferior, culture-less, without *Geist*. Yet, black agency survived the tortuous African blood stained water of the Atlantic. Like jazz (with its improvisatory structure and chromatic form), the blues (with its ontology of lyrically holding at a distance incredible pain and sorrow), and rap music (with its *phat* beats, lyrical braggadocio, and in yo face street reality), AAL is a significant site of black cultural innovation, syncretism, and survival, laden with situated epistemological insights. There is no other way to honor the work of Geneva Smitherman, to explore the "language-gaming" of everyday black folk, without directly and unapologetically entering into the dynamic, rhythmic, ritual and cognitive spaces of African American linguistic expressiveness.

Hence, from the very giddayup, that is, befo I bees gittin into some really dope cultural, historical, philosophical and linguistic analyses, let's engage in a lil bit of naming and claiming. Word! The power of *Nommo*. Geneva Smitherman (aka Docta G) is an educational activist, a word warrior, a language rights fighter, a linguist-activist, and a linguistic democratizer. Can I get a witness? Yeah, that's right. She is the legitimizer[6] of AAL. The shonuff sista from the hood who is cognizant of what it means to be a

New World African, to be linked to that shonuff black space of talkin and testifyin, stylin and profilin. AAL is the language of her nurture.[7] She was, after all, baptized "in the linguistic fire of black Folk."[8] Believe me, for if I'm lyin, I'm flyin, she knows the source of those deleted copulas ("The coffee cold."), those post-vocalic –r sounds ("My feet be *tied*," not "tired"), redundant past tense marking ("I likeded her," not "liked"), few consonant pairs ("Those tesses was hard," not "tests"), stylizations, and rhetorical devices.

Docta G operates within that unique African American space of performative "languaging," a space of agency, contestation, self-definition, poiesis, and hermeneutic combat. She is all up in the cultural sphere of ashy knees, nappy hair and how we be actin so saddity. Ah, yes, and she knows about the hot comb as a cultural artifact of self-hatred, a form of hatred instilled through the power of colonial white aesthetics. She *member* where she come from. She got no desire to front. Docta G's medium *is* the message. She avoids what linguist-philosopher John L. Austin refers to as the "descriptive fallacy," which involves the assumption that the main function of language is to describe things. Through the incorporation of AAL *flava* in her written works (and no doubt in her lectures), Docta G is *doing something* with those words and phrases. Her writings, in short, are demonstrative enactments of the historical, stylistic, political, communicative, cognitive and social ontological power of AAL. Docta G is the lion who has learned how to write, how to narrate a counter-historical narrative, and how to recognize and theorize a counter-language. A meta-linguist, she is a cultural, ethical, and political theorist. If push comes to shove, she'll "choose goodness over grammar."[9] She knows that the politics of language policy is a larger question of the politics of reality construction, historical structuring of society, race, class, and Anglo-linguistic imperialism. As such, she moves between both the sociolinguists (who stress social and ethnic language) and the Cartesian or Chomskyan linguists (who stress "ideally competent" language). She knows that the right to speak AAL is a question of linguistic freedom, agency and justice. A Womanist, moving within that bold, self-assertive and *we-affirming* space of sistas like Angela Davis, Alice Walker, Patricia Hill Collins, Sojourner Truth, and Harriet Tubman, Docta G is responsible, in charge and serious. She's no prisoner of the academy; rather, she is existentially and politically committed to the black community, its survival and the continual actualization of its cultural generative force. Smitherman maintains that a womanist denotes an "African-American woman who is rooted in the Black community and committed to the development of herself and the entire community."[10] African American women, empowered by their womanist consciousness, were well aware that white feminists had failed to critique, self-reflexively, the normativity of their own whiteness. Epistemologically, black womanists occupied their own subject positions, positions that did not square with the theorizations of white middle-class women. You dig (Wolof: *dega*) what I'm sayin? Can I get an Amen?

Docta G, "daughter of the hood,"[11] raised in Brownsville, Tennessee, was culturally immersed in the rich locutionary acts of black folk. Y'all wit me? I'm pointing to the significant links between Docta G's biographical *location* and how this influenced her later theorizations about AAL. Consistent with feminist, Womanist, social constructionist and postmodernist insights, one's social location is a significant hermeneutic lens through which to understand one's theorizations. By emphasizing one's social location, one is able to avoid the obfuscating process of reification. As social constructionists Peter L. Berger and Thomas Luckmann maintain, "Reification is the apprehension of human phenomena as if they were things, that is, in non-human or possibly suprahuman terms."[12] In short, the lived-context, as existential phenomenology stresses, is always already presupposed in relationship to epistemological claims.

Docta G, daughter of the black ghetto, daughter of Reverend Napoleon, was an early witness to the illocutionary and perlocutionary acts of a linguistically rich black family, a sharecropping community, and a Traditional Black Church (TBC). For example, she knows the power of tonal semantics, a significant feature of AAL that moves the listener through melodic structure and poignant rhetorical configuration. She relates that her father once expressed the following theme in one of his sermons: "I am nobody talking to Somebody Who can help anybody."[13] Geneva, monolingual and from the sociolinguistic margins, was well aware of what it meant to be deemed a problem, to endure the pain of being told that her speech was "pathological," "wrong," "inferior," "bad," and "derelict." Having gone North (or was it simply up South?) where she attended college, Geneva had to pass a test "in order to qualify for the teacher preparation program."[14] Given the then oppressive and racist language policy, a policy that stressed the importance of teachers being able to speak the language of those who "carry on the affairs of the English-speaking people,"[15] Geneva did not pass the speech test. Docta G explains:

> We found ourselves in a classroom with a speech therapist who wasn't sure what to do with us. Nobody was dyslexic. No one was aphasic. There was not even a stutterer among us. I mean here was this young white girl, a teaching assistant at the university, who was just trying to get her Ph.D., and she was presented with this perplexing problem of people who didn't have any of the communication disorders she had been trained to deal with.[16]

Although Geneva eventually passed the test by simply memorizing the pronunciation of particular sounds she needed to focus on, she came to interpret this experience as key to stimulating her politico-linguistic consciousness. She relates that "it aroused the fighting spirit in me, sent me off into critical linguistics and I eventually entered the lists of the language wars."[17] Clearly, this experience created in Geneva a powerful sense of agency and praxis. On the strength! You know it. As Kenyan philosopher and literary figure Ngugi wa Thiong'o argues, "There is no history which is purely and for all time that of actors and those always acted upon."[18] Uhm talkin bout a Womanist, Docta G. You know, the chief expert *witness* for the linguistic intelligence of Black children, the one who has made it her political project to challenge effectively the totalizing systems of Euro/Anglo-linguistic cultural normativity. You betta act like you know. She fightin against African American *linguistic* erasure. Naw, even more so, she fightin *for* African American hue-manity.

Docta G reveals that AAL is not some broken, ersatz sign system relegated to the confines of ghetto life; rather, AAL is the language of black America.[19] Docta G is up on it; she operates in that deeply deep space of African American signs and symbols, a semiotic space where individual words and phrases carry the weight of an entire worldview. As Frantz Fanon asserts, "To speak a language is to take on a world, a culture."[20] I'm talkin bout an entire life-world where folk gotta live under conditions of much oppression, at the bottom, where black bodies and souls constantly struggle to move within a compressing and collapsing social cosmos. Sendin out an S.O.S. call. There appears to be a Blue Shift in the black existential universe. But as we move to the center of it all, to the heart and soul of these historicizing, proud black people, we notice a dynamic process of reconstitution, reinterpretation, being and becoming. We be a praxis-oriented people who are defined by our communicative acts, our existential improvisatory modes of being, forms of world-making, and ways of renarrating, over and over again, our historical and spiritual links to Africa and the Americas.

Toasts. Yo mamma! Some Baaaaad people we be. Coded language. Gangsta limp. Bloods and Crips. Lightin up that spliff. Yo, it's a Philly blunt! Catchin the spirit. Is it glossolalia or scatting? The Amen corner. Bench walkin preachers. "This ain no prayin church." "Naw, we a prayin church, Reb. Preach Brotha!" Call and response. Moans, shouts, and groans. All of these significations are capable of establishing a psychocognitive communal dynamic of shared cultural, religious, and intrapsychological meaningfulness.[21] In the fields, in the storefront church, or from the lips of the Godfather of funk, it's all good. The sacred and secular always already organically fused. As Docta G notes, "It is, after all, only a short distance from 'sacred' Clara Ward's 'I'm climbin high mountains tryin to git 'Home' to 'secular'

Curtis Mayfield's 'keep on pushin / can't stop me now / move up a little higher / someway or somehow.'"[22] Tarrying all night long. Those black bodies, forming a deep and harmonious *Mitsein*, will move and groove until the break of dawn. These bluesified, jazzified, funkified, spiritualized, and aestheticized sites of existence.

Damn she slammin! She's a brick. Uhm talkin boodylicious. Shakin that jelly. Ask Destiny's Child. Movin those hips. You know it didn't start with Elvis. Boodylicious! Aesthetics? Erotica? You tell me. I gots to come clean. Does the French naturalist Georges Cuvier fall within the same cipha with Sir Mix-A-Lot? Baby Got Back. Steatopygia? Cuvier came with all his racist porno-tropes, gazing with those medical eyes that saw a collage of "abnormal" buttocks and genitalia. Big ups to Sarah Bartmann. They called her "Hottentot Venus." Josephine Baker knew how to *work it*. Sistas know *Cosmo* ain representin. Big ups to the sistas who realize that aesthetics is political. The Sistas got some high standards, too. They ain no skeezers. You know you gotta show respect. Industry funded, paid for images got U hooked, Brotha. Believin all that hype, throwin all that chedda, tryin to bling bling yo way to a piece of that pie. Do I see Cuvier behind yo gaze? Brothas gotta come real, his shit gotta be tight, no wack raps allowed. It ain all bout the benjamins! Is it Johnny Walker Red or a forty-ounce? Let's pour a lil bit for the brothas who ain heah. Singin doo-wop in some back ally. That's the way it usta be. Or rappin, freestylin, on some urban street corner. Even the Hawk, you know, Joe Chilly, don't stop these Brothas from talkin that talk. Yo, you gotta represent. The power of *Nommo* within these tight, fluctuatin, surreal, inviting and dangerous streets can save yo life. Ask Malcolm, not X, but Little. He was out there. You know, my man Detroit Red. He was tryin to make that chedda. The trickster. You've got to be improvisational on these chocolate city streets, constantly in existential negotiation, takin no shorts. In these streets, somethin always bout to kick off. It's summahtime and brothas be rollin tough, posse-style. Many, they be frontin, though. Whether duping Mister Charlie, ole Massa, or The Man, black folk be flippin the script. The power of improvisatorial negotiation. Thelonius Monk, he is a child of the first twenty Africans to arrive. The Middle Passage. Negotiating. Creating. Makin somethin outta nothin. Learning how to play those microtones and enact those micro-disturbances of white hegemonic power. Black folk bees some BaddDDD people, all decked out in their marvelousness, their terribleness, contradictoriness, pains and pleasures. Ask DMX, he know WHO WE BE. From Africa to America, black people bees tellin stories within stories. The African Griot. Field holler. A Blues song. A Jazz improvisation. Reb in the house! Revolutionary politico-poetics. Rap music. Big Momma's linguistic and paralinguistic style. And you know she got much Mother-wit. This is a complex, continuous and contiguous historical

cipher. The power of *Nommo* as both constant and constative. Sonia San-
chez shonuff knows this; Larry Neal and surrealist Ted Joans *still* knows it;
and Amiri Baraka's vociferations tell it all. Yo, Docta G, kick the ballistics:

> The emergence of the Black Freedom Struggle marked a fundamen-
> tal shift in linguistic consciousness as Black intellectuals, scholar-
> activists, and writer-artists deliberately and consciously engaged in
> an unprecedented search for a language to express Black identity
> and the Black condition.[23]

The entire cadre of the Black Arts Movement knew a change had to
come. This ain just braggadocio, although we can do that, too. You smell
me? Hips in motion with some serious attitude. Deconstructed linearity.
Cakewalking, Swinging (just to say alive), bopping, grooving, hip hopping
and Harlem shakin. Cool and hot expressiveness ever so fused. Talkin shit.
Sometimes wino-style. Richard Pryor had a comedic-dramatic feel for all this
marvelous Black everydayness; he was all up in the *Lebenswelt* of black folk.
Playin some craps. Heah come the PO-ice! Multiple sites of keepin it real:
the Amen corner, barbershops, hair salons, the safe space of the kitchen,
pool halls, clubs, street corners, and back allies. Cell phones and pagers in
this postmodern urban space. Boody call. "It's my shorty, I gotta go. Shoot
some hoops later. Peace out." "Damn, dog, I think you must be whupped."
These are the speech acts of everydayness, the *lingua franca* of so many of
my peeps. But not everything is linguistically permissible within this space.
Within the framework of speech act theory, there are definite *felicity conditions*. Black people be movin in that rich semiotic space, suspended and
immersed in webs of meaning, as Max Weber and Clifford Geertz would say.
You might ask, why the delineation of the above culturally thick, multiply
semiotic, and intertextually rich streams? Answer: Docta G's work demands
it! She writes:

> In my own work, I have very consciously sought to present the
> whole of Black Life, and the rich continuum of African American
> speech from the secular semantics of the street and the basketball
> court to the talkin and testifyin of the family reunion and the
> Black Church.[24]

This cultural space is thick, hypertextual, protean and diachronic. It
is a cultural semiotic tale, a narrative force, told and lived by a people who,
despite their horrendous experiences during the Middle Passage, the failures
of Reconstruction, the presence of lynched black bodies (or strange fruit),
the water hoses, and "Nigger dogs" during the 1960s, see it as they duty to
keep keepin on, keepin their "eye on the sparrow," and gittin ovuh. That's

right: *AND STILL WE RISE!* Docta G knows that "niggers is more than deleted copulas."[25] To get a clear sense of the diachronic structure of AAL, it is important to understand the historicity and dynamic remaking of African folk in racist America; indeed, there is the need to be fully cognizant of what America bees puttin black folk through. As I have suggested, Docta G is hip to the particular forms of life of so many African Americans. She is all up in the epistemological, ontological, and cultural "language-gaming" of black folk, from the pulpit, within the everyday urban and rural spaces of African American linguistic performativity, to the complexity and aesthetics of talkin shit, to rapese. She recognizes that it is not simply an issue of getting at the lexical core of what makes AAL unique and legitimate, but it is an issue of "whose culture?" and "whose values?" and "whose identity?" Peep the insightful lines where she elaborates, "The moment is not which dialect, but which culture, not whose vocabulary but whose values, not *I* vs. *I be*, but WHO DO I BE?"[26] It is a question of the axiological, linguistic and cultural ontology of identity. But to get at "WHO DO I BE" involves moving beyond the discourse of pathology and what W. E. B. Du Bois referred to as our being defined as *a problem* vis-à-vis white folk. Therefore, Docta G is engaged in a project that is fueled by de-pathologization, celebration, and reclamation of African American humanity and identity. In sum, then, Ima have to continue writin a *responsible* article that captures the broad scope of what Docta G bees droppin.

At this juncture, I briefly explore, in an expository, synthetic, and interpretive fashion, various aspects of Docta G's critical corpus: (1) the significance of the existentially terrifying journey from Africa, through the Middle Passage, and to the so-called New World, which will provide historical insight into the psycho-linguistic rupture, although not resulting in a complete cultural severance, caused by the malicious regime of white racism; (2) the significance of *Nommo* or the Word for Africans in America, and how *Nommo* is linked to the protean and resistant/resilient power of African/African American identity; and, (3) the structure of AAL in terms of significant lexical, phonological, stylistic, and semantic features, and what this means in terms of resisting/combating Euro/Anglo linguistic imperialism and hegemony.

Throughout Docta G's critical oeuvre she makes constant reference to 1619. For example, she notes:

> The first cargo of African slaves to be deposited in what would become the United States of America arrived at Jamestown in 1619. From that point until the beginnings of the movement to abolish slavery in the nineteenth century, whites, by and large, perceived of America's African slave population as beasts of burden, exotic sexual objects, or curious primitives.[27]

In short, within the racist epistemological regime of white racism, these Africans were not *different*, but were deemed as constituting an *ontological deficiency*.[28] "We are trapped," according to Docta G, "in our own historical moment and wish to understand that."[29] In order to understand this historical moment, however, and Docta G is well aware of this, black folk must understand their historical journey across space and time. It involves the narrative of black folk's "unfinished business of what it means to be and talk like home."[30] Again, back to the connection between ontology, identity, and language. Docta G agrees with Fanon that white colonialism forces black folk to question their sense of identity: "Who am I?"[31] After all, the institution of American and European slavery, with their disciplinary strategies and practices, was designed to instill in Africans a sense of inferiority and ontological servitude, to deracinate any sense of African pride, cultural identity, and home. This motif of "home" has been a rich trope for black folk in America; for in their various stages of identity formation (African, Colored, Negro, black, African American) they have sought ways of negotiating a sense of themselves and a sense of *place* and *reality*. Docta G writes, "The societal complexity of the Black condition continues to necessitate a self-conscious construction of reality."[32]

Africans were taught to internalize negative images of themselves, to "know" themselves as chattel and property. This process was evident during the Middle Passage. During the voyage, Africans (Ashantis, Ibos, Fulanis, Yorubas, Hausas, etc.) were subjected to tight forms of spatialization. The Middle Passage was itself part and parcel of a disciplinary practice to construct the black body/self as a *thing*, to encourage Africans to begin thinking of themselves in subhuman terms. Black bodies were herded into suffocating spaces of confinement. Think here of the physically tight, economically impoverished, spaces of contemporary urban black America. On the slave ship Pongas, for example, 250 women, many of whom were pregnant, were forced into a space of 16 × 18 feet. Feminist and cultural theorist bell hooks writes:

> The women who survived the initial stages of pregnancy gave birth aboard the ship with their bodies exposed to either the scorching sun or the freezing cold. The number of black women who died during childbirth or the number of stillborn children will never be known. Black women with children on board the slave ships were ridiculed, mocked, and treated contemptuously by the slaver crew. Often the slavers brutalized children to watch the anguish of their mothers.[33]

An African slave trader tells of 108 boys and girls who were packed into a small hole:

> I returned on board to aid in stowing [on the slave ship] one hundred and eight boys and girls, the eldest of whom did not exceed fifteen years [old]. As I crawled between decks, I confess I could not imagine how this little army was to be packed or draw breath in a hole but twenty-two inches high![34]

Molefi Asante captures the terror of the Middle Passage where he writes:

> Imagine crossing the ocean abroad a small ship made to hold 200 people but packed with 1,000 weeping and crying men, women, and children. Each African was forced to fit into a space no more than 55.9 centimeters (22 inches) high, roughly the height of a single gym locker, and 61 centimeters (24 inches) wide, scarcely an arm's length. There were no lights aboard the ships, little food, and no toilet facilities.[35]

The Middle Passage was a voyage of death, bodily objectification, humiliation, dehumanization, geographical, and psychological dislocation. It was a process of cultural disruption, which involved a profound sense of religious, aesthetic, linguistic, teleological, and cosmological disorientation. In the "New World," we were sold from auction blocks; the black body/self became a blood and flesh text on which whites could project all of their fears, desires, ressentiment, fantasies, myths and lies. For example, white fears and perversions created the myth of the so-called "Negro rapist." In 1903, Dr. William Lee Howard argued that Negro males attack innocent white women because of "racial instincts that are about as amenable to ethical culture as is the inherent odor of the race."[36] In 1900, Charles Carroll supported the pre-Adamite beliefs of Dr. Samuel Cartwright. The Negro was described as an ape and was said to be the actual "tempter of Eve."[37] The so-called "sciences" of physiognomy and phrenology, with their emphasis on the prognathous jaw of Negroes, were said to clearly support the "primitive" nature of African people. In short, the black body/self, within the scientific discursive space of whiteness, which embodied a racist epistemology, was constructed as a mere object of the white racist gaze. The black body/self was subjected to the tactics of what philosopher Michel Foucault termed *anatomo-politics*, that is, those disciplines that operated on the body, regulating and subjecting the black body/self to white racist theorizations.[38] Docta G is well aware of the historical existence of scientific racism where she notes:

> In the years just before the Civil War (roughly the 1840s and 1850s), scientific theories of racial superiority located social and

behavioral differences between members of the human species in genetic factors, which became the basis of studies of black slaves.[39]

Through the powerful structuration of the white gaze, the black body/self was codified and typified as a subhuman, savage beast devoid of culture. Dr. Paul B. Barringer drew from the Darwinian emphasis on heredity. According to the insights of historian George M. Frederickson, Barringer argued:

> The inborn characteristics of the Negro had been formed by natural selection during "ages of degradation" in Africa and his savage traits could not have been altered in any significant way by a mere two centuries of proximity to Caucasian civilization in America.[40]

Historian Joseph A. Tillinghast also theorized within the framework of Darwinian theory. For Tillinghast, "The Negro character had been formed in Africa, a region which supposedly showed an uninterrupted history of stagnation, inefficiency, ignorance, cannibalism, sexual licence, and superstition."[41] And Scottish philosopher David Hume (1711–1776), in his "Of National Characters," maintains:

> I am apt to suspect the Negroes, and in general all other species of men (for there are four or five different kinds) to be naturally inferior to whites. There never was a civilized nation of any other complexion than white, nor even any individual eminent either in action or speculation. No ingenious manufactures amongst them, no arts, no sciences. In Jamaica indeed they talk of one Negro as a man of learning; but 'tis likely he is admired for very slender accomplishments, like a parrot, who speaks a few words plainly.[42]

The idea was to "demonstrate" (although we know it was to rationalize white wicked deeds) that Africans had no language (perhaps a few words only), no history, no identity, and no peoplehood. But I/we must admit that them white boys was droppin some weak, mythical, indefensible, pseudo-scientific, shit.

What is clear is that the newly arrived Africans found themselves in a hostile and dangerous world of anti-blackness, a world that refused to recognize the complex cultural and subjective *here* from which Africans viewed the world and hated their captivity and oppression. "It was the practice of slavers to mix up Africans from different tribes."[43] Africans were forced into unfamiliar groupings so as to eliminate any sense of community, cultural, *linguistic* or otherwise. The objective, despite, paradoxically, the racist belief that Africans were devoid of any complex linguistic-communicative practices, was to prevent them from communicating, from gaining any sense of group identity, and, hence, suppressing any possibility of rebellion/overthrow. Consistent with Hume's belief that Africans spoke "a few words plainly," Docta G notes that in 1884, J. A. Harrison held that African American speech was "based on African genetic inferiority."[44] For Harrison, much of Negro talk was "baby-talk."[45] Docta G concludes:

> Blinded by the science of biological determinism, early twentieth-century white linguistic scholars followed Harrison's lead, taking hold of his baby-talk theory of African American speech and widely disseminating it in academic discourse. The child language explanation of Black Language is linguistic racism that corresponds to the biological determinist assumption that blacks are lower forms of the human species whose evolution is incomplete.[46]

Such beliefs, however, were not limited to white racist "academics." As African American linguist and anthropologist John Baugh correctly points out:

> The racist literature about blacks and black speech in particular should, of course, be dismissed in any serious analysis of the subject, but we must appreciate that the opinions expressed by white supremacists—while often absurd—reflected the feelings of a majority of white Americans.[47]

Finding themselves within this colonial context, a space of white supremacy (read: anti-blackness), what were Africans to do? Torn from their own rich soil, and transplanted within this blood-soaked soil of America, Africans, with their magnificent oral tradition, rich cultural modes of being, non-white constructions of reality, and their own conception of what it meant *to be*, had to make sense out of this imposed and absurd situation. *They had to survive* the existential horror and meaninglessness of white America. "But that is the essence of the Black experience: to make a way out of no way."[48] Keep in mind that American slavery also was reinforced through the use of nondiscursive forms of brutality and oppression. It wasn't all about white racist abstract theory. Frederick Douglass knew all too well of the physical horrors of plantation life. He was torn from his mother at a very young age. The idea here was to eliminate any sense of biological and familial continuity, to attempt to break the spirit of oneness. In terms of sheer physical brutality, Douglass, who Docta G groups within the black intellectual tradition of Du Bois, Carter G. Woodson, and Lorenzo Turner, given his understanding of the rich oral/aural tradition of black people,

tells of the story of old Barney receiving thirty lashes on his black flesh by
Colonel Lloyd.[49] He tells of Demby who disobeyed an order given by Mr.
Gore and was shot in the head as a result. Douglass says that "his mangled
body sank out of sight, and blood and brains marked the water where he
had stood."[50] Or, think of the young black girl, Douglass' wife's cousin, who
had fallen asleep while watching Mrs. Hick's baby. Mrs. Hick "jumped from
her bed, seized an oak stick of wood by the fireplace, and with it broke the
girl's nose and breastbone, and thus ended her life."[51]

To be enslaved was to be subjected to terror. You had your teeth
knocked out, permanently separated from your family, burned to death,
castrated, lynched; you watched your mother or sister raped, beaten, and
shackled. This was an everyday reality and a constant live possibility for
Africans bought to the "New World." But this is the historical space that
must be explored, if only briefly, to understand the force of our *languaging*. Docta G is mindful of this: "I say . . . we can not talk about Black
Idiom apart from Black culture and the Black experience."[52] Continuing
with Douglass, Smitherman locates a significant aspect of our oral, aural,
musical, and narrative motifs, viz., the use of song as a counter-hegemonic
expression. These black bodies, locked down, with very little space within
which to move, must have had rich (Ghanaian, Dahomeyan, etc.) musical
fire shut up in they bones. Memory. Retentions. Identity. Douglass dispels
the false notion that enslaved Africans were "happy darkies" who sung their
time away. Indeed, on the contrary, singing, which was a powerful semiotic
marker of our enduring ability to create visions of counter-reality, solidarity,
memory, and agency, was an illocutionary form of expression, communicating discontentment and protestation, which had a significant perlocutionary
impact on the psychology of the enslaved. Douglass:

> The songs of the slave represent the sorrows of his heart; and
> he is relieved by them, only as an aching heart is relieved by its
> tears . . . [the songs] told a tale of woe . . . they were tones loud,
> long, and deep; they breathed the prayer and complaint of souls
> boiling over with the bitterest anguish. Every tone was a testi-
> mony against slavery, and a prayer to God for deliverance from
> chains. . . . To those songs I trace my first glimmering conception of
> the dehumanizing character of slavery. . . . Those songs still follow
> me, to deepen my hatred of slavery, and quicken my sympathies
> for my brethren in bonds.[53]

Hence, even our "musicking" was a form of communication. But there
were times when we had to code our language from the ofay. This is just
one, although very important, semantic register of the Africans creation

of a counterlanguage.[54] Docta G points to an example of a stanza from an old black folk song that includes the expression "not turn her." This was a brilliant coded way of referring to the revolutionary freedom fighter "Nat-Tur-ner." Docta G goes on to argue that many of the Negro spirituals were not speaking about other-worldly affairs, but about the historically concrete affairs of black people, in the here and now of their servitude. Hence, though the lyrics (overheard by whites) suggested a *vertical* metaphysics that spoke to God, the lyrics contained a powerful social and political *horizontal* message that spoke to the urgency of escape. Docta G:

> The slaves used other-worldly lyrics, yes, but the spirituals had for them this-worldly meanings [What I be callin a "horizontal message."]. They moaned "steal away to Jesus" to mean stealing away FROM the plantation and TO freedom (that is, "Jesus"). They sang triumphantly "this train is bound for Glory," but the train they were really talking about was the "freedom train" that ran on the Underground Railroad. The symbolic Underground Railroad was actually a revolutionary network of escape routes and schemes devised to assist slaves fleeing to the "glory" of freedom in Canada and the North. "Go down, Moses, and tell Ole Pharaoh to let my people go." Moses—black freedom fighter Harriet Tubman, the "conductor" of the Underground Railroad, who in her lifetime assisted more than 300 slaves to escape. She would "go down" South and by her actions "tell" white slavers (Ole Pharaoh) to let her people go.[55]

This is one example of what I mean by the dynamics of linguistic resistance. Africans were able to use the language of white folk, curving it, warping it, and twisting it against them. This was/is a form of linguistic resistance/combat and overthrow. In yo face style. Swish, two points! Docta G notes:

> When an enslaved African said, "Eve'body talkin bout Heaben ain goin dere," it was a double-voiced form of speech that *signified* on the slaveholders who professed Christianity but practiced slavery. This Africanized form of speaking became a code for Africans in America to talk about Black business, publicly or privately, and in the enslavement period, even to talk about "ole Massa" himself right in front of his face![56]

Of course, when the ofay caught on, Black folk had to change the word, expression. We talkin bout a dynamic process heah. Concerning the two-pronged dimensions of language, Ngugi argues:

Every language has two aspects. One aspect is its role as an agent that enables us to communicate with one another in our struggle to find the means for survival. The other is its role as a carrier of the history and the culture built into the process of that communication over time.[57]

Ngugi sees these two aspects of language as forming a kind of dialectical unity.

Despite the long journey across the Middle Passage, one way that Africans were able to negotiate ways of surviving was through dynamic semiotic and linguistic modalities, to communicate with one another (in Pidgin and Creole) in a common struggle to stay alive. As Marlene Nourbese Philip notes:

In the vortex of New World slavery, the African forged new and different words, developed strategies to impress her experience on the language. The formal standard language was subverted, turned upside down, inside out, and sometimes erased. Nouns became strangers to verbs and vice versa; tonal accentuation took the place of several words at a time; rhythms held sway.[58]

Africanized SAE also functioned as a medium of black culture and reminded black folk of the historicity of their African identity. Hence, the complete cultural rupture that was intended for enslaved Africans simply failed. "Using elements of the white man's speech, in combination with their own linguistic patterns and practices, enslaved Africans developed an oppositional way of speaking."[59] I see this as a dynamic process of sublation, which understands the African experience in America as a process of negation and preservation. No matter how much of WHO WE BE was negated, through a disruptive and colonialist "synthesis," we preserved significant and powerful elements of our rich historical past. *Hallelujah, thank the Lord!* Yes, we got soul and we SUPER BAD! Soul, according to Docta G, involves "a worldview that is not only God-centered, but includes the vision that Goodness and Justice is gon prevail."[60] She links soul with the dynamic philosophical category of style, which is rich with aesthetic, political, and ontological overtones. In other words, style is the dynamic expression or articulation of the motif of overcoming. She concludes: "If you got soul, yo style oughta reflect it."[61] But whassup wit all dis philosophical talk? Well, it's bout black folk. Their linguistic preservation and combativeness constitutes their style, which is deeply reflective of their souls. Yes, the souls of black folk. Du Bois be down wit it. Therefore, we need to move within that space of soul and style where our collective languaging is a commentary on both.

Contrary to the white colonialist view, Africans did not get off that Dutch ship in Jamestown without any sense of identity and culture as manifested in and structured through language. The many millions that were brought over in chains after 1619 also arrived with their nuanced cultural practices and religious worldviews as mediated through unique linguistic rules and styles. As *homo narrans* (creators of their own meaningful oral-narrative existence) and *homo significans* (creators of signs and symbols that ordered their reality), Africans already had their language and hence their own theory of reality. On this score, language is the medium through which reality is constructed. Language, then, shapes the contours of one's metaphysics. Africans had to feel a profound sense of cognitive and metaphysical dissonance within the white colonial order of things in America, with its strange language, and hence, its imposing and extraneous view of reality. As Docta G reminds us, "Language represents a society's theory of reality. It not only reflects that theory of reality, it explains, interprets, constructs, and reproduces that reality."[62] Although Docta G thinks that the Whorfians (followers of B. L. Whorf) overstate the importance of language vis-à-vis the construction of reality, she maintains:

> Reality is not merely *socially*, but *sociolinguistically* constructed. Real-world experience and phenomena do not exist in some raw, undifferentiated form. Rather, reality is always filtered, apprehended, encoded, codified, and conveyed via some linguistic shape.[63]

So as to clarify the sociolinguistic "determinist" implications of Docta G's position, it is important to note that she *does not* say that consciousness and ideology are supervenient on sociolinguistic factors. She is careful to say that it is her "contention that ideology and consciousness are *largely* [my emphasis] the products of what I call the 'sociolinguistic construction of reality.' "[64]

Attempting to understand this new colonial reality within the framework of their understanding of *Nommo*, the power of the word, black folk had to feel a sense of double consciousness or what Docta G refers to as the phenomenon of "linguistic push–pull."[65] Through the power of *Nommo*, Black folk *performatively* spoke (and continue to speak) a new reality and a new sense of identity into existence. Crossing the horror of the Middle Passage—which could take anywhere from 35 to 90 days, and having to contend with feces, lice, fleas, rats, disease, and dying black bodies—failed to break the power of the African spirit; failed to silence the power of *Nommo*, which said "NO!" to white imperialism, "NO!" to white cultural hegemony, "NO!" to colonial brainwashing, and "NO!" to linguistic-cultural dispossession. There was a "deep structural" cultural awareness that the *word* can radically alter the *world*.[66] Docta G notes:

> The oral tradition, then, is part of the cultural baggage the African brought to America. The pre-slavery background was one in which the concept of Nommo, the magic power of the Word, was believed necessary to actualize life and give man mastery over things.[67]

She further notes:

> In traditional African culture, a newborn child is a mere thing until his father gives and speaks his name. No medicine, potion, or magic of any sort is considered effective without accompanying words. So strong is the African belief in the power and absolute necessity of Nommo that all craftsmanship must be accompanied by speech.[68]

Nommo is an essential ontological register of WHO WE BE. *Nommo* is capable of concretizing the black spirit in the form of action, action that is necessary within the framework of a contentious and oppressive alien cultural environment. It was imperative that Diasporic Africans create *syncretistic constructions of reality* vis-à-vis "deep structural" linguistic-cultural (African) patterns and practices acting as the general framework through which new cultural elements were absorbed, synthesized, and reconfigured. This process is less like a Kuhnian paradigm shift and more like a form of "adaptive fusion." It is a fusion (don't let the jazz motif pass you by) that bespeaks the ability of black folk to keep keepin on in the face of oppression and white terror. This process of fusion is indicative of the fact that black folk live their lives within a *subjunctive* (indicative of our *possibilities*) ontological mode of ex-istence. Docta G observes that African American Language (or what she also refers to as black English, black idiom, African American English, African American Vernacular English, Ebonics) "reflects the modal experiences of African Americans and the continuing quest for freedom."[69] Given the emphasis on the power of *Nommo* and the sheer protean and meta-stable force of African linguistic-cultural, psychological and existential endurance, what then is AAL? The Docta is worth quoting in full:

> THE EBONICS SPOKEN in the US is rooted in the Black American Oral Tradition, reflecting the combination of African languages (Niger-Congo) and Euro American English. It is a language forged in the crucible of enslavement, US-style apartheid, and the

struggle to survive and thrive in the face of domination. Ebonics is emphatically *not* "broken" English, nor "sloppy" speech. Nor is it merely "slang." Nor is it some bizarre form of language spoken by baggy-pants-wearing Black youth. Ebonics *is* a set of communication patterns and practices resulting from Africans' appropriation and transformation of a foreign tongue during the African Holocaust.[70]

From jump street, let's dispel certain assumptions. AAL ain no slang. "True, Black slang is Black Language, but all Black Language is not Black slang."[71] Also, we must not conflate AAL with Nonstandard American English. As for the latter, examples are "the pronunciation of 'ask' as 'axe,' use of double negatives, as in 'They don't know nothing,' and the use of 'ain't.' Such features of American English often are *erroneously* characterized as Ebonics. They are not."[72] Keep in mind that Ebonics is known for its multiple negatives (this really frustrates the gatekeepers of European American Language [EAL]), not simply the double negatives disapproved of by EAL. Docta G provides an example of multiple negation from a member of the TBC sometime during the 1960s: "Don't nobody don't know God can't tell me nothin!" And drawing from Lonne Elder's play, *Ceremonies in Dark Old Men*, Docta G provides another example: "Don't nobody pay no attention to no nigga that ain't crazy!" Mutiple negation, in this example, signifies a form of linguistic, sociopsychological resistance. Docta G explains:

> Because "nigger" is a racialized epithet in EAL, AAL embraces its usage, encoding a variety of unique Black meanings. And "crazy niggas" are the rebellious ones, who resist racial supremacist domination and draw attention to their cause because they act in ways contrary to the inscribed role for Africans in America.[73]

Another point to keep in mind is that "US Ebonics, aka African American Vernacular English, did not completely originate in British English, nor in other white-immigrant dialects from the seventeenth century."[74] For those who are proponents of Euro-Anglo linguistic hegemony, the state Anglicist ideologues, those who control the army, navy, major television stations, major news outlets, major publishing houses, curriculum planning, legal and corporate languaging, educational policy/policing, it's all bout the politics of erasure, rejecting Africanized linguistic-cultural legitimacy and the impact of the Africanist influence in America. In short, Euro-Anglo linguistic hegemony (*the* hegemonic tongue) is a form of colonialism and linguistic racism. As Docta G points out, however, there are syntactic patterns that are not to be found in older Anglicized syntax, but are found in West African languages. She gives as an example, "Me massa name Cunney

Tomsee." The linguistic phenomenon of making a statement without the obligatory copula "is not a pattern of older British English dialects."[75] Docta G provides another example of a sentential construction without the use of the verb to be, which is required in English, given by an enslaved African who was located in the Dutch colony of Suriname in South America: "Me bella well" ("I am very well"). "He tall," "She my lady," and "She real phat" (no copulas) are also allowable forms of expression in West African languages.

Let's move to the aspectual verb. Docta G kicks it this way:

> This use of the verb "to be" [in AAL] derives from an aspectual verb system that is also found in many African languages, in Creole language forms of the Caribbean, in West African Pidgin English, and in the Gullah Creole spoken by blacks living on the Sea Island along the southeastern seaboard of the United States. Its use conveys the speaker's meaning with reference to qualitative character and distribution of an action over time.[76]

As an example, she provides, "He be hollin at us." This is the durative use of "to be"; it indicates iterativity or actions that are ongoing. "The sista be lookin fly" is also illustrative of iterativity. Docta G argues that the use of the verb system here demonstrates an "implied racial resistance," particularly in the light of the racist control of AAL by white America's linguistic rejection of such a verb system.[77] The "Standard English" verb system does not capture past, present and future tense all at the same time. Consider the expression, "It bees dat way sometime." Here we have two African language features. First, "bees" is used as a habitual condition; and, second, "dat" is used instead of "that," because West African languages do not have a "th" sound; that is, the initial voiced *th* is realized as *d*. The reader will also note that in AAL the final *th* is realized as *f*, *t*, or *d* (e.g., "up souf" for "up south," and "wit" or "wid" for "with"). Wid regard to the expression "It bees dat way sometime," however, Docta G draws a very interesting distinction that has rich philosophical implications. She distinguishes between "language" and "style." In the above example, language points to "bees" as an instance of iterativity. Style, however, points to a *Weltbild*, a way of picturing the world or a world picture. She argues that if we take the expression ("It bees dat way sometime") as "the total expression," then "the statement suggests a point of view, a way of looking at life, and a method of adapting to life's realities."[78] Her point here is well taken. When Nina Simone sings "It bees dat way sometime," there is the sense that life just ain fair. Docta G explains: "To live by the philosophy of 'It bees dat way sometime' is to come to grips with the changes that life bees puttin us through, and to accept the changes and bad times as a constant, ever-present reality."[79] I would only add that this expression is explosive with a surplus of significations. In this single locutionary act, we find a rich narrative of black existence in America. It is not only descriptive, but prescriptive, suggesting how life ought to be approached. Implicit in its description is the power of the reality of existential fissure and fracture.

From what has been delineated above, it is clear that as a people we are capable of living through white hatred, improvising our way in and out of American existential angst, and embracing and transcending our existential blues precisely by singing (languaging) them. The point here is that *Nommo* is operative here as a site of rupture. "It bees dat way sometime" expresses the power of the word to move black folk toward a greater sense of community and collective hope and resistance. It's important that we recognize the symbolic weight of the locutionary act, for it speaks to the power of our ancestors to cope, endure, and survive. In other words, "It bees dat way sometime" points to the heteronomy of oppressive forces that attempt to subdue black people, but the logic of the expression also sounds a clarion call for autonomy and is indicative of an existential transversal process that moves black people closer to a sense of home. Docta G is all up in the deep epistemological implications of this African American linguistic thang where she states:

> What uhm runnin on you is bout a cognitive linguistic style whose semantics bees grounded not only in words but in the socio-psychological space between the words. In sum: a Black-based communications system derived from the oppressor's tongue—the words is Euro-American, the meanings, nuances and tone African American.[80]

It is precisely these meanings, nuances and tone that are a threat to white America. For to control our own language is to control how we see ourselves, it is to some extent to explode the pathology of our double consciousness. Psychologist Robert Williams, who actually coined the term *Ebonics*, states:

> I think that Ebonics is a threat to white supremacy in this society because it means that we have invoked the Second Principle of the *Nguzo Saba, Kujichagulia* or self-determination, in that we are creating and defining our own reality so that that becomes threatening to white America.[81]

Another important point regarding the verb system of AAL can be examined in relationship to Docta G's contention that we should refer to black English as a "language" as opposed to a "dialect." The importance of this insight, and, hence, her reconceptualization of black English, is important in terms of African American praxis. The reader will note that I have used African American *Language* throughout the article, because I believe that this is the position that Docta G has come to embrace. However, in 1970, Docta G thought that the black English sentential construction, "The coffee cold" was not very different from the white English version, "The coffee is cold." This was because Docta G relied on the explanatory rules provided by the transformational-generative grammar framework whereby a deletion rule, permissible in English, "had been applied, so that the speaker went from 'The coffee is cold' to 'The coffee's cold,' to dropping the /'s/ "in pronunciation, thereby producing 'The coffee cold.' "[82] Docta G realized that even the distinctiveness of black English's rhetorical style and communication patterns failed to get at the distinction in meaning between "The coffee cold" and "The coffee be cold."[83] Later realizing the insights of linguist Sista Beryl Bailey, Docta G came to understand that:

> There are indeed deep-structural linguistic differences, in addition to "deep" differences in rhetorical style and strategies of discourse. I began to speak of the "language," not the "dialect," of Black America. In time, I came to think of this linguistic phenomenon not only as a "language," but as a language that could be a vehicle for unifying America's outsiders and consequently as a tool for social transformation.[84]

Always with her eye on the larger political ramifications of language, Docta G insightfully notes:

> Since linguistics cannot offer the definitive word on language-dialect differentiation, it ultimately comes down to who has the power to define; or as Max Weinreich once put it, the difference between a language and a dialect is who's got the army.[85]

My sense is that when Docta G uses the expression "deep-structure," she should not be taken to mean that speakers of EAL and AAL are somehow constituted by *racially distinct* bioprograms. My sense is that, for Docta G, AAL has a deep-structural component in that African American languaging (as in the example, "The coffee be cold") should not be reduced to mere surface features of English, that is, that sentential constructions in AAL are merely surface representations of other sentential constructions in

English. *Africanized* English is so deeply sedimented with African conceptions of the self, reality, time, and social norms of social interaction, and
other modes of spiritual and cultural comportment, that there is something
radically distinct—perhaps at the very psycho-linguistic (cultural) deep
structural level—about AAL vis-à-vis EAL. Docta G, she postulating "that
the two different speech communities employ differing thought patterns and
conceptions of reality and that these differences are reflected in different
styles of discourse."[86] Take for example the speech act, "What's happenin?"
The expression is not simply indexed to the present moment. The question
could refer to what happened already or what might be kickin off later. The
point here is that the question "What's happenin?" assumes a culture, a fluid
nexus of meanings, norms, and philosophical conceptions. Docta G advises
that you got to get down wit the symbolic system at work here. She notes:

> See, in the Traditional African World View, time is cyclical, and
> verb structure is not concerned with tense, but modality or aspect.
> So "What's happenin?" could mean what happened in the past,
> what's happenin now, as well as what's gon happen in the future.[87]

Nevertheless, to refer to AAL as a *language*, to buttress this claim
with solid historical and linguistic-cultural research, legal and institutional
support, is a danger to white America; for to use the term *language* is to
suggest an entire cultural identity, a co-equal language (vis-à-vis EAL), and
a legitimate mode of reality construction. (Whether its AAL or Gikuyu,
it's all about the activity of self-empowerment and self-definition.) It is
to put to rest the deficit model of African American speech events, and,
by implication, put to rest the deficit model that links AAL to inferior
cognition, and, indeed, to call attention to the fact that we as a people
constitute a NATION. Big Ups to our Nation Language advocates and
theorists[88]; they deserve their *propers*. By the way, are you *down* with AAL
as a Nation Language?

Let's talk a lil mow bout *AALanguagin*, some of its rhetorical devices.
Take *call and response*. Here we have a powerful communication device
utilized in both "secular" and "sacred" spheres of communication interaction. In the latter case, in the TBC, I recall my uncle, Revered Matt,
preachin: "Church, y'all don't heah me today!" The church folk would
respond, "Preach!" Indeed, it was deemed a "dead" church if this dynamic
of call and response, this *co-signing* and *co-narrating* of a shared communicative reality, failed to take place. There were even times when the music
played by the pianist would seem to respond to his homiletic call. In the
secular sphere (keeping in mind that the sacred and the secular constitute an organic unity in much of the African American life-world) "the

audience might manifest its response in giving skin (fives) when a really down verbal point is scored. Other approval responses include laughter and phrases like 'Oh, you mean, nigger,' 'Get back, nigger,' 'Git down baby,' etc."[89] Cognoscente of our Passage, our power to Africanize and reconfigure American and European physical and cultural spaces, Docta G notes that call and response "is a basic organizing principle of black American culture generally, for it enables traditional black folk to achieve the unified state of balance or harmony which is fundamental to the traditional African world view."[90] Indeed, call and response is symbolic of a profound level of intersubjectivity and linguistic-communal performativity that acknowledges the *ex-istence* (not locked in a private Cartesian sphere) of both speaker and listener. *Rhythmic pattern* is also a key feature of AAL. Again, let's return to Revered Matt. After walking the benches (I mean, he be done got the spirit), and while the church folk up on they feet, he might say, rhythmically and melodically, in an almost "singing voice," "I-I-I-I-I-KNOOOOOW. YESSSSS-I-I-I-KNOOOOOW." The perlocutionary force of this form of languaging would set the church off. Half the church would git happy, deacons, members of the choir, even ushers would be dancin and shoutin in the aisles. And in a *proverbial* speech act, someone might shout, "My name is written on high," liquid joy flowin and streamin down they face. Docta G is on it: "The preacher will get a rhythm going, conveying his message through sound rather than depending on sheer semantic import."[91] The power of sound. System. Sound reasoning. Don't you go *soundin* on me. The power of an elongated *hum* can carry the pain and suffering of an entire people or signify a nod of epistemic approval.

Semantic inversion is similar in intent to the use of coded language. The idea here is to take familiar words from EAL and superimpose radically different meanings on them. For example, to be *down* with something is actually to be *up* with it, in support of it. To be *bad* is to be *good*. This linguistic practice is the same whether in Wolof, Mandingo, Ibo, or Yoruba. Docta G points out that it's the same linguistic process, but a different language.[92] She elaborates: "This linguistic reversal process, using negative terms with positive meanings, is present in a number of African languages—for example, the Mandingo *a ka nyi ko-jugu*, which literally means "it is good badly," that is, "it is very good.""[93] Again, here we have an instance of Black folk in America exercising linguistic resistance and agency, a practice of baffling and excluding the oppressive ofay.

Indirection is a linguistic species of coded language and semantic inversion. It thrives off of circumlocutory rhetoric. You known Black folk gotta move in non-linear lines lest the evil spirits catch them. Docta G points to an example where Malcolm X gave a speech in which he opens by acknowledging his friends, sisters, brothers, and others, but goes on to acknowledge his enemies. "Not only is Malcolm neatly putting down his enemies in the audience without a direct frontal attack," according to Docta G, "he is also sending a hidden message (to those hip enough to dig it)."[94] Malcolm, in other words, is *signifyin* on those possible Black traitors ("Black Judases") sitting right there in his midst. But not only is circumlocutory rhetoric an important attribute of AAL, our language soars to the heights of *exaggeration*, another AAL discursive marker. Yo, we bees all up in the bombastic, grandiloquent, magniloquent, highfalutin, sonorous realm of talkin that talk. MLK, Jr., once referred to an issue as being "incandescently clear."[95] Docta G:

> Sometime the whole syntax of a sentence may be expressed in an elevated, formal manner, as in this invitation from a working-class black male: "My dear, would you care to dine with me tonight on some delectable red beans and rice?"[96]

And then there is that space of *braggadocio*. There are multiple signifiers within this space. "I'm the greatest!" Ali in the cultural mix. Stag-O-Lee. Jack Johnson. Rap ciphers where brothas be dropin some serious science, cultural codes, and philosophy. There are powerful tales of African folklores that narrate great escapes. Shine. Toasts. The Bad Nigga. Keepin Mista Charlie, Massa, or Miss Ann on they toes. Docta G: "Whether referring to physical badness, fighting ability, lovemanship, coolness (that is, 'grace under pressure'), the aim is to convey the image of an omnipotent fearless being, capable of doing the undoable."[97] The dynamic of *narrativizing* is also a salient feature of AAL discursivity. It involves explicating some event, some situation, in the style of the traditional African griot. The point here is that such existential events are constructed within a narrative structure, moving within a deep cultural semiotic space of familiarity. As contemporary philosophers begin to reassess the significance of the epistemological explanatory power of narrative, we been done engaged in this hermeneutic process. Peep Ice Cube's narrative flow, talkin wid dat AAL flava:

> How you like me now? I'm in the mix, it's 1986, and I got the fix . . . /Dropped out the 12th cause my welfare's shorter than a midget on his knees . . . /Fucked up in the pen, now it's '94, back in L.A. and I'm fallin in the door/Everybody know I got to start from scratch . . . /No skills to pay the bills/Talkin bout education to battle inflation/No college degree, just a dumb-ass G . . . /I got a baby on the way/Damn, it's a mess/Have you ever been convicted of a felony?—Yes!/Took some advice from my Uncle Fester, all dressed up in polyester/"Welcome to McDonald's. May I please help you?"/ Shit, what can I do?[98]

Some just don't want to recognize that rap is the next step in our historical journey as masters of the Word. Rap ain no aberration. These complex brothas and sistas, engagin and pushin the discursive boundaries of what is said/sayable, articulating, through *Nommo*, what is beautiful, marvelous, mendacious, ugly, corrupt, fucked up, and surreal, are still moving Black folk in the direction of *home*. Docta G knows that rap and Hip Hop bees part of that *Nommo* continuum, that African sense of existential and communal balance. Those stylizations (linguistic, bodily, aesthetic, sonic, spiritual, metaphysical) coming out of those hood spaces/places and hooded faces, they must be reflections of soul. And U know yo style oughta reflect it. Word! Docta G:

> Rap music is rooted in the Black Oral Tradition of tonal semantics, narrativizing, signification/signifyin, the Dozens/playin the Dozens, Africanized syntax, and other communicative practices. The Oral Tradition itself is rooted in the surviving African tradition of "Nommo" and the power of the word in human life.[99]

Let's rap/wrap it up. Docta G has shown that black folk have always already been pushin the language envelope. Black folk have been fightin on all fronts, the physical, geopolitical, metaphysical, philosophical, aesthetic, religious, political, ideological, psychological, spiritual, symbolic, economic, hermeneutic, academic, linguistic, iconic, and more. Through all of these wars, we have managed to maintain a sense of ethics, humanity, dignity, and sanity. Damn! We talkin bout folk who simply refuse to die. Don't even talk about givin up! What manner of people DO WE BE? Protean. Always already in struggle, always already beginning some new shit, conceptualizing some new order of things, some other/alternative/unheard of/unimagined/unexplored reality and mode of being. We bees doin da unthinkable. Must be *magical* and *real*. We always pushin. Whether its remaking and reconfiguring some superimposed language, creating musical instruments from some old found object, doctoring up a traditional instrument, because you know we gotta hear that twang and chromatic sound, or pushin the bounds of what it means to be human and democratic, we up on it, way out in front. Blusing. Bopping. Moving. Rapping. Hip Hopping. Historicizing. Morphing. Always in the process of red-shifting, even when we be down. And, yes, LANGUAGING. We are still in process. What next? Can't be sho. But I'll C U when WE get there. As Docta G says, stay tuned.

ACKNOWLEDGMENTS

I would like to thank Geneva Smitherman for her rigorous philosophical and political contributions to Africana philosophy through her work in linguistics. There is a need for more African American philosophers to explore her work in terms of its significance for and impact on Africana philosophy. I would also like to thank African American linguists John Baugh and H. Samy Alim for encouraging me to write this piece and for recognizing the importance of Smitherman's work in linguistics, philosophy, education, politics, cultural studies and psychology. This chapter was previously published in *Journal of Speculative Philosophy* 18, no. 4, 273–299. Copyright 2004 by the Pennsylvania State University. Reproduced by permission of the publisher.

NOTES

1. George Yancy, "Between Facticity and Possibility." In *The Philosophical i: Personal Reflections on Life in Philosophy*, ed. George Yancy (Rowman & Littlefield, 2002). Also see my articles "Ebonics Went to Court in Michigan, And Won!: A White Judge Ruled in 1979 that Black English was More than Faulty Dialect," *The Philadelphia Tribune* (January 3, 1997); "U.S. Founders Began Suppression of Our African Speech Patterns," *The Philadelphia Tribune* (December 31, 1996); "Among Ourselves, the 'N' Word Carries Warmth," *The Philadelphia Tribune* (September 8, 1995); and, "'Nigger': Not What's Said, But Who and How," *The Philadelphia Tribune* (December 31, 1993).

2. Russell A. Potter, *Spectacular Vernaculars: Hip-Hop and the Politics of Postmodernism*, (Albany, New York: State University of New York Press, 1995): p. 58.

3. Frantz Fanon, *Black Skin, White Masks*. Trans. Charles Lam Markmann. (New York: Grove Press, Inc., 1967): p. 36.

4. Fanon, *Black Skin, White Masks*, 18, my emphasis.

5. Becky Brown, "'Talk That Talk!': African American English in its Social and Cultural Context" in *Radical Philosophy Review*, Vol. 4, No. 1&2, 2001: pp. 59–60

6. Geneva Smitherman, *Talkin That Talk: Language, Culture and Education in African America* (London and New York: Routledge, 2001): p. 347.

7. Smitherman, *Talkin That Talk*, p. 343.

8. Geneva Smitherman, *Talkin and Testifyin: The Language of Black America* (Boston: Houghton Mifflin; reissued, with revisions, Detroit: Wayne State University Press, 1977): p. 242.

9. Smitherman, *Talkin That Talk*, p. 349.

10. Geneva Smitherman, "A Womanist Looks at the Million Man March." In *Million Man March/Day of Absence* Edited by Haki R. Madhubuti and Maulana Karenga, (Chicago: Third World Press, 1996): p. 104.

11. Geneva Smitherman, *Black Talk: Words and Phrases from the Hood to the Amen Corner*, (revised, updated edition, Boston and New York: Houghton Mifflin, 2000): p. xiii.

12. Peter L. Berger and Thomas Luckmann, "The Dehumanized World" in Walter T. Anderson (ed.) *The Truth About the Truth: De-Confusing and Re-Constructing the Postmodern World* (New York: A Jeremy P. Tarcher/ Putnam Book): 1995, 36.

13. Smitherman, *Talkin That Talk*, p. 222.

14. Ibid., p. 1.

15. Ibid., p. 2.

16. Ibid.

17. Ibid., p. 3.

18. Ngugi wa Thiongo, *Moving the Centre: The Struggle for Cultural Freedoms.* (Portsmouth, New Hampshire: Heinemann Educational Books Inc., 1993): p. 131.

19. Smitherman, *Talkin That Talk*, p. 350.

20. Fanon, *Black Skin, White Masks*, p. 38.

21. Smitherman, *Talkin That Talk*, p. 222.

22. Smitherman, *Talkin and Testifyin*, p. 56.

23. Smitherman, *Black Talk*, p. 4.

24. Smitherman, *Talkin That Talk*, p. 8.

25. Ibid., p. 58.

26. Ibid., p. 66.

27. Ibid., p. 70.

28. Ibid., p. 71.

29. Ibid., p. 113.

30. Smitherman, *Black Talk*, p. 38.

31. Smitherman, *Talkin That Talk*, p. 317.

32. Ibid., p. 43.

33. bell hooks, *Ain't I A Woman: black women and feminism.* (Boston, MA: South End Press, 1981): pp. 18–19.

34. Molefi K. Asante, *African American History: A Journey of Liberation.* (Maywood, New Jersey: The Peoples Publishing Group, Inc., 1995): p. 61.

35. Ibid., p. 59.

36. George M. Frederickson, *The Black Image in the White Mind: The Debate on Afro-America Character and Destiny, 1817–1914.* (Hanover, NH: Wesleyan University Press., 1971): p. 279.

37. Ibid., p. 277.

38. Michel Foucault, *The History of Sexuality* (Volume I). Trans. Robert Hurley. (New York: Vintage, 1990): p. 139.

39. Smitherman, *Talkin That Talk*, p. 71.

40. Frederickson, *The Black Image in the White Mind*, p. 253.

41. Ibid.

42. Cornel West, *The Cornel West Reader.* (New York, NY: Basic Civitas Books, 1999): p. 83.

43. Smitherman, *Talkin and Testifyin*, p. 7.

44. Smitherman, *Talkin That Talk*, p. 72.

45. Ibid.

46. Smitherman, *Talkin That Talk*, p. 73.

47. John Baugh, *Black Street Speech: It's History, Structure and Survival."* (Austin, TX: University of Texas Press, 1983): p. 14.

48. Smitherman, *Talkin That Talk*, p. 240.

49. Frederick Douglass, *Narrative of the Life of Frederick Douglass, An American Slave, Written by Himself.* Edited with an Intro. by David W. Blight. (New York, NY: Bedford/St. Martin's Press, 1993): p. 49.

50. Ibid.,, p. 52.

51. Ibid., p. 53.
52. Smitherman, *Talkin That Talk*, p. 57.
53. Smitherman, *Talkin and Testifyin*, pp. 48–49)
54. Smitherman, *Talkin That Talk*, p. 19.
55. Smitherman, *Talkin and Testifyin*, p. 48.
56. Smitherman, *Talkin That Talk*, p. 19.
57. Ngugi wa Thiongo, *Moving the Centre*, p. 30.
58. Potter, *Spectacular Vernaculars*, p. 57.
59. Smitherman, *Talkin That Talk*, p. 19.
60. Ibid., p. 344.
61. Ibid.
62. Ibid., p. 99.
63. Ibid., p. 43.
64. Ibid., p. 96.
65. Ibid., p. 146.
66. Ibid., p. 54.
67. Ibid., p. 203.
68. Ibid.
69. Ibid., p. 101.
70. Ibid., p. 19.
71. Smitherman, *Black Talk*, p. 2.
72. Smitherman, *Talkin That Talk*, p. 20.
73. Ibid., p. 272.
74. Ibid., p. 20.
75. Ibid., p. 31.
76. Ibid., pp. 136–137.
77. Ibid., p. 272.
78. Smitherman, *Talkin and Testifyin*, p. 3.
79. Ibid.
80. Smitherman, *Talkin That Talk*, p. 351.
81. This statement appears in my recent article, "The Scholar Who Coined the Term Ebonics: A Conversation with Dr. Robert L. Williams, *Journal of Language, Identity, and Education*, Volume 10, Number 1, January-March 2011, 41–51; cited on page 45.
82. Smitherman, *Talkin That Talk*, p. 15.
83. Ibid.
84. Ibid., p. 16.
85. Ibid., p. 139.
86. Ibid., p. 140.
87. Ibid., p. 358.
88. For example, see Kamau Brathwaite's *History of the Voice: The Development of Nation Language in Anglophone Caribbean Poetry* (New Beacon, 1984).
89. Smitherman, *Talkin That Talk*, p. 64.
90. Smitherman, *Talkin and Testifyin*, p. 104.
91. Smitherman, *Talkin That Talk*, p. 64.
92. Smitherman, *Talkin and Testifyin*, p. 44.

93. Ibid.
94. Smitherman, *Talkin That Talk*, p. 220.
95. Ibid., p. 217.
96. Ibid.
97. Ibid., p. 219.
98. Ibid., p. 275.
99. Ibid., p. 269.

CHAPTER SIXTEEN

LANGUAGE, POWER, AND PHILOSOPHY

Some Comments on the Exclusion of Spanish from the Philosophical Canon

Elizabeth Millán

It is no secret that philosophy in the United States is far from inclusive. The reasons are many, yet the rigorous assessment of some of those reasons is beyond the grasp of the philosopher's analysis. However, there are some rather obvious limitations concerning the ways in which philosophy is conducted in the United States, which any philosopher interested in truth and justice should comment on and critique. The exclusionary practice that I discuss is one that results when an entire tradition is silenced. This silencing is rooted in a glaring limitation of philosophical practice in the United States: the problem of language. We come to this problem via a narrative that excludes far too many voices from the canon of philosophy. Certain philosophers are quite fond of claims that philosophy was born with the Greeks and reached its culmination in Europe and then in the United States. I take my work in Latin American philosophy to be part of the process of rectifying what we might call philosophy's "mendacious cultural autobiography."[1]

Philosophy's mendacious tale of its birth in ancient Greece to its culmination in western Europe not only oversimplifies a more complex state of affairs, it also is perniciously exclusionary. The exclusion is far-reaching and contaminated at every level with falsehoods. The "Ancient Greece to western Europe" story of philosophy is filled with lofty claims regarding the "authentic" roots of philosophy, and a sudden shrinking of Europe to a collection of just three countries and their languages: France, Germany, and England. So, French, German, and English receive special status as "philosophical" languages, a status honored in graduate programs where the study of such languages is part of the serious training students undergo to become masters or doctors of philosophy. Spain and Spanish disappear from the map of philosophy, and, of course, so does all of Latin America. This slighting of Spanish as a philosophical language is just one of many acts of exclusion that have led important philosophical voices to be silenced and our path to truth to be truncated. Moreover, those of us who want to include this language and these voices are looked upon as confused nomads who have lost our way, unaware of what "true" philosophy really is and of where the boundaries of the sacred territory lie.

The silencing of the Spanish-language tradition can be corrected, or so I argue. We need to accomplish the following:

1. Cure ourselves of the historical amnesia under which we suffer.

2. Remove the pugnacious philosophical minutemen who patrol the borders of our field and open those borders to include more voices.

3. Strive for a true cosmopolitanism in philosophy, one that would liberate us from the exclusionary (and often downright racist) gaze that has infected philosophy.

These are just three of the steps that will make an important voice of philosophy audible; a voice that speaks in Spanish, but is no less philosophical than any English, French, or German philosophical musings.

THE PROBLEM OF HISTORICAL AMNESIA

I begin with a focus on a problem that is a serious hindrance to the very recognition of Spanish-language intellectual traditions: the problem of historical amnesia. Cuban essayist, Roberto Fernández Retamar, in *Caliban*, which he describes, not without a certain tone of understatement, as "a simple essay on Latin American culture" (as if anything about Latin American culture could possibly be simple),[2] complains of the "relative oblivion into which the work of the Cuban hero [Jose Martí] fell after his death."[3] In particular, he is shocked that so careful a scholar as the Dominican, Henríquez Ureña, had made observations about Martí's positions that were "completely erroneous." He writes:

> Given the exemplary honesty of Henríquez Ureña, [the mistakes] led me, first to suspect and later, to verify that it was due simply to the fact that during this period the great Dominican had not

read, *had not been able to read*, Martí adequately. Martí was hardly published at the time. "Our America" is a good example of this fate. Readers of the Mexican newspaper *El Partido Liberal* could have read it on 30 January 1891. It is possible that some other local newspaper republished it, although the most recent edition of Martí's *Complete Works* does not indicate anything in this regard. But it is most likely that those who did not have the good fortune to obtain that newspaper knew nothing about the article—the most important document published in America from the end of the past century until the appearance in 1962 of the Second Declaration of Havana.[4]

Fernández Retamar draws attention to what has been a serious problem for the reception of much Spanish-language philosophy, namely, the absence of authoritative editions, seriously hindering scholarship in the field. Until a given tradition is deemed worthy of attention, critical editions remain scarce. Fernández Retamar also remarks that even the names evoked by Martí, as he makes claims that the inhabitants of "our America" are descended from "Valencian fathers and Canary Island mothers and feel the inflamed blood of Tamanaco and Paramaconi coursing through our veins" will be unfamiliar references to most readers in Latin America.[5] Fernández Retamar claims that this lack of familiarity "is but another proof of our subjection to the colonialist perspective of history that has been imposed on us, causing names, dates, circumstances, and truths to vanish from our consciousness."[6]

Fernández Retamar diagnoses a serious malady, something that, in another article, I dubbed, "a great vanishing act."[7] This vanishing act has nothing to do with spells or magic, but rather with something far less enchanting: exclusion and the invisibility born of such exclusion. The historical vanishing act of people, places, and events of Spanish America has had a deleterious effect on attempts to build a canon, to assemble a history of philosophy for the region. This vanishing act has given rise to a host of enduring problems the most salient of which is the invisibility of an entire philosophical tradition. This invisibility is one reason why the question: Does a Latin American philosophy exist? endures. The question, as Fernández Retamar points out, is related to the "irremediable colonial condition," of those countries emerging from colonialism, which have been "ineptly and successively termed *barbarians, peoples of color, underdeveloped countries, Third World*," a condition that has led to the view that intellectual activity carried out beyond the borders of the "civilized" world is "but a distorted echo of what occurs elsewhere" [*un eco desfigurado de lo que sucede en otra parte*].[8] The upshot of such a dismissive view of the intellectual products of the "Third World": If Latin American philosophy exists at all (and the same would hold true of all philosophies of the Third World), it deserves no serious attention from the First-World philosophers, because it is merely derivative, and contributes nothing original to the philosophical discussions that shape "real" philosophy of the First World.

Alas, vestiges of this sort of dismissive treatment are all too prevalent in the academic world today. For example, Latin American philosophy and Spanish-speaking philosophers remain ghettoized. We have special committees to oversee the treatment of Hispanics in philosophy, in part because inclusiveness of this group cannot be taken for granted. We have to market sessions at the American Philosophical Association so that they will appeal to mainstream philosophers: Logic in Brazil is a crowd pleaser, whereas the topic of indigenous thought in America draws only a few eccentrics. The theme of German philosophy in the Americas is seen as more valuable than addressing the problem of modernity in Latin America, for the stentorian philosophical voice of the German tradition inevitably overpowers the muffled voice of the Latin American tradition. Paying serious attention to something like the problem of modernity in Latin America would surely be a sign of progress, of an overcoming of the "colonial condition" in which Latin American philosophy has been placed, for it would present Latin American thought in an autonomous way, a way that frees it of the ghetto where it remains silent and isolated.[9]

SPAIN AS THE OTHER OF EUROPE— LATIN AMERICA AS THE OTHER OF SPAIN

Another force fueling the invisibility of the Spanish-language philosophical tradition is a perception of Spain as non-European, not part of the Europe that exists in the wake of the philosophical map drawn to keep out the barbarous elements from west of the Pyrenees. In his essay, "Against the Black Legend," Fernández Retamar addresses the common link of exclusion that exists between Spain and Latin America:

> It is not surprising, given its origin, that the Black Legend should find a place among the diverse and permanently unacceptable forms of racism. We need only mention the sad case of the United States, where the words, "Hispanic" or "Latino" as applied to Latin Americans—to Puerto Ricans and Chicanos in particular—carry a strong connotation of the disdain with which the apparently transparent citizens of that unhappy country habitually deal with persons "of color." It may be useful, as well, to recall a statement attributed in its classical form to Alexandre Dumas: "Africa begins

at the Pyrenees." The sacrosanct West thus shows its repugnance toward *the other*, which is not itself, and finds the embodiment par excellence of this *other* in Africa, whose tortured present was *caused* by Western capitalism, which "undeveloped" it in order to make its own growth possible.[10]

The Black Legend was sparked by Bartolomé de las Casas' account of the devastation the Spaniards wreaked on the indigenous cultures of Latin America, and it served to demonize Spain.[11] Fernández Retamar attempts to clear Spain's name in order to reclaim Latin America's Iberian heritage. To be sure, the relation of Latin American philosophy to the European tradition is a complicated one. Simón Bolívar addressed the difficulty early in the region's period of nation-building. In the famous *Carta de Jamaica* we find the following description of an identity crisis that continues to plague the citizens of Latin America:

> [W]e scarcely retain a vestige of once was; we are moreover, neither Indian nor European, but a species midway between the legitimate proprietors of this country and the Spanish usurpers. In short, though Americans by birth we derive our rights from Europe.[12]

Just as the people of the newly liberated territories of Spanish America struggled to define themselves in terms of their position between two distinct cultural legacies, Latin American philosophy also struggles with the tensions born of its hybrid identity. Within the peculiar map of philosophy, this hybrid identity becomes even more complicated. Even today, philosophy in Latin America has a notable Franco-German tone.[13] The value of the Latin American philosophical tradition still is not fully recognized, either in the United States or in Latin America, and if one wants to do work in this area, there must be a justification for it. In contrast, the value of Anglo-American, French, and German philosophy is taken to be self-evident. Part of what it means to be a good philosopher, even in Latin America, is to be acquainted with figures such as Kant, Hegel, Nietzsche, Derrida, even Davidson or Searle—Zea and Martí just don't have the same currency. In part, this is because Zea and Martí don't speak the "right" language. As Gloria Anzaldúa points out: "By the end of [the 20th century], Spanish speakers will comprise the biggest minority group in the U.S., a country where students in high schools and colleges are encouraged to take French classes because French is considered more 'cultured.'"[14] Anzaldúa is concerned with what she calls "linguistic terrorism" and the slighting of those who speak "español deficiente" or the Spanish of America. If Spain's geographical location places it on the margins of Europe, Latin America's colonial location places it at the margins of "civilized" culture. What Anzaldúa observes about the status of the French language as "cultured" and the Spanish language (and the Spanish of America in particular) as beneath that level of culture, could be said of the perception of philosophy with those adjectives. For example, French-language philosophy is considered more "philosophical" than Spanish-language philosophy, which is why the inclusion of Spanish-language philosophy requires justification in graduate programs and philosophy curricula, whereas, as I have emphasized, the value of the Anglo-American, French, and German traditions is taken as self-evident.

Part of the reason that the French and German philosophical traditions found a welcome reception in Latin America is because those traditions were seen to come "with no strings attached," that is, to represent intellectual traditions not sullied by the colonial baggage that a relation to Spain would carry. Yet, Latin American philosophy is a philosophy carried out in Spanish (and Portuguese), and so it remains bound to Spain (and the Iberian peninsula) and is victimized by the same Eurocentrism that excludes Spain (and by association, Latin America) from entrance to the archons of philosophy.

What we need, if we really want to rid the field of philosophy from the ghettos that isolate and silence important voices is a more critical approach to philosophy itself. The work of Jacques Derrida offered important tools in this direction. As he indicates in the last interview he did before his death: "Deconstruction in general is an undertaking that many have considered, and rightly so, to be a gesture of suspicion with regard to all Eurocentrism."[15] Derrida carefully unpacks the relation between deconstruction and Europe. He writes:

> What I call "deconstruction" even when it is directed toward something from Europe, is European; it is a product of Europe, a relation of Europe to itself as an experience of radical alterity. Since the time of the Enlightenment, Europe has undertaken a perpetual self-critique, and in this perfectible heritage there is a chance for a future. At least I would like to hope so, and that is what feeds my indignation when I hear people definitively condemning Europe as if it were but the scene of its crimes.[16]

So, although deconstruction attacks Eurocentrism, it acknowledges itself as part of the European tradition, but as that part of the tradition engaged in a constant state of self-critique. Latin American philosophy is European too, but just as Bolívar so trenchantly captured with his reference to Latin Americans as "Americans by birth and Europeans by right," Latin

American philosophy is of mixed Euro-American lineage and so in questioning Europe, it questions itself. Its hybrid identity and its failure to fit on the traditional map of philosophy have led to a crisis of identity which has generated what might be called an excessive cycle of self-criticism and self-questioning within its philosophical tradition.

Aspects of this self-criticism are healthy, but some aspects are the result of certain pathologies that plague the field of philosophy. Philosophers are obsessed with boundaries and borders—the tighter the better. And it is not just voices that speak in other languages that are silenced or dismissed when the map of philosophy is drawn too narrowly. Plenty of German-speaking philosophers have sought to exclude other German-speaking philosophers. We can think of Kant's critical project and the leading role that borders play in the drama of his critiques. For Kant, boundaries are linked to progress and security in philosophy: Only with the proper boundaries in place can philosophy retain its place as the queen of the sciences. Philosophers who play with these boundaries are immediately looked on with suspicion. An obsession with strict boundaries is one of the reasons why philosophers have tended to be uncomfortable with moves to bring other disciplines into close company with philosophy. This explains the unhappy fate of the early German Romantics. Their call for the unification of poetry and philosophy led, until quite recently, to their banishment from the field of philosophy.

The task of those who we may call the philosophical border police reached its pinnacle with the development of analytic philosophy.[17] Carnap tried to run Heidegger out of the territory of philosophy. Some strands of analytic philosophy involved such a reductionist view of the tasks of philosophy (linguistic analysis, conditions of verifiability, etc.) that the borders of philosophy became drawn so narrowly that many important voices were cast aside as nefariously nonsensical or irrational.[18] Of course, we need some limits to guide our philosophical investigations—the right borders can help to keep the field healthy and progressive, but when the boundaries are drawn too rigidly, then philosophy risks becoming a most barren, desolate field. The philosophical minutemen of our tradition do great harm to the field of philosophy as they proliferate hierarchies based on power rather than philosophical quality. We do need some borders in place to define the field of philosophy, and surely also criteria to distinguish the value of various contributions to the field. This is not the place to discuss the details of how to erect the borders of philosophy or how to generate a list of criteria for assessing the value of a given contribution, but one thing is clear: Blanket condemnations of all foreign contributions (or those that don't come in the languages of English, French, or German) should have no place in shaping our field.

TOWARD A NEW INTERNATIONALISM FOR PHILOSOPHY

The presence of voices that speak languages other than English, French, and German to the field of philosophy will help us move to a new, enriching level of internationalism. In his foreword to *Caliban*, Frederic Jameson emphasizes, referencing Goethe's sense of world literature, that world literature "has nothing to do with eternal invariants and timeless forms, but very specifically with literary and cultural journals read across national boundaries and with the emergence of critical networks by which the intellectuals of one country inform themselves about the specific intellectual problems and debates of another."[19] From this observation he concludes:

> We, therefore, need a new literary and cultural internationalism which involves risks and dangers, which calls us into question fully, as much as it acknowledges the Other, thereby also serving as a more adequate and chastening form of self-knowledge. This "internationalism of the national situations" neither reduces the "Third World" to some homogenous Other of the West, nor does it vacuously celebrate the "astonishing" pluralism of human cultures.[20]

We can apply Jameson's insights to the field of philosophy. Part of the reason for the exclusion of Spanish-language philosophy from the professional canon in the United States is the result of a rather provincial notion of philosophical internationalism, a provincialism that reduces the so-called Third World to a group of second- or even third-rate copies of French, German, or Anglo philosophical currents. One balm against this sort of myopic view of the philosophical world is to take a closer look at intellectual history and to make a commitment to including more voices in philosophy. We can take our cue from Martí, who was well aware of the importance of intellectual history:

> To know one's country and govern it with that knowledge is the only way to free it from tyranny. The European university must bow to the American university. The history of America, from the Incas to the present, must be taught in clear detail and to the letter, even if the archons of Greece are overlooked. Our Greece must take priority over the Greece which is not ours. We need it more. Nationalist statesmen must replace foreign statesmen. Let the world be grafted onto our republics, but the trunk must be our own.[21]

In the spirit of Martí's claim, I call for a move to integrate more languages into our canon of philosophy. I have been arguing for one excluded language and its tradition: the Spanish-language philosophical tradition. The attention to Spanish as a philosophical language and to the traditions of the nations of the Spanish-speaking world is no move toward making philosophy nationalistic. Quite the contrary, the move toward inclusion of more voices is part of a project of creating a world philosophy.

Although he is deeply committed to the Latin American cause (and to the Cuban Revolution), Fernández Retamar is clear that dedication to a true intellectual internationalism should trump merely national interests:

> My wish is not, and never was, to present Latin America and the Caribbean as a region cut off from the rest of the world but rather to view it precisely as a part of the world—a part that should be looked at with the same attention and respect as the rest, not as a merely paraphrastic expression of the West.[22]

The internationalism that Fernández Retamar returns to is just the call that I think we need to take up if we want our field to be engaged in the sort of internationalism that will breed an inclusive canon in which no tradition is made to vanish.

CONCLUDING REMARKS

Paul Gilroy notes that specialist and nationalist gazes are obstacles in the way of developing a truly international intellectual dialogue.[23] When philosophers erect boundaries that replicate what the nation-states put into place, the philosophical lens becomes myopic. Long before Gilroy voiced his concerns regarding overspecialization, José Enrique Rodó warned us of this danger. In his essay, *Ariel*, written in 1900 to alert Latin Americans of the perils that the United States (symbolized as plodding, monstrous Caliban) posed to their culture (symbolized as the pure creature of spirit, Ariel), we find this impassioned statement on the price of progress:

> Unhappily, it is in civilizations that have achieved a whole and refined culture that the danger of spiritual limitation is most real and leads to the most dreaded consequences. In fact, to the degree that culture advances, the law of evolution, manifesting itself in society as in nature to be a growing tendency toward heterogeneity, seems to require a corresponding limitation in individual aptitudes and the inclination to restrict more severely each individual's field of action. While it is a necessary condition to progress, the development of specialization brings with it visible disadvantages, which are not limited to narrowing the horizon of individual intelligence and which inevitably falsify our concept of the world. Specialization, because of the great diversity of individual preferences and habits, is

also damaging to a sense of solidarity. Auguste Comte has tellingly noted this danger in advanced civilizations. In his view, the most serious flaw in a state of high social perfection lies in the frequency with which it produces deformed spirits, spirits extremely adept in one aspect of life but monstrously inept in all others.[24]

Rodó's insight is an important one, and although he was concerned with Latin American culture, his insight helps us identify a problem facing philosophy in the United States and the sort of limitation that threatens to make of our field an impoverished, overspecialized area that will produce deformed spirits, extremely adept in one area of philosophy and monstrously inept in all others. The monsters born of the overspecialization of philosophy are many: The ones I have tried to battle in this chapter include a historical myopia, an exclusionary gaze, and rigidly prohibitive borders for a field that should be ever striving to expand and grow. Taking the tradition that speaks in the Spanish language seriously would be one small step in helping to correct a tendency toward just the sort of spirit squeezing overspecialization against which Rodó warned. Opening the field of philosophy to more voices will diversify the canon of philosophy and lead us to question some of the criteria that have been used to justify the exclusion of entire traditions from that canon.

ACKNOWLEDGMENTS

I have had the good fortune to consider these issues in a wide array of forums over the past few years. I would like to thank my fellow participants at a roundtable held in Chicago in April 2006 on "Inclusiveness Issues in the Profession" sponsored by the American Philosophical Association's Committee on Inclusiveness and the Committee on the Statue of Women and from the session on *The Writer as a Philosopher in Latin America* at the American Philosophical Association Eastern Division Meeting, held in Washington, DC in December 2006. Thanks also to the students at the University of Oregon who attended my talk "Towards a New Philosophical Internationalism," and to John Lysaker for inviting me to participate in his seminar on Latin American philosophy. I also thank my undergraduate and graduate students at DePaul, who have been wonderful interlocutors as I developed my thoughts on these matters.

NOTES

1. I borrow this phrase from Cuban essayist Roberto Fernández Retamar, who brings it up within the context of dismantling the myth "according to which

Reason was revealed to Greece, became an Empire in Rome, and assimilated a Religion that was destined after several centuries in hibernation, to reappear like an armed prophet in the works of the (post-barbarian) Westerners, who were to spend the next several centuries fulfilling the onerous mission of bringing the light of "civilization" to the rest of the planet. If any country permits us to unmask the genial fraud implicit in this "history" appropriated by the developed Western bourgeoisie, it is Spain—a fact that no doubt has contributed in no small measure to the denigration it has suffered at Western hands. I do not pretend to be an expert on the matter, but common knowledge is sufficient to begin to rectify this mendacious cultural autobiography" ("Against the Black Legend," in Roberto Fernández Retamar, *Caliban and Other Essays*, translated by Edward Baker, foreword by Frederic Jameson (Minneapolis: University of Minnesota Press, 1989), p. 63). I refer to Fernández Retamar throughout this chapter, not without awareness of his dubious standing in the eyes of some thinkers. Jorge Edwards, for example, describes him as a "fierce bureaucrat of literature," a standing that freed him of any suspicion by the Castro regime and essentially made him untouchable (Jorge Edwards, *Persona Non Grata: A Memoir of Disenchantment with the Cuban Revolution*, translated by Andrew Hurley, preface by Octavio Paz (New York: Nation Books, 1991), p. 139). There are moments in his work when Fernández Retamar obviously allows his enthusiasm for the Cuban Revolution to lead him into making quite biased claims, but I think that many of his points do stand up to strong critique and his insights can serve as tools to help us deal with the unjust position in which the Latin American intellectual tradition finds itself.

2. Roberto Fernández Retamar, *Caliban and Other Essays*, translated by Edward Baker, Foreword by Frederic Jameson (Minneapolis: University of Minnesota Press, 1989), p. 29. Cf. *Todo Caliban*, prólogo de Frederic Jameson (San Juan: Ediciones Callejón, 2003), p. 71.

3. Ibid., p. 17./*Todo Caliban*, op. cit., p. 49.

4. Ibid., pp. 17–18/ *Todo Caliban*, op. cit., pp. 49–50. The last bit of this claim is just the sort of hyperbole that would have led Edwards to describe Fernández Retamar as a "fierce bureaucrat of literature." Whether or not we agree with all of what Fernández Retamar claims in this passage, the problem that he is diagnosing is one that deserves our full attention for it has seriously hampered the reception of much Spanish-language philosophy, namely, the absence of scholarly editions of work from the tradition's leading thinkers. For too long, having access to central philosophical texts of the Latin American philosophical tradition was indeed a matter of good fortune.

5. Ibid., p. 19/*Todo Caliban*, op. cit., p. 53.

6. Ibid. "Esa carencia de familiaridad no es sino una nueva prueba de nuestro sometimiento a la perspectiva colonizadora de la historia que se nos ha impuesto, y nos ha evaporado nombres, fechas, circunstancias, verdades" (*Todo Caliban*, op. cit., p. 53).

7. See, Elizabeth Millán-Zaibert, "A Great Vanishing Act? The Latin American Philosophical Tradition and How Ariel and Caliban Helped Save It from Oblivion," *CR: The New Centennial Review*, nol. 7, n. 3 (2008): 149–169.

8. Roberto Fernández Retamar, *Caliban and Other Essays*, op. cit., pp. 3–4. *Todo Caliban*, op. cit., pp. 21–22.

9. Some thinkers have done this, yet the philosophical world is slow to catch on to their work. See, for example, Julio Ramos, *Desencuentros de la modernidad en América Latina. Literatura y política en el siglo xix* (México: Fondo de la cultura económica, 1989, 2003). In English as *Divergent Modernities: Culture and Politics in Nineteenth-Century Latin America*, translated by John D. Blanco (Durham: Duke University Press, 2001). Of course, a focus on the problem of modernity is not the only way to liberate Latin American philosophy from its colonial condition. Recent work by thinkers such as Linda Alcoff and Jorge Gracia on the problem of race has done much to highlight the unique philosophical contributions of the Latin American philosophical tradition.

10. Fernández Retamar, *Caliban and Other Essays*, op. cit., p. 63.

11. See, *The Devastation of the Indies: A Brief Account*, translated by Herma Briffault, foreword by Bill Donovan (Baltimore: The Johns Hopkins University Press, 1992).

12. Simón Bolívar, "Jamaica Letter," in *Latin American Philosophy for the 21st Century*, edited by Jorge Gracia and Elizabeth Millán-Zaibert (Amherst, NY: Prometheus Books), pp. 63–66, at pp. 65–66.

13. When I taught in Venezuela at the Universidad Simón Bolívar in 1998, I gave seminars on Kant and the early German Romantics, and even a course on Bertrand Russell. The students were not interested in anything on Leopoldo Zea, José Enrique Rodó, José Martí, Domingo Faustino Sarmiento, or Andrés Bello, to name just a few of the central figures of the Latin American tradition.

14. Gloria Anzaldúa, *Borderlands/La Frontera: The New Mestiza* (San Francisco: Aunt Lute Books, 2007).

15. Jacques Derrida, *Learning to Live Finally: The Last Interview*, translated by Pascale-Anne Brault and Michael Naas (Hoboken, NJ: Melville Publishing House, 2007), p. 40. I am grateful to Michael Naas for bringing this text to my attention.

16. Ibid., pp. 44–45.

17. For more on this, see Jochen Hörisch, Theorie-Apotheke: Eine Handreichung zu den humanwissenschaftlichen Theorien der letzten fünfzig Jahre, einschließlich ihrer Risiken und Nebenwirkungen (Frankfurt am Main: Eichborn Verlag, 2005), esp., pp. 35–44.

18. An excellent example of such a view is Rudolph Carnap's, "Die Überwindung der Metaphysik durch die logische Analyse der Sprache," *Erkenntnis*, 2 (1931): 219–41. Translated by Arthur Pap as "The Elimination of Metaphysics through Logical Analysis" in *Logical Positivism*, edited by A.J. Ayer (New York: The Free Press, 1959): 60–81.

19. Roberto Fernández Retamar, *Caliban and Other Essays*, translated by Edward Baker, Foreword by Frederic Jameson (Minneapolis: University of Minnesota Press, 1989), xi.

20. Ibid., xii.

21. José Martí, "Our America," in José Martí, *Our America: Writings on Latin America and the Struggle for Cuban Independence*, translated by Elinor Randall et al. (New York: Monthly Review Press, 1977), p. 88. Cited by Fernández Retamar,

Caliban and Other Essays, op. cit., p. 21. See also, José Martí, *Obras Completas,* Volume III, edited by Jorge Quintana (Caracas: Litho Tip, 1964): 105–12. "Conocer el país, y gobernarlo conforme al conocimiento, es el único modo de librarlo de tiranías. La Universidad europea ha de ceder a la Universidad Americana. La historia de América, de los incas a acá, ha de enseñarse al dedillo, aunque no se enseñe la de los arcontes de Grecia. Nuestra Grecia es preferible a la Grecia que no es nuestra. Nos es más necesaria. Los políticos nacionales han de reemplazar a los politicos exóticos. Injértese en nuestras Repúblicas el mundo; pero el tronco ha de ser el de nuestras Repúblicas" (p. 108).

22. Fernández Retamar, op. cit., p. 55/*Todo Caliban,* op. cit., p. 129.

23. Paul Gilroy, *The Black Atlantic. Modernity and Double Consciousness* (Cambridge: Harvard University Press, 1993).

24. José Enrique Rodó, *Ariel,* translated by Margaret Sayers Peden, foreword by James W. Symington, prologue by Carlos Fuentes (Austin: University of Texas Press, 1988), pp. 42–43. Disregarding Carlos Fuentes aesthetic assessment of Rodó's style (in the prologue of the aforementioned volume, Fuentes calls *Ariel* "a supremely irritating book" whose "rhetoric is insufferable"), I would like to give the citation in Rodó's beautiful Spanish:

Por desdicha, es en los tiempos y las civilizaciones que han alcanzado una completa y refinada cultura donde el peligro de esta limitación de los espíritus tiene una importancia más real y conduce a resultados más terribles. Quiere, en efecto, la ley de evolución, manifestándose en la sociedad come en la Naturaleza por una creciente tendencia a la heterogeneidad, que, a medida que la cultura general de las sociedades avanza, se limite correlativamente la extension de las aptitudes individuales y haya de ceñirse el campo de acción de cada uno a una especialidad más restringida. Sin dejar de constituir una condición necesaria de progreso, ese desenvolvimiento del espíritu de especialización trae consigo desventajas visibles, que no se limitan a estrechar el horizonte de cada inteligencia, falseando necesariamente su concepto del mundo, sino que alcanzan y perjudican, por la dispersión de las afecciones y los hábitos individuales, al sentimiento de la solidaridad. Augusto Comte ha señalado bien este peligro de las civilizaciones avanzadas. Un alto estado de perfeccionamiento social tiene para él un grave inconveniente en la facilidad con que suscita la aparición de espíritus deformados y estrechos; de espíritus 'muy capaces bajo un aspecto único y monstruosamente ineptos bajo todos los otros' (José Enrique Rodó, *Ariel,* edición de Belén Castro (Madrid: Catedra, 2004), p. 155).

CHAPTER SEVENTEEN

LINGUISTIC HEGEMONY
AND LINGUISTIC RESISTANCE

<hr>

English, Spanish, and American Philosophy

José Medina

Can we express the same meanings in whatever language we choose to use? Does the use of English versus Spanish make any difference? Is our linguistic choice just a matter of convenience for reaching one audience versus another? Is a philosophical discourse listened to and understood in the same way no matter in what language it is expressed? Do bilingual audiences attach the same experiential and philosophical significance to the speech of a philosopher who speaks in English or in Spanish, or who goes back and forth between the two languages? Does it matter whether she speaks with an accent? In this chapter I develop a Bourdieuan analysis of linguistic diversity in academia, more specifically, an analysis of the differences between English and Spanish in American philosophy. I develop my account of the significance of linguistic differences in three stages. First, I offer a critique of two semantic models that distort the cultural and socio-political significance of linguistic differences, and I develop an alternative semantic model grounded in the pragmatist tradition. Second, using my pragmatic semantic model, I sketch an account of *linguistic resistance* that offers a robust notion of discursive responsibility and underscores the possibilities for transformation that exist in our cultural practices, including our philosophical practices in the Americas. Drawing on the work of Gloria Anzaldúa, I call attention to the critical and transformative potential of linguistic *mestizaje*. Finally, I elucidate what is at stake in the use of English and Spanish in American philosophy.

MONOPOLY, "FREE TRADE," AND NEGOTIATION

The francophone African diaspora achieved some unity and developed a powerful race consciousness through black literary voices writing in the French language. Jean-Paul Sartre recognized the crucial role that French played in the articulation of black consciousness and black solidarity by the Negritude poets. He argued that the language of the oppressor and colonizer offered possibilities for resistance and subversion that the national and autochthonous African languages could not afford. As Sartre puts it:

> Having been dispersed to the four corners of the earth by the slave trade, blacks have no common language: in order to incite the oppressed to unite, they must necessarily rely on the words of the oppressor's language. And French is the language that will furnish the black poet with the largest audience, at least within the limits of French colonization.[1]

But Sartre also recognized the problems of using a hegemonic, colonial language for the liberation of colonized peoples. By establishing a particular language (French, Spanish, or English) as the "official" and "standard" language of a globalized community, this community retains the mark of an empire, the heritage of a colonial power, and thus inherits a particular power dynamic that empowers some and disempowers others. In this way, through language, "the colonist has arranged to be the eternal mediator between the colonized"; through the (sometimes forced, sometimes self-imposed) use of a hegemonic language, the colonist "is there—always there—even when he is absent, even in the most secret meetings."[2] But does it really make any difference which language one uses? Why should the language in which the colonized subject chooses to speak matter at all? Sartre answers that it matters because "this syntax and vocabulary—forged thousands of miles away in another epoch to answer other needs and to designate other objects—are unsuitable to furnish him with the means of speaking about himself, his own concerns, his own hopes."[3]

Frantz Fanon also saw the linguistic trap that the use of the French language poses for African diasporic subjects. The imposition of French (or Spanish, or English, for that matter) as the official language in the colonies was indeed a crucial part of the colonization of non-Western peoples. As Fanon's analysis underscores, the imposition of colonial languages facilitates crucial psychological aspects of the process of subjection and subjugation of Third-World subjects; for, to use a language "means above all to assume a culture, to support the weight a civilization," "to speak a language is to take on a world, a culture."[4] The imposition of a Western colonial language on

Third-World subjects contributes to the internalization of power structures and cultural standards, of Western ideals and values. It contributes to the whitening of the psyche of back subjects. It imposes a culture and a way of life as standard, and it presents particular kinds of subjectivity as *normal*, and different ones as *deviant*. As Fanon puts it, "the Negro of the Antilles will be proportionately whiter . . . in direct ratio to his mastery of the French language." Fanon also notes, "The Antilles Negro who wants to be white will be the whiter as he gains greater mastery of the cultural tool that language is."[5]

So Fanon agrees with what I described here, following Sartre, as the linguistic "trap" set up by colonial powers. But, at the same time, Fanon also emphasizes that this is not an inescapable trap: Escaping it—he seems to suggest—requires the interrogation and challenging of certain assumptions about who owns the language. For example, Fanon calls our attention to the pervasive assumption that francophone black people speak a language that does not belong to them, a foreign tongue; or that they speak it in a way that perverts it, with a foreign accent. But now (even if not before) this language belongs to them as well, for, even if French used to be the language of the metropolis, the reality is that it is now also the language of the colonies.[6] We need to resist not only the (forced) use of hegemonic languages by making room for other languages, but also and more importantly, we need to resist the hegemonic assumptions about these languages and about their past, present, and future. In fact, one could argue that the central problem lies not so much in the use of *hegemonic languages*, but rather, in the *hegemonic uses* of a language.

I want to call attention to the fact that English seems to have become the most powerful *hegemonic language*, but also, I want to underscore the fact that there are certain *hegemonic uses* of the English language in economic, political, and cultural domains (including that of academia and of philosophy, more specifically): uses that are *exclusionary* and lead to an *unequal* distribution of symbolic power and agency among subjects, contributing to the *differential authority* of their voices. In the postcolonial globalized world of today, English has become the hegemonic language. Even when it is not explicitly declared the official language of socioeconomic and cultural transactions, it is nonetheless very often used as the standard language in most international affairs. In academia, English has become the *lingua franca* of the world. It is important to note that by allowing a language to occupy this position of hegemony, speakers become disproportionately empowered and disempowered: Speakers whose native languages are other than English are—whether explicitly or implicitly—forbidden to use their native tongues; and if they speak English with an accent, no matter how fluently, they are perceived as not owning the language in which they speak. We can define a hegemonic language as the language that monopolizes expressive resources and control most of the "linguistic markets" in which our expressive lives unfold. So a language is hegemonic if it dominates a vast array of linguistic contexts, and if speakers in those contexts (or hegemonic spaces) are forced to adopt that language.

Pierre Bourdieu's sociological account of language is helpful here.[7] Bourdieu studied the sociological formation of "linguistic fields" or "linguistic markets" in which symbolic agency is exercised and power relations are formed, legitimated, or reinforced. In these linguistic markets speakers can do better or worse depending on whether their modes of expression conform with what is considered appropriate language, that is, whether their vocabularies, syntactic structures, accents, etc, correspond to the linguistic usage that has the highest recognition and authority in those contexts. Speakers can accumulate "linguistic capital" by doing well in those markets in which their uses of language can yield profits, or they can become increasingly marginalized and "linguistically dispossessed" if they lack the linguistic resources and competences that are esteemed and positively appreciated in the linguistic markets in which they enter. The overall value of one's modes of expression is what Bourdieu calls one's *linguisitc capital*, which determines the *profits* that one can make in linguistic exchanges. These profits can be gains in social status and influence, but sometimes they are directly economic profits: for example, the profit of the use of language in a job interview (i.e., speaking with certain diction, in a masculine or feminine way, using certain terms, etc). Bourdieu talks about the linguistic capital that particular individuals accrue in their lives and exhibit in their symbolic performance, but he also talks about the linguistic capital that groups have or lack, which consists in the linguistic resources appropriated by that group (whether of their own making or taken from others) and which members of that group can partake in to a greater or lesser extent. The notion of linguistic capital can be used to identify different forms of cultural disenfranchisement and marginalization by being differentially deprived of symbolic agency.

Bourdieu's analysis shows that there is always linguistic oppression and dispossession when a particular use of language (e.g., a particular dialect and accent, particular choices of words, particular grammatical constructions, etc.) is established as the only *proper* and *legitimate* use of language, all the others being considered deviations or perversions. The imposition of an official and legitimate use of language—a standard usage—involves the disciplining of speaking subjects, the construction of subjects and citizens. This is illustrated by Bourdieu's sociohistorical account of the formation of the French language from the fourteenth century on.[8] According to Bourdieu, maintaining the linguistic unity of a community always involves (some degree of) "linguistic domination," that is, it involves the *imposition* of a *legitimate* language, the privileging of a particular set of uses; for "integration into a single 'linguistic community'" is always "the product of political domination that is endlessly reproduced by institutions capable of imposing universal recognition of the dominant language."[9] A dominant way of speaking and writing is maintained and transmitted from generation to generation by a complex network of formal and informal, public and private, practices and institutions, which include schooling, the family, religion, the labor market, and so on. The reproduction of the legitimate language is accomplished with the collaboration of academic, cultural, and educational institutions that domesticate language and fix usage by sanctioning certain uses of language as legitimate and others as illegitimate.

As seen in the case of the Negritude movement discussed by Sartre and Fanon, the imposition of certain modes of expression is especially problematic when the imposed language is not the language of the cultural milieu of the subjects who are forced to use it. In this sense, it is troublesome that English is the only language used in the academic discussions of Hispanic issues and of Hispanic philosophy in this country. Especially now that Hispanics are becoming the most numerous minority of the United States, it is troublesome that the language(s) of their philosophical tradition(s) and the language(s) of their cultural practices are excluded from most official contexts of public life, including academic settings. It also is troublesome that Hispanics lose linguistic capital if they speak with an accent or if they let Spanish or nonstandard uses of English penetrate their discourse in academic settings, as if the mixing of linguistic resources automatically devalued one's speech, as if the preservation of the purity of the English language (i.e., of what has become the proper use of English in academia) were an absolute value. The issue of linguistic *mestizaje* and of the proliferation and hybridization of linguistic markets within philosophical communities are the topics of the last section. In order to pave the way to that discussion, for the remainder of this section I address the issue of who (if anybody) owns a language. Are linguistic resources owned by the ethnic groups in which they originated? Or do they belong to everybody? Does English belong to the Anglos? Does Spanish belong to Hispanics? I argue that there are serious problems with the view that languages can be monopolized, but also with the view that they belong to no one in particular or to everybody equally, that is, the view that languages are universal instruments that anybody can use in the same way and without impediment in the "free trade" of ideas and cultural products. As an alternative to these inadequate semantic views—the Monopoly Model and the Free Trade Model—I propose a Negotiating Model, which accounts for linguistic interaction without assuming the exclusivity or the universality of linguistic resources.

Languages cannot be monopolized. The Monopoly Model depicts each language as inextricably tied to the ethnic group in which it originated. The problem with this view is not that there are no cultural ties between a language and the group in which it originated—there are, and very important ones at that. The problem is that these ties are not so rigidly established, so unchangeable, as to guarantee *exclusive* use; they cannot be the basis on which to claim exclusive rights and maintain monopoly. The key issue is whether a linguistic capital can be claimed as the *exclusive* possession of a group, or rather, alternatively, as something *sharable*, as a cultural contribution of a group that can be used and enjoyed by other groups as well. Cultural critics such as David Hollinger[10] have assumed that all appeals to the linguistic or cultural capital of an ethnic group or race are intrinsically exclusionary. But, as I argued elsewhere[11], this is not necessarily the case. It is true that the proprietary language of "linguistic capital" and "cultural heritage" does have exclusionary connotations. But claiming one's language or culture as one's own does not have to be done to the exclusion of others; claiming one's heritage doesn't have to be exclusionary if one is willing to share. It is certainly possible to call attention to the link between certain linguistic and cultural resources and the practices and traditions of one's group, while offering these linguistic and cultural resources as contributions for the use and enjoyment of other groups.

But we have to be careful in how we construe the sharable nature of language, because we run the risk of going to the other extreme in our escape from the misconceptions of the Monopoly Model. This other extreme in the spectrum would be the one that asserts that languages are universal property and belong to no one in particular, thus severing all cultural ties between languages and the ethnic groups in which they originated. We can call this view the Free Trade Model, for it construes linguistic markets as completely unconstrained and unregulated spaces where every speaker has full autonomy and freedom to use any language she pleases in whatever way she pleases. This model is problematic because it makes us blind to issues of linguistic dispossession (or differential access to linguistic resources) and cultural exploitation, and to the many ways in which linguistic interactions and the structured setting in which they take place can be built on (and used to maintain) relations of oppression. Here, I call attention to two central problems for the Free Trade Model: cooptation (which also can be called the problem of appropriation, incorporation, or assimilation); and illusory equality (i.e., creating a false sense of free trade that hides disparities in cultural agency and in access to linguisitc resources).

Cooptation does not always take the form of blatant exploitation and ideological instrumentalization. It can consist simply in a reabsorption (often quite unintentional) of new meanings into the mainstream, in the neutralization of their subversive power. New constellations of meanings are sometimes redirected by users who put them at the service of old ideologies, and thus lose their transformative potential. Even allies of disempowered groups often fall victim to the problem of cooptation, indulging in problematic forms of appropriation or assimilation without even being aware of the problem. Consider, for example, the concepts of Liberation Theology developed by an application of Marxist and critical theory to Latin American realities by Enrique Dussel and others.[12] This is one of the few Latin American philosophical movements that has received some worldwide attention, but the specificity of its concepts often is lost in the Anglo literature because they are assimilated to other movements and applied to other cultural realities, without paying much attention to the originating cultural contexts these concepts come from. I am not, of course, denying the importance of drawing interconnections among movements of liberation and sharing philosophical resources, but this can be done without erasing differences. However, in their translation and use in the English literature, the critical concepts of Liberation Theology tend to lose their particularity and to become reabsorbed in a preexisting ideology of liberation. In this way the specificity and density of Latin American experiences of oppression are lost. (And I argue that there is no universal, free-standing experience of oppression, but particular forms of oppression tied to particular social locations and experiential standpoints.) This is simply an illustration of how even sympathetic and friendly users of transformative meanings can contribute to their cooptation. And there are of course the more problematic cases of appropriation and cooptation in which the linguistic tools of the oppressed are used by the oppressor in such a way that they lose their critical and liberating power completely and are put at the service of opposite ends, ultimately solidifying the relation of oppression. There is a wealth of evidence in Cultural Studies that underscores how the cultural representations of marginal voices—the literary and artistic works of minority group—are repackaged by the mainstream media for the mass consumption of publics that are not challenged or critically enriched by these diverse voices.[13]

A second problem of the Free Trade Model is that it rests on a socially and politically dangerous illusion: *the myth of equality*—what Bourdieu calls "the illusion of *linguistic communism*."[14] It is of paramount importance to recognize that in actual linguistic communities there is no equal access to linguistic resources: There are differences in upbringing, in schooling, in access to higher learning, and more generally in the social environment in which one leads one's life; and these differences result in the mastery of different vocabularies and rhetorical devices, in different pronunciations, dictions, and writing styles, and in different discursive competences. It is important to note that language is not used in an abstract space of logical relations, but in a social space that is structured by power relations. In linguistic markets some people accumulate gains and accrue linguistic capital, whereas others accumulate losses and thus become linguistically dispossessed. The phenomenon of linguistic dispossession becomes invisible in a view of language that ignores the unequal distribution of linguistic resources in actual linguistic communities. The alleged universal access to linguistic resources is a distracting and dangerous illusion: It creates an illusory sense of equality that hides conditions of oppression and distracts us from the cultural dispossession of particular groups, from the roots and consequences of their disempowerment in linguistic practices.

As an alternative to the Monopoly and Free Trade models, I propose a Negotiating Model for the understanding of linguistic resources and their availability. I sketch this model through a discussion of two conditions for the responsible and critical use of linguistic resources: the Reconstruction Condition and the Openness Condition.

In the first place, a responsible use of a symbol requires some familiarity with its historicity and projectability. A crucial part of this familiarity is an informed and critical sense of the symbol's origin and trajectory—often multiple origins and multiple trajectories. Critical symbolic agency and responsible use require the kind of critical reflection that pragmatists have called *reconstruction*. The required familiarity with the historicity and projectability of symbols can only be achieved through a process of reconstruction that is both backward-looking and forward-looking, involving both genealogical reflection and a critical exploration of possibilities for resignification. So I term this first condition for responsible symbolic agency *the reconstruction condition*.[15] This condition, uncontroversial as it may seem at first glance, would not be accepted by everybody. In particular, it would be rejected by proponents of the Free Trade Model, such as Hollinger.[16]

For better or for worse, linguistic resources don't belong to all of us equally. But this does not mean that we cannot all use them or enjoy them; we can, but we will do so differently. As articulated here, the notion of a linguistic capital refers to the range of potentialities that have been (or can be) expressed and realized by the members of a group. These potentialities need to be uncovered and appropriated through a genealogical and projective reconstruction, for the members of the group are not automatically aware and in control of their linguistic capital. Also, as argued previously, the potentialities of a linguistic capital are never the *exclusive* property of a single group and its (actual and possible) trajectories are always open to *negotiation*, to complex processes of intra- and intergroup negotiations. Openness to these negotiations is the second crucial condition for responsible symbolic agency that I want to identify and briefly discuss.

The *openness condition* for responsible symbolic agency is grounded in a general point about the relational nature of language,[17] namely: that our singular voices are always entangled with the voices of others, and that it is important to recognize these relations and to be open to a process of negotiation and mutual influence with these plural and heterogeneous voices. This relationality is crucial given the nonexclusionary view of linguistic capital I have articulated here. On my view, given the relations of mutual influence between groups and their languages, we cannot make sense of the development of each group and its linguistic capital independently of other groups and their linguistic capitals. Especially in today's globalized world and multicultural societies, groups develop together, and they become mutually enriched or impoverished in and through their interactions. Plural linguistic communities need *open* symbolic negotiations in which linguistic resources are used flexibly and fluidly, without agents being handicapped or paralyzed by linguistic differences. Languages should not be construed as fixed structures that rigidly constrain speakers, as if they were strait jackets. Rather, they should be thought of as sets of living practices that function both as enabling and as constraining conditions of people's agency. Although linguistic differences can be obstacles and problems that affect people's abilities to listen to, speak to, and understand each other, linguistic diversity also is (and more importantly) a source of mutual cultural enrichment for the people exposed to it. In this sense, although bilingual speakers—as many Hispanics are—often have special problems and disadvantages in their linguistic agency (concerning their accents, the exclusion of some of their modes of expression, what is lost in translation, etc.), it is important to recognize that they also have advantages and special assets and abilities to enrich and diversify cultural contexts. Bilingual speakers also are well positioned to be subversive agents who can interrogate and challenge hegemonic languages and hegemonic cultural spaces. To these subversive negotiations I now turn.

SUBVERSIVE NEGOTIATIONS:
LINGUISTIC RESISTANCE AND MESTIZAJE

It is important to call attention to *subversive negotiations* that have a critical and transformative potential: negotiations that are *critical* because they offer resistance to hegemonic languages and hegemonic linguistic contexts; and negotiations that are *transformative* because they diversify and rearticulate linguistic practices. I explore some specific aspects of linguistic resistance and transformative negotiation in the concluding section, focusing on American philosophy and its cultural practices in the United States. As a preface to that discussion, in this section I sketch an account of certain forms of linguistic dissidence and resistance that can subvert and reshape cultural practices. For this I draw on the pioneering and inspiring work of Gloria Anzaldúa.

As suggested at the end of the last section, my negotiating model of linguistic agency emphasizes that we need to keep the cultural dialogues in and across linguistic communities as open as possible, without constraining and disciplining their diversity, that is, the plurality and heterogeneity of their voices. In other words, we need to keep our dialogues *polyphonic*. We have to be prepared to fight *homogenizing* and *normalizing* tendencies that erase differences.[18] As we saw in the previous section through Bourdieu, the social shaping and unification of a language and the domestication of the identities of its speakers go hand in hand. Coercive social and cultural forces and institutions (from school to the family and the media) are responsible for the standardization of language and the homogenization of mainstream identities. These coercive forces—which can come from inside one's own group or community as well as from other social units—limit the self-expression of individuals and groups. They often restrict, handicap, and even preclude the emergence and development of alternative identities that can be subversive and transformative. A crucial part of this social and cultural process of disciplining identities and taming their polyphony is the attempt to subdue and domesticate new languages and dialects that people develop to express their experiences, ideals, values, needs, interests, and so on. These new linguistic formations (new language games) can facilitate the rearticulation or reconstruction of established communities or cultural groups and the creation of new ones. Therefore, keeping cultural dialogues open is a prerequisite for the flourishing of new identities. But how does one resist the taming of one's tongue?

Of special interest here are *frontier identities*[19] and *border languages*. These are the languages and identities of those who live at the limits or borders between communities or cultures—*en la frontera*. In *Borderlands/La Frontera*, Anzaldúa examines the development of her own language and her own identity growing up between two cultures along the U.S.–Mexico border. She tells us that at the core of her Chicana identity is a cultural and linguistic duplicity that makes her a stranger even to the members of the cultural group to which she belongs. Those who have frontier identities often display signs of cultural otherness in their faces and bodies, in their manners and comportment, and in their speech. These are signs that often come under attack, being subject to the domesticating social and cultural forces that conspire to erase them. Our bodies and habits are disciplined; our tongues are tamed. In this respect, Anzaldúa talks about the concerted efforts "to get rid of our accents," which she describes as a violent attack on one's identity and basic rights: "Attacks on one's form of expression with the intent to censor are a violation of the First Amendment. *El Anglo con cara de inocente nos arrancó la lengua*. Wild tongues can't be tamed, they can only be cut out."[20]

It is important to note that the efforts to tame one's tongue do not come only from outside one's group or family. Anzaldúa poignantly remarks that her Chicana tongue is not only tamed—and ultimately "cut out"—by the Anglos, but also by other Hispanics. Chicano Spanish is not recognized and respected by many other Spanish speakers: "Even our own people, other Spanish speakers, *nos quieren poner candados en la boca*. . . . Chicano Spanish is considered by the purist and by most Latinos deficient, a mutilation of Spanish."[21] And this scorn and disciplining efforts come not just from other Spanish speakers, but from Chicanas and Chicanos themselves, who have internalized the alleged inferiority of their language and, ultimately, of their identity. "Chicanas who grew up speaking Chicano Spanish have internalized the belief that we speak poor Spanish . . . we use our language differences against each other."[22]

The domestication of a border language such as Chicano Spanish leaves its speakers tongue-tied, speechless, indeed as if their tongues had been cut out, for they are rendered unable to express themselves in their own ways. The social stigmatization and exclusion of their forms of expression amount to the marginalization of their very identities: "If a person, Chicana or Latina, has a low estimation of my native tongue, she has also a low estimation of me. . . . I am my language. Until I can take pride in my language, I cannot take pride in myself."[23] This moment of self-empowerment through one's tongue is a moment of cultural pride and cultural affirmation. It involves a demand for *linguistic solidarity*, for the formation of a proud linguistic community liberated from self-hatred, a community in which the marginalized tongue finds a home and a family. Anzaldúa makes this point in very Wittgensteinian terms, calling for the construction of a "We"—*un* "*Nosotras*"—around a common tongue that corresponds to a shared form of life. She writes: "Chicano Spanish is a border tongue which developed naturally. . . . *Un language que corresponde a un modo de vivir*. Chicano Spanish is not incorrect, it is a living language."[24] On Anzaldúa's view, language must be adequate to the life experiences of the people who speak it; there is no sense in calling Chicano Spanish deficient just because it does not conform to some canonical rules (whose rules?). She remarks that this language "sprang out of the Chicano's need to identify ourselves as a distinct people": "for a people who cannot entirely identify with either standard (formal, Castillian) Spanish nor standard English, what recourse is left to them but to create their own language? A language which they can connect their identity to, one capable of communicating the realities and values true to themselves. . . . We needed a language with which we could communicate with ourselves, a secret language."[25]

Anzaldúa emphasizes that language can be both unifying and divisive: We often use our linguistic differences against each other, but we also develop language as a site of solidarity for the formation of group identity. The relations between cultural and linguistic differences do not have to be necessarily antagonistic and oppressive; these relations can also be productive. Anzaldúa's account recognizes that cultural borders and the cohabitation of different forms of life can have a *special kind of linguistic productivity*: "at the juncture of cultures, languages cross-pollinate and are revitalized; they die and they are reborn."[26] A border tongue can be characterized for its special kind of creativity. As Anzaldúa's discussion suggests, language can be an ethnic home or cultural cradle. As she puts it, "for some of us, language is a homeland closer than the Southwest."[27] It is for this reason that she finds it impossible to separate her language from her ethnic identity: "Ethnic identity is twin skin to linguistic identity—I am my language. Until I can take pride in my language, I cannot take pride in myself."[28]

The task of cultural self-affirmation through language is a complex and always ongoing task. It is extremely complex because it has to be constantly diversified, making sure that no voices are left out. As Anzaldúa points out, "there is no one Chicano language just as there is no one Chicano experience."[29] Even for a single individual, taking pride in one's tongue is typically not a single, unified task, but a plurality of tasks, with multiple fronts, for we speak in many tongues: "because we are a complex, heterogeneous people, we speak many languages."[30] For this reason, because of the unavoidable and indomitable diversity of human experience, there is no sense in talking about the *purity* of a language or the *purity* of an identity. Languages and identities are not only intrinsically diverse, but also necessarily open to change. The development of language and identity constitutes a never-ending task, for languages and cultural identities are *living* things that are always changing.

Resisting the reification and homogenization of languages and discursive contexts is a pressing task for which we are all collectively responsible, as individuals and as communities. But it is indeed not an easy task. In and through cultural dialogues we need to secure recognition and respect for all languages and expressions of identity but especially for those that have been silenced, for those subjects and groups left without a voice, for those whose experiences depart from normalized cultural expectations and whose identities do not fit into the established cultural molds available to them. There are cultural identities that need a new language to express themselves and the creation of a supportive community in which to flourish, identities that—without special attention and care—are doomed to isolation and silence because they will remain marginalized and tongue-tied. Keeping cultural dialogues polyphonic involves a process of constant interrogation and challenge, a process of *resistance*, of *radical but immanent critique* of our linguistic and cultural practices and the ways in which they include and exclude people. We need to destabilize whatever cultural borders or frontiers are erected, whatever relations of inclusion and exclusion are established in our linguistic communities. We have to make it possible for people to develop their own ways of expressing themselves and of articulating their experiences, problems, interests, and so on. We have the individual and collective responsibility to do everything we can to keep cultural dialogues open and to allow for the identities of groups and individuals to be *polyphonic*, that is, to contain a (diverse and heterogeneous) plurality of voices. We must keep tongues untied. We must make our cultural dialogues polyphonic. Of course, open and polyphonic dialogues do not guarantee cultural solidarity, social justice, the mitigation of oppression, and the flourishing of happier cultural groups. The achievement of these goals is never guaranteed. But what untying tongues and having polyphonic dialogues can do is to increase the capacity that groups and individuals have to negotiate their languages and the symbolic articulations of their experiences.

The affirmation of linguistic differences and the hybridization of languages are acts of linguistic resistance that can have benefits for all speakers and not only for those whose modes of expression are deemed deviant and marginalized, for these acts diversify discursive contexts and practices and they destabilize hegemonic languages and the monopolization of linguistic capitals. It is important to note the role that institutions play in maintaining linguistic hegemony and the monopolization of linguistic capitals—public and official institutions (the state, the law, the school, etc.) as well as private and informal ones (the family, the church, entertainment activities and clubs, etc.). But, by the same token, these institutional frameworks and the institutional practices that take place within them can also play a crucial critical and transformative role, that is, a role in *resisting* linguistic hegemony and monopolization. It is of crucial importance to identify the role that institutions can play in linguistic resistance and *mestizaje* if they are made polyphonic, that is, genuinely open to linguistic diversity and experimentation. In particular, I want to call attention to the role of institutions of higher learning (such as the university) in producing respectable subjects with rich symbolic agency and great linguistic capital. In this context, I emphasize the importance of allowing Spanish as well as other languages in discursive contexts within academia, and also the importance of allowing for the hybridization of languages or linguistic *mestizaje*. More specifically, in the concluding section, I briefly discuss linguistic diversification and mestizaje in the teaching and practice of philosophy. What is the role that philosophy and philosophers can play in this?

ENGLISH AND SPANISH IN AMERICAN PHILOSOPHY

Why aren't Spanish and Portuguese used more often by Hispanic philosophers in the United States? An important part of the answer to this question is that there is nothing to gain and there is much to lose by doing so in the established linguistic markets of academia: One can lose one's linguistic and cultural capital without any gain to compensate for the loss. Why run that risk? Why make oneself vulnerable? A motivation for doing so is the importance—perhaps even urgency—of creating new linguistic markets and transforming the existing ones. But this requires crucial changes in the linguistic attitudes and habits of Hispanic philosophers, who are often reluctant (typically not by choice or by accident, but by training and social pressure) to use Spanish or Portuguese even when they can. That has been my experience in the years I served on the American Philosophical Association's (APA) Committee on Hispanic Philosophy and in the conferences on Hispanic philosophy I have attended. Why do we, Hispanic philosophers in the United States, typically not use Spanish or Portuguese among ourselves even in informal discussions or private meetings where everybody speaks the language(s)? Why is it so rare for us to introduce philosophical terms in Spanish or Portuguese when we are addressing a mixed audience, even though it is standard practice to do so in German or French? I first call attention to the problems and obstacles that account for this. I then turn to a more positive discussion—the analysis of the positive side of the issue of linguistic diversification and mestizaje in philosophy—by asking the following questions. What can we do to disrupt the linguistic habitus of mainstream philosophers in the United States? What are the positive steps that can be taken to make room for Spanish and other languages in academic philosophy? What discursive contexts and practices can be established so that these different languages can not only coexist but also interact and mutually enrich each other? What new linguistic markets can be inaugurated to facilitate the interpenetration of these languages in a productive way?

There are two obstacles that stand in the way for the use of Spanish (and Portuguese)[31] in philosophy. A first cultural obstacle that stands in the way of appreciating Hispanic philosophy and the use of Spanish in philosophical contexts is the *foreignness* associated with Hispanic identity and everything relating to it—its cultural traditions and any sign of Hispanic identity (e.g., speaking English with a Hispanic accent). Given this, there is an implicit social and cultural pressure to hide or at least deemphasize one's Hispanicity. There is considerable pressure for *passing* as an Anglo if one can, or at least for not calling excessive attention to those aspects of oneself that can make one deviant and marginal, resulting in the loss of linguistic and cultural capital. As Jorge Gracia has argued since his first book on the subject,[32] unlike other minorities in this country, Hispanics are perceived as foreigners, as not belonging here, not even as second-class citizens, but as noncitizens, as never fully achieving citizenship, no matter what their papers say and how many generations their families may have been in this country. This is supported by sociologists and legal theorists who have studied the most widespread stereotypes that stigmatize minorities in the US and contribute to their unjust treatment. In *Profiles in Injustice*,[33] David Harris discusses different negative stereotypes that inform and underlie racial and ethnic profiling, lifting the presumption of innocence and curtailing the rights and liberties of certain groups. Among these pernicious stereotypes we find the perceived foreignness of Hispanics: they are often the object of the suspicion of not being a citizen and, moreover, of being an illegal immigrant. This systematic suspicion applies especially in some geographical and cultural contexts—for example, along the southern U.S. border.[34] The stereotypes and stigmatizations that circulate in society in general indirectly affect how signs of Hispanicity are read everywhere, even in academic contexts—for the ivory tower is not after all completely impenetrable and isolated. The general presumption in most contexts is that being perceived as a Hispanic is risky and can potentially bring negative implications. Showing signs of Hispanicity, letting your Hispanic identity inform your speech, has at least the danger of diminishing or compromising your status and cultural capital.

Associating signs of Hispanicity with your ways of doing philosophy can therefore contribute to create the appearance that your philosophy is foreign, not relevant, and not properly classified as *American*. Yet, although this is indeed an important factor, it does not fully explain the marginalization of Hispanic philosophy and of ways of doing philosophy in Spanish and Portuguese.[35] For philosophizing in French and German does certainly create the appearance of foreignness, but it does not automatically diminish the linguistic and cultural capital of those who do it, and very often it can result in an increase of intellectual authority and cultural capital. Let's consider a second obstacle that Hispanics face in academic philosophical contexts, which can shed light on the marginalization and lack of appreciation for their philosophical traditions.

This second obstacle is the lack of recognition and respect that Hispanic cultural traditions have received in the Anglo-American world. This lack of appreciation has cast doubt on whether Hispanic *thought* can be considered *philosophy* properly so called. Until very recently intellectuals in this country had a very minimal awareness of Hispanic philosophy, its concepts, authors, and philosophical schools. Until recently, there were very few books available in Hispanic philosophy: Very few translations of Hispanic authors—even major ones—and very few anthologies and monographs analyzing and discussing philosophical movements in the Hispanic world. This is slowly changing, but the availability of Hispanic philosophy in print is still pretty dire. And besides this minimal awareness of and exposure to Hispanic philosophy (or perhaps because of it), there are also very negative attitudes towards it. In fact, it is not difficult to find in U.S. philosophy departments (still today, although things are changing) some people who are convinced that there is no such thing as Hispanic philosophy. (I myself have been told this.) It is also troublesome that one of the available text-books in Hispanic philosophy, Susana Nuccetelli's *Latin American Thought*,[36] takes this skeptical and condescending position as its starting point, let-ting it structure the analysis and discussion of Latin American thinkers (who have to earn the honorary designation of "philosophers" if their ideas are proven to be sophisticated enough). It is bothersome that one of the available volumes in Latin American philosophy is entitled "thought" and that the author assumes the burden of showing that, despite appearances, the Latin American thought developed from the Mayans to this day really amounts to a philosophical tradition.[37] Although ultimately claiming that there is in fact Latin American philosophy—surprising as this may seem to some—Nuccetelli's book encourages the reader not to make such a risky assumption until evidence is offered in its favor, as if the fact that there have been "philosophers" (intellectuals so described) and "philosophical" debates (discussions so described) in the Hispanic world for centuries was not sufficient prima facie evidence.

There is an inadmissible cultural arrogance in the assumption that only European (excluding Portuguese and Spanish) philosophy is philosophy properly so called, whereas other philosophies are only alleged philosophies that still have to prove themselves. This arrogant attitude underlies many aspects of the institutional frameworks in which philosophers are trained.[38] We should be attentive to the fact that these negative cultural attitudes of condescendence and skepticism are often internalized by marginalized minority subjects who adopt it toward themselves. This leads to an "inferi-ority complex," which Fanon analyzed so brilliantly for colonized peoples. As he explains it, racist ideologies make people assume that the Negro "has no culture, no civilization, no 'long historical past.'" Negroes themselves internalize this assumption and thus they throw themselves into a misguided enterprise: "to prove the existence of a black civilization to the white world at all costs."[39] This burden of proof should not be assumed because to assume it is already to concede too much to racist, ethnocentric, and xenophobic ideologies.

I now turn to a more positive discussion about what to do. What can we do to change the exclusion of languages other than English? What measures can be taken to promote the linguistic diversification and mestizaje in philosophy? What can we do to change linguistic attitudes and habits? What are the concrete steps that result in the transformation of the philo-sophical establishment, making it more agreeable to linguistic differences and more friendly to non-English-speaking philosophers? Jorge Gracia is one of the few Hispanic philosophers in the United States who has written passionately and eloquently on this issue. In *Latinos in America: Philosophy and Social Identity*,[40] Gracia suggests concrete steps that we should take to promote Hispanic philosophy and to increase the philosophical and cultural capital of Hispanics in the United States, earning recognition and respect for their philosophical traditions and creating spaces for their cultural agency to flourish unimpeded. He proposes ten concrete initiatives that we should concentrate our efforts on.[41] Among these initiatives are Gracia's recommendations to begin or continue the following: the publication of translations; developing reference works (such as a dictionary of Hispanic philosophy, a directory of Hispanic philosophers, etc); producing serious scholarship in the history of Hispanic philosophy; designing courses on Hispanic philosophy; continuing the APA Newsletter on Hispanic philosophy; creating professional journals and monograph series in this area; and participating in the Society for Iberian and Latin American Thought. Gracia also warns us that we should be careful that these measures are not taken in such a way that Hispanic philosophy is segregated from the philosophical canon. Special efforts have to be made to ensure that Hispanic philosophy is properly integrated in the academic linguistic markets, avoiding the formation of a ghetto for so-called non-Western philosophies (although unfortunately this seems to be happening already).[42] Some parts of the philosophical establishment are more receptive and easier to change than others. For example, professional associations such as SPEP or SAAP have been more open to include sessions on Hispanic philosophy in their main programs, whereas the APA includes them only in group meetings, contributing to the problem of segregation and ghettoization recognized by Gracia.

I wholeheartedly support Gracia's suggestions, but I think we have to go further, beyond institutionalized practices, to break cultural hegemony and to transform linguistic attitudes and habits. The diversification of American philosophy has to happen from the inside and in a variety of ways, which include additions to the philosophical establishment as well as critical cultural interventions and subversions. Not only must we open new linguistic markets, but we must also change existing ones with internal contestation and subversive moves, which should include linguistic resistance. An important part of this is linguistic hybridization or mestizaje, that is, introducing Spanish (and Portuguese, etc.) terms and expression in the vocabulary of mainstream philosophical discussions. Also, the linguistic resistance to hegemonic uses of language in American academia should include challenging cultural assumptions in English and identifying the limitations of contemporary English. This is what Sartre claimed that the Negritude poets did with the French language: They identified its silences, urging us to "make silence with language" in order to eventually give voice to those who did not have it in this language; they created "short-circuits of language," speaking "this language in order to destroy it."[43] Since I began this chapter with Sartre, I think it is fitting to end with him as well. What he says about the critical and transformative use of language by Negritude poets is very instructive: "since French lacks terms and concepts to define negritude, since negritude is silence, these poets will use 'allusive words, never direct, reducing themselves to the same silence' in order to evoke it."[44]

These subversive negotiations within the interstices of a hegemonic language are something that Gloria Anzaldúa did brilliantly, mixing academic English and her Chicano Spanish and calling attention to limitations, exclusions, and silences that haunt the use of English in academia. Using language in creative ways in order to transform it, Anzaldúa's use of language is poetic and subversive in this sense. Besides the linguistic mestizaje produced in these subversive negotiations, Anzaldúa also used English against itself, not to destroy it, but to renew it, exploiting its interstices and its silences, and encouraging us to experiment with the various languages and dialects in which our multilayered and diverse lives unfold. This is a call we need to keep responding to if we are going to find a home in American philosophy and in its linguistic markets, that is, if we are going to make our philosophical discourse our own and not a mere mask that disguises (or even erases) cultural identities and differences. As I have suggested, a small but important step in that direction is the use of Spanish terms of art developed in the philosophical traditions of Iberian and Latin American countries: for example, Dussel's "liberación," Mariátegui's "socialismo heroico y creativo," Martí's "raza," Ortega's "razón vital," and Unamuno's "sentimiento trágico," to name a few. As of today, these coined expressions in Spanish do not carry with them the same linguistic and cultural capital that technical terms in French or German do. But it is up to us to change that (although of course the collaboration of multiple constituencies in philosophical communities, taking up and echoing the use of these terms is necessary). The proliferation and hybridization of linguistic markets within philosophical communities can play a crucial critical role in the diversification and enrichment of American philosophy. And besides the intellectual benefits for all that we can find in these critical interventions, they are also required by justice, that is, for the desperately needed creation of more just, equal, and open communities that respond to and repair exclusions and silences. In this sense I want to link the linguistic resistance I have discussed with a larger form of social and political critique of which it is part. Linguistic resistance should be put at the service of cultural and ideological resistance, which involves—among other things—unsettling cultural assumptions, violating fixed expectations, disturbing the status quo and not letting received views go unquestioned. In short, linguistic resistance is necessary in order to fight cultural hegemony: we cannot let the philosophical establishment (and the social and cultural powers that shape it) set the agenda for us and fix the language in which we must speak. In this sense, linguistic resistance is an exercise in self-empowerment, in reclaiming one's own modes of expressions and remaking one's own linguistic agency.

NOTES

1. Jean-Paul Sartre, (2001), "Black Orpheus," in Robert Bernasconi (ed.): *Race*. London & New York: Blackwell, p.121.

2. Ibid.

3. Ibid.

4. Frantz Fanon, (1967), *Black Skin, White Masks*. New York: Grove Pres, pp. 17–18 and p. 38.

5. Ibid., p. 18 and p. 38.

6. Sartre made this claim in *Orphée Noir* when he writes: "It is not true, however, that the black expresses himself in a 'forcign' language, since he is taught French from childhood and since he is perfectly at ease when he thinks in the terms of a technician, of a scholar or of a politician" (p. 122). Although Fanon takes issue with Sartre's views in this paper, he does seem to agree with Sartre's central claim about language in this passage.

7. See esp. Pierre Bourdieu (1991) *Language and Symbolic Power*. Cambridge, MA: Harvard Univeristy Press.

8. Bourdieu observes that "the common language which was developed in Paris in cultivated circles [was] promoted to the status of official language" (p. 48); and the other side of this historical process of instituting an official language was that the popular and purely oral uses of all the regional dialects degenerated into *patois*, that is, into nonsensical, corrupted, or simply vulgar speech.

9. Bourdieu, Language and Symbolic Power, p. 46.

10. David Hollinger, (2000), *Postethnic America: Beyond Multiculturalism*. New York: Basic Books.

11. José Medina, (2004), "Pragmatism and Ethnicity: Critique, Reconstruction, and the New Hispanic," *Metaphilosophy* 35, 115–146.

12. See Enrique Dussell (1985) *Philosophy of Liberation*. Maryknoll, NY: Orbis; Enrique Dussell (1995) *The Invention of the Americas: Eclipse of 'the Other' and the Myth of Modernity*. New York: Continuum. See also Linda Alcoff and Eduardo Mendieta (2000) *Thinking from the Underside of History*. New York: Rowman & Littlefield; Eduardo Mendieta (1997) "Identity and Liberation," *Peace Review* 9 (4), 494–502; and, Eduardo Mendieta (2003) *Latin American Philosophy: Currents, Issues, Debates*. Bloomington: Indiana University Press.

13. Fanon's *Blask Skin, White Masks* can be considered as a pioneering study of cases of cooptation of this kind (especially in his discussions of the commodification of African art as well as in his critique of Sartre's use of Negritude poetry).

14. Bourdieu, Language and Symbolic Power, p. 43.

15. This condition would be impoverished if it is understood only individualistically or academically: it is not only the task of individuals but also that of a

community of users to critically inspect trajectories of use in a variety of ways (not just through the philological studies of academics, but also artistically, politically, and socially, reaching all the corners of the cultural life of the community).

16. According to David Hollinger, the ethnic roots of cultural products (including language) do not play an active role in their appreciation and can become obstacles for their use and enjoyment; they are something accidental to be transcended, mainly negative (biased) aspects to be overcome. In this sense Hollinger refers to examples of cultural products that, despite the ethnic specificity of their origins, have become the universal patrimony of mankind: for example, the scientific and artistic achievements of Ancient Egypt. But the crucial mistake here is to think that one *cannot* make cultural products available universally and at the same time develop an appreciation for their ethnic ancestry, that we have to choose between these two things, that one can only be done at the expense of the other. This error gives plausibility to the claim that the cost of expanding the availability of cultural products is to detach them from their ethnic roots and to minimize the value of their ethnic aspects. But this is simply wrong. In fact, making cultural products available outside the cultural contexts in which they were developed, far from being incompatible with, actually *requires* an appreciation of their ethnic ancestry. Such an appreciation is a precondition for the *full* enjoyment and the *responsible* use of these products. See David Hollinger (2000) *Postethnic America (Revised Edition)*. New York: Basic Books.

17. I have formulated a polyphonic view of symbolic agency that elaborates this point. See chapter 3 of *Speaking from Elsewhere: A New Contextualist Perspective on Meaning, Identity, and Discursive Agency*. Albany, NY: SUNY Press (2006).

18. Parts of what follows are drawn from chapter 6 of my book, *Language: Key Concepts in Philosophy*. London & New York: Continuum (2005).

19. As I have argued in my article, "Identity Trouble: Disidentification and the Problem of Difference," *Philosophy and Social Criticism* 29 (6), 657–82, (2003), all of us have multiple identities and are members of multiple groups. As Gomez-Peña puts it, "we are all members of multiple communities, at different times and for different reasons. Most communities in the 90s are fragmented, ephemeral, dysfunctional, and insufficient. They can only contain and 'include' selected aspects of ourselves." See Guillermo Gomez-Peña *Dangerous Border-Crossers*. New York: Routledge, 2000, p. 277. So, *frontier identities* and *border tongues* simply make explicit and perspicuous the tensions and problems that to some degree affect all languages and identities.

20. Gloria Anzaldúa, (1987), *Borderlands/La Frontera: The New Mestiza*. San Francisco: Aunt Lute Books, p. 76.

21. Ibid., pp. 76–77.

22. Ibid., p. 80.

23. Ibid., pp. 80–81.

24. Ibid., p. 77.

25. Ibid.

26. Ibid., p. 20.

27. Ibid.

28. Ibid., p. 81.

29. Ibid.

30. Ibid., p. 77.

31. Although I believe these obstacles apply quite similarly to Portuguese and Spanish, from now on I focus on the latter only because it is the language I know best.

32. Jorge Gracia, (2000), *Hispanic/Latino Identity: A Philosophical Perspective*. Oxford: Blackwell Publishers.

33. David Harris, (2003), *Profiles in Injustice: Why Racial Profiling Cannot Work*. New York: New Press, Norton & Co.

34. Harris (2003) discusses contemporary contexts in which the presumption of innocence is systematically lifted for certain groups: Arabs at the airport, Mexicans at the southern U.S. border, and those who commit the "offense" of "Driving While Black" are suspected of being up to no good and treated as guilty until proven innocent. As noted by Harris, a political effect of the so-called "war on terrorism" has been the proliferation of widespread suspicion against those cultural Others who exhibit racial, ethnic, and religious differences.

35. There are of course many accounts of what counts as Hispanic or Latino philosophy and of whether the use of Spanish and Portuguese can be considered necessary and/or sufficient conditions for this type of philosophy. For systematic discussions of these issues see Jorge Gracia, (2000), *Hispanic/Latino Identity: A Philosophical Perspective*. Oxford: Blackwell Publishers; and, Jorge Gracia, (2008), *Latinos in America: Philosophy and Social Identity*. Oxford: Blackwell Publishers.

36. Susana Nuccetelli, (2002), *Latin American Thought: Philosophical Problems and Arguments*. Boulder, CO: Westview Press.

37. Worse yet, Nuccetelli's first two chapters are devoted to the question of whether Latin American Indians such as the Mayans could be said to have thought and rationality. This was indeed a question taken very seriously which structured philosophical debates for centuries; and, therefore, it deserves a historical treatment, but not a philosophical revival as a contemporary issue. For the elaboration of this critical point as well as others, see my critical review of Nuccetelli's book in my article, "Contexts, Practices, and Identity: Comments on Susana Nuccetelli's Latin American Thought," APA *Newsletter on Hispanic/Latino Issues in Philosophy* 2 (1), 126–29, (2002).

38. For example, it is not uncommon to find philosophy graduate programs in which French and German are the only contemporary foreign languages accepted for the satisfaction of foreign-language requirements. It was this way in my own department at Vanderbilt University until recently. It's also not uncommon to hear something like the following (and I myself heard this from a well-intentioned colleague): "But these are the only modern European languages that have a philosophical tradition, aren't they? Is there a philosophical tradition in Spanish? Tell me. I just want to be enlightened."

39. Fanon, Black Skin, White Masks, p. 34.

40. Gracia, Latinos in America.

41. See chapter 8, section VII, "Incorporating Latino Philosophy into the Philosophical Canon," in Gracia *Latinos in America*.

42. Gracia remarks that "this is what has happened to some non-Western philosophies, Chinese and Indian, for example, for these are part of the curriculum

but they are segregated within it. It is practically unheard of that texts from Chinese and Indian philosophy are discussed in general courses in philosophy, such as metaphysics, epistemology, ethics, aesthetics, and so on. Even in introductory courses, these philosophies are ignored, and the textbooks for these courses seldom, if ever, include texts from these traditions. The same could happen to Latino philosophy."

43. Sartre, "Black Orpheus," pp. 122–23.

44. Ibid., p. 123.

CONTRIBUTOR NOTES

Jesús H. Aguilar is associate professor of philosophy at the Rochester Institute of Technology. His areas of research and teaching include Latin American philosophy, philosophy of art, philosophy of action, and philosophy of mind. His philosophical contributions have appeared in journals and volumes like *Variaciones Borges, Human Studies, Philosophical Review, dialectica, Philosophia,* and *The Blackwell Companion to Latin American Philosophy.* His most recent co-edited books are *Causing Human Actions* (MIT Press) and *New Waves in Philosophy of Action* (Palgrave-Macmillan). He has been the recipient of several awards and fellowships like the Fellowship Award for the Summer Institute in Cognitive Neuroscience by Dartmouth College, and the Fellowship Award for the NEH Summer Institute in Latin American Philosophy by SUNY-Buffalo. He was also a member of the American Philosophical Society Committee on Hispanics.

Linda Martín Alcoff is professor of philosophy at Hunter College and the CUNY Graduate Center. Her writings have focused on social identity, epistemology and politics, sexual violence, Foucault, and Latino issues in philosophy. She has written two books: *Visible Identities: Race, Gender and the Self* (Oxford 2006), *Real Knowing* (Cornell 1996); and she has edited nine, including *Thinking From the Underside of History* co-edited with Eduardo Mendieta (Rowman & Littlefield, 2000), *Singing in the Fire: Tales of Women in Philosophy* (Rowman & Littlefield 2003), *Feminist Epistemologies* co-edited with Elizabeth Potter (Routledge 1993), *Blackwell Guide to Feminist Philosophy,* co-edited with Eva Feder Kittay (2006), *Identity Politics Reconsidered* co-edited with Michael Hames-Garcia, Satya Mohanty and Paula Moya (Palgrave, 2006).

Lewis R. Gordon is Laura H. Carnell Professor of philosophy and director of the Institute for the Study of Race and Social Thought and the Center for Afro-Jewish Studies at Temple University. He also was president of the Caribbean Philosophical Association (2003–2008). He is the author and editor of many books, and most recently *An Introduction to Africana Philosophy* (Cambridge UP, 2008), and with Jane Anna Gordon, *Of Divine Warning: Reading Disaster in the Modern Age* (Paradigm Publishers, 2009), and coeditor, also with Jane Anna Gordon, of *A Companion to African-American Studies* (Blackwell Publishers, 2006), which was the NetLibrary Book of the month in February 2007.

Jorge J. E. Gracia is SUNY Distinguished Professor and holds the Samuel P. Capen Chair in Philosophy. A graduate of Chicago and Toronto, he is the author of more than a dozen books and two hundred articles, and has edited two dozen volumes, in such areas as metaphysics, philosophical historiography, and medieval philosophy. Recently, he has also been working on race and ethnicity. Among his most recent books are: *Latinos in America* (2008), *Surviving Race, Ethnicity, and Nationality* (2005), *Old Wine in New Skins* (2003), *Hispanic/Latino Identity* (2000), and *Metaphysics and Its Task* (1999). He is currently working on a book on categories.

Bill E. Lawson is Distinguished Professor of philosophy at the University of Memphis. He has published articles on the urban underclass, John Locke's theory of political obligation, social contract theory and African Americans, jazz, and urban environmental philosophy. He is the author (with Howard McGary) of *Between Slavery and Freedom* (1992), editor of *The Underclass Question* (1992), co-editor (with Frank Kirkland) of *Frederick Douglass: A Critical Reader* (1999), co-editor (with Laura Westra) of *Faces of Environmental Racism* (2001), and co-editor (with Donald Koch) of *Pragmatism and the Problem of Race* (2004).

Nelson Maldonado-Torres is associate professor of Latino and Hispanic Caribbean Studies, and the Program in Comparative Literature at Rutgers University. He also has taught critical theory of religion at Duke University, and comparative ethnic studies at the University of California, Berkeley. He works on theories and philosophies that address problems and questions related to the intersection of knowledge, ethics and politics on the one hand, and race, gender, nation, and empire on the other, particularly in connection with critical theory, phenomenology, postcolonial studies, and modern religious thought. He is the author of *Against War: Views from the Underside of Modernity* (Duke UP, 2008), editor of an issue on Caribbean philosophy in the journal of *Caribbean Studies* (2005), and coordinator of the web dossier on "Post-continental Philosophy" in the Web journal *Worlds and Knowledges Otherwise*. In 2005, he co-edited with Ramón Grosfoguel and José David Saldívar the book *Latin@s in the World-System: Decolonization Struggles in the 21st U.S. Empire* (Paradigm Press).

Donna-Dale Marcano teaches feminist philosophy, philosophy and race, and philosophy of human rights at Trinity College in Hartford, Connecticut.

She has published various articles on philosophy and race and is the co-editor of *Convergences: Black Feminism and Continental Philosophy* (SUNY Press, 2010).

Oscar R. Martí has taught at the City College of New York, San Diego State University, UCLA, the Universidad Nacional Autonoma de Mexico, Goddard College, and is currently Associate Professor of Chicana/o Studies and the director of the Center for Ethics and Values at the California State University, Northridge. A fellow at the UCLA Institute for American Cultures Studies, and a Fulbright Scholar, he has published extensively in the United States and abroad on Latin American philosophy, and on the history of philosophy in the eighteenth and nineteenth centuries.

John H. McClendon III is professor in the Department of Philosophy at Michigan State University. McClendon's areas of expertise include African philosophy, philosophy of African American studies, Marxist philosophy, and the history of African American philosophers. He is the author of C.L.R. *James's Notes on Dialectics: Left Hegelianism or Marxism-Leninism* (Lexington Books 2005) and is currently completing a manuscript, *Conversations with My Christian Friends*; this text focuses on African Americans from the standpoint of the philosophy of religion.

José Medina is associate professor of philosophy at Vanderbilt University. He works in philosophy of language, social and political philosophy, philosophy of race, and philosophy of culture and ethnicity, with a special focus on Wittgenstein, American philosophy, gender theory, and Hispanic philosophy. His research in theories of meaning and theories of identity has focused primarily on the intersections between heterogeneous and multiple dimensions of identity such as gender, sexuality, race, and ethnicity. Medina's publications include the single-authored books *Speaking from Elsewhere* (SUNY Press, 2006), *Language* (Continuum, 2005), and *The Unity of Wittgenstein's Philosophy* (SUNY Press, 2002). He has also published two edited volumes: *Truth: Engagements Across Philosophical Traditions* (Blackwell, 2005; co-edited with David Wood); and *Identity and Ethnicity* (*The Journal of Speculative Philosophy* 12, April 2004). Some of his most recent papers on theories of meaning and identity have been published in "*Inquiry, Metaphilosophy,* and *Philosophy and Social Criticism. Symposia on Gender, Race, and Philosophy* dedicated an issue (May 2005) to the discussion of his article "Identity Trouble" (see http://web.mit.edu/sgrp). Medina also has published articles in *Cognition, Dialectica, International Journal of Philosophical Studies, International Philosophical Quarterly, Journal of Pragmatics, Philosophical Forum, Philosophical Investigations,* and *Philosophical Studies* (among other professional journals).

Eduardo Mendieta is professor of philosophy at Stony Brook University. He was written on Latino/as and race, the Frankfurt School, Latin American philosophy, and postcolonialism. He is the author of *Global Fragments: Globalizations, Latinamericanisms, and Critical Theory* (SUNY, 2007), and is co-editor with Stuart Elden of *Reading Kant's Geography* (SUNY, 2011).

Elizabeth Millán is professor of philosophy at DePaul University and has also taught at the Universidad Simón Bolívar in Caracas. She has held research fellowships from the National Endowment for the Humanities and the Alexander von Humboldt Foundation. Her research interests are Latin American philosophy and German philosophy, and she regularly publishes work in these fields. Recent publications include: *Friedrich Schlegel and the Emergence of Romantic Philosophy* (2007); with Bärbel Frischmann, *Das neue Licht der Frühromantik/The New Light of German Romanticism* (2008). Her articles have appeared in CR: *The New Centennial Review, The Goethe Yearbook, Yearbook on German Idealism,* and *Fichte Studien*.

Charles W. Mills is John Evans Professor of Moral and Intellectual Philosophy at Northwestern University. He works in the general area of oppositional political theory, and is the author of five books: *The Racial Contract* (1997), *Blackness Visible: Essays on Philosophy and Race* (1998), *From Class to Race: Essays in White Marxism and Black Radicalism* (2003), *Contract and Domination* (with Carole Pateman) (2007), and *Radical Theory, Caribbean Reality: Race, Class and Social Domination* (2010).

Gregory Fernando Pappas is associate professor of philosophy at Texas A & M University. He has written numerous articles on Latin American and American philosophy. He is a Ford Foundation recipient and winner of the 2005 APA prize in Latin American thought. His articles have appeared in such journals as *Philosophy and Social Criticism, Social Theory and Practice, History of Philosophy Quarterly, Transactions of the Charles Peirce Society,* and others. He is the author of *John Dewey's Moral Theory: Experience as Method* (Indiana University Press).

Ofelia Schutte is professor of philosophy at the University of South Florida in Tampa, where she teaches Latin American philosophy, European continental philosophy, and feminism. She is the author of *Beyond Nihilism: Nietzsche without Masks* (1984) and *Cultural Identity and Social Liberation in Latin American Thought* (1993), as well as numerous articles and book chapters in her areas of specialization. She is also co-editor of *A Companion to Latin American Philosophy* (Wiley-Blackwell, 2010). A symposium on her work was featured in *Hypatia: A Journal of Feminist Philosophy* (19:3, 2004).

Her current interests include postcolonial theory, Latin American feminism, and recent work by Cuban women writers.

Jacqueline Scott is associate professor of philosophy at Loyola University of Chicago. She has published several articles on Nietzsche as well as on race theory. She is co-editor with A. Todd Franklin of *Critical Affinities: Nietzsche and African American Thought* (SUNY 2006). She is currently working on a manuscript entitled, *Nietzsche's Worthy Opponents: Socrates, Wagner, the Ascetic Priest and Women*.

George Yancy is currently associate professor of philosophy at Duquesne University and Coordinator of the Critical Race Speaker Series at Duquesne. He is the author of *Black Bodies, White Gazes: The Continuing Significance of Race*, which in 2008, received an Honorable Mention from the Gustavus Myers Center for the Study of Bigotry and Human Rights. He is also author of *Look, A White! Philosophical Essays on Whiteness*. He has edited twelve influential books, three of which have received CHOICE Awards. Yancy was recently nominated for Duquesne University's Presidential Award for Excellence in Scholarship.

INDEX